Volume TWO

MEASURING
EGO
DEVELOPMENT

Scoring Manual for
Women and Girls

Jane Loevinger

Ruth Wessler

and

Carolyn Redmore

MEASURING EGO DEVELOPMENT

Volume TWO

 Jossey-Bass Inc., Publishers

615 Montgomery Street · San Francisco · 1970

MEASURING EGO DEVELOPMENT
Volume Two: Scoring Manual for Women and Girls
by Jane Loevinger, Ruth Wessler, and Carolyn Redmore

Jossey-Bass, Inc., Publishers
615 Montgomery Street
San Francisco, California 94111

Library of Congress Catalog Card Number 71–92891

International Standard Book Number ISBN 0–87589–069–5

Manufactured in the United States of America
Composed and printed by York Composition Company, Inc.
Bound by Chas. H. Bohn & Co., Inc.

JACKET DESIGN BY WILLI BAUM, SAN FRANCISCO

FIRST EDITION

Code 7011

THE JOSSEY-BASS BEHAVIORAL SCIENCE SERIES

General Editors

WILLIAM E. HENRY, *University of Chicago*

NEVITT SANFORD, *Wright Institute, Berkeley*

Preface

A reader cannot just pick up this second volume of *Measuring Ego Development* and use it to score sentence completion tests, even if he has administered exactly this form of the test. The scoring manual is both more and less than that: less, in that one must first have a thorough mastery of the conception of ego development; more, in that the technique it presents does not apply only to the particular stems illustrated.

This manual is constructed explicitly for our Form 9-62 for women. Other forms that we use are presented in Appendix B of Volume One. We mimeograph our protocol forms as follows: The stems are numbered and listed on the left side of the page to leave as much space as possible for each response. Two-page forms have eighteen items per page; three-page forms have ten items on the first page and thirteen items on the second and on the third pages.

From a number of studies not yet reported, some of them still in progress, we believe the method is generally valid for other stems and also for men and boys. With new groups or new stems, interrater agreement will probably be slightly lower; however, disagreements of a full step or more should not increase appreciably. (In a full-step disagreement one rater, for example, gives a response an I-3 rating, another rater gives an I-4; or one rater gives an I-3/4 rating, another an I-4/5.)

A clinician or research worker who wishes to use our method but who wants to substitute a few stems of his own must make the total number of stems remain exactly thirty-six since our ogive scoring paradigm assumes a thirty-six item test. If additional, unscored stems are included, they should follow the test to be scored. Anyone altering the test should take care, as we have done, to arrange the items to minimize sequential or interconnected responses since each response should be independent of the others. Before deleting or altering any stem, the user should read the item manual for that stem in this volume.

Before using the scoring manual, the rater must master the conception of ego development that is the basis and the tacit component of the method (Chapters One and Four of Volume One), and he must also master the scoring method per se (Chapters Five and Six of Volume One). In doing so, he will complete the exercises of Appendix C and Appendix D, which have been designed to substitute for the more usual projective test workshop. We suggest that he not look at any scoring keys until after completing eighteen items of Appendix C. Then he can correct those ratings and proceed to the remaining block of eighteen items. After correcting all ratings in Appendix C, he should repeat the procedure with Appendix D.

The rater can evaluate his own performance by computing the percentage agreement between his ratings and ours for each item. Although the scoring keys give categories as well as I-levels to help the rater follow our reasoning, in lieu of a more personal tutorial, only I-level is considered in evaluating the percentage agreement. The distribution of percentage agreement per item is comparable to the distributions displayed in Table 13 of Volume One. Preliminary results with new raters in our own group indicate that he should do appreciably better with the exercises of Appendix C than the percentage agreements shown in Table 13, with a median close to 0.9, because the responses in Appendix C have been chosen to be rather easy to classify. If he computes the same statistics for his item ratings for Appendix D, he should find his distribution of percentage agreement per item comparable to the distributions displayed in Table 13 since for these real protocols many responses are difficult to classify.

Percentage agreement is not entirely satisfactory as an evaluation of the skill of a rater since it does not take into account the magnitude of the errors. To do so one must correlate his ratings with ours. (To correlate, transform the ratings to an ordinal scale. I-2 becomes 1, Delta becomes 3, I-5 becomes 9, I-6 becomes 11, I-3/4 becomes 6, and so on.) Distributions of correlations obtained will be comparable to those in Table 14 of Volume One. The median correlation for Appendix C may be higher than those shown in Table 14; however, if the same correlations are computed for the item ratings of Appendix D, they can be expected to be directly comparable to those of Table 14.

Finally, the rater's TPRs for Appendix D can be compared with ours. This comparison will result in a single correlation coefficient which can be evaluated against those of the self-trained raters shown in Table 17 of Volume One.

Although these evaluative checks are somewhat tedious, they are much simpler than devising one's own checks of interrater reliability. Under no circumstances should a rater who finds himself doing better than previous raters omit the remainder of the exercises in Appendices C and D. They have been designed as a whole.

JANE LOEVINGER
RUTH WESSLER
CAROLYN REDMORE

St. Louis, Missouri
February 1970

Contents

Using the Scoring Manual

The format of the scoring manual is the same for every item. Detailed, necessary instructions for use of the item-by-item manual are given in Chapter Five of Volume One. Here we merely explain the format. Introductory comments to each item tell what kinds of responses are given and what aspects of the response are related to I-level for that stem. Most scored levels also have introductory comments, partly expository but also intended to draw attention to clues for difficult discriminations. Each scored level contains several categories of response, usually followed by some examples. Where the category title begins without a dash and with a capital letter, it is our description of the responses included. Where the category title begins with a dash, it is the same as or similar to one or several observed responses. Category titles are essentially correct in grammar and orthography rather than verbatim as written.

Examples listed under a category title are given exactly the way the subject wrote them. We have intentionally retained errors of spelling, punctuation, and grammar to convey the flavor of real responses. Where we had a choice, we used responses free of errors rather than similar ones with errors. Illustrations include typical and marginal examples for the categories.

Where there is a possibility of confusion between a category at one level and a similar category at another level, cross-references follow the category titles. Similar categories within the same level are not listed since the purpose is to discriminate between, not within, levels. Where unclassified responses are listed, they have been observed two or three times, or they are meant to be discriminated from a category at another level, or they are theoretically interesting. A single star before a category title means that about 3 per cent or more of a large heterogeneous sample can be expected to give a response in that category. Two stars indicate that about 10 per cent or more will so respond.

Volume TWO

MEASURING
EGO
DEVELOPMENT

Scoring Manual for
Women and Girls

Raising a Family—

T<small>his</small> stem has a high pull. It elicits some touching responses clearly expressive of the highest I-levels. Also, contingent and qualified responses, found at I-3/4 and I-4 and higher for other stems, here appear at all levels. (This shows that the usual findings are not entirely an artifact of correlation with intelligence.) The terms of the contingent and qualified responses are trite and banal at low levels: "is hard but fun work" and "is nice if you don't have two many" both come from I-2 protocols, though they are scored I-3; "is not a picnic but its rewards are bountiful" is a similar thought from an I-4/5 protocol, scored I-4.

Below I-3 the predominant responses are slight variations on fun and hard work; both responses occur, though rarely alone, as high as I-4/5 or I-5. These responses seem to represent a single concept: the activities of life are divided into those that are fun and those that are hard work, and the only difference is which class raising a family belongs in (probably depending on whether the subject is an unmarried girl or a mother). The fun cliché is so common that it is classed I-3. "Hard work" and its contrary are classed Delta. The contrary of fun in relation to this item changes subtly for many I-3 subjects, from work to a difficult problem. Of course many responses ("is not easy") are ambiguous with respect to this distinction.

Though responsibility is ordinarily an I-4 concern, it is a cliché here and occurs at all levels, though most typically at I-3. Responsibility in conjunction with a contrasting idea, such as enjoyable or rewarding, is rated I-4 or higher. Seeing both positive and negative aspects, rare below I-3 for other items, here occurs at all levels and is scored as a category at I-3 and higher, depending on content.

Distinctive of subjects at the I-4 level and above are conceptual complexity and revelation of affect. Conceptual complexity can be shown by mentioning at least three distinct traits or attributes in one connection. Another form of complexity is seeing raising children in terms of the relation between the parents; this contrasts with seeing father only as a provider or an assistant at I-3. Interpreting the stem in terms of watching growth and development seems to be exclusively a high level (above I-4) concern, as it is for other stems.

I-2

The most common response at this level is hard work (Delta). The categories "is good, OK" and "is bad, no good" are all-purpose responses slightly inapropos here. Possibly because of the difficulty of the grammatical form, there are an unusual number of responses that are simply associations. Failure to complete a grammatical sentence does not suffice to justify an I-2 rating; "to be brought up to complete school and to be loved" comes from an I-3/4 subject.

1. —is good, OK (I-3, 1)
   is good and you should do the best you can
   is allright with me
   is fine

2. —is bad, no good
   is no good buseness
   is a bad problem
   is a horror

3. Redundant or inappropriate associations
   having children

> *by working and feeding them*
> *to learn your chinldren how to act*
> *right like your supposed to*
> *is a fundamental idea*

DELTA

The self-centered, self-interested attitudes of the Delta subject are elicited by this stem: raising a family takes money and is hard work. A self-protective attitude can be expressed in terms of demanding obedience, hence a dominance-submission view of family structure, or in terms of hostile humor, often directed against the tester.

*1. —is hard, a hard job, lots of work (I-3, 4; I-3/4, 8)
   is hard for a young girl
   it can be a very hard job sometimes
   is a tough job
   is hard for most parents

2. —is not much fun
   doesn't sound very fun to me
   is some fun

3. —is easy, not hard
   Is not so very hard

4. —takes money (I-3, 7; I-4, 6)
   you would have money to eat and buy things
   is nice if you can afford children
   is expensive
   is a hard job if you have no money

5. Self-protective attitude
   I want my family to obey me
   do not let children run the household

6. Hostile humor
   is easy on ADC
   is for Catholics

I-3

We can separate I-3 responses into those similar to I-3 responses to other stems and those reminiscent of higher levels on other stems. In the former group are those mentioning a superficial positive or negative aspect of raising a family: fun, wonderful, important, a job, difficult, and similar responses. In the latter are stereotyped versions of I-4 concerns, including responsibility and goals. Also in the latter group are statements of contingency and responses combining both positive and negative aspects; for this stem such responses are given at all levels, though there are no categories below I-3. The contrasting elements reveal the subject's conceptual structure; at I-3 and lower levels the opposite of fun is hard work rather than sorrow or problems. Contingencies classed at I-3 all involve fairly concrete factors: the person, the size of the family, help, whereas at I-4 and higher rewards and enjoyment are contingent on how one goes about raising a family. At I-3 father is rarely mentioned, and then only as provider or as assistant.

**1. —is nice, pleasant, wonderful, fun, and so on ʿ(I-2, 1; I-3/4, 2)
 is very exciting
 is the best thing that can happen to a girl
 is a delightful experience
 is going to be fun

 2. —is important (I-4, 1)
 is a matter of importance to any woman's life
 is an important occupation
 is very necessary to the American life

**3. —is a responsibility, a problem
 requires a lot of responsibility and love
 takes a great deal of responsibility especially if there are
     children in the family
 is a very big undertaking
 is an individual problem

 4. —is a job, a chore ʿ(Δ, 1; I-3/4, 8)
 is a woman's job
 is an everyday job
 is quite a task
 is Not so bad, but It's a big Job sometimes

*5. —is difficult, tedious, not easy
 is a serious thing
 can be a struggle
 can be nerve racking at times
 is Hectic
 is difficult in these times

*6. —is wonderful, nice, fun, but hard, difficult, a job ʿ(I-3/4, 5;
     I-4, 4)
 would be fun yet hard work

is a hard, but pleasant chore
is difficult and brings happiness

7. Fun, nice, and so on, contingent on person, concrete factors
   (Δ, 4; I-4, 6)
   is nice for those that love kids
   is swell if you have the right kind of help
   should be a pleasure for every normal person
   would be fun if the person is capable of taking responsity
   can be difficult if you don't have a husband to help you out

8. —is every girl's (woman's) goal, dream, desire
   is something to look forward to

*9. —is what I want, intend to do; something I look forward to
   (I-3/4, 4, 10)

10. Concrete reference to own status (I-3/4, 11)
    yes
    no family
    I don't have one as yet to raise
    I think I would like only have 1 child
    If I had my way I would have had more children
    isn't hard to mother because she has three children

11. —should be done the right way
    is to bring them up in the way that god would have them go
    to be brought up to complete school and to be loved
    is not very easy, we should have had more training in school
    Is not a problem, a family is what you make it

Unclassified
    keeps a home together

I-3/4

The inward turn of the I-3/4 is shown here. The opposite of joy is sorrow or heartache, the opposite of pleasure is problem or headache, contrasting with the I-3 subject for whom the opposite of pleasure is hard work (backache?). At I-4 the joy is not so much contrasted with as tempered by responsibility, and many responses of this type at I-4 combine three different ideas. Although we do not score on single words, *experience* is used more often and more meaningfully at I-3/4 than at lower levels; raising a family is an experience to go through rather than just something one does or wants to do. The I-3/4 woman also puts raising a family into general perspective, seeing it as part of life (not further specified) or as compared with other jobs.

*1. —is, can be rewarding, satisfying
      most satisfactory feeling
      is a necessary and rewarding experience
      makes life worth living
      is the most gratifying thing

*2. —is interesting, challenging, a rich experience (I-3, 1)
      is an interesting job
      is a happy challenge

 3. —is something everyone should experience
      is what every women in life should want to do
      is something every girl should think about

 4. —will be an experience for me (I-3, 9)
      is an experience I have yet to go through

 5. —has its joys and sorrows, problems and pleasures (I-3, 6;
      I-4, 4)
      is a beautiful experience with many problems
      happy and unhappy
      has moments of joy, happyness and sorry
      is a big job with many joys as well as heartaches
      can be a joy as well as a headache

 6. —takes love, patience, understanding (I-4, 7)
      takes lots of love and patience
      is not an easy job it take time & patience
      requires loving patience
      is a combination of love and discipline

 7. Compared with other careers or jobs
      can be almost as hard as doing well in any career
      is a career in itself and has both joy and sorrowful moments
      is the most responsible job
      is a vocation of high esteem

 8. —is a full time (lifetime) job (Δ, 1; I-3, 4)

 9. —is part of life, love (I-4, 1)
      is a woman's main purpose in life

10. —is one goal (I-3, 9; I-4/5, 4)
      is one of my aims
      is one thing I hope to do in the future
      *is one of my ambitions in life but one which I wonder if I
          shall ever accomplish*

11. Personal evaluation, general (I-3, 10)
   would have been a joy to me
   sounds like a fine idea now
   does not appeal to me
   means a lot to me
   is not the pleasure anticipated

Unclassified
   is a variety of things
   I am trying to

I-4

At I-4 raising a family is put into social perspective in more explicit terms than at I-3/4; it "is one of the most important things a person can do." The nature of childrearing is distinguished from what people may think or how the subject herself may react. How much fun it is is contingent not just on money or help but on how it is done. Where ideas are combined, they are not polar opposites, or at least not trite ones; responsibility is contrasted with enjoyment, hectic with dull. The change away from polar opposites is shown also by combining three aspects. Highly discriminating categories are based on the introduction of new terms: maturity, privilege, duty, self-fulfillment, and mutuality. Mutuality may be expressed in terms of husband and wife sharing an experience or responsibility, that both parents are required, cooperation is required, and so on. Explicit parallel mention of husband and wife or of mother and father is indicative of this level; merely substituting the word parent for mother or woman in responses otherwise classed lower does not suffice. "Is hard for most parents" is scored Delta.

1. —is a most rewarding (enjoyable, important) part of life
   (I-3, 2; I-3/4, 9; I-4/5, 4)
   is the most enjoyable time of life
   is one of the supreme joys of life
   must be a most satisfying way of life
   is one of the most important things a person can do
   is one of life's greatest experiences

2. —is a privilege, blessing, gift; a duty
   is a duty that should be taken seriously

3. —is a fulfilling (enriching, enlightening) experience
   very fullfilling. It completes a woman

is an experience all its own that you must have to be really happy
is instructive

4. —is stressful, time-consuming, challenging, but rewarding, a joy (at least one alternative classed singly above I-3) (I-3, 6; I-3/4, 5; I-4/5, 5)
   is a pleasurable, time-consuming experience
   may be hectic, but never dull
   is not a picnic, but its rewards are bountiful
   is a joy, a challenge, and occasionally a heartache
   is a very exacting but exciting and rewarding job

5. —is enjoyable, fun, rewarding as well as a responsibility
   is an enjoyable responsibility
   is a great responsibility, but rewarding in so many ways
   is difficult, enjoyable, expensive, and a great responsibility

6. Enjoyment contingent on how done (Δ, 4; I-3, 7; I-4/5, 2)
   is fun if you let it be
   can be quite fun and satisfying if handled in the right way
   is fun if you try your best
   can be a wonderful experience if all work together

7. —requires maturity, sacrifice, and other qualities (I-3/4, 6)
   is a responsibility for mature persons
   is certainly no job for an irresponsible person
   is a tremendous challenge, even to a mature, responsible adult

8. —requires both parents, mutual cooperation; is an experience for both husband and wife
   is a joint effort of both husband & wife
   is a two-way deal
   is the most important project a man and woman can undertake
   it take a Mother and father to do a good job and love and understanding
   is one thing every married couple wants to do

9. —is complex, complicated
   is a highly involved undertaking
   is not easy because there are so many conflicts and contradictions in the world today
   I find it very Important and difficult with so many things to influence children

10. Seen in terms of social class, society
    is a more complex process in an urban community than in a rural area
    is more of a concern to the 20th century parent because of our present mode of living
    is an important part of one's contribution to society and fulfillment of himself
    is the extension of one's self into the future
    will be an extremely hard job in this society as far as raising your children the way you want them

11. —is more difficult than people think

12. Difficult, but (personal reaction) (I-4/5, 1)
    is a hardship I hear, but I'm looking forward to it
    is a very serious problem as I've found out from just having my 5th baby
    Is not an easy thing to do but I try to do the best thing and wisest things in every decision

13. —takes planning
    takes a lot of careful planning and organizing
    should be planned and thought out carefully before bringing children into the world

Unclassified
    is beyond my ken, being single. However, I have some very definite ideas of how it should be done

I-4/5

Most of the responses classed I-4/5 are unique elaborations of themes found at the I-4 level. Two new elements are role conceptualization and seeing raising a family as fulfilling a basic natural need, as distinct from a wish.

1. Personalized description of problem to be coped with (I-4, 12; I-5, 2)
    calls on all your resources! But I would trade the assignment for anything
    is a job that I would give a million dollars to have. I love children, and all the responsibilities that go with raising a family
    is a real joy, especially for me for I almost gave up hopes of having a child

is something that I want to do very much because I think I
will be happiest & most fulfilled by doing this, however, I
realize that it is not going to be easy
involves a real investment of oneself

2. Outcome contingent on how done (I-4, 6)
   well is a woman's most important job
   is a full-time project and can be most rewarding when en-
   deavor is enthusiastic
   intelligently, takes love, patience, and understanding

3. —is a basic need
   is a difficult task, yet a natural one for women. All women
   desire the love & responsibility of a family

4. —is one aspect of marriage, one role (I-3/4, 10; I-4, 1)
   should be the most fulfilling role a woman can play
   is a definite facet of married life

5. Combination of at least three diverse ideas (including at least
   one at I-4) (I-4, 4)
   requires love, good humor, and practicality
   requires great maturity and accepting personal responsibilities
   and sacrifices
   requires that a women have many facets: homemaker, confi-
   dante, spiritual and emotional well being and an ability to
   adapt
   means sacrifice, time, frustrations and most of all the giving
   and sharing of love
   is a full-time job, interesting, rewarding, but hectic and awe-
   some at times

Unclassified
   of bears is difficult; however, rearing humans is even more
   difficult

I-5

The responsibility accepted as a cliché at I-3 and weighing heavily
at I-4 may be partly renounced at I-5 and I-6. One watches and accepts;
one learns humility. There is greater tolerance for ambivalence than at

lower levels. Feelings are vividly expressed in context of appreciation for complexity.

1. Sensitivity to growth and change
   is a real attribute in life. It is wonderful to see a family grow and prosper
   is a wonderful experience for me. I enjoy my children's progress so much
   is a responsibility and a challenge to do the best you can to help children become useful adults and well adjusted in society

2. Open acknowledgment of negative affect in positive context (I-4/5, 1)
   must be a rewarding thing. I have no children but sometimes envy those who do have
   is both exciting and boring—husband and wife are joined together in a way that can never be duplicated when children arrive
   is a full time job full of joys and sorrows and regrets for certain mistakes on my part
   is a fulfilling experience, but not always a happy experience
   is a great challenge, usually ending in heart ache and disappointment

Unclassified
   is a challenging, delightful, humbling and satisfying experience
   must be one of the most challenging, trying things if done properly, but it must also be the very most rewarding and self-satisfying too
   requires sufficient maturity of each parent and a loving, stable relationship between them
   after marriage, is woman's basic traditional role. This tradition is being modified, but is still true for most women

I-6

There are no categories at this level, but the following responses are illustrative. One looks for combinations of elements such as toleration of ambiguity, renunciation of manipulation, time perspective, orientation towards process and development, conceptual complexity, and vivid communication of affect.

can break your heart and be wonderful too. One sometimes learns almost too late to accept and love and not try to change

challenges one to test the theories he has held and to find practical ways to implement his philosophy; therefore it is process in completion of one's development

I<small>TEM</small> **2**

Most Men Think
That Women—

T<small>his</small> stem calls for stereotypes, hence has an I-3 pull; so we may expect I-3 answers even from those at higher levels. But socially accepted stereotypes include mutual exploitation of men and women, as well as banal idealization. Thus there may be responses at high levels difficult or impossible to distinguish from Delta answers. We partly overcome this difficulty by using fine shades of meaning and language, distinguishing "are stupid" (Delta/3) from "are dumb" (I-3) from "are less intelligent than they are" (I-4). In part, however, this remains as an element of error.

In addition to the item pull, other factors contribute to error. The most obvious is that the different subjects do in fact know different kinds of men. Any attempt to take this factor into account almost certainly would introduce more error than it eliminates; so we exclude this consideration.

A subtler factor is that the question may be interpreted various ways. Some women indicate that they are reporting the popular stereotype, others that they are reporting concerning men in their own families. Most don't say which they are doing. Still more complex possibilities may be hypothesized, such as projection of the woman's own self-image. Again, these possibilities cannot be taken into account except as they are explicitly stated, thus actually changing the response. As a rule, these various possibilities are not differentiated at the lowest levels. The clearer the distinction between what one man thinks and what another does, between what men think and what women are really like, the higher the rating. One should avoid, however, awarding a premium to sophisticated lingo about stereotypes. Moreover, merely counterposing a different stereotype does not raise the rating: "are crazy, but I think that the men are crazy" comes from an I-2 subject.

Other factors that determine the rating are how differentiated, abstract, and inward is the trait in terms of which women are judged, and expressing discordant attitudes or complex contingencies in a single response. Going up the scale, one finds increasing distance from the war between the sexes and from unrealistic idealization of women. Many high responses have a light touch.

I-2

Most responses by I-2 subjects represent variations on the theme, good-bad. Some such responses, for example, nice, pretty, are frequent at other levels and scored accordingly. Those not only relatively but absolutely more frequent at low levels are scored here.

1. Primitive moral dichotomy: good, bad
   are bad but some are good
   are no good
   are mean, but beautiful

2. —are fools, crazy, nuts ($\Delta/3$, 1; I-3, 4)
   are crazy, but I think that the men are crazy
   are crazy sometimes
   are nuts, crazy and stupid

3. Derogatory names
   are sluts because the drink wine
   are lieer
   are to timers and some gets alone good

4. —are sweet (I-3, 1)

DELTA

Responses classed here, partly on a theoretical basis, concern either sexual exploitation of women by men or financial exploitation of men by women. Their greatest absolute frequency is at I-3/4, where they are relatively more frequent than at I-3. They are classed here somewhat arbitrarily, as there is no psychometrically satisfactory way of dealing with them.

1. —are good for just one thing; are to play with (I-3/4, 7)
   are just something to use &
   are all play
   should do what ever they want them to
   to sleep with
   are only to take out & have fun & leave them

2. —are easy; can be had easily (I-3/4, 10)
   are a push over
   are helpless. They can do what ever they want to them
   are easy. But they are very mistakend

3. Are out to exploit men (I-3, 9; I-3/4, 8)
   are always wanting to spend their money
   are craftier than they are
   are mearly around to get what they can off of them
   are gold diggers what tried to be smart

DELTA/3

Two categories go here because of greater relative frequency below I-3. "Stupid" occurs also at I-3 and I-3/4. "Good looking" rarely occurs above I-3, where it belongs a priori.

1. —are stupid (I-2, 2; I-3, 3, 4)
   are stupid and sometimes buitiful
   are defenceless and stupid
   are stupid and ugly, some do

*2. —are good looking, beautiful, attractive, lovely, pretty (I-3, 1)
   are usually pretty
   is beautiful or have good shape
   are beautiful & love them & will do anything they say

I-3

Responses here deal with global, stereotyped, conventional attributes without qualification: wonderful, necessary, silly, weak. Some faults are tied to concrete behavior: extravagant, gossip. The I-3 subject may also give global comparisons, "are all alike," "are inferior." At higher levels such comparisons are spelled out, usually in terms of capabilities. Woman's traditional social role may be mentioned: women should stay at home and not be dominating.

*1. —are nice, wonderful, great, all right (I-2, 4; Δ/3, 2; I-3/4, 1)
   are something pretty special

2. —are necessary, important, essential (I-4, 4)

3. —are smart, not smart (Δ/3, 1; I-3/4, 4; I-4, 5)

*4. —are silly, dumb, ignorant (I-2, 2; Δ/3, 1; I-3/4, 2)
   don't know what they are talking about
   dont know any thing
   are full of hot air

5. Cannot do things right (general) (I-3/4, 4)

*6. —are inferior, not their equals (I-3/4, 4, 7)
   ar not up to their standards
   are of the lower class

7. —are weak, fragile, delicate
   are the weaker sex
   are fragile and should be taken care of
   are weaker and more stupid then they

8. —are gossips, talk too much
   are too talkative and nosy
   are gossipers and stubborn which is wrong (most of the time)

9. —are expensive, extravagant (Δ, 3; I-4, 5)
   are spendthrifts
   have a way of being extravagant

10. —are to be married, should be wives, mothers (I-3/4, 11; I-4/5, 4)
    are just a person that should get married and have children

11. —should stay home, do the housework, raise the children (I-3/4, 11; I-4/5, 4)
    belong in the home rather than out in the business world
    should be home with the children
    Should stay home and be there when he get there
    chief cook & bottle washer

12. —are too bossy; try to dominate; shouldn't be boss (I-3/4, 6, 7; I-4, 9)

     are taking over
     should not be head of the family. I agree
     are too forward and outspoken
     are trying to compete with them

13. —should help, work with men; are helpful
     helpers
     are for marring and to help them along the way

14. —have it easy; are lazy
     loaf too much
     sit around all day
     have a easy life (if she doesn't have to work and can stay home all day.)

15. Global comparison
     are basically alike
     are something apart
     are different from them

16. Rejection of stem (I-3/4, 12)
     I wouldn't explain this one
     ?

I-3/4

Although the I-3/4 subject responds to this item mainly in conventional terms, she talks of traits a little more abstract, more inward, and more differentiated than does the I-3 person. There is a glimpse of the relation between men and women in the shift from women are wonderful (I-3) to women are nice to have around (I-3/4). Some categories, that women should be subservient, that they want to snare men, and direct references to sex, are hard to distinguish from similar ones at the Delta level; since the differences are not clear-cut, there are inevitable mistakes.

1. —are nice (fun, good) to have around (to be with); are good companions; are interesting (I-3, 1)
     are important to have around
     are good company

2. Conventional faults of women (I-3, 4; I-4, 2)
     scheme
     are vain and gossipy
     are spoiled creatures

are somewhat silly and frivolous
are cloth horses
are scatterbrain
are self-centered
too demanding and somewhat stupid
are jealous of one another

*3. —are poor drivers
     drivers are dangerous

4. —are capable, less capable, not very capable (I-3, 3, 5, 6; I-4, 5)
     are not quite quallified for most things
     are incapable of doing the same jobs as them
     are not capable of anything other than being a housewife
     use better judgment

5. Are different emotionally
     are not as stable as themselves
     worry too much over trivial things in life
     are too serious
     are too sensitive
     are shallow
     are emotional
     are soft hearted

6. —should be (are) feminine (I-3, 12)
     are too masculine
     should be women

7. —should serve them, be subservient; are made for them (Δ, 1; I-3, 6, 12; I-4, 9)
     are slaves
     are for their pleasure
     are here just to take care of the house and watch the children
     are the pawns of men
     are to be taken for granted
     are common and can be treated in any way
     should be under them

8. —are out to snare, marry men (Δ, 3)
     are after them; that is, if they're single
     are marriage conscious

9. —are interested in them
     are competing for their attention
     are trying to make many impressions on them

10. —are sexy, afraid of sex (Δ, 2; I-5, 3)
    are cold sexually
    are sex-crazy

11. Abstract or evaluative view of her duties (I-3, 10, 11; I-4/5, 4)
    are very good cooks
    never forget any thing and cook three meals a day
    do a good job of raising their children and keeping their home
    should take all the responsibility by them self
    should stay home and let the men make the most decisions
    are to keep the family happy and togather
    that work make poor housekeepers and mothers

12. —I don't know what they think; I haven't thought about it
    (I-3, 16; I-4, 10)

I-4

The I-4 person is concerned with differentiated traits not likely to be mentioned by lower level subjects in response to this item, such as respect, responsibility, and the problem of dependence. References to ability at lower levels are vague, using words like stupid, dumb, smart, as much pejorative as descriptive. At I-4 more specific descriptions of abilities are given, in terms of intelligence, logic, common sense. More humor is evident in responses such as "are a necessary evil," and "make the best wives." Coping with complexity is seen in responses referring to women's complexity, conflicting attitudes toward women, that men may not admit their admiration, that men do not all think alike, and that men may view women as individuals.

1. —are to be loved, admired, respected
    are precious and something they could cherish
    deserve respect and attention
    should be on a pedestal
    are made for love and responsability

2. Conflicting attitudes (I-3/4, 2; I-4/5, 2, 3)
    are a necessary evil
    are interesting but dependent
    are nutty but nice!
    are gossips and try to boss them around too much but what would they do without them
    are too mannish, yet try to be too sexy
    are inferior them, but are appreciated

3. Will not admit they admire us
   are necessary and nice even if they kid us and tell us we aren't
   are as equal as them but just don't want to admit it
   are pretty great although they don't always act like it or seem to think so

4. Important to life, happiness, society (I-3, 2)
   are a very necessary part of living
   are quite essential to happiness and success

*5. —are less intelligent; less capable in business, finances, special fields (I-3, 3, 5; I-3/4, 4; I-4/5, 4)
   are not too bright
   should take a second seat as far as work and mental ability are concerned
   are slightly retarded
   tend to be irresponsible in household finances
   can not add or keep a checkbook accurately
   have less brains than they really have
   makes poor leadership

6. —are illogical, lack common sense
   do not think in a logical pattern
   dont have enough practical sense to do things correctly

7. —are complex, hard to understand; don't understand them (I-4/5, 1)
   are unpredictable
   are confusing at times
   can't understand their needs and hopes
   are complicated creatures

8. —are equal to men; are human, individuals
   are just as good and have equal rights just as they do
   can be judged like themselves
   are necessary and treat them as equals
   are human, just as they are

9. —are dependent, helpless; should be dependent (I-3, 12; I-3/4, 7)
   need to be protected
   enjoy being dominated
   are wonderful people who need them
   aren't independent enough
   are too independent
   are to be helpmates rather than indepent

10. Men do not all think alike (I-3/4, 12; I-5, 2)
are angeles and the greatest and others don't
my husband I can only speak for think most women are the
greatest thing could have ben made
are, according to their own experience or culture

Unclassified
make the best wives

I-4/5

While the statement that men think women belong in the home is a commonplace at I-3, only at high levels does one find career versus homemaking discussed in terms of women's rights and abilities. A combination of a favorable and an unfavorable attitude toward women can be found at I-4, but this is sharpened to a paradox at I-4/5, or a contrasting of two or more ideas, with the terms of at least one of them itself at I-4 level. Some responses indicate a clear distinction between physical and psychological qualities.

1. —are puzzling, mysteries (I-4, 7)
are mysteries but interesting
are puzzling but nice to know

2. Paradoxical views (I-4, 2; I-5, 2)
should be dependently independent
are either too dumb, or too intelligent
are delightful and maddening creatures

3. Contrasting ideas (at least one at I-4 level) (I-4, 2; I-5, 2)
should be poised and intelligent
are difficult to understand, but wonderful to be with
should be feminine, honest, and interesting
should be intellectually stimulated and also be a good companion
should be put on a pedestal because they are the so-called weaker sex
all worship them and are totally dependent on men
are meant to be used for their own pleasure and weren't meant to be loved or respected
are necessary in the present day economy but resent their intrusion

4. Have a right (do not have a right) to a career (I-3, 10, 11; I-3/4, 11; I-4, 5)

*belong in the home, in spite of the fact that they may be
equally as, or even more, capable than the men themselves*
*have earned the right to participate in most fields and inter-
ests that were once available only to men*
*are their equals in most fields and admire those in the pro-
fessions*
*belong at home and not working unless they have real skill in
the field in which they work*

5. Physical qualities distinguished from psychological ones
   are objects to be admired physically
   *are biologically inferior to men, but find out that such is not
   the case*
   *are somewhat fragile, but medical science tells us the female
   is the stronger sex*

I-5

Most characteristic of responses at this level is some way of indicating that the stereotype is a stereotype. This does not necessarily mean
rejection of it; in fact, explicit, usually somewhat humorous, acceptance
of the stereotype is more characteristic of this than of lower levels. There
is also concern for the relation between men and women, and particularly
for sexuality as part of a broader relation.

1. Stereotype may be justified
   are rather difficult to understand—and in many cases We are!
   are sentimental and quite emotional which is often the case
   *are poor drivers, and you know I think so too when I observe
   some of their antics!*
   *are meant to care for them, attend to their needs. I feel this
   is at it should be, and American women could on the whole
   pamper men more*

2. Evaluation of or distance from stereotype (I-4, 10; I-4/5,
   2, 3)
   must be perfect or so it seems
   *have intellectual and emotional characteristics related to their
   sex*
   *are more talkative than men & the weaker sex, its question-
   able whether they believe the latter*
   *are better than they really are; they do not see the faults
   which women find with other women*

are basically intelligent, and a needed part of their world, contrary to the popular "Madison Ave." concept of women as sex symbols

should be more gentle, idealistic and dependent than is possible

are, should be, or should act as if they were inferior to men

are in general more illogical than are men in general

have little or no business sense and no understanding of mechanics. They believe a vast difference exists between male and female logic

are slightly inferior in some aspects, but I think they love them for this and are glad it's that way!!

3. Sexuality seen in interpersonal context (I-3/4, 10)

should stay at home and raise a family, and be good wives (and lovers!)

are no good if their relations extend to more than 1 man. I think it depend on the treatment given her by the 1st man

are alike but they are wrong some devotes their lives to one man other are likewise that goes for them too

Unclassified

are worthwhile to be with, but depending on the type of man and type of woman thinkings differ

I-6

The responses illustrating this level combine elements of the I-5 and I-4/5 responses. One notes mutuality and a concern for the relation between the sexes, humor, paradox, and awareness of the stereotype as such.

Unclassified

are partners who bring a new perspective and different point of view into focus

are beautiful, desirable, "motherly," dependable, good chauffeurs, cooks, leaders in the community, and almost as capable as they are

are necessary evils when considered collectively, and are wonderful when considered individually (that is to say—wife, mother, sister, lover.)

When They
Avoided Me—

The most common completion to this stem refers to hurt feelings, particularly at I-3, I-3/4, and I-4. At I-2 the corresponding response is "they made me upset," and at Delta, "I get mad." The I-3 subject may report feeling bad, or stress the aspect of social rejection. More differentiated feelings (lonely, depressed) are classed at I-3/4, while at I-4 the idea of hurt feelings is often combined with another thought. At I-4/5 there are different feelings, depending on the situation, while at I-5 conflicting feelings are reported.

Some version of the statement that "it doesn't bother me" is also common, absolutely more frequent in the I-3, I-3/4 range, rare above it, but relatively more frequent at lower levels. A group of responses interpreting the situation so as to exclude hostile intention is classed I-4, while acceptance of the situation without denying hostile intent is I-4/5.

Leaving, ignoring them, and avoiding them are more frequently mentioned than are feelings below I-3. An I-2 version is to go home or to go to mother. At I-3 one leaves, or goes on one's way, at I-3/4 one leaves them alone or turns to others. The I-4 person finds other interests. Related ideas are avoiding or ignoring them (I-3), ignoring the situation (I-3/4), and pretending not to notice (I-4). These themes, leaving, ignoring, avoiding, are rarely found above I-4.

At high I-levels the characteristic responses represent search for reasons, a theme rarely found on protocols below I-3. The corresponding category at Delta is that there is something wrong, or they are doing wrong. "I wonder why" is a frequent and poorly discriminating category, found from I-3 through I-5, and classed I-3/4. General and vague statements about causation, in them or in the subject, are classed I-3/4. A determination to find out the reason, or to improve oneself, or a statement of psychological causation in them, is rated I-4. At I-4/5 there is a category accepting responsibility but without excessive self-blame—perhaps the subject has been unintentionally snobbish, she says. At I-5 alternative causes are considered.

Conceptual complexity, combining two or more thoughts into a single response, characterizes virtually all high level ratings for this stem.

I-2

Responses classed at this level may be dependent in tone, "I cried and ran to mommy," or they may be global and impoverished. "I try to get along with them" involves a misperception of the situation, as if the subject is still involved in friendly interaction with the others, unlike "I just tried to be more friendly" (I-3/4).

1. Dependent response: go home, run to mother
   I went home and cried
   I feel sorry that I did something wrong so I go home

2. —I do nothing
   I could do Nothing about it

3. —I try to get along with them

4. —they made me upset
   upset

5. Impoverished associations
   enemies
   Jelioeus
   sad

DELTA

The Delta subject may make somewhat paradoxical responses, asserting that it was they, not she, who suffered, or say that she laughed. The latter is not the same as saying she smiled, which may be a conscious defense or facade. "I get mad" (Delta) is more specific than "upset" (I-2) but less so than "my feelings are hurt" (I-3/4). The Delta subject knows something is wrong but is more likely to think it is they than herself.

1. —I get mad; I knew they were mad (I-3, 2)
   raise hell
   I get real mad and leave the house
   I get mad, if he's the one I like
   I get furious

2. —I laugh, was glad (I-3/4, 3)
   Im happy
   I laughed because my intentions were to avoid them

3. Revenge (I-3, 6)
   I turned the tables

4. They were the only ones who got hurt
   they didn't know what they were missing

5. —something is wrong; they are doing wrong (I-3/4, 7, 12)
   I think there is something wrong

Unclassified
   they avoided my dog also
   I am always avoided when Im among professional models who knows me because I allways stand out front
   I gathered they feel guilty of the lie they told about our group
   they make me feel shame

DELTA/3

Denial that unpleasant feelings have been aroused occurs fairly frequently at I-3 and I-3/4 but relatively more frequently below I-3.

*1. —it doesn't bother me; I don't care (I-4, 2)
so what?
I forget them
it really doesnt matter
I dont really mind Some times
I don't worry

I-3

For the I-3 subject social exclusion is a major problem, and this aspect will often be stressed: "I felt unwanted"; "I think they don't like me"; "I must not of been attractive." The I-3 person may evade the question or state that she evades the situation, by going on her way, avoiding them, or ignoring them. Because the avoidance is viewed as something "they" did, rather than as an interaction in which she is involved, the I-3 person is more likely to say "I ignore them" than "I ignored it" (I-4).

*1. —I feel rejected, unwanted, shunned, left out, out of place
I felt slighted
I felt as if I wasn't wanted

2. —I resent it; I don't like it (Δ, 1)
I get a little angry
I felt put out

*3. —I feel sad, funny, bad; I worry (I-3/4, 2)
I was unhappy
they bother me
it worried me
I felt disturbed

4. —I was surprised
I was amazed
it surprised me

*5. —I ignore them; pay no attention (to them) (I-3/4, 4)
I look over them
who? I guess I just ignore people who avoid me

*6. —I avoid them (Δ, 3)
I did likewise
I refused to see them

*7. —I leave, go on my way (I-4, 8)
I went on to my job
I just get up and leave the room, I hate to be avoided
I smiled and kept on my way

8. —I don't need them
   I say for get them
   I thought they could go jump in a lake
   I thought the hell with them and walked away

9. —they don't like me
   I feel they dont like me or are tired of me
   they must not like me or my personality
   if they do its because I not the type they like I guess
   I think they hate me
   I'm not their type or they aren't my type of person

10. —I'm not attractive
    I feel something must be wrong with my appearance
    sometimes you be avoided by not being neat, by you personality

11. —I had BO, halitosis
    I wondered if my deodorant was strong enough

12. Mention of specific situations
    the time I had a surprise party
    when I was in lower grades at school
    *when I arrived at the hospital I thought I would deliver in
    the waiting room*

13. —it never happened; I can't remember
    nobody ever did
    I feel unrelax in case they would, but they don't
    I have never been aware any-one did

14. Evasion
    ?
    you tell me
    no comment
    can't think of anything

Unclassified
    I spoke to them
    I went on talking
    I prayed for them
    maybe they won't the next time

I-3/4

The most frequent response, hurt feelings, occurs mainly at I-3, I-3/4, and I-4, and is placed here as compromise. When the thought is combined with another, clearly different one, the rating is I-4. More differentiated feelings are also classed here, contrasting with feeling bad or sad at I-3. The subject at this level may blame herself or them; in either case she tends to see behavior as having reasons, though, typically, rather vague and general ones. Subjects describing their response to the situation talk of leaving them alone, turning to others, or being even more friendly.

*1. —I felt (was) hurt (I-4, 1)
   it hurt my feelings
   I feel hurt and rejected
   I was hurt and wanted to cry
   I felt like crying

*2. Differentiated feelings: lonely, depressed, embarrassed, disappointed, and so on (I-3, 3)
   I felt as if I was different and not as good as them
   I felt very self-conscious
   I was insulted
   I felt I could die
   I felt rebellious
   I felt lonely and unwanted, and I felt no love anywhere

3. Being nice, forgiving, friendly (at all costs) (Δ, 2)
   I made a point of talking to them the next time that I saw them
   I turned the other cheek
   I try my best to make friends
   I simply smiled

4. —I ignore it, pay no attention (to the situation) (I-3, 5)
   I ingore they silly act
   I tried to ignore it

5. —I turn to others
   I went over to someone else
   I talked to someone else
   I had to find new friends
   thought nothing of it—found someone friendly and forgot the others

6. —I left them alone, didn't want to be around them
   I withdrew
   I did not wish to see them again
   I kept to myself

7. —I wonder what I did wrong; what is wrong with me (Δ, 5; I-4, 3)
   I wondered if I did something wrong
   I wondered what was the matter with me

I wondered about myself
I wonder what my trouble is

8. Acceptance of blame: know I have done something wrong; deserved it
   I feel that I have done something to cause this
   I knew that I must have done something wrong
   I probably deserved it
   I feel it is my fault
   I felt I had offended them
   I often felt there was something wrong with me

*9. —I wonder why; asked why; tried to find out why (I-4, 4)
   I questioned them as to why
   I would try to find out why
   I felt a need to find out why
   I was puzzled
   I couldn't understand why
   I became confused as to why they did this to me

10. —I began to analyze myself
    examined my conscience
    I began to study my personality
    I study myself
    I start looking for my faults

11. They had reasons (vague and general) (I-4, 4)
    I could generally see their reasons
    I tried to understand they had a reason to do so. or otherwise why should they do so

12. Fault lies within them (Δ, 5; I-4, 6)
    I don't feel they understand me
    I was rather disappointed in them
    , they made a mistake
    they had their wrong idea of choosing the right one for the job

I-4

Where the I-3/4 subject sees behavior as having vague and general reasons, the I-4 person looks for specific reasons, whether in herself or the others. Specific psychological mechanisms may be ascribed to them; if the fault belongs to the subject she tries to correct it. She distinguishes feelings from actions. This may take the form of recognizing the avoidance but denying hostile intent, or of recognizing her own hurt feelings but covering them up. Responses classed above I-4 are almost all combinations. The simplest combination, hurt feelings plus some other thought, is classed I-4. However, "I feel hurt and rejected" is considered almost redundant and is classed I-3/4, 1.

1. —I felt hurt (bad, sad, upset) and (another response) (I-3/4, 1)

   I felt hurt and wonder what I have done to cause this

   I got angry, and hurt

   I avoided them too, but I couldn't help being a little sad

   I became hurt and do things that are meant to hurt my parents but I always end up in trouble

   I became very upset and tried to figure out why they treated me that way

2. Attempt to cover up feelings, not let it bother me; pretend not to notice (Δ/3, 1)

   I tried not to think very much about it

   I tried to brush it off

   I try to convey the impression that it doesn't bother me

   I didn't let it bother me

3. —I wonder what I had done (no mention of "wrong"); if I had offended them (I-3/4, 7)

   I wonder if there is some way I have offened them

   I try to think weather or not I have mistreated them

   I tried to figure out what I had done to rate this treatment

   I wondered what I had done

4. —I wonder about, try to find out the reason (I-3/4, 9, 11)

   I began to wonder what the reason was for avoidance

   wanted to know the reason why and how I was to blame

   I questioned their reason

   I asked them their reasons for doing it

   I try to find out their reason

   I took stock of myself to find possible reasons

5. Attempt to change self, make self more acceptable

   I think there's something I done or said wrong and try to be a little better

   I cannot remember being "avoided"—if this should happen I'd try to "prove myself" to the group

   It may be an indication that some type of self improvement may be necessary either in appearance or personality

   I want to find out why and correct it

6. Psychological causation in them (I-3/4, 12)

   I thought they were imature

   I felt they had some guilt complex

   it is a personality defect

   I thought they were manifesting personal conflicts and problems

7. Denial of hostile intention

   I assumed they were busy with other responsibilities and couldn't take time to talk

   it was not an indication of deliberate hostility

   it was because they didn't know me

   I trusted it was because they had not seen me

   I did things to have them notice me

   I make myself known

8. —I found other interests, went off by myself (I-3, 7)

   I did something else

   I amused myself

   I busied myself with browsing around the garden, til they finished their discussion

   I continued my project

9. —I don't force myself on them

   I just let them go their way as I don't believe in pushing yourself where you're not wanted

   I had no hurt feelings, will not force myself on anyone, have to be liked for what I am

I-4/5

Answers classed here may express alternative responses to the situation, in some cases contingent on the person involved, in others expressing time perspective. Two categories involve a kind of acceptance of the situation, in one case without denying the hostile intention, in the other accepting responsibility but without excessive self-blame.

1. Alternative responses to situation

   I was sometimes angry—other times I didn't care

   I sometimes ignore them, and at other times try to become friends

2. Response contingent on persons involved, on reasons

   it doesn't bother me unless my husband would, and he doesn't

   I didn't care unless they were my friends

   it would depend on the ones involved. an my opion of them how I felt

*I felt disturbed because I could not understand the reason
why*
I knew why so it usually didn't bother me

3. Expressions of time perspective
    my first response was to try to ignore them
    *at first it didn't bother me, but after a while I became quite
    concerned*
    I withdrew, and avoided any future confrontations
    *it made me feel funny inside, and I told myself I would never
    avoid others*
    I began to stay away from their company entirely

4. Responsibility without too much guilt
    I thought I had inadvertently offended someone
    *I found I had been rather snobism to them, although unin-
    tentional*
    I am hurt, but I feel I have perhaps been unpleasant
    *I suddenly realized I brought it on by being indifferent to
    them on previous occasions*

5. Acceptance of avoidance, without denying the intention
    *I ignored it and did not let it interfere with my friendliness
    toward them*
    I felt our interests were not commonly shared
    I knew I wasn't welcome in their "clique"
    I took it for granted I was no longer needed
    I make it possible for them to do so gracefully
    *, I decided that they knew something about me which I was
    not aware of*
    I oblidge and avoid them
Unclassified
    I felt a failure as a true friend

I-5

We class at this level responses that indicate coping with conflicting feelings; those examining alternative constructions of causation, in
self, in others, and in chance factors; and some in which the conceptual
complexity is displayed by coping with reasons for, feelings about, or responses to the situation simultaneously.

1. Alternative constructions of the situation
    I wondered what the reason was. Whether it was something

I had done, some unrelated feelings they had, or if it were just by chance

I wondered why they did—was it me? or was it them? or something else

I wondered if it were due to my deficiencies or theirs

2. Coping with conflicting feelings

   I felt ashamed and mad at the same time because they felt they were better than me and I didn't feel that they were

   I felt depressed & withdrawn, there was this swelling inside me that wanted to strike out at them for hurting me and then there was this conflict inside of me telling me to be nice to them

3. Compound responses: reasons and feelings

   there was usually a good reason and although I didn't like it too well, I usually forgot about it

   I felt they didn't want to talk to me for some reason. I might have felt hurt or indifferent toward them

   I wondered what I might have done to repel them and which of their needs I had failed to satisfy

ITEM 4

If My Mother—

This stem calls for a statement about mother, followed by a contingent statement, usually about the mother, the subject, or family relationships. The complex format results in few responses repeated verbatim. The rating task is difficult, with many categories and many responses that fit no category. Tending toward low ratings are threats, demands, unmodulated complaints against the mother (rather than statements of her faults), statements about actions, and undifferentiated moods (happy, glad, sad, mad). Tending toward high ratings are movement away from egocentricity, differentiated traits and feelings (sincere, liberal, prejudiced, affectionate), statements about the mother's specific faults rather than total hostility to her, psychological causation, concern for interpersonal relations as such, and rarely, recognition of inner conflict. References to father and his relation with mother usually contain implication of concern for relationships or diminished egocentricity or both.

This stem seems to stir up a childish plaint, something like "If mother would only help me, everything would be OK," or "If mother is nice, I'll be happy (good)." At the I-2 level the stem may be turned into an impulsive outburst, such as a demand ("would only come with my clean clothes"), or a threat ("died, I would too"). At the Delta level the mother may be seen as an aversive controlling agent ("would only free me") or as a scapegoat ("would straighten out I wouldn't be here"). Generally there is a less helpless tone to the Delta responses. At the I-3 level frankly dependent responses occur but the complaining, demanding tone is infrequent. Most responses continue to be of the form of how mother can make me happy. Where mother can make me happy by relaxing or not worrying, it may be left ambiguous whether this is for my good or for hers. If the statement or context clearly indicates that the mother is being asked to change for her own good, the rating is I-4 rather than I-3.

The categories at I-3/4 involve a minimal variation on the I-3 theme that if mother would only do something, I would be happy. There may be a shift from concrete actions to moods and feelings, or a diminution of egocentricity, such as in the desire to help her. At the I-4 level the variations on the original theme are greater, and typical I-4 themes, such as achievements and interests, are introduced. A subtle change is from the mother's traits making the subject happy or unhappy to the effect the mother's traits have on the relation between mother and subject. Mother may be blamed for subject's problems, even with bitterness, but there must be some element of indirect or more or less psychological causation, rather than simply casting mother as giver or withholder. Above I-4 there is acceptance of mother as a real person with good and bad traits, which may be described without evaluation, or ambivalence may be acknowledged. One may express appreciation for her as an individual in terms comparable to those used for other friends or relatives. Most responses at the I-5 level are not recognizable as variations of the child's plaint.

Because of the lack of replication, there is a temptation to interpret the categories in terms of topic. However, similar topics are found at different levels, and it is chiefly the manner of treating the topic that differentiates levels.

I-2

Subjects from practically the whole range of levels give responses that begin with "died, ..." These responses are classed according to their independent clauses. The version at I-2, "dies, I would too," can be interpreted as remnant of a symbiotic relation, as an expression of total dependence, or as a threat to compel the mother to stay alive.

1. Mother as source of supplies (Δ, 1; I-3, 9)
   go down town I want her to buy me a dress
   gives me the money I'll go
   would only finish my sweather!
   brought me a sweater I will thank her
   let me go on a shopping spree I would me happy
   could make cothes I'd have a hole wardrobe
   was my size I would wear her cloths
   was living I would be very happy to get that motherly love
   Come over today I will ask her to bake some cookies
   has any money I would like to see it once in awhile

2. —died, I would too (I-3, 3; I-3/4, 5)
   died, I would kill myself
   die I couldn't make it

3. Immediate reaction to mother hitting (no time perspective) (Δ, 3)
   ever hit my father. I'd be afraid
   hit me I'd cry
   ever even touched me I'd possitively leave

Unclassified
   is a short fat lady
   is good to me our be to you

DELTA

The Delta subject resents control, where a few I-3 subjects demand it. The Delta person blames mother for causing trouble, contrasting with complaining about specific faults at I-3/4 and more indirect and psychological causation at I-4 and above. A Delta person may bargain for some advantage or promise reform as soon as she is freed from present predicament; she will be grateful in the future, where high level subjects regret not having shown gratitude in the past. Dependent complaining is similar to the I-2 view of the mother as a source of supplies; at I-2 one gets actual things, usually clothes or money. Greater preoccupation with the mother's sexual and aggressive transgressions at low levels is apparent, but it is not clear whether this is a manifestation of low level, a cause of it, or a correlate, perhaps due to socioeconomic status.

1. Dependent complaining (I-2, 1; I-3, 9)
   should stay home and take care of us childrens and cook and
   see that they go to school
   would only take me shopping
   would only baby sit more often
   could only get the ironing done
   dosen't get those P. J.'s I'll die
   wood alway ask my Husban before take my baby home with
   her, and stop ask me all the time

2. Resentment of control (opportunistic tone) (I-3, 7, 16)
   would keep her mouth shut, things would be fine
   tells me I can't date, I do it anyway
   were dead I would be boss
   would listen
   went out of town for a while I could have a good time
   let me get married
   would give me priviledge, I would stay home

3. Immediate reaction to mother's anger (not differentiated reactions) (I-2, 3; I-3, 11; I-3/4, 10)
   yells at me, I yell back
   hollers, I get mad
   argues I shut up
   get mad at me I stay out of her way
   hollars I just agree with her to shut her up
   was mean I would be mean to

4. Crude blaming of mother (opportunistic tone) (I-3/4, 9)
   acted like a mother I would like her
   had told me so
   would stop drinking everything would be all right
   were alive I would be in worse trouble
   would have been more of a mother when I was little
   had been a real mother I wouldn't be the way I am
   would straighten out I wouldn't be here
   had of loved me more

5. —ran around with other men, I'd leave
   ran around with other men I wouldn't want her for a mother
   loved only my father then I would to

6. Exploitative use of mother, for example, to gain freedom
   would only free me
   would talk with my aunt I will go home
   would any be able to take me from here

(*Mrs.* [deleted] *is just like a mother*) *would board me or
adopt me I would do my best to show my gratefulness
were to give me a thousand dollars and asked it back I would
go to Europe and wait until she forgot it*

Unclassified
*drinks it makes me mad
could see this form, she'd laugh*

I-3

Many responses at this level focus on specific actions and they are
often self-centered, though they lack the short-term opportunism of the
Delta subject. Expressions of frank dependence on the mother's help
occur at almost all levels and are classed here as a compromise. The statement that the subject would be happy (or, rarely, unhappy) if mother
had another baby is also frequent and nondiscriminating. Preoccupation
with obedience, disobedience, strictness, leniency, and raising children
the right way are typical of I-3. At this level, strictness and leniency are
seen in terms of making the subject a better behaved child. Where indirect effects are attributed to the mother's discipline, the rating is I-4.

*1. —were here (alive, younger), I'd be happy (I-3/4, 2, 4, 13;
    I-4, 1, 8)
    *were here I would enjoy myself
    and father were here I would be happier
    were younger we'd have more fun
    were living, I would spend many hours doing things with her
    live With me I be hoppy*

2. —were here, alive, younger, more modern (unelaborated)
    (I-3/4, 4)
    *was with me now
    could be with me more
    would only understand times have changed*

3. —died (were ill, left), I'd be sad (I-2, 2; I-3/4, 5)
    *was gone I don't know what I would do
    died, I would cry
    left home, I would be very upset*

4. —were in better health, I'd be happier
    *were feeling better, I wouldn't worry so much
    were not always getting tired I would be happier
    was well & able to go out & enjoy herself*

5. —were sick, I would worry, try to help '(I-3/4, 1)
   is sick I am always there to help her
   were to get hurt I would stay here

6. —tells me to do something, I do it; punishes me, I accept it
   [(I-3/4, 1)
   talks I listen
   said something I usually obeyed
   scolds me, I feel it is for my own good
   says it's so then it is true

7. Disobedience (Δ, 2; I-3/4, 10; I-4, 9)
   called me I wouldn't answer
   lectures me, I shut my ears to her
   scolded me, I talked back

8. Mother should control me; should have told me the facts of
   life (I-4, 14)
   would have refused to let me marry it would have made my
       happy
   didn't ask me she'd never get me to do any work
   were stricter, I'd like it better
   is too lenient, sometimes I might take advantage of her
   had disciplined me more, I feel that i would have been a
       much better child

9. Frank dependence on mother's help (I-2, 1; Δ, 1)
   was alive she could be most helpful
   has time she will do some shopping for me
   couldn't sew, I would be at a loss
   were here, she'd help me get well
   could only help me
   could only sew

*10. Subject's happiness contingent on mother's specific, concrete
   actions (I-3/4, 12)
   had another girl I would be happy
   worked I wouldn't like it
   could see her grandchildren I would be very happy
   marries again, I'll be happy
   buys a new car, I'll be very happy
   would spend her money it would be fun

11. Subject's mood reflects mother's (Δ, 3; I-3/4, 7)
   is happy, so am I
   is unhappy I am very depressed

is happy, I feel content
worries, I worry

12. Concrete activities shared with mother
    were home, I'd go there for dinner
    goes somewhere she envites me
    goes shopping I like to go with her
    and I get a chance, we're going on a vacation this summer
    writes me, I'll answer

13. Descriptive statement: mother is good, nice, wonderful, and so on '(I-4, 5)
    She's all right
    my mother is nice. I don't know how to answer
    Could bare 14 children she is pretty wonderful
    is kind and generous
    is a good mother

14. —loved, knew me better (I-3/4, 9)
    love me as much as my sister
    thought more like me, we could get along better

15. —would only relax, not worry, think before speaking (I-4, 2)
    would calm down
    would not worry about me so much
    would be more content

16. —would quit nagging me; would leave me alone, I'd be happier (Δ, 2)
    would only quit worrying me
    didn't fuss so much, I'd be happier
    wouldn't sometimes scream
    would not yell and scream at everything wrong I do, I would
    be much happier

17. —was mean (got drunk, swore), I'd hate her (leave home, die)
    slapped me I would break down
    was like some parnets I would hate her
    was ever unkind, I would be shocked
    yells at me for doing something I didn't do I get upset

18. Concrete contingencies
    eats too much she gets fat
    remarried I'd have a stepfather
    were living she'd be a grandmother
    would get a job we would have more money

were younger, we'd look just alike
is not at home I can't get in

19. Wish mother would stay the same (I-3/4, 6; I-4, 5)
    stays the way she is, I will always love her
    I wouldn't change her
    weren't my mother I'd be sad

20. —my mother is dead
    Don't have one

21. Matter of fact reference to test
    could only read this whole test
    saw these statements, she'd be amused
    saw this she would wonder

I-3/4

At this level there is a shift from action to somewhat differentiated feelings and from exclusive concern with self toward more concern for the mother or for the relation with the mother. Complaints about mother are couched in terms of traits or quasi-traits, most often, "were only more understanding." At I-3/4 dependence on the mother is less a need for her help or discipline and more an emotional dependence. Where the I-3 subject may report her mood as directly reflecting her mother's the I-3/4 person sees a slightly more indirect effect, with mother's mood causing an effect but not necessarily a direct reflection in the subject. In place of outright disobedience at I-3, the I-3/4 subject may express resentment of correction or resistance to advice, but there is at least a hint of its being on principle rather than on impulse.

1. —needs something, I try to help her (I-3, 5, 6)
    asked me to do anything in the world for her I would try
        to do it
    had a problem I would try to help her solve it
    was to call me I would go see what she wanted
    needs me I'm always available

2. —were closer, I would be happier (I-3, 1)
    didn't live so far away
    would be alive I would like to live near her
    lived closer I would not feel lonely so much

3. —comes to visit, I will be happy
    does not visit us I shall be hurt

didn't call me often, I'd miss it
would only take time out to talk with me

4. —were younger, we'd be closer (I-3, 1, 2)
   were younger we might get along a little bit better

5. —died (left), I would feel lost, lonely (I-2, 2; I-3, 3)
   ever left or died, I would miss her terribly as we are very
   close
   died it would be a long time before I accepted it
   moved out of town I would be lonesome
   would die I wouldn't want to live anymore. I would probably
   go nuts

6. —was any different, I wouldn't like it (I-3, 19; I-4, 5)
   was any different than she is, we wouldn't know her
   was any different I wouldn't need her. She's just fine the way
   she is

7. Effect of mother's mood on subject's (not reflection) (I-3, 11)
   looks mad, I am hurt
   is unhappy, I become very concerned
   is upset I know it
   doesn't care, I don't
   is patient, I do love her

8. Thoughts or feelings about mother's physical appearance
   would lose a little weight, she would be very attractive
   would forget about her grey hair she'd be fine
   were thinner, she would be a lot more comfortable
   wanted to, she could learn how to set her own hair
   ever dyed her hair, I would disown her

9. Complaints about mother's faults (traits) (Δ, 4; I-3, 9, 14;
   I-4, 13; I-4/5, 3)
   were only more understanding
   were less selfish, she would be happier
   wasn't so lose handed she would be better off
   had a sense of humor it would be more fun to be with her
   was more patient I could discuss matters with her better
   could solve her problems, she might be happier
   were not so dominering I would be happier
   bought clothes for me, they would be the wrong size
   wouldn't be so nervous she wouldn't get so mad as easily as
   she does

could only understand my personal feelings
would give me credit

10. —scolds me, I get angry; gives advice, I resent it (Δ, 3; I-3, 7)
    tells me something I don't think is right, I let her know
    told me what to do today, I would listen, but do as I pleased

11. —knew; finds out
    knew the things I have done she would disown me
    even knew
    was here she might know
    only knew, it would break her heart
    finds out, I'll be in trouble
    would see the way I really keep house, I would die

12. Mother's happiness contingent on concrete events (I-3, 10)
    were married, she'd be much happier
    didn't have to work, she would be happier
    were teaching school, she would enjoy it greatly
    and dad would go out more often it would be fun for them
    could get me married, she'd be happy
    could see my brother clean and tidy for once, I know she
      would be happy

13. —were living, things would be different; were different, I
    would be different (I-3, 1)
    were alive, I'd be a different person, personality wise
    had lived, life might have been a little easier

I-4

Among the new elements at the I-4 level are time perspective, indirect effects of the mother's actions or personality, regret for lost opportunities, and conceiving impulse control as a problem. We differentiate
"get mad at me I stay out of her way" (Delta) from "gets mad at me I
give her time to cool off before argueing" (I-4) on the last point, seeing
it as a problem of control.

1. Mother's feelings if she were here, living (I-3, 1)
   were alive she would encourage me
   was alive she would love her grandchildren because she was a
      very affectionate mother
   were here she'd love St. Louis
   were alive she'd be fascinated with current changes
   were alive, she'd be proud of me

2. —would relax (worry less), she would be better off (I-3, 15)
   would just learn not to worry about petty litle details!
   would be more calm, she wouldn't have high blood pressure
   would not worry about Kevin she would be happy
   didn't get angry & upset over nothing it probably would help her a great deal

3. Wish mother were more active, outgoing, less prejudiced, had broader interests (I-4/5, 2, 3)
   would only make friends and meet people
   only had some interests to occupy her time
   were only as gay as she used to be
   broadened her outlook she would be a happier person
   didn't have such petty prejudices, she'd be all right

4. Wish mother had more education, better opportunities
   had the opportunities I have had she could do even more than she has done
   If my mother had a chanc like I did she would be very lucky

5. Idealization of mother (affect-laden, individualized) (I-3, 13, 19; I-3/4, 6)
   were any better she'd be an angle
   stays just like she is she would still be a wonderful mother
   were perfect, I couldn't love her any more
   and dad weren't so great I don't know what I would do

6. Mother's effect on family, father
   is away for a lengthy time the family circle seems incomplete
   is sick or aggrevated the whole house is upset
   were still liven today our family would be better
   was hurt, I know our family would not be able to manage successfully
   didn't feel like she does, dullness would come over the home

7. Appreciation or evaluation of relation to mother (I-4/5, 2)
   sister, and I weren't as close as we are, I wouldn't be near as happy as I am
   is not as close to me as I hope my girls will be
   only really cared about me and not just for her sake I would be very happy
   loved me in a noncontrolling way, I would have been happier
   didn't love me, I would lose a lot of security in my life

8. —were here, I'd be unhappy (I-3, 1)
   were here we'd probably argue
   lived near or with me I would be a nervous wreck

were living near, I'd move
were living further from me we would get along better

9. Impulse control as a problem (I-3, 7)
   were a little less impulsive, it would probably be better for her
   had exercised more self-control
   becomes angry I close my ears off until I can talk to her
   sensably
   gets mad at me I give her time to cool off before argueing
   gets angry, she never stays so very long

10. Respect for mother's opinions, advice, guidance
    has an opinion about the things I do, I give it strong consid-
    eration
    disagrees with me, I look at her point of view
    counselled me I'd probably agree

11. Identification of self with mother (I-5, 1)
    were me, what choices would she make?
    were like I am, we would not get along as well as we do
    were in my place, I'de be real mean to her

12. Guilt, wish for mother's forgiveness (I-4/5, 1; I-5, 2)
    were living I'd show her how much I appreciate her love and
    sacrifice
    is angry with me when I leave the house, I cannot enjoy my-
    self until I apologize
    were alive I would be more understanding of her now. I wish
    she were

13. Subject's (father's, etc.) problems blamed on mother's per-
    sonality, past mistakes (I-3/4, 9)
    wasn't such a cold fish, we'd all be better adjusted
    had not worked, I would probably not be so highly emotional
    loves my father more, we would have had a much happier
    home life
    had been easier to get along with my father wouldn't have
    drank so much
    had been always understanding I probably would like more
    women
    had told me the things about entering womanhood, I would
    have known what to expect
    had understood me more—I would have understood myself
    sooner

14. Indirect effects of strictness, leniency, being raised right (I-3, 8;
    I-4/5, 1; I-5, 4)

was stricter I would not be as independent

had been more lenient, I might never have finished college

had not have been strict I may would have turned out a bad woman

had not raised me the way she did I certainly would have made many more mistakes

would not be as lenient as she is we would actually do better

had been more strict I would have accomplished more

Unclassified

were taking this test, she would be quite sincere

were here I'd like you to meet her

was older I feel she would not have been as liberal as she is

I-4/5

At the I-4/5 level the mother-child relation is seen in terms of two interacting partners. Subject gives evidence of greater distance from her feelings, which are just one aspect of the interaction. Mother is now seen as an individual with problems apart from the relation with the subject. There are indirect effects of past relations, beyond the obvious strictness-lenience aspect, and anticipation of future events. Complex psychological causation, however, is rated I-5.

1. Gratefulness for mother's past influence (I-4, 12, 14)

    had not instilled in me a great feeling for love and affection, I would not feel as secure and satisfied as I do

    could know how much she has influenced my life, I think she would be pleased

    had not stimulated my interests, would I be what I am?

    had not encouraged many of the things she did, I might not have been successful in school

2. Relation contingent on mother's differentiated traits and attitudes (I-4, 3, 7)

    had understood me better and been satisfied with my accomplishments we might have had a better relationship

    would be more human we could get along better

    were less of the "old school," we might have a closer relationship

    were not so broad minded and understanding it would present problems in our home since she lives with us

    were more open minded and less conventional, we would get along more peacably

were not such an introvert, my parents would be much happier

3. Traits affecting mother's achievements; mother's work affecting her relations (I-3/4, 9; I-4, 3)

had been more aggressive she might have "done big things"

had more self-confidence she would make better use of her many talents

had a job I believe she would be more content at home

didn't have to work so hard at her office, she might be less irritable at home due to fatigue

did not work we could share many more happy hours of pleasure

4. Anticipation of mother's old age

can live to a good age and enjoy good health, I shall be very happy

remains well and active, I will be happy

ever lost interest in what was happening, I'd be surprised and worried

wants to make her home with us when she reaches the dependent stage she knows she is invited. But she won't give up easily for her independence is second nature

5. Dependence, independence as an emotional problem

had been less protective I feel I would have assumed a greater independence at an earlier age

were less dependent upon her children, it would be easier for them to break away

could only know there are many things I have to do that she may not like

would realize that I must make certain decisions be myself or with my fiance, I would appreciate it

Unclassified

showed me that she always wants me to be happy I will be a happier person

were to change so that our relationship would differ it would be tragic

is mad at me I sometimes feel mad and sometimes hurt

could give of herself and be appreciated she was happy

isn't careful, she takes on too much responsibility

I-5

At the I-5 level, the mother is seen as an individual, functioning in one or more possibly conflicting roles other than that of subject's mother.

The subject can mention in a single response both her mother's faults and her own love, thus expressing openly her ambivalence. Mother is cherished or appreciated or criticized as an individual, just as one cherishes or criticizes other friends and relatives. Subject may become aware that barriers to a deeper or happier relation lie within herself rather than in mother. Interpersonal relations and communication are highly valued.

1. Role conception (I-4, 11)
   were less a "career woman" and more woman my dad would be happier
   would or could stop working and act as a grandma I would certainly apprec. it
   were my daughter, I wonder how I would treat her
   were only a little less of the "martyre" type, yet I admire, miss and love her

2. Importance of communication with mother (I-4, 12)
   and I could "communicate" better and more often we'd both be happier
   could only know how many things I would like to tell her and how difficult I find it to say all that is in my heart
   were still alive I could appreciate her more and express my appreciation to her. I wish it were the case

3. Circular causation
   were able to find any real happiness in her life, all who are around her would benefit
   were different, I would be different too. If she were more interested, I'd care more. If she'd care more, I'd be more interested
   would allow me to live my own life, we would both be much happier

4. Complex psychological causation (I-4, 14)
   would return to school and occupy her mind as she does her time, she would be a happier person
   had not been raised as she was, I feel I probably would've been quite different
   hadn't married so young (19) and had had less than her five children I may have looked forward to a family
   had understood her underlying motives better, she might have been a happier person
   had been punitive toward or untrusting of me when I was an adolescent, I would not have the self confidence I now possess

Unclassified

> *gets upset I feel personally responsible since she is such a sensitive—actually delicate woman*
>
> *was changed I wouldn't like it, she is fine, not perfect, but a "person" not just a woman with husband an children*
>
> *insisted on dictating the direction my life should take I would have to assert my independence*

Being with
Other People—

This stem has an I-3 pull. Being with others is the I-3 subject's *modus vivendi* in most cases. For her, being with others is fun, helps her personality, makes her feel wanted as part of a group, and passes the time. Most subjects below I-3 also give such responses, especially variations of "is a lot of fun" and "makes me feel good," but there are some expressions of I-2 and Delta concerns, the more distinctive for not being called for by the stem. Most responses at all levels are positive. Negative reactions are classed according to the kind of awareness of inner life they reveal and other usual criteria. As one rises to I-3/4 and I-4, there are more differentiated reports of inner reactions, and particularly above I-4 there is greater conceptual complexity. This may be shown as concern about the relations with other people as such, as distinct from merely being with them, or in terms of contrasting solitude with company and expressing appreciation of both, or in terms of expressing contrasting reactions.

I-2

The global, all-purpose responses "is nice" and "OK" are less appropriate than the more conventional "makes me happy" and "is lots of fun" (I-3). Statements of contingency are found at all levels for this item, as the unclassified examples show.

1. —is nice, OK (unelaborated) (I-3, 1)
   I guess its alright

2. —isn't for me (Δ/3, 1)
   makes me sick
   anoys me
   gives me the creeps

3. General description of good or bad behavior
   I am very mean
   I would try to be on my best behavor
   you would have to act nice

Unclassified
   is nice if their boys
   is okay if it isn't too bad

DELTA

The contingency found at the Delta level, "is swell if they are the right one," may indicate that the way to get ahead is to be with the "right class of people," or that one can keep out of trouble by avoiding the wrong crowd. Whether it indicates opportunism or evasion of responsibility for one's own behavior, this category is highly discriminating.

1. —is swell, all right, fun if they are good, the right type (I-3, 9)
   makes you feel good if your with the right crowd
   means a lot to me if they are the right class of people

Unclassified
   is fine (but not behind bars)
   is nice when your parents aren't around
   I will watch myself

DELTA/3

Listed here are some categories relatively more frequent below I-3 than at or above I-3. The reason is not clear.

1. —makes me nervous (unqualified) (I-2, 2; I-3/4, 4)
   scares me
   frightens me
   make me fill nervous

2. —is a chance to make new friends (I-4, 7)
   makes you know them better
   is good because you get to make friends
   is a lot of fun and you get to know them
   to be friend and have fun

3. —helps me (I-3, 3, 4)
   are so helpful to me

I-3

Almost half of all subjects respond with banal expressions of fun or approval (I-3, 1 and 2). These categories are therefore poorly discriminating, but may make the test less discomfiting than would be a succession of highly discriminating items. When one of these extremely popular responses is combined with another thought, scoring depends on the other thought. For the I-3 and Delta subject, adjustment to the group is an end in itself; being with other people helps one to that end.

**1. —is good, wonderful, enjoyable, exciting, fun, a pleasure (I-2, 1; I-3/4, 3; I-4, 1, 3)
   is nice sometimes
   is good for people at times
   is a good feeling
   is the best thing to do

**2. —makes me happy; I enjoy; I have fun; is what I like (I-4, 4)
   I like to be
   turns me on
   helps me have fun
   gives me great pleasure

3. —helps your personality; helps you socially (Δ/3, 3; I-4, 8)
   helps me look at myself and build up my personality
   helps us to mature socially

4. —you learn a lot; helps you to understand them (Δ/3, 3; I-4, 2, 7)
   helps me I learn through others
   I always learn something

5. —makes me feel wanted, part of the group, sure of myself (I-3/4, 5)
   is fun and a person knows she or he is wanted

6. —makes time pass faster
   is my favorite past-time
   is fun when you don't have anything special to do

7. —is better than being alone (I-3/4, 6)
   is more fun than just being with one or two
   is better than being on a date. I enjoy being in groups more

8. —is boring, tiring, irritating
   sometimes bores me
   is sometimes nerve racking, especially if they're loud
   at times is too much bother

9. —is all right, fun, etc. if you know them (Δ, 1; I-3/4, 8)
   I am cramped if I don't know them

10. Enjoyment contingent on numbers or ages
    is fun if they are my own age ecpesially when there is a crowd
    is a wonderful experience, except when its in a crowd

I-3/4

While the I-3 person may say that being with others is fun "at times" or "sometimes," the possibility of alternative reactions is carried a little farther at I-3/4, with responses of the type of sometimes yes, sometimes no. Naming two (or more) alternative reactions raises the level to I-4. An unqualified expression of being nervous or frightened is so frequent below I-3 that it is scored Delta/3. More differentiated inner perceptions ("shy," "self-conscious") as well as qualified expressions of nervousness ("often makes me nervous") are classed here. The categories are not sharply discriminating, and I-3 cases occur in both. Loneliness, as distinct from being alone, is an I-3/4 idea, as is having problems.

*1. —is important, necessary, essential
   I like very much and need
   means a lot many times

2. —is not important to me

makes me no difference
is not one of my problems

3. Is desirable at times, not at others (I-3, 1; I-4, 5)
   is good at sometimes times but at other times it's not
   some time I enjoy they company other time no
   can be overdone
   is fine if its not constant

4. —makes me self-conscious, shy, uneasy; sometimes makes me
   nervous (Δ/3, 1)
   gets on my nerves sometimes
   I am backward
   scares me if I don't know them
   gives me an empty feeling inside because I would sooner read
      a book than mix with a crowd

5. —gives me a sense of security (I-3, 5)
   sometimes gives a secure feeling

6. Prevents loneliness (I-3, 7; I-4/5, 1)
   i like a lot. Sometimes it gets lonly at home

7. —helps me to forget my problems
   helps me to forget things that annoy or make me sad

8. —is fun, enjoyable, etc. if you like, understand them (I-3, 9;
   I-4, 6)
   is fun if they are good friends
   is important and I enjoy it if I like their company

I-4

At I-4 being with other people is a means to the end of a deeper experience of life, contrasting with the I-3 view of it as a means to the end of group adjustment. Obviously many responses are equivocal with respect to this distinction, and the rules for classifying them must be correspondingly arbitrary. The I-4 subject not only has a richer, more differentiated inner life than those at lower levels; she is interested in the inner life of others. Thus she may use social interaction to see things through another's eyes. She is aware of differences in mood but (for this item at least) tends to express those differences in rather commonplace terms. What is commonplace here is essentially what can be found in category titles at this and lower levels for this item.

    *1. —is stimulating, challenging, rewarding, interesting, a pleasant experience (I-3, 1)

is satisfying, some time
is generally refreshing
is usually a pleasant experience

2. —is a learning experience; is an education itself; is itself an experience (I-3, 4)

3. —is one of life's pleasures (I-3, 1)
   has been an important factor in my life
   at times is essential to happiness

4. —relaxes me; cheers me up; brightens the day (I-3, 2)
   is fun and peps me up
   is a good way to overcome the blues
   makes me feel fresh and alive
   makes me feel better

5. Affects me differently at different times (I-3/4, 3; I-4/5, 4)
   can be interesting, exciting, dull, or however I wish to make it
   sometimes I feel relaxed, sometimes tired, and sometimes bored
   is enjoyable at times, necessary at times, and undesirable at other times
   can be very plesant or tiring
   is sometimes stimulating and other times boring
   can be stimulating & boring

6. Enjoyment contingent on inner qualities (I-3/4, 8; I-4/5, 2, 3)
   is enjoyable if I'm in the mood
   is something I enjoy if they are happy, Christian people
   is fun if everyone is their self and not too sophisticated
   whom I know and am comfortable with is relaxing

7. Helps you learn about other kinds of people, their problems, and so on (Δ/3, 2; I-3, 4)·
   is a great experience to discover different types of people and personalities
   is one way of finding you're not the only one with problems
   is always a pleasure to me, for I am the person that hates being alone, and am always interested in learning interests of other people
   makes me feel bad, I see myself as I would like to be

8. Helps one to a broader view of life, deepens one's personality (I-3, 3)
   helps one to realize to accept life and change only what is to be changed

stimulates one's thinking and emotional reactions
enlightens me, give me new ideas thought and the like

9. Opportunity for expression, comparison of ideas
   is a challenge to put what you know and think against what
   they know and think
   and sharing fun and ideas with them to me beats having all
   the money and success in the world

10. —is natural, a part of life, normal, healthy
    is part of growing up
    is generally a normal desire
    is part of the social animal
    is necessary for a person to remain normal
    is a sign of health

I-4/5

Touchstones of responses above the I-4 level are concern for the interpersonal relation as such; contrasting attitudes, often contingent on mood or compatibility; contrasting the need or desire for company with that for solitude or privacy. Almost all responses are uniquely phrased. There is an elusive common element in the unclassified responses at I-4/5, implicitly contrasting being with other people with having a genuine relation with them.

1. Contrasted with desire for solitude or privacy; need for both
   (I-3/4, 6)
   can be gratifying at times—then too at times I wish I could
   go to the moon
   is great. I like to be alone sometimes but not too often
   is more enjoyable when one has privacy available at other
   times
   too much doesn't leave one to think much alone

2. Enjoyment contingent on relation: compatibility, feelings
   aroused (I-4, 6; I-5, 1)
   usually lifts my spirits if they and I are at all compatible
   is nice if you can feel at ease and are around the kind you
   like and those you can learn to like
   sometimes makes me want to cry because I feel they really
   don't want me

3. Stimulation, satisfaction contingent on inner qualities (I-4, 6)
   can be satisfying or disappointing—depending on the people
   and one's own mood

stimulates me only when we have something in common

is stimulating and interesting if the other people are interesting

4. Contrasting reactions (not including banalities such as fun, boring) (I-4, 5)

is the source of our great pleasure and most nerve-wracking worry

can be comforting or troublesome

can be the best or the worst feeling—it depends

can be everything from torture to sheer delight

Unclassified

is often a defense against being alone with oneself

is not always an answer to loneliness

is not always communicating with them. I often prefer to observe them

I-5

At I-5 appreciation of the worth of other people may transcend the issue of compatibility. "Relationships with people give life meaning" is characteristic. All the unclassified responses at this level are conceptually complex. Most of them elaborate an idea which would by itself be classed at I-4/5. Many of these responses came from I-6 protocols, but there does not seem to be a clear rule for distinguishing I-5 from I-6 responses.

1. Appreciation of other people's worth, one's own need for relations with others (I-4/5, 2)

is something that I have to have my friends mean an awful lot to me

sometimes upsets me or sometimes is something I really need. A lot depends on who the other people are

is my cup of tea I don't like to be alone. Having children really fills the gap

is a joy since relationships with people give life meaning

is something I like very much because people are a new adventure every time you meet someone new or converse with any human successfully

is often a wearisom waste of time; however, I occasionally discover an involvement with others that I find reassurance in

Unclassified

helps one to develop himself socially, mentally and emotionally

*is something I enjoy but if they are strangers I have a tend-
ency to shy away from them which gives the impression
that I'm a snob*

*makes for a good time. But you sometimes need privacy, and
married couples need time to be "two" alone*

*can be the most enjoyable experience, whether one is actively
engaged with them or just observant—at least most of the
time. I like to be alone at times too*

*is necessary for real living provided a person can also live
with himself*

*is tremendously stimulating, but much of the world's work is
done in loneliness*

*is generally a pleasure, can be a great solace in time of need
or loneliness but may be a bore, depending on the occasion
and people involved*

The Thing I Like About Myself Is—

For many of our early samples this item was the first one on the form. That was a mistake. We had to learn to start with a less threatening item, just as the early intelligence testers learned to ask children to point to the eyes and nose of a doll rather than to their own. The answers evoke a wide range of qualities, with no one predominant or even frequent; this in itself shows that the item is challenging.

One response to the challenge is more or less to reject the item. Omission is not frequent, but there are an appreciable number of responses like "nothing" (I-2), "everything" (Delta), "myself" (I-3), "I don't know," and "you wouldn't want me to be conceited would you" (I-3/4). They are about as scorable as more germane replies.

Easy distinctions based on content do not separate levels. Many responses ("my sense of humor," "I get along with others," and references to appearance) occur in indistinguishable form over a wide range. The discriminating power of the item is increased by taking into account afterthoughts and subordinate clauses. "I'm nice" is scored Delta, but "I'm nice—I really am nice to others, especially good friends and near strangers" is scored I-4 on the basis of distinguishing degrees of acquaintanceship; the response actually comes from an I-6 protocol. Although references to appearance are scored Delta/3, the response "the softness of my skin (This sounds conceited)" is scored I-3/4.

Topics that recur at different levels permit one to trace in capsule some aspects of ego development. Morality progresses from cleanliness (I-2) to being nice to others (I-3) to being honest and trustworthy (I-3/4) to following one's own convictions (I-4). Capacity for interpersonal relations changes from other people get along with me (Delta) to I try to please others (I-3) to I get along with others (I-3/4) to respect for their point of view (I-4) to conceptualizing the qualities in oneself that enable one to understand others (I-4/5). Adjustment proceeds from "that I know I can get a lot of guys to like me" (Delta) to being happy and having fun (I-3) to getting along with others (I-3/4) to ability to adjust or cope with situations (I-4) to quite varied expressions of a zest for life (I-4/5).

For most subjects below I-3 and to a considerable extent at I-3 one likes things about oneself that are simply given: "my height," "my nose," "that I am like by others," "being a woman," and "my background." At I-4 and above responses in terms of passively received gifts are rare. What one likes about oneself is always something in which one participates more or less actively: interests, efforts, relations with others, and self-reliance. Thus the item illustrates growth in sense of choice and control over one's destiny. One subject responded, "my mind; a gift I know, but don't have to work too hard to get things." Thus she is both conscious it is a gift and answering in terms of active participation.

I-2

The response "nothing" is not uncommon, particularly among adolescents. It may of course be indicative of depression rather than I-level; the rest of the protocol can be counted on to indicate the distinction. Responses classed here are stated as fact ("I am clean") rather than as goal ("that I try to keep myself clean at all times" I-3).

1. —nothing, not much (I-3/4, 11)
   nothing much

2. —I am cute, good looking (Δ/3, 1)
   that I think I am pretty

3. Primitive socialization of impulses or bodily processes (Δ/3, 2)
   I am clean
   not drinking

DELTA

The Delta person is likely to deny faults and defects. She may claim, perhaps sarcastically, exaggerated virtues valued by the culture ("I am so lovable"), but these are things one does not say about oneself. In contrast with "that I like people" (I-3) or "my ability to get along with people" (I-3/4), she may state "that most people can get along with me." What is liked is thus not part of oneself but displaced to others' reactions to the subject.

1. —everything
   everything with nothing lacking
   all of me

2. —I'm nice, good, charming, sweet (I-3, 1, 2)
   my sweet disposition
   I am so lovable
   my charming personality
   I am good at times and I am short

3. —people like me; people get along with me (I-3/4, 1)
   that people say I am very nice

4. Manipulativeness and deception
   that I know I can get a lot of guys to like me
   the way to handle boys
   my ability to keep secrets that people tell me

5. —I am not conceited (I-3/4, 8)
   that I'm modest

6. —I am lucky

Unclassified
   I respect those who respect me

DELTA/3

Responses concerning physical appearance, most often singling out one feature ("my legs," "my body"), are common at I-3 and below. Where they occur with another remark, scoring is based on the other part.

*1. Appearance (I-2, 2)
   that I am skinny and don't have to worry about weight loss
   my smile
   that I have finally goten over being tall
   my eyes

2. Neatness (I-2, 3; I-3, 9)
   that I am neat

Unclassified
   I take after my father

I-3

The qualities mentioned at I-3 are often social ones, sense of humor, nice to others, like people. Of the more abstract traits, there are practicality and efficiency and not having a bad temper. Such responses as being a woman, having a nice husband, and family background, are similar to mention of appearance (scored Delta/3 but frequent at I-3) in that they are things given rather than striven for. Having a family or friends (I-3) is distinguished from dedication to or appreciation of family or friends (I-3/4), admittedly at times a difficult distinction.

*1. Pleasing social personality: sense of humor, friendliness (Δ, 2; I-3/4, 2; I-4, 3)
   I laugh a lot
   that I am happy
   I am gentle
   sometimes my personality

*2. Social virtues: kind, nice to others; try to please them (Δ, 2; I-3/4, 3, 4, 6; I-4, 1, 10)
   I am a true friend
   being fair to everyone
   I'm considerate
   I help others
   my desire to please people
   that I try not to be unkind to people

that I try to like everyone
that I am understanding

3. —I like, enjoy, am interested in others (I-3/4, 2, 4)
   that I like people and go out of my way to meet them
   the way I usually enjoy being with people
   that I like fun with everyone

4. —I have fun; I like things
   I like doing everything
   that I can have fun almost anywhere I go

5. Calmness, don't get upset, self-control (I-4, 4; I-4/5, 4)
   that I never get too mad
   I don't panic easily
   I am trying to overcome my quick temper
   my patience

6. Traits dealing with level-headedness, practicality, efficiency, dependability, ambition
   my ability to use good common sense
   that I am firm
   my sense of responsibility
   I have an organized mind
   my ambition to get ahead in this competitive world

7. —I mind my own business
   that I do not bother about every day life of other people

8. Specific actions
   I wash clothes good
   I have manners at the table
   the way I act when I meet new people
   the way I sleep so soundly
   I make good grades
   that I don't have very much to say to anyone unless they say something to me
   that I don't talk about myself

9. —I try to be neat, clean (Δ/3, 2)
   that I try and keep myself clean at all times
   that I try to keep everything neat

10. Being a woman, girl, wife, mother
    that I am what I am—a woman

11. Having a home, family, children, friends (I-3/4, 4, 5)
    I married a nice person
    that I've got a twin brother

12. Background, religion, training, heritage (I-4, 2)
    my high cheek bones & my inheritage
    my belief
    I was raised in a very nice home

13. —I am healthy, normal

14. —I am old fashioned

15. Individuality, independence (not elaborated) (I-5, 1)
    I am an individual
    I am somewhat independent

16. —myself
    that I am what I am

I-3/4

At this level the things liked about self mostly are wishes or actions rather than something just given. One is able to love, gets along with others, puts one's family first, and tries to help others. The moral virtues are Boy Scoutish, a step above the I-3 being nice to others but below the I-4, who has self-evaluated standards. The reflexive traits at I-3/4 for this item are self-respect and self-confidence. The self-consciousness and lack of self-confidence often mentioned at I-3/4 for other stems would of course not fit the stem. Note that "I respect those who respect me" is scored Delta; it represents a different usage of the term respect.

*1. —I get along with others (Δ, 3)
    my ability to get along with little children
    I try to get along with everyone
    I am so easy to get alone with

2. Ease of conversation, making friends (I-3, 1, 3)
    being able to talk to almost anybody
    that I love to meet new people and I make friends easily

3. Desire to help others (I-3, 2; I-4, 1, 10)
    that I get pleasure out of helping others
    that I try to do my best to make others as happy as possible

4. Being able to love; show love; feel warm (I-3, 2, 3, 11)
    my love for children & people
    I look nice for my husband & show him that I love him
    that I have love for God, my family & my fellow man
    I feel warm toward people

5. Dedication to family; appreciation of friends and family (I-3, 11)
   I always try to make my familey first
   that I am a very good wife, mother and housekeeper
   that I am trying to make a good home
   that I have contributed to having a happy marriage
   the type of friends with whom I have become acquainted

6. Moral virtues: honest, unselfish, trustworthy, frank (I-3, 2; I-4, 2; I-4/5, 1)
   sincerity
   my ability to cooperate
   that I always try to be honest with others

7. Self-respect; self-confidence (I-4, 5)
   I Need Not be ashamed of most things I do

8. —I don't want to seem conceited; unassuming, not proud (Δ, 5; I-4, 6)
   that I don't like to talk about my better ways
   that I try not to put on airs to impress someone
   the softness of my skin (This sounds conceited)
   I can't always think of anything and besides, you wouldn't want me to be conceited would you

9. Abilities (not elaborated) (I-4, 7)
   my talent
   I am very capable
   my intelligence

10. Realistic
    My will to face reality
    being able to take life as it comes

11. —nothing in particular; don't know (I-2, 1)
    not to unusual
    cant come to mind
    ?
    hard to say because now that I think of it I don't know much of anything outstanding about me

I-4

At I-4 morality involves one's own philosophy, rather than taking over prescribed virtues (I-3/4). Being nice to others now involves seeing from their point of view. Self-criticism is characteristic, as well as need for achievement. Perhaps ability to adjust or cope with situations is the equivalent of the I-3/4 getting along with people. While "individuality" and "independence," as one-word responses or simple, unelaborated ideas, are scored I-3, "adaptability" and "my flexibility" are scored I-4. Apparently the subjects have some meaning of individuality and independence quite different from that of the raters; such self-descriptions appear on protocols otherwise very conventional. Perhaps adaptability and flexibility in common speech differ somewhat less from the usage of the raters. The response "my sense of humor" (I-3) is nondiscriminating, occurring from Delta at least through I-5. We know from the remainder of the protocol that different sorts of things are considered humorous at different levels. Some less trite ways of talking about a sense of humor are classed here. Conceptual complexity appears in making distinctions between appearance and feelings and in distinguishing degrees of intimacy.

1. Respect for others: sensitivity to their needs, feelings, reasons (I-3, 2; I-3/4, 3)

   my ability to understand why people do what they do sometimes

   that I like most people and try hard not to be critical

   that I can be straight to the point without hurting anyone

   my ability or rather my determination to be abjective and non judgmental when evaluating a clients situatuion

2. Inner moral standards; my own beliefs (I-3, 12; I-3/4, 6)

   my philosophy of life

   my conscientiousness. Knowing what is right from wrong and then a will to do right is so important for anyone

   my ideals

   that I have perseverance and courage, and follow my own convictions

3. —my good nature; my optimism (I-3, 1; I-4/5, 1)

   the ability to laugh at myself

   my ability to laugh with others instead of at them

   my ability not to take life too seriously

   my sense of the ridiculous

   the fact that I can usually try to see the good side of things

   that I recover from disappointments easily

4. —my ability to adjust, cope with different situations (I-3, 5; I-4/5, 4)

   my flexibility

   adaptability

that I usually try to find a logical way to handle any difficulty as soon as it arises

that I am unselfish, and quite adaptable

5. Self-reliance; self-sufficient (I-3/4, 7)

    I try to solve my own problems before asking for help

    that I'm independly able to make a living with my own trade

6. Self-improvement; see own faults, limitations (I-3/4, 8; I-4/5, 1)

    that I know I am never too old to learn something. And I am willing to hear other out

    that I'm self-critical

    that I'm trying to make something of myself

7. Abilities and interests (specified) (I-3/4, 9; I-4/5, 2)

    my interest in so many different things

    I have the ability to be interested in really good books and projects

    that I can play the piano

    my capabilities as a housewife

8. Desire for, concern with accomplishment; ability, effort to get things done

    determination

    my perseverance

    that I never give up

    that I always like a challenge

    my efforts to do well

    that I'm easy to make friends and I'm a good worker

9. Distinguishing appearance or actions from mood or feelings

    that I am moody which can be quite deceptive

    I am most becoming when I am happy

    an ability to look and act composed on some occasions when I'm not

    my control of appearance and expression

10. Contribution to society (I-3, 2; I-3/4, 3)

    that I'm in a worthwhile career

    I enjoy being useful and busy

    I try to be worthwhile

Unclassified

I'm nice—I really am nice to others, especially good friends and near strangers

that I do not find it difficult to talk to people I know only slightly or not at all
I seem to receive more in this life than I deserve

I-4/5

To be honest with or objective about oneself is rated here, contrasting with being honest about others (I-3/4) or objective about them (I-4). New elements at this level are (rare) responses indicating some emancipation from the standards adhered to below the I-4 level, and a zest for life, usually given unique expression.

1. —that I am honest with myself, objective about myself (I-3/4, 6; I-4, 3, 6)
   that I don't try to lie to myself
   my honesty when dealing with other people as well as myself

2. Interpersonal ability (I-4, 7)
   that I can work in groups with others to arrive at a solution to a problem
   that I think I can sympathize with other people and am able to feel what they feel (empathy?)
   my reaction to people which makes for warm relationships
   although my own ideals are very high, I think that I can understand and relate to others who feel differently
   my ability to take a sincere interest in other people
   my ability to get along with my close friends and maintain a friendship for a long time
   I seem to have a way of "getting through" to other people

3. Freedom from conformist and materialistic standards
   I don't wonder constantly how others see me. Most often I couldn't care less
   I am completely free of materialistic and "high" aiming goals

4. Ability to tolerate stress (elaborated) (I-3, 5; I-4, 4)
   that I can react casually and appropriately and produce even under sever pressure
   my ability to relax and rid myself of many unimportant tense moments
   that I am relatively serene and able to take things in my stride
   I do not panic in times of crises

5. Zest for life
   the thrills I get by such tomboyish things as jumping on a trampoline

the ability to reach out for new experiences
that I truly enjoy meeting people, going places, and keeping
an ever growing list of interests
the fact that I am often most content when doing everyday,
seemingly unimportant tasks
that I can usually find something happy and stimulating dur-
ing the day—almost always

Unclassified
having parents who allowed me to make my own decisions
early
my mind; a gift I know but don't have to work too hard to
get things
what I consider my honesty and integrity, perhaps false
gradually learning to be independent

I-5

There is relatively little in the way of specific new content expressive of the I-5 level. Responses classed at I-5 combine several thoughts each of which separately would be classed lower; these contain themes referring to social and to internal aspects and imply a complex and differentiated conception of oneself.

1. Concern for individuality and identity (I-3, 15)
   that I am an individual and am liked for that reason above
   all else
   the freedom I have to choose the way of life I wish and to be
   an individual
   my ability to love without losing my identity?? (Oh yeah?)

2. Combination of at least three different traits (at least one
   at I-4)
   my ability to organize & what I hope is genuine humility &
   a basic compassion for people
   I care about ideals as well as practicalities, I'm willing to be
   an outsider if it means compromising something I hold very
   dear. But I can compromise
   that like most people, I like to do many different things, I
   find many things in life that are humorous as well as seri-
   ous, and I believe in God
   my sensitivity to the world around me, to people's feelings,
   and my sense of humor
   my life—the family into which I was born, the socio-economic

background, the opportunities I had—still have, my education, intelligence, my marriage, my philosophies, and goals

my honesty and my real affection for and interest in people

that I can adjust myself quite well usually in different situations and societies and usually do not have much difficulties in being accepted or to accept others as they are

Unclassified

that I like all humanity, I'm glad to be one with them

my abilities to face the actualities, sometimes pleasant, often not, about life and myself

My Mother and I—

In rating this item
we are judging ego development, not the quality of the mother-daughter
relation. While the subject's I-level puts some limits on the relations open
to her, it is only one factor in any of them. We look therefore for different ways of describing similar situations, whether close and loving or distant or quarrelsome.

This stem provides little opportunity to express low I-level, but
there are many scorable high-level responses. Virtually all subjects consider this a question about the relation; thus those who turn it into a
statement about physical distance can be assumed to be expressing a limi-
tation in their interpersonal capacity, hence limited ego level. A statement
about behavior in common but not together ("drink") reflects a low
level by similar reasoning.

Among the least differentiating categories are "are close," "get
along well" (I-3), and "are friends" (I-3/4). Expressions of petulant

quarreling, without statement that these quarrels are limited in time or concern only some aspects of the relation, are rated below I-3; they are relatively if not absolutely more frequent below that level. We may contrast the Delta category, "don't get along" or "have arguments," with the I-3/4 category that includes "do not agree about all matters" and "disagree about spending money"; the latter contrasts also with I-4, "have differences of opinion," and "have different values."

Omissions of response to this stem come more often from protocols below I-3 than above, though the rating is I-3 as in the case of other items. Omission may be another way of coping with the situation described by some respondents in terms such as "separate when I was small" or "my mother is dead" (I-3) and by others as "never knew each other" (I-4). To say that one never knew one's mother is to indicate that even though one has nothing to go on, it is conceived as a potential interpersonal situation rather than merely physical separation.

I-2

The typical I-2 response to this stem is a positive one, for example, "get along real well." Such responses, however, are classed at I-3. Only global, somewhat inappropriate "OK" is classed at this level. When the I-2 subject gives a negative response it is likely to be "fight." Even where the subject means quarrel (Delta) rather than actual physical combat, the response itself is intemperate when worded thus. Also classed at this level are those responses describing behavior common to both subject and mother. These appear to be crude attempts to describe similarity, and are differentiated from responses classed Delta/3 that are concerned with doing things together, "clean house together on Saturday."

1. —fight
   fight sometimes

2. —OK, all right
   are OK all of the time
   is OK sometime
   are alright

3. Behavior in common (but no implication this is done together) (Δ/3, 1)
   drink
   go swimming alot
   go to work at the same time

Unclassified
   are the same

DELTA

Subjects at the Delta level, like those at I-2, usually give responses classed at the I-3 level. Classed here are responses indicating a complete submersion in the mother-daughter conflict without any qualification indicating a limit of the time or occasion or intensity of the conflicts. Time references are unusual below I-3; hence any reference to time, even "have never gotten along," raises the response to I-3/4.

1. —quarrel; argue; don't get along (unqualified) (I-3/4, 3)
   have many arguements
   don't get along together
   are always arguing
   hate each other

Unclassified
   dont get in trouble at all because I love her and she loves me
   get along when she has money
   can get along wonderfully when we have too
   are the same sex

DELTA/3

The category "do things together" contrasts with one at I-2 that lacks the implication "together" and one at I-3 that adds mention of enjoying it. These responses occur in similar terms from I-2 through I-4, and are classed here as a compromise.

*1. —do things together (I-2, 3; I-3, 4)
   clean house together on Saturday
   are going shopping tonight
   had lunch yesterday
   were planning a trip
   went to Church
   go shoping and I like it when she buys me candy

I-3

The most frequent categories of response are clichés about the quality of the relation, "are close, not close," "get along well." Responses in these categories come from the entire range of I-level. Two action-oriented categories concern talking and enjoying doing things together. The latter must be distinguished from the category, "do things together," classed at Delta/3. Doubtful responses ("like to clean the house") are classed here if they involve feelings about the activities. Several categories refer to physical closeness or distance, including one that states that the mother is dead. The statement "are like sisters" is classed here whereas the comparative "are more like sisters" is placed at I-3/4. Comparisons classed here are superficial, mostly referring to physical appearance.

**1. —are close, not close; were, have been close, not close
  are very close together
  are as close as anything
  are as close as sisters
  are not very close
  are distant
  were never close
  were close before she died

**2. —get along well
  get along fabously
  get along well most of the time
  get along ok

3. —love each other
  were devoted to each other
  care a lot for each other
  liked each other

*4. —have fun together; enjoy each other's company; enjoy doing things together (Δ/3, 1; I-4, 11)
  have fun talking in whatever we do
  are constantly joking with each other
  had lots of fun together most of the time, until shortly before her death
  enjoyed fishing
  gad about
  loved to take trips together
  love to go antiquing
  if were living would be very happy together

5. —talk
  were discussing my roomate
  talk together a great deal
  always have women to women talks
  talk a lot about my problems
  talked quite freely and openly
  often talk about world problems

6. —are like sisters (I-3/4, 7)
   were like sisters

*7. Superficial comparison (I-3/4, 8; I-4, 11)
   are said to look alike
   were both grey-haired at 22
   have large family
   wear the same size dress
   both have the same religion

8. —live together; don't live together; are separated (I-4, 7)
   live in the same house
   are in separate countries. I am here and she is in Africa
   are far apart
   separt when I was Small

9. —don't see much of each other (I-4, 7)
   see each other once a year—she lives in Florida
   never get to see each other

10. —my mother is dead (I-4, 7)
    I do not rebember my mother
    Don't have one
    were never together since she died when I was 2 yrs. old

Unclassified
   make up 1/3 of my family
   are mother and daughter

I-3/4

Most categories here represent slightly more precise versions of I-3 categories. Where the I-3 subject and her mother were close, the I-3/4 subject says they are friends, or understand each other, or were close at a particular time of life. (The "good friends" responses are found at all levels.) A compound of I-3 categories is "close though separated." A category concerning not getting along represents a qualified version of a theme found at the Delta level. The relation with the mother may be compared with other relations, at this level only in banal terms such as "close" or "get along." Comparison of mother and subject, given only in superficial terms at I-3, appears in global terms here: alike or different. Comparisons of personality, interests, and values typify the I-4 level.

**1. —are friends; are companions
   are sometimes pals

are pals not just mother and daughter
are like best friends which is okay with me
would have been good companions

2. —understand each other; do not understand each other
   always had an understanding
   have mutual understanding
   just don't understand each other

3. —argue; don't get along (qualified or sense of time implied)
   (Δ, 1; I-4, 8)
   often argue
   do not get along at times
   don't get along too well
   are not getting along
   did not get along
   can No Live together eaisly

4. —were close at a particular time (I-4, 3)
   were very close when I was living at home
   were always very close when I was just a little tyke
   were very close after my father died

5. —are close though separated; miss each other
   are apart, but are still close
   miss each other we live miles apart
   are yet close, even if we are not in the same State

6. —argue but get along (I-4, 12; I-4/5, 1)
   don't always agree with each other, but I like to listen to her
   advice
   are very close but we also have many spats
   seem to be close sometimes but we have our misunderstandings
   agree on many things but misunderstand on others

7. Relation with mother compared with other relations (I-3, 6)
   were always closer than my father and I
   are very close as she is with the rest of her children
   Always understands each other and are close but I was always
   a Daddy's child
   got along much better than my friends & their Moms
   are as close as a mother and daughter can be
   have always been close, but we are not like sisters
   get along better than average
   were more like friends than relatives
   are more like sisters

8. Global comparison: are alike, not alike (I-3, 7; I-4, 10, 11)
   have a lot in common
   are alike in many ways
   are different
   have very little in common
   are similar types of women
   are not close, nor are we alike in any way

I-4

Responses at this level often concern the quality of the relation, but are in some way more complex than those at I-3. The complexity may take the form of less banal expression (respect or appreciate rather than get along or are close) or closeness may be seen as contingent on growing older or other circumstances. However, if the only contingency is the mother's death ("were close before she died"), the rating is I-3. Comparisons are qualified rather than absolute ("are very much alike yet very different"). The most characteristic responses at this level compare mother and subject in terms of ideas, problems, feelings, traits, or values.

1. —have a good, close, open relationship
   have a very fine relationship
   relate well
   have a very mature relationship
   enjoyed a happy relationship, especially when I was in my late teens
   have a great companionship and understanding

2. —respect, appreciate, are good for each other
   enjoy, appreciate, and even help each other
   have a respect for each others views
   argue, but love and respect each other
   are very good for each other

3. —are closer; get along better (I-3/4, 4; I-4/5, 3)
   were much closer as we grew older
   are closer now that I've left home
   have become closer during my college years
   get along better now that I'm older
   are not really very close but we are improving

4. Wish for greater closeness
   should have a more confidential relationship

*don't get along as well as I think we should. I don't feel able
to tell her everything I do*

5. Contingent relation
   get alone pretty well as long as we are not alone
   *do not get along too well if we live in the same household for
   very long*
   get along good if my brother isn't around

6. Distant relation; cannot communicate
   are unable to communicate very well
   *are quite distant in relation to feelings and expressing thoughts
   in personal subjects*
   have never had a close relationship

7. —never knew each other well (I-3, 8, 9, 10)
   knew each other a short time, She died young

8. —disagree; have differences of opinion (I-3/4, 3)
   differ
   think different
   disagree about the type of man I should marry
   don't see eye to eye

9. Sharing of ideas, problems; think alike
   *are very close and I can tell her anything knowing she will
   always listen to me*
   *get along very well, confiding in each other and working out
   little problems and doing things together*
   *can share things (such as ideas, etc.)—that I can share only
   with her*
   sometimes set down, and talk out our problems
   can talk things out
   share different views on various subjects
   understand one anothers problems

10. —have different (similar) ideas, values, opinions (I-3/4, 8)
    have different standards of right and wrong
    believe differently
    were worlds apart

11. —are similar (different) in personality, feelings, interests (I-3,
    4, 7; I-3/4, 8)
    are very much the same emotionally
    are very congenial
    share some unfortunate traits
    enjoy good music

both enjoy cooking a great deal and trading recipes often
both like clothes of good quality and taste
are very different in our interests and abilities

12. —are alike yet different; get along well although we are different (I-3/4, 6; I-4/5, 1)
    are alike in many ways; yet so different in others
    *are not very much alike, although we get along together very
    well*
    have different interests, but still have much common ground
    *don't have much in common, but she is the best person in the
    world*
    have some things in common, but generally do not think alike

13. —do things similarly, differently
    handle my son differently
    do not go about things in the same way

14. —work well together
    work as a team
    would work well together

I-4/5

On many items a combination of two or more different aspects leads to I-4/5 or I-5 ratings; for this stem there must be contrasting of different aspects to justify an I-4/5 rating. Two categories here deal with change in the relation over time. One deals simply with improved relations, "have become friends now that I'm grown," and is differentiated from the similar category at I-4 in that subject does not use the cliché "are closer" or "get along better," indicating a more personal evaluation of the change. The second category contains a more complex view of the relation. The relation has improved because of mutual problems, hardships, or experiences, thus implying not only a change in the relation but in each of the members. The final category, too close or too much alike, represents a further departure from conventional views.

1. Contrast of different aspects of relation (I-3/4, 6; I-4, 12)
    were not alike in any way but I loved and admired her
    have personality clashes, but she is there when needed
    are independent though devoted
    *are alike in many ways yet differ and disagree without too
    much*
    understand each other's shortcomings and respect one another

*look alike but I do not have the energy or as as good outlook
on life as she does*

*are very close but do not manifest our feelings in actions or
even words*

were different in externals; similar in temperament

get along well but secretly she get my ire up at times

*sometimes disagree on basic issues but remain the dearest of
friends*

*are very close. We trust and confide in each other and respect
each others idea. We do argue but not often*

2. Close relation a result of mutual hardships, problems, experiences

*have a better relation since I've been married because she can
understand my problems better*

have been brought closer together through hardships

became close to one another only when she was old and ill

*shared many experiences together which endeared us to each
other*

*have always been close, but now are very, very, close since my
father died*

3. Quality of relation or feelings improved over time (I-4, 3;
I-5, 2)

have become better friends now that I'm grown

are more equal since I've gone to college

*have a much better relationship now than we did when I was
an adolescent*

are more understanding of each other than 5–10 yrs ago

*have more and more in common and have grown closer as I
have grown older*

are becoming closer as I mature in my understanding of her

4. —are too close, too much alike

*have always been very close—possibly too much so for our
own good*

are very much alike even though I don't like to think so

*like each other but we are so much alike that we get into
each other's hair at times*

Unclassified

*have often sit down and talked of becoming a woman and
mother*

used to talk for hours and "solve the world's problems

*are much alike in temperament but I realized this only after
I was grown*
*are in a way like sisters in that we talk on any subject and
aren't ashamed*

I-5

The elements of responses at the I-5 level are similar to those at the I-4/5 level, coping with ambiguity, contradiction, and complexity of causation, and seeing oneself in perspective, most often time perspective. Responses classed here, however, are often more unique and vivid in their evocation of feeling. Complex notions of psychological causation justify an I-5 rating. All responses classed here involve at least two ideas.

1. Role differentiation
    *have always had a pleasant relationship, although she depends
    on me for decisions*
    don't get along in our personal lives—only in business
    *have not only a "family" relationship and love, but also a
    companion, intellectual admiration and relationship*

2. Complex psychological causation; relation or comparison in perspective (I-4/5, 3)
    *share many of the same feelings so that we cannot work to-
    gether easily*
    *love one another but do not understand each others ideas or
    happiness*
    *don't understand each other and expect too much from one
    another*
    are very close—psychologically on the same wave length
    *had many mutual character traits, yet our total personalities
    were very different*
    *belong to different generations, with the usual difference in
    behavior and morals*
    *get along very well now because I finally understand that par-
    ents are not expected to be perfect and her little habits
    don't bother me*

3. Complex relation with unique and vivid feelings
    *do not get along as well as most mothers and daughters, but
    our love for each other is deep*
    *got along very well, we had a deep love and respect for each
    other as people*

should have been closer. Why we weren't I don't know, except I was always afraid of disappointing her and as an adult I never wanted to burden her with my problems

don't always get along well together, I try to understand her but I let her get on my nerves too easily

can become petty and quarrelsome—yet each can bear their innermost hearts to the other without fear—we know, till death, each is for the other

love one another; we know how to laugh when we approach a point of needless dissention

are quite, different in temperament, ideals, thoughts in general and I don't feel I have ever really gotten a chance to know her

I-6

To rate a response at I-6 one would look for a combination of I-5 ideas, or the problem of identity in context of I-5 ideas, as in the response illustrated.

Unclassified

get along, but I need to get away to develop myself. I praise her because she is a woman, and a person. I am a person, but not yet a woman

What Gets Me into Trouble Is—

This item is given differing interpretations at different I-levels. At low levels it is taken to mean something like "The kind of trouble I get in is—" or "I blame my troubles on—." At high levels the meaning becomes more like "My trouble is (I tend to)—." At low levels blame is put on situations and on other people; "trouble" means getting caught. At high levels there is self-criticism. When self-criticism occurs at I-3, it tends to concern specific actions; at I-4 it tends to concern traits or tendencies. Emotions are mentioned in a small percentage of cases: temper occurs at all levels but is classed I-3; love is mentioned at I-3, needing love at I-4. Worrying and shyness appear at I-3/4, insecurity and inadequacy at I-4, and unique responses referring to depression and loneliness occur at I-5. These deeply

84

felt responses, as well as others with a light touch ("something that rarely concerns me greatly," I-4), are a long way from those that blame others or that see the problem as one of getting caught ("not minding," Delta/3).

Talking is a frequent response at I-3 and, with appropriate variations, at all higher levels. Below I-3 it usually is "my (big) mouth," a version that does not seem to occur above I-4 but is very common at I-3. Sex, like temper, is the kind of thing that does indeed give trouble to all sorts of people. The I-2 version is "boys"; at Delta it is the wrong people or reference to subject's body. The latter responses parallel "my mouth"; it is as if, while not blaming another person, one blames one's own body, which is not quite part of the self. Interpersonal concerns are evident at all levels for this stem, but concern for achievement is marked only at I-4, though there are references to not studying at I-3, and one I-2 subject said "school."

I-2

There are three kinds of responses here: the usual good-bad category, blaming other people, and physical expressions of aggression. Sexual acts are implied in many of the responses, since the other people blamed are usually specified as "boys." Many responses at I-3 and below mention a concrete thing or situation. "My telephone" (I-3) can be considered an example of ordinary ellipsis. The response "school" (I-2) seems more illogical.

1. —boys; friends; other people (Δ, 1)
   my sister
   my husband
   someone else
   Bad people

2. —fighting (I-3, 3; I-3/4, 12)
   that my brother and I get into fights
   when I slap my sister
   hitting my little brother

3. —being bad; being good (Δ/3, 1)
   badniss
   when I am bad
   I am to nice

Unclassified
   school

DELTA

Although there are marginal cases, blaming others takes a slightly different form at Delta than at I-2. It is not a bad person but bad company, the group per se, that leads me astray. The subject's body is referred to also as if it were another party to lead her astray. A problematic category is "ideas, thinking," which one can rationalize by saying that the subject believes the thought leads directly to the act of transgression, as if there were no possibility of control. However, this category is not frequent or altogether convincing. The response "my imagination" occurred on a Delta protocol, but "my vivid imagination" occurred on an I-5 protocol and can plausibly be classed at I-4/5, 1.

1. —being with the wrong people, different people (I-2, 1)
   the car and going out with a boy of a different religion
   running around with the wrong group
   when I am with a group of girl
   Bad company

2. Body leads to sexual trouble (I-3, 13)
   my figure
   what my sister call trouble for me is that I talk with my eyes
      they say to men I don't really mean. (Smile)
   this flesh of mine
   my natural impulses
   kicks

3. Getting caught
   my friends edges me one to things and gets in trouble
   I can't tell a fib without smiling
   my brother blames everything on me
   i'm always late and then I lie to get out of trouble
   when my brothers or sisters tattle on me, and I don't have a
      way out
   my sister she told

4. Running away; restricted freedom
   my step father, he speck for me to stay in the house all day
      & night
   running
   that I love my freedom

5. —ideas, thinking (unelaborated) (I-4, 11)
   my mind

6. Hostile evasion (I-3, 14; I-4, 13)
none of your business
you

DELTA/3

The responses at this level, which carry the connotation of disobeying specific rules of specific authorities, are found in the range I-2 to I-3/4 and are classed here as compromise. Perhaps it is only coincidence, but we have not seen these responses on a protocol classed Delta, though they do appear at Delta/3.

1. —doing wrong, misbehaving (I-2, 3; I-3, 7; I-3/4, 15)
that sometimes I make the wrong step
doing things and being with people I'm not supposed to be with
I get into to much mishtauf
when you don do righ

2. —disobeying, not minding (I-3, 6)
I sometimes never obey my parents and not listen
not doing what I'm told

I-3

By far the most common response to the stem is "my big mouth" and its variants. Although it occurs as low as I-2 and as high as I-4, it is a distinctively I-3 response, with most of the other cases at Delta/3 and I-3/4. Misdemeanors acknowledged at I-3 tend to be rather specific actions, contrasting with description of the same behavior in terms of traits at higher levels. Such traits or prototraits as are described here are vague and global ("my attitude") or banal ("my temper").

**1. —my mouth; my sharp tongue; talking (unelaborated)
my big mouth

*2. —talking too much, too loud (I-3/4, 1)
I talk too loud & get on my husbands nervous
my talkativeness

3. —talking back; not listening; arguing (I-2, 2; I-3/4, 7, 12)
that I am sassy to my parents
(smart-allec-ness)
my sister; we have our little spats
to quarrel with my husband

*4. —my temper; impatience (without indication that subject tries to control it) (I-4, 6)
losing my temper
getting mad a people
I do not have enough patience with my family

5. —my disposition, attitude, selfishness, and so on (unelaborated)
being crabby
wanting to have my own way

6. Specific actions disapproved by parents, husband, and so on (Δ/3, 2)
not telling my parents where I am going
when I don't get home when mom wants me to
talk to long over the phone
break-ing something
falling a sleep watching TV
losing keys
my telephone

7. Taboo behavior: smoking, swearing, cheating, and so on (Δ/3, 1)
when I lie to cover up the truth

8. Late, and so on (I-3/4, 10)
coming home late because I lose track of time
staying out too long
I'm not very prompt always

9. Not doing specific things thoroughly
not studying enough
when I don't do a good job in cleaning the kitchen
not writing enough letters
not having dinner on time

10. Self-indulgence (instances, not as a trait)
not being able to say no to a sales pitch
Watching T. V. too much
*I drink too many Cokes and that makes my husband mad
  at me*
too much booze
eating too much

11. Rudimentary self-criticism, action-oriented (I-4, 3)
being lazy
idleness
no work

I don't know about many things
forgetting things
I never talk back
talking about others
not thinking

12. —being too good to my children (I-3/4, 13)
give in to my children
Taking up for the children
my children problem
I give my children to much

13. —love (Δ, 2)
too much love for my children
thinking about the boy I love
my love for animals

14. —nothing; I don't get into trouble (Δ, 6; I-4, 13)
(I can't think of anything)
not one Thing

Unclassified
my imagination
driving my car

I-3/4

Most of the categories at the I-3/4 level are slightly more differentiated versions of the ideas at the I-3 level. A new element is the explicit avowal that what gets me into trouble is my own responsibility. This seems to be the idea behind the heterogeneous responses classed as "The things I do" (not itself a response). If we contrast "driving my car" (I-3) with *"hating ironing"* (I-3/4), we note more explicit self-blame in the latter, as well as reference to feelings, not just actions. These considerations are germane for handling unclassified answers.

1. —saying the wrong thing; speaking at the wrong time (I-3, 2; I-4, 5)
talking when I should be listening
talking to much and talking out of turn
is saying things that shouldn't be said
my inability to know when to keep quiet

2. —saying things I don't mean; not saying what I mean
not saying what I think
not talking when I should

not expressing myself and feelings well
my inability at times to find correct expressions

3. —not being able to say no

4. —worrying, nervousness (I-4/5, 2)
   getting shook on the job
   trying to do things when I get nervous
   my fears

5. —self-consciousness; I'm shy (I-4, 9)

6. —expecting too much of myself (I-5, 2)
   high expectations

7. —sarcasm (I-3, 3)
   my sometimes sarcastic manner

8. —my stubbornness (I-4, 3)

9. —spending money; not paying bills on time
   probably the use of charge accounts
   not haveing enough money to pay the bills at times
   not paying bills right the minute my husband thinks I should

10. —too little time; hurrying (I-3, 8; I-4, 1)
    my time runs out
    a tight schedule
    when I hurry too much

11. Being too sociable; not doing chores
    over extending my friendship to new acquaintances
    visiting my neighbors
    my desire to spend too much time with other people
    spending too much time reading when I should be helping
      with other chores
    the amount of time I am not at home and the lack of chores
      I do

12. Teasing; bossing; interfering with others (I-2, 2; I-3, 3)
    bossing my brothers & sisters around too much
    I worry about other people not getting work done at work

13. —trying to help others; not wanting to hurt people's feelings
    (I-3, 12)
    being too sorry for other people's troubles
    getting too involved with other people
    the fact I don't like to criticize others
    to avoid hurting people I sometimes lie at my own expense

14. Backhanded compliments
   that I try to please everyone
   my trust in human beings
   truthfulness
   being to soft harted
   that Im too sincere
   being favering others & nectlect my self

15. The things I do (Δ/3, 1)
   doing what I want to do
   doing what others do
   trying to do what I think others want me to do
   cause I want let people tell me what to do
   not doing what I know I should
   doing things I should not do
   when I goof!
   trying to decide what's best to do
   not doing what's best for me

16. —myself; my responsibility
   me
   my own mistakes

Unclassified
   hating ironing

I-4

At I-4 subject is worried not about how much or how loud she talks but about what she is saying ("too outspoken"). Getting into trouble at this level tends to be an inner event. Responses generally refer to feelings, traits, and standards: achievement, consideration for others, and impulse control.

*1. — procrastination; disorganization (I-3/4, 10)
   I try to do too many things
   my habit of putting things off until the last minute
   that I do not get everything done that should be done
   planning more activities than I can easily handle with my housework
   trying to please too many people and making too many commitments

*2. —my frankness; being too outspoken
   saying what I think
   that I am not always diplomatic

my lack of tack
a definite opinion or stand, at times
that I cannot remain silent when somebody talks stupidly

3. Self-criticism: traits and attributes (I-3, 11; I-3/4, 8)
   my forgetfulness
   inappropriate self-discipline
   passiveness at the wrong time
   being too much of a doormat
   carelessness
   being deceptive
   my impatience, and over-optimism
   my over-enthusiasm & aggressiveness
   my lack of motivation at times

4. —impulsiveness; lack of foresight; snap judgments
   that sometimes I jump to the wrong conclusion
   my sudden assumptions that usually need further clarification
   and validity
   my inability to carefully avoid situations that may be trouble
   producing
   I sometimes act impetously

*5. —speaking before thinking; acting before thinking (I-3/4, 1;
   I-4/5, 3)
   not stopping to think before leaping
   speaking the first thing that pops into my mind
   my rapid reply to people
   starting to tell something I've heard and not being sure of
   the conclusion

6. —lack (loss) of self-control (I-3, 4)
   loosing my patience
   my quick temper under minor circumstances
   I talk too much and get angry too quickly

7. —I keep my feelings bottled up; let them out all at once
   not being able to hurt anyone's feelings, and always keeping
   my feelings locked up inside

8. —sensitivity; my emotions (general) (I-5, 4)
   my big mouth and show of feelings
   I at times get moody
   Leting things I cannot control, get under my Skin
   my sensitiveness

9. —my lack of self-confidence; insecurity (I-3/4, 5)
   my feelings of inadequacy

10. —my need for love, attention
    I don't like to be left alone
    when I feel not wanted

11. Problems with learning, thinking (elaborated) (Δ, 5)
    I wonder if I'll be able to learn all I am suppose to learn
    often my differences in thinking
    my lack of creativity and imagination

12. —my wide interests
    my liking for so many different things
    my career and its demands

13. Evasion (without verbalized hostility) (Δ, 6; I-3, 14)
    wish I knew
    what I am trying to discover
    something that rarely concerns me greatly
    the least of my worries
    what I least expect

Unclassified
    saying things which I really don't mean, and regretting it
    I tend to offer advice and wind up either with a job to do, or
    people mad

I-4/5

At the I-4/5 level there appears concern about realistic coping with life expressed in general terms or in terms of worrying about trivia; the unique self-perceptions that accompany this concern at the I-5 level are lacking. The I-4 interest in impulse control and consideration for others is here carried one step further to a concern for how one's behavior affects or appears to others. Some unclassified responses are recognizable as significant elaborations of ideas classed at lower levels. While we do not have explicit categories for two or three ideas in a single response, in doubtful cases the mentioning of contrasting ideas may be decisive, as in some of the unclassified examples.

1. Not coping with reality (general) (I-5, 1)
    my inability to realize I'm headed for it
    my big mouth and not being able to except what I really have
    to do
    my tendency to put off or avoid unpleasant experiences

2. —worrying about trivialities (I-3/4, 4)
    that I get too nervous and excited about things which I ob-
    jectively know are unimportant

*my jumping to conclusions and getting excited—internally—
about trivialities*

*my taking some things too seriously which could best be not
worried about*

*is worrying about the tiny little things and also not being hard
enough on myself at times*

3. Consideration or awareness of one's social impact (I-4, 5)

*that I speak too quickly without thinking what it might sound
like*

*my tendency to speak too quietly which annoys other who
have to ask me to repeat what I've said*

*doing what is wrong and thinking I can get away with it be-
cause I don't look the type to do wrong*

*that often I think and talk too fast too far afield, and some-
times others don't see the significant things I'd like to talk
about*

*that I like to know a person well before I become a "close"
friend and therefore I may appear disinterested in some
people*

*my inability to express sympathy when someone in my family
is not feeling well*

*trying to agree with two people who are having problems with
each other*

*my awful habit of confiding in people and trusting those I
hardly know. I usually end up starting rumours about someone, often myself*

*that I say things alot of time without thinking about them,
often hurting other people. Sometimes I don't do (or do)
things I should, not intentionally, but I still get into trouble*

Unclassified

my demand to maintain my independence in all situations

*my sarcastic tongue. Hypocrisy is not part of my make-up.
Diplomacy should be practiced more but I consider that a
form of hypocrisy*

*talking! (Unless someone labels something as confidential—I
don't always take care in discussing same. When they do I
am careful.) I can't think of any real trouble, but I sometimes realize I should not have told so much*

*intermittent periods of laziness and dislike of work (also dis-
interest)*

*something another person will have to help me evaluate as I
cannot call any facet of my life a "trouble area"*

> *a tendency to procratinate, then exert double effort and go without sleep to meet deadlines*

I-5

At the I-5 level concern about realistic coping is expressed in terms of unique and vivid self-perceptions. Expecting too much of others and being impatient with their faults is an aspect of this problem; the latter are among the few responses repeated in similar terms by several subjects at this level. As at I-4/5, mention of contrasting ideas may be decisive in awarding an I-5 rating to marginal responses (*"my impatience,* impractibility, perfectionism"). We have not found distinctive I-6 responses.

1. Not coping with reality (unique self-perceptions) (I-4/5, 1)
    sometimes being satisfied with daydreams instead of dealing with things as they really are
    first impressions I have of people and cannot change even when they are untrue
    I think too much and become paralyzed for action
    sometimes I think I am too analytical about things and myself
    not being able to face the disappointments and failures of my life
    overconcern with myself so that I loose faith in what I know to be ultimately true and good

2. —expecting too much of others; being overly critical (I-3/4, 6)
    my quick temper and impatience with others' shortcomings
    my impatience, impractibility, perfectionism
    my tendency to control situations and people on the premise that I can do a better job than they
    that at times I am too idealistic and don't realize others aren't as tolerant as I am

3. —fighting for ideals; standing up for principles
    my preoccupation with principles
    my honesty in matters involving injustice and pettiness
    becoming interested in things to the point that I must act responsibly
    my desire to put my point across to people with "closed" ears, my independence and liberal ideas, my willingness to go to bat for the underdog
    being too sympathetic to causes

4. Unique and vivid emotions; inner conflict (I-4, 8)

> *depression which occurs so seldom that it tends to frighten
> and "throw" me because it is unfamiliar*
>
> *my groveling attitude toward myself*
>
> *heartbreak—loneliness, or a need for someone to* love me
> alone
>
> *I'm basically dishonest—and I get in trouble because I dislike
> dishonesty and stifle my impulses*

Education—

At the lower levels education is viewed as a thing one has; at the higher levels it is seen as a continuing process. Need for more education can correspondingly be stated as a wish to have it (Delta/3) or as regret for not having continued (I-4). A similar contrast is between education as what happens in school and as something continuing throughout life.

At the I-3 level education is almost uniformly seen as desirable, essential, necessary, important, though it may be expensive or difficult. Expressions of distaste for education are rare in any group and occur almost exclusively on low (below I-3) protocols; however, critical remarks about education as an institution occur at the I-4 level.

Education is seen at all levels as having instrumental value. At the lowest levels it is seen as useful to get a job; at the I-3 level it is seen as one important factor in getting a job and particularly as affecting the desirability of the work obtained. At the I-3/4 level it is important for

97

advancement, at I-4 for personal growth. At the I-5 level education helps one to cope with life's problems, to find self-fulfillment, to understand oneself and others. But at this point the instrumental value of education is almost identical with seeing it as intrinsically valuable.

The main contribution of this item seems to be in discriminating individuals below I-3 and above I-4. Discrimination between I-2 and Delta categories is somewhat arbitrary.

I-2

Almost everyone in the I-2 and Delta range talks of education as a *thing* that you *get* in *school* and then you *have*. Their answers are distinguished from similar I-3 answers in one of several ways: by redundancy (I-2); by expressions of distaste for education or of not getting along in school; and by bland and vacuous positive remarks, which miss the point of the I-3 notion of education as important.

1. —is fun; is no fun; is hard (Δ, 3)
   is fun and hard
   is fun to do things that you want to
   is no fun but it gets done

2. —is good for you (Δ, 1; I-3, 1, 3)
   is good for me
   is very could for people

3. —helps you learn; helps in school
   would help me better in school & finish school
   learning
   is good for me because it helps me learn and no more things
   I need to Larn more

DELTA

The most difficult category to differentiate is the one that declares education is good for getting a job, compared to a similar I-3 category. The shade of meaning that distinguishes Delta responses is the implication that education is *only* good for getting a job.

1. —is good, nice, fine; is good to have (I-2, 2; I-3, 7)
   is o. k.
   is a fine thing
   is a very good thing

is nice to have
is I good thing for a person to have

2. —is good for getting a job (I-3, 5)
   I think Education is good for finding a job
   is very nice to have if you ant got it you can't get a job
   is what we need to get a job

3. —is boring; is for the birds; is not good (I-2, 1)
   is okay but not necessary
   and me don't get along too good
   is very boring and worth-less
   is useless and a lot of bother
   is rotten at our age and we shouldn't get homework
   is for the birds. But I like it

4. —is needed but I don't like it (I-4, 6)
   is something I can take or leave, although I'd like to pass
   is a drag but important
   is good, although I hate it, because where would the world be
   without it

DELTA/3

Responses concerning wanting, needing, and getting more education are classed here as a compromise. In contrasting this category with regret for not having finished school at I-4, one looks at this level for signs that education is a thing that one gets, at I-4 for a greater sense of responsibility and choice.

*1. —I wish I had more; I need, will get more (I-4, 14)
    is what I want most at this time
    I want to go to high school
    something I never got, but I wish I had an Education
    is very important because I want to finish it

I-3

The current ideal of a number of years of schooling as essential for everyone and an uncritical, idealized view of education are characteristic of this level. Education is interpreted as school attendance, which has practical usefulness; one can get a better job with it than without it. Difficulties in obtaining an education are occasionally specified, but not till the I-4 level are they contrasted with rewards.

**1. —is essential, necessary, important (for me) (unelaborated)
(I-2, 2; I-3/4, 1)
is of the utmost importance
is a must
means a great deal to me
is the most important thing to me

*2. —is necessary, important nowadays, in the world today
(I-3/4, 8)
is a very important and useful thing today
means a lot today
is a thing that we must have in order to live in the world today
is a must for today's living
is very ensential in todays world

*3. —is necessary, important, good for everyone, for special groups
(I-2, 2)
everyone needs
is necessary for girls
is a necessity for all U. S. citizens
is very important for children
is the most fundamental needed among todays teen-agers

4. —is something everyone should have (I-3/4, 7; I-4, 5)
is a great field that everyone should obtain
I think everyone should graduate high school
I think you should have one

5. Is important in looking for or getting a good job (Δ, 2)
is so important when looking for employment
is a must, in order to make a good living
is an essential requirement in acquiring a good job

6. —is useful (I-3/4, 2, 4)
is something everyone can use
helps everyone

*7. Idealization: is wonderful, desirable, great, etc. (Δ, 1; I-3/4, 6)
is a pleasure
is a blessing
is beneficial
is the greatest thing on earth

8. —is expensive; is good if you can afford it

9. —is hard to get

10. —is sometimes difficult (I-4, 6)
    is sometimes frustrating
    is sometimes traumatic

*11. Statement of completed education
    *High School and I am going to a summer school workshop
    for piano*
    I have just graduated from senior highschool
    8 Gr
    one semister colledge
    *I had ten & 1/2 years of schooling and someday I will get
    that last year. Because it's important*
    I haven't mutch Education

Unclassified
    is learning and experiencing

I-3/4

At this level education's importance is viewed in terms of life or the future. The statement "all should have as much as possible" (I-3/4) indicates a shift away from thinking of education as a concrete entity, as in "everybody should have one" (I-3). A similar shift away from a concrete view is indicated by the statements that education is worthwhile, a goal, or an asset.

1. —is a necessary, essential, important part of (my) life (I-3, 1)
    is a very important step in life
    will be an important factor in my life
    is an important segment in my life
    is of primary importance all through life

*2. —is necessary, important, for success, for the future (I-3, 6;
    I-4, 1)
    is the key to success
    is a good way to advance
    *is important to be able to lead a prosperous, happy life and
    to support oneself*
    is a thing to be used to get ahead and profit by
    for a sucure future
    is very important and invaluable to one's future
    is a preparation for life
    is the key to a great future for everyone

3. —is a valuable possession, an asset; is a goal (I-4, 13; I-5, 1)
    is man's greatest fortune

should be a prized possession
is a real asset all through life
is very desirable & a goal for all members of my family
is the one ultimate goal everyone should have

4. —is worthwhile; is worth it (I-3, 6)
   is time well spent
   is invaluable
   is valuable
   is worth time and effort spent
   is a worth while pursuit

5. —can't be taken away

6. —is interesting (I-3, 7)
   is very interesting if you like school
   is fine if you're interested

7. Everyone should have as much as possible (I-3, 4; I-4, 5)
   is very important. I enjoy school and think that all teenagers should go as far as they can in school
   I think everyone should have a high school education and some college if possible
   I think is try to learn all you can and go as far as you can

8. —is more important now than ever before (I-3, 2)

I-4

At this level education is viewed as an experience that affects a person's inner life. It is no longer merely a number of years of useful schooling. Its importance lies in stimulation and potential enrichment for the individual. It influences a person's whole life, making it more worthwhile and enjoyable. The seemingly contradictory idea, that education itself is not enough, expresses the same underlying idea: just going to school a certain number of years does not suffice. The I-4 subject, like the I-3, believes that education is important for everyone. She views it, however, as a privilege or opportunity that should be *available* to everyone, including women. She may comment on the significance of education in improving society or express the need for improvement of the educational system.

1. Is important for social goals (I-3/4, 2)
   is the standard for strong America
   is one of the primary ways of solving social problems
   to the extent of capability for all is essential ingredient of democratic society

is gate to welfare of mankind

would decrease the rate of illiteracy and the number of un-skilled unemployable, people

is of major importance for peace

should have been used more widely for the uplift of minority groups

2. Should be improved (I-4/5, 3)

   is being neglected in the U. S.

   will get quite poor if the type and quality of teachers does not improve

   certainly does vary in quality

   seldom lives up to its goals

3. —is more than book learning; can be gained in different ways

   is more than just knowledge

   is extremely important but useless without some common sense

   is school is not sufficient in itself

   is not just what they teach at school

4. —is an opportunity; must be worked for, taken advantage of

   is very important, and worth working for

   must be searched for

   is a great advantage provided us and should be regarded as such

   is a priviledge and not a right!

   is something everyone should strive to attain

5. —should be available to all (I-3, 4; I-3/4, 7)

   is something everyone should be exposed to no matter what their color, rel. etc.

   is for everyone who wants it

   should be provided with equal opportunity for all

6. Valuable but difficult (Δ, 4; I-3, 10)

   is hard and lots of work but in the long run is worth it

   is something that I like in and of itself but I sometimes wish there weren't so darned much of it

   is a challenge but also a necessity

   is an ongoing, stressful but rewarding experience

7. —is a process, an ongoing process (I-4/5, 1)

   is definitely an ingoing process which must have frequent re-visions

   is a constant process not limited to a classroom

8. —is satisfying, stimulating, enriching
   is a source of satisfaction in the present and for the future
   is exciting and valuable
   is an enjoyable way to be exposed to new ideas and areas of thought

9. Leads to growth, improvement; prepares one for life (I-4/5, 2; I-5, 4)
   is for learning and development
   is a crucial part of development
   is essential in gaining maturity
   is important for advancement and to develop one's capabilities
   prepares one to face the world

10. —is important for women as well as men; is important for raising a family
    is essential for men and women—compulsory for men—the more the better
    is very important to both a man and woman, sometimes I think equally important
    means a great deal to me, so I will be able to help my children

11. —is a way of solving problems; opens doors (I-5, 3)
    helps one achieve insight into problems
    is like a pair of glasses—you see things through it which you have never seen before

12. —is not an end in itself; is not enough
    is important, but not the end
    is not the cure for all the worlds troubles
    in itself is not enough to get one through life

13. Seen in relation to other personal goals and values (I-3/4, 3; I-5, 1)
    is the most important thing along with being able to love
    has become an indicator of status in some circles
    is the foundation for a socially and financially secure life
    is important or high in my hierarchy of values
    is the basis for everything

14. Regret about insufficient education (sense of responsibility implied) (Δ/3, 1)
    wish I had taken advantage of getting a better education
    I wish I would have taken subjects I could use in raising my family and used my time better when in school
    is something I think people should do more about instead of just think. I should have finished highschool anyway

*Is a wonderful thing I wish that I had completed my last
year 12th*

I-4/5

A large proportion of protocols at the I-4/5 and I-5 levels give
unique and clearly high-level responses to this stem; they are rated I-5.
At I-4/5, both for logical and psychometric reasons, are classed responses
that resemble those found at lower levels as well as having elements of a
high response.

1. —should never end; continues throughout life (I-4, 7)
   is a lifelong process
   continues everyday
   *is a process that should continue long after one's formal edu-
   cation has been completed*
   *You can never have enough of it. Life should be a process of
   learning as much as you can about anyting at all*

2. —is essential for a full life, for enjoyment of life (I-4, 9;
   I-5, 4)
   is an important tool for leading a useful and interesting life
   is a means of developing an individual's potential for living
   helps a person become himself
   opens new avenues of thought and produces more joy in living
   is a must because the more I learn, the more I enjoy life
   *is very important if one wants to feel he is making the most
   of his life*
   *is necessary now but the general trend of education should be
   training for life not a profession*

3. Not always what it seems to be (I-4, 2)
   *is a terrific experience but does not always represent what it
   seems to*
   *or the concept of it, not infrequently impresses me as being a
   gigantic fraud*

Unclassified
   *is a most vital part of our lives; it's a pity we often dont
   realize it until it is too late*
   *is necessary. What we learn is not as important as the fact
   that we are learning how to think for ourselves*
   *is a process which gives you the facts and lets you draw your
   own conclusions*
   determines the type of life a person will lead

is most important to find one's place in life
could be the key to many things. But those who seemed to
need a key the most are in terrible situations with respect
to the facilities available to them

I-5

At this level education is seen as leading to a deeper understanding of oneself and others, as helping one to cope with life, as leading to creativity, self-fulfillment, and deeper values; hence, education is intrinsically valuable. Thus at the I-4/5 and I-5 levels education is not a thing that one has or gets, once and for all, nor is it identified solely with school and intellectual achievement apart from interpersonal relations and emotional involvements.

1. Education is intrinsically valuable, admirable (I-3/4, 3; I-4, 13)

   seems valuable in itself
   will help me all though life. I am not being educated because I have to, but education is a wonderful thing
   and, the love of it, is a priceless inheritance
   is one of the things I value very highly, and I admire people with seemingly good educations
   looms for me as very important and engendering great respect. I always admire those well-educated persons I know
   is a fetish of mine. No sacrifice will be too great to assure college educations for my own children
   is the epitomy of civilization—the highest value and most important goal
   can be a means or an end depending on other characteristics of those who pursue it

2. Is important socially and in individual lives

   is as basic for an individual as it is for masses if there is to be progress
   is in human nature, and the most important way to progress and to cultivate individual & society

3. Helps you cope with life (original, elaborated) (I-4, 11)

   is learning to solve problems in a better way—to know what needs doing when and how to do it
   is very important to mankind as it helps people to know what has happened, be aware of what is happening and what he could do to influence future happenings

*is the most important gift a person may be given to keep him
from going adrift in a rather cruel and lonely world*

*is important so that one has the ability to carry on an inter-
esting and accurate conversation even if he isn't the most
intelligent person in scholastic studies*

*is a value usually believed in in most "civilized" societies; it
provides people with knowledge which helps them to cope
with life*

4. Leads to self-fulfillment, self-understanding, new values (I-4,
9; I-4/5, 2)

*means a lot to me—I'll stagnate if I never do anything crea-
tive*

is a necessary part of my development as a unique individual

*is the hope of civilization if developing values are also con-
sidered as a part of education*

*is the development of the entire man, physical, mental and
spiritual*

*is very important. It helps make you the best possible person
for yourself and your husband, and your future family*

*is necessary for self-understanding and is experienced formally
and informally*

*is necessary to enjoy life to its fullest and to get the most
from oneself*

*is the most important thing for a well rounded individual and
opens many new and exciting doors to him*

*is rewarding only if you learn to see things in a variety of
ways and can have feelings for other peoples beliefs*

Unclassified

*is both a stimulation to growth and method for accumulating
knowledge for future use*

I-6

Unclassified

*is a many splendered thing. It is also a necessity, a responsi-
bility and at times a trouble, a sadness*

When People Are Helpless—

Τhis stem offers easy and obvious answers for subjects at the conformist level, and at the same time provides opportunity for high-level subjects to express their sensitivity to others' feelings and their respect for others' need for autonomy. Major themes through all or almost all levels are helping, how I feel, how they feel, and why they are helpless. The helping theme by far predominates. How they feel may be bad (I-2) or unhappy (I-3) or some subtler possibilities (afraid, I-3/4; unrealistic, I-4) that are consequences of helplessness rather than mere translations into feelings of the fact of helplessness. A few categories are concerned with causes, though none rated below I-3.

I-2

The most differentiating I-2 category for this item is the set of responses that make sense only if the stem is read as "When people are helpful—." The other types of response are restatements of the stem and translations of the fact of helplessness into feeling bad or sick.

1. —they feel bad, sick (I-3, 6, 8)
   it make some people feel sick

2. Redundancies (I-3, 3)
   they cant do anything
   because they can't help it
   that can't care for themselves

3. Stem apparently misread as "helpful"
   they are nice
   that would be very kind of them
   they are my friend
   you thank them
   you prease it
   i feel pretty good
   is good

Unclassified
   they are no good
   they would be better off dead
   They are not a good friend

DELTA

The Delta person seems to perceive helpless people as making unlimited demands, and she may respond in terms of the complementary need to defend herself against such demands.

1. —they want you to do everything
   they expect everyone to wait on them
   they don't have to do work
   they sometimes think you are to break your neck to help them

2. —they are looking for sympathy (I-3/4, 8)
   they look for pity

3. Self-defensive responses (I-4, 16)
   I laugh

I try not to think about it
there are nurses
I feel sorry for them but wouldn't do anything
will not help
they annoy me
I dont like to be bothered with them

Unclassified
everything falls apart

I-3

The predominant responses at I-3 are various statements of the rule that one should help them, plus "I feel sorry for them." Concrete causes and consequences are stated: jobs, money, sickness, crying. Some I-3 subjects think the helpless just do not try, while others think the remedy is kindness and cheer. "They should be taught to help themselves" must be distinguished from categories at I-4 and I-5 concerning help directed toward self-help. The I-3 version contains as a subtle paradox one of the central dilemmas of ego development: how to teach reliance on self rather than on the teacher.

**1. —I help, enjoy helping them; I try to help them, help if I can (I-3/4, 1)
I try my best to help
I like to lend a hand
I try to be of assistance if possible
i do what i can to help them
I try to come to their rescuit
I do all I can

**2. —they should be helped; others, you, we should help (I-3/4, 2; I-4, 2)
help them
they must receive outside help
someone should come to their aid
it's nice to lend a hand
you should try to help them, because they can't help them-
you should do the best for them that you can
don't laugh at them help them
   selves
see what you are able to do for them
others are there to help

*3. —they need help, attention (I-2, 2; I-3/4, 7; I-4, 3, 4)
they need all the help they can get

4. —they need someone (to help them) (I-3/4, 6, 7)
they need friends
they need someone to talk to
it's good if they have someone to depend on

*5. I feel sorry, sad; it is sad (I-3/4, 8)
I feel sorry for them
it is a shame
it is unfortunate
it makes me unhappy

6. —they are sad, unhappy; they cry (I-2, 1; I-3/4, 5)
they are sometimes miserable
they tend to cry

7. —they are handicapped, not useful, a burden
they are a hinder to others
it is a handicap
they are not useful to others or their self

8. Specific, concrete reasons (or consequences) (I-2, 1)
because they are jobless
when they are sick
they usually need money
they are usually sick

9. —they are lazy, don't try (I-3/4, 11, 12)
when they don't do for themselves
its because they don't try
only If they want to be
they haven't tried hard enough to help themselves

10. —be kind, considerate (I-4, 8)
they need a kind word and consideration from others more
fortunate
I try to give some comfort
I try to cheer them up, if I can
, your kindness does a world of good

Unclassified
they should be taught to help themselves

I-3/4

The notion that help should be offered, appearing at I-3/4, shows a shift away from the I-3 rules-of-conduct approach toward a recognition, more explicit at higher levels, that the helpless person must remain the origin of his own destiny. A search for causation and an awareness of inner feeling are both found here, but only in vague and banal terms. The notion that one should not take advantage of helpless people we have seen on a Delta/3 protocol and on several I-4 protocols, while one I-4/5 subject stated, "they are frequently taken advantage of by those in power." Hence this category is not highly discriminating and is classed here as compromise.

**1. —I want to help them (I-3, 1; I-4, 1)
    I can't do enough for them
    I want to go to their rescue
    I feel sorry for them and I would like to help them
    you feel that you must and want to help
    I want to do something for them
    I want to reach out to them

2. —help should be offered (I-3, 2; I-4, 2)
    it is wise to offer assistance
    I feel they should be offered help even if they don't ask for it
    those who are not should offer assistance
    I offer whatever assistance I can

3. Society should help (I-4, 3)
    they are still a part of society
    the community should extend a willing hand
    I think all humans should pitch in and help the other person

4. —they should seek help
    they should turn to someone for help

5. —they are afraid, hopeless; they feel lost (I-3, 6; I-4, 11)
    they sometimes feel that there is no hope
    they become scared
    they may become anxious
    they feel alone

6. —they are dependent on others (I-3, 4)
    they become dependent
    they rely on others
    they look to one another
    they can't be independent

7. —they need care, protection; they should not be taken advantage of (I-3, 3, 4)
    they must be protected
    , no one should step on them

>*There should be a place for them and so some one can care*
>   *for them*
>*others tend to take advantage of them*

8. —I feel pity; they are pitiful, pathetic (Δ, 2; I-3, 5; I-4, 10, 16)
   I pity them
   they are to be pitied
   it is pathetic

9. —I feel helpless (too) (I-4, 14)
   it makes me feel helpless

10. —I wonder why
    I ask "why," & "can they help themselves?"

11. —it is their own fault (I-3, 9)
    , it may be because they want to be this way
    it is usually because they don't want to be helped
    they have no one to blame but thier own selves

12. —they should try (I-3, 9; I-4, 18)
    they will try anything

I-4

This stem elicits an unusually large number of I-4 categories. The most frequent category at this level is "I feel a need to help," similar to the popular I-3/4 category, "I want to help," but more suggestive of introspection. Some I-4 categories elaborate this theme in one of two directions, either concern for the inner feelings of the subject or of the helpless person, in more differentiated terms than at lower levels, or mentioning a principle (duty, right) which calls for helping the other. Causes, consequences, and contingencies are discussed in other categories.

1. —I feel a need to help (I-3/4, 1)
   my heart goes out to them and I must help
   I feel the need to assist them, if it is at all possible
   I have this need to help them
   feel a great urgency to make them comfortable and happy
   they bring out the mother instinct in me

2. —it is our duty, obligation, responsibility, privilege to help
   (I-3, 2; I-3/4, 2)
   I feel that it is my place to help them
   I feel obligated to do what I can to help
   it is others responsibility to God and to himself to do what
   * he can*

*I feel that it is a great privilege & honor if I am physically,
emotionally, or financially able to help them*

3. —they deserve help (I-3, 3; I-3/4, 3)
   they are entitled to help
   they should be able to turn to other people and receive help

4. —they need support, understanding, professional help (I-3, 3)
   they should be counseled
   they need reassurance
   they often need the help of a disinterested person
   try to understand the problem
   they need sympathetic attention
   they usually evoke sympathy (but need understanding)

5. Concern with manner in which help is given (I-4/5, 2)
   they should be understood and helped in that way
   I try to help, however, with much tact
   *they need to be offered help in a positive manner & one they
   are able to accept*
   I tried to help them in every way possible—not sympathy
   I always wonder why and how they could best be helped
   one needs to be careful how one helps them

6. —I try to help them help themselves; they need help toward
   self-help (unelaborated) (I-4/5, 2; I-5, 1)
   I want to help them find a way to help themselves
   I wish I could help them to become more self-sufficient
   *they should be given help and encouraged to do for them-
   selves*
   they need to be shown a way to help themselves
   they need assistance in order to regain their strength

7. Help contingent on circumstances (I-5, 2)
   *I sympathize, unless they are unwilling to try to help them-
   selves*
   *I like to help them, I mean if they're really are helpless. Some
   people are helpless because they want to be, and then I
   don't like to help them*
   *I will try to the best of my ability to help those who are mo-
   mentarily "helpless"*
   I want to help them even if they're strangers
   *I try to give them a hand. But if they aren't willing to help
   themselves well then I'm not going to waste my time*

8. Concern for their feelings, wishes (I-3, 10; I-4/5, 2)
   I am especially afraid of hurting them
   I try to make them feel less helpless by reassuring them and
      giving them confidence
   a kind word or helping hand can give them strength
   , they should not be pitied or helped, unless they ask for it
   you must help them if they wanted it or like it
   they do not like charity, they are usually very proud

9. —they should not be pitied; pity isn't helpful
   I sort of pity them but don't let them know this
   they don't need pity
   I don't show it, but I feel sorry for them. I don't show it be-
      cause pity in such a case isn't at all helpful

10. —I feel compassion, sympathy (I-3/4, 8)
   I have empathy and sympathy
   compassion is a must
   my sympathies are aroused

11. —they feel frustrated, dependent, troubled, etc. (I-3/4, 5)
   frustration is almost inevitable
   it is a very empty & useless feeling
   they feel inferior
   —they often come to realize how completely helpless they
      really are with only themselves to rely on—
   they often become defensive
   they feel defeated and dejected & want to be helped

12. They may become unrealistic
   they may be too disturbed to be rational in the situation
   they can lose sight of their wants & desires
   they can't see the trees for the forest

13. —they need faith, belief
   they turn to God first
   they need other people and a belief in a higher being
   they often times draw closer to God
   they can find help in prayer

14. —I want to help, but it's hard, I can't always; I feel bad if
   I can't help (I-3/4, 9)
   so am I. I wish I could help them. I try to, but I don't feel
      capable
   I try to help them but I do not always succeed

It gives me a very helpless feeling myself because I want to do all I can to help but there usually isn't much for a girl to do

I feel a deep desire to be able to help them and become annoyed at myself if I lack the proper information to do so

& there is little I can do, I begin to feel very inadequate

I am happy if I am able to help them; if I cannot, then I am bothered, at least for a time, about their state

15. Helping seen as reciprocal

I like to help them, because one of these days I might need help

I think others should help, because others appericate others help

I want to help them as much as I can. I put myself into their place and I know that I would want help to

I remember my own feelings of frustration and helplessness and I want to help them

16. Introspective personal reaction (Δ, 3; I-3/4, 8; I-5, 3)

I think about why I'm not helpless

I often get myself too involved in trying to help them

I sometimes dislike them

I am thankful many times over that my inflictions are few

it does nothing to me

I am drawn to them

I often feel ridicule toward them

I become sometimes too anxious about their situation

it affects me very strongly and I want to hold out my hand to them and help them

I feel religious. Whenever I see a helpless person I pray to God and ask him to give these people help. I always feel sorry

17. —there is a reason for it (I-4/5, 3)

the cause may vary

a number of factors may be operating

sometimes it is not their fault

it is often because of circumstances they can not help

18. —I want to stimulate them to try (I-3/4, 12)

, there must be a reason, find it, show their weakness, and push them into getting out the helpless state by themselves

I try to do my best to influence them to go on and try and try for where there is life there is hope!

I-4/5

The marks of this level are complex notions of causation, unrealized potential, help that preserves dignity and independence, and explicit concern for the relations between people, in terms such as involvement and basic goodness. Although the lines are not sharp, giving help in such a way as to preserve dignity or restore independence (I-4/5) is distinguished from a similar category at I-4 (help toward self-help) in indicating, at least minimally, that helping may have its own hazards.

1. —they should make the most of their own abilities, potential
   they ought to look first to themselves for their own latent potential
   they should make the most of facilities they do have
   , there is always some positive factor somewhere on which to build

2. Concern for dignity, independence (I-4, 5, 6, 8; I-5, 1)
   I want to help them become more self-confident & independent
   they should be given help, with attention to the preservation of their dignity
   we must help them, but not do everything for them or they may never overcome their helplessness
   they can defeat themselves for future helpfulness if they become defeated
   there ought to be a means of helping them so they can get on their own again
   they should still be treated like human beings and every effort should be made to give them a feeling of personal worth
   they should seek some assistance to learn how to be more independent

3. Complex causation (I-4, 17; I-6, 1)
   there are reasons for it that they are not always capable of discerning
   there is always some cause, which altho we can't always understand, we must try to
   they are usually asking to "please" be involved with others
   they usually have a feeling of desertion by other people even when it does not occur
   it is frustrating to the point of disintegration of personality and confidence

Unclassified

> *they are dependent upon the chance that people will let known their basic goodness*
>
> *they are fooling themselves because people are rarely truly helpless*
>
> *they react by crying, becoming mad, or try to become helpful*
>
> *it is the duty of a progressive social order to lend a helping hand*

I-5

The help toward self-help theme at I-4 more or less combines with the I-4/5 theme of help that preserves dignity and independence in the corresponding category at I-5. To merit an I-5 rating the response should not sound like a cliché; also, it should emphasize that they must find their own means, or else that where potential is lacking, protection should be provided. The other responses at this level contain by implication some evidence of inner conflict. In view of the wide range of high-level responses to this item, these categories are probably not exhaustive.

1. They need help toward self-help (elaborated) (I-4, 6; I-4/5, 2)

   > *the greatest effort is to find a beginning avenue in which they climb out of this state*
   >
   > *they should be aided and encouraged to find ways to help themselves*
   >
   > *it is sometimes better to help them realize that there are something that they can do for themselves and they are not as helpless as they feel*
   >
   > *they need to be guided to help themselves, or if necessary must be helped by others*
   >
   > *they often need someone to assist them, thus enabling them to help themselves if possible*
   >
   > *it is best to aid them to help themselves than to prolong their helplessness and dependency on others*
   >
   > *they should be helped to understand why they are that way and what they can do to correct this condition*

2. Mixed feelings; alternative feelings (I-4, 7)

   > *I feel sorry for them, want to help, don't want to be a "do-gooder," determine if it's their fault. If it is their own fault, I leave them alone*
   >
   > *I pity them and admire those who try to change their situa-*

tion. I have no respect for those who exploit their help-lessness

I feel sorry for them, but I also feel helpless because I can't help all the people who are in need of it

3. Self-critical introspective reaction (I-4, 16)

I have an inclination to be unsympathetic and this makes me unhappy with myself

I try to aid them, but sometimes if I don't like them I don't help them. (Thats why I don't want to be a social worker.)

I feel very sorry for them and want to do something for them. I feel guilty sometimes because I don't think it effects me enough

I think of them as a worry although I know its selfish I do it physically I am full of pity and nausea, mental helplessness (retarded ect.) reduces me to tears and tends to give me a leaning toward belief in mercy killing, tho my morality will never accept it

I-6

The single category classed here contains responses that contrast alternative ways of viewing the situation. Each of the responses summarizes several contrasting points of view that lie behind many categories at lower levels. Note that the elements of the responses are themselves high, as they contain reference to possible causes and to potential for development. Contrast the response, "they react by crying, becoming mad, or try to become helpful" (I-4).

1. Alternative constructions of situation (I-4/5, 3)

, it may be because they lack self-confidence, the will to help themselves, or knowledge of the solution to their difficulty

they need others help to grow and become more self sufficient, if there is potential for development. Lacking potential they need protection

Women Are
Lucky Because—

Probably more because of the grammatical form than because of the emotional connotations, this stem elicits more responses that are not quite logically germane than most others. "Because" is used in the sense of psychological causation, which some subjects at the lowest level do not seem to grasp. Responses that seem to mean "When women are lucky—" are classed I-2. Above I-2, responses that seem to be triggered more by the word "lucky" than by the sense of the stem are rare, but occur at least through the I-4/5 level. At Delta people are seen as either lucky or unlucky, as if it were something that occurred once and for all. At I-3 there may be evasion or rejection

120

of the stem. The statement that women are not lucky occurs over a wide range, but centers at I-3/4. At I-4 and higher the notion of luck is turned aside in some manner.

The stem invites a statement about the advantages of being a woman. Turning this into advantages over men sounds and may be Delta, but there are also I-3/4 categories of that type. At the I-3 level the stem is usually turned into a banality; "It's nice to be a woman because—" and the completion is usually superficial, obvious, or redundant. I-4 responses more clearly imply comparison or contingency, as if the stem read, "There are good and bad aspects to being a woman; the good ones are—"; "One way in which women are more fortunate than men is—"; "Women are more fortunate than they used to be in that—." Responses above the I-4 level show appreciation in nonstereotyped terms for unique privileges of her sex, either alternative ways of life open to her or emotional relations she may have with her family.

I-2

The identifiable I-2 completions to this stem are mostly logically defective. To the I-2 subject being lucky means getting nice things, being happy, and doing what you want to. Since things are not usually like that, such responses make better sense as completions of "Women are lucky when—" or "Those women are lucky who—." The response "they don't have any children" makes no sense unless interpreted this way.

1. Wishes (I-3/4, 8)
   they get nice things
   she can get a good man and Be happy
   there content
   they wish for something
   they always go to stores and buy things
   the huband give them moeny
   they get to do the things they want
   men don't hit them

2. —they can't have babies
   they can't give children
   they don't have any children

Unclassified
   they are niser than boys
   because they are ladies

DELTA

An occasional subject at Delta indicates that she sees people as either lucky or unlucky. More typically, their answers reveal that they see work as onerous and money as desirable. Paradoxically, the responses, "they don't have to work so hard," or "they don't have to work like men," are rated Delta, while the apparently simpler thought, "they don't have to work," is rated Delta/3. Although we first noted the distinction empirically, the reason is clear. No one believes that women in general do not have to work. Therefore "they don't have to work" means they do not have to take a job (I-3) or make a living (I-3/4). Thus the Delta idea is that they just work less. To be pampered, to get their way, and to play on the sympathy of men are part of one conventional conception of femininity and appear at I-3/4; however, exploitative use of sex is classed Delta, but it is a rare response.

1. —they don't have to work like men, as hard (unqualified) (Δ/3, 1; I-3, 8, 9)
    they dont have to do hard things
    they don't have to build houses and all that
    they don't have to carry heavy things
    they don't have to work as hard as men
    they can usually get away from heavy work

2. —they get the pay check
    they get to handle the money
    they can get married and live off the men

3. People are lucky or unlucky
    some women are lucky
    we are always getting lucky breaks
    I don't know why they are lucky. I don't think they are lucky.
       I don't think I am lucky
    the lord bless them. I gess

Unclassified
    They rule men with sex
    they can usually get by with more things than men

DELTA/3

Categories at this level contain responses found relatively more often below I-3 than at I-3 and I-3/4. They have a narcissistic and passive dependent tone that contrasts with the more positive and interpersonal aspects of being a woman stressed at I-3 and higher. There is a big jump

between "they don't have to work" (Delta) and "they don't have to go
out to work unless they want to" (I-3), for the latter response indicates
that some people may actually enjoy working.

1. —they don't have to work; they can stay home and let their
   husbands work (Δ, 1; I-3, 8, 9)
   they get to stay home and watch T. V.
   they don't have to go out and work
   they can stat at home
   they don't have to work all their life like a man
   sometimes they don't have to work
   *they are taken care of either by their parents or by their
   husbands*

I-3

The two most frequent categories, accounting together for almost
1/5 of all responses, are "they are women" and "they can have babies."
Both responses occur on protocols from I-2 to I-4/5, both peak at I-3,
but of course they do not contribute much to the discriminating power
of the item. "They are women" occurs on more low protocols and fewer
high protocols than "they can have babies." Taken together, the categories at I-3 reveal a conventional, superficial picture of what being a
woman is. The advantages for which the I-3 woman is grateful are more
likely to be conveniences and services than opportunities. The cliché "they
are the weaker sex" appears here, though as an answer it is somewhat
paradoxical.

**1. —they are women; they aren't men (I-4, 16)
   they are females

*2. —they can have babies (I-3/4, 1; I-4, 3)
   they can bring children into the world
   they can bear children
   we can have children
   they can become pregnant

3. —they can raise a family (I-3/4, 1, 2)
   they rear children
   they can riase a very nice faimly

4. —they have children to love them
   they have the love of a child

5. Functions in the family—superficial, stereotyped aspects
    they get to choose the interior decorations of their home
    we can have a fine family and be happy
    of her role as homemaker and mother
    they have nice children and a happy home and try to support them
    their place is in the home
    they are supposed to stay at home and raise the family
    they usually have nice husbands and healthy children

6. Appearance—explicit aspects (I-3/4, 13)
    they wear prettier clothes
    they don't have to shave!
    they have long hair
    they get to wear skirts
    styles have changed
    they are beautiful. At least some are
    they get to wear makeup

7. —they can go out; they can get married (I-3/4, 4)
    they get to go out with men

8. —they don't have to go out to work unless they want to (Δ, 1; Δ/3, 1; I-3/4, 12)
    They doesn't have to work unless they don't ever want anything
    , as a rule, they can either stay at home or go out and work if they wish

9. —they can take it easy (Δ, 1; Δ/3, 1; I-3/4, 7)
    at times their lives are easier than men's
    they can enjoy the leisures of life
    they have so many conveniences
    they usually get help
    they do not have it so hard a the man does

10. —they can do as much as a man can; they have modern advantages (I-3/4, 10)
    of present day conditions
    of all the things in the world now
    they can get an education today
    they can do so many thing for them self
    they can earn a living
    they have the advantages of modern facilities, which weren't available years ago
    because they have a change to get a job sooner than men
    they have some advantages

11. —they don't have to go into the army
    they don't go to war
    they don't get drafted

12. —men have to pay for the dates
    they don't have to spend money when they go out on a date

13. Superiority to men, competitive tone (I-4, 13)
    because we are the most precious creatures on earth
    they usually can do more than a man, and don't have to go
       to work
    most of them can out smart men
    they are the fairer sex
    of their personality
    they are made of sugar and spice and everything nice
    because some are refined
    they are basically good
    they are strong

14. —they can show their feelings (I-4, 14)
    they can cry
    they can cry without feeling ashamed
    whenever things are bothering them they let them out in the
       open and men do not

15. —they are the weaker sex (I-3/4, 9; I-4, 15)
    they are suppose to be the weaker sex

16. —they are, can be feminine
    nothing is so much fun as being feminine

17. —they can make a man happy
    they are man's glory
    they are helpful to men
    they can give their husbands pleasure and bear children &
       keep a house

18. —I don't know (I-3/4, 14)
    no comment
    I haven't figured this one out yet
    ?

Unclassified
    they think they are
    they live longer than men
    Girls are lucky because—they are able to feel happy about
       lots of things and it is lucky
    they can have much more fun than men

I-3/4

The categories at 1-3/4 differ from the corresponding ones at I-3 in the direction of more affect, being more interpersonal, and having more active connotations (being a mother rather than just having a baby, but raising a family and being loved by a child are empirically located at I-3). The ideas of choice and responsibility occur more clearly at I-3/4 than at I-3, often with use of those words, and they are specified still more clearly at I-4. One kind of femininity is seen in those I-3/4 subjects who say "they can be pampered," or that they take advantage of being "the weaker sex" to "get their way." Although there is a manipulative and narcissistic tone to such responses, they do not have the hostile or predatory tone typical for the Delta level; at any rate, empirically they are good indicators of the I-3/4 level.

1. —they can be mothers (I-3, 2, 3; I-4, 3)
    they have an opportunity to be a good wife a mother
    they can have children. And be good mothers

2. —they can spend more time with their children (I-3, 3; I-4, 2)
    they get to stay home more than the husband an get to know the kids better
    they can stay home & take care of there family, not getting out & working everyday
    they are the ones that get to take care of the children. While there father can't

3. —family life centers around them
    They really are the person who the whole family looks up to for the decisions

4. —they have men; there are men (I-3, 7)
    of men
    there are so many men around
    there are still a few real men in the world
    they can fall in love with men
    they have men to marry

5. —men love, need them
    they have a husband to love them & to look after them
    they can feel wanted and loved
    they are loved
    men turn to them
    they are cared for

*6. —they have men to lean on; men take care of them (I-4, 15)
    they can depend on men

they have men to protect them
they have wonderful husbands to help with problems
marry the right guy and you're secure for the rest of your life
they have somone to depend upon for their living

7. —they are pampered, catered to, given attention; they are treated well, with respect (I-3, 9)
   they are respected where I come from
   they are supposed to be waited upon
   they can be treated daintily
   its like being a queen
   so many businesses today cater to their tastes
   they are courted
   they are shown courtesies (men open doors, etc. for them)
   if a man is a gentleman he will treat her nicely and make a comfortable home for her

8. —they can get their own way (I-2, 1; I-4, 9)
   they can wrap men around their little finger
   they usually can get what they want if they go about it in the right way
   they can wheedle anyone into anything
   most often their husbands give in to them and they don't have to fight in wars
   of their persuasive powers
   they rule men

9. They can take advantage of being the weaker sex (I-3, 15; I-4, 15)
   they are the weaker sex and can play on the sympathy of our men
   they can hide behind ignorance
   through marriage many stupid women succeed in life by having a man do their thinking
   they can use their feminity to gain their goals

10. —they have experiences, privileges, choices that men do not (unelaborated) (I-3, 10; I-4, 1, 7)
    there are a few things they can do that no one else can

11. —they don't have all the responsibilities a man does (I-4, 11)
    they don't have to carry as big a load, as men
    they are usually not under as much pressure as men
    they don't have as much to worry about as men
    they don't have half a rough life like a man does

*12. —they usually don't have to support a family (I-3, 8)
most of them do not have to earn a living or join the millatary
they are not the bread winners

13. —they have more choice in appearance (I-3, 6)
they have more freedom in beauty than men have. (cosmetics, fashion, etc.)
their fashions are so varied and colourful
they have more choice when it comes to clothes

14. —I don't think they are lucky (I-3, 18; I-4, 17)
Are they?
no opinion. Don't believe they are "lucky" for any reason in particular
don't you believe it
ha—
I don't agree . . . it's a man's world!
men may think so. But I don't

I-4

Responses at I-4 can be broadly categorized in terms of traits, experiences (often affective), social expectations, and availability of choices. Emotional differences might be classed as differences in traits or in experiences. Among their unique experiences are that they are the source of life, emotional aspects of childbearing and childrearing, childrearing seen in terms of effort, process, outcome, responsibility, influence, or in terms of a larger social context. Rather than simply saying that women are weak or dependent (I-3), these are given as social expectations: "they are considered the more fragile sex," "they are not expected to be so aggressive as men," they do not have to be competitive. A somewhat different aspect of social expectations is their freedom from certain responsibilities or pressures, stated more specifically than at I-3/4. Saying that women are lucky because they are now equal to men in terms of freedom, independence, and the like implies comparison with their status in former times. The I-4 notion that working or serving others is a privilege or opportunity contrasts with the notion at I-3 and below that work is onerous.

1. Childbearing seen as experience, privilege, joy, blessing (I-3/4, 10; I-4/5, 1; I-5, 2)
they can enjoy the wonders of holding a newborn baby
they have the pleasure of having babies
they have the God-given ability to have children

they can experience motherhood

they have that wonder power of birth and they should try an use it

they have the opportunity of knowing their baby 9 months longer than the father knows him

they can feel life during pregnancy which must be a good feeling and men are deprived of that

2. —they can be close to, enjoy their children (I-3/4, 2; I-4/5, 1)

    they get to make over their children more than men

    they have the children to keep them happy, most of the times

    they can be close to their families

    they have the joy of having babies and therefore being closer to the child

3. —they can give life (I-3, 2; I-3/4, 1)

    they can fullfill God's purpose of creation

    they truthfully are the tree of fruition in a family

    they are the main source of life

    they are the means of new flesh and blood in the world

4. Raising a family in terms of effort, process, outcome

    if they really try can raise a loveing family and have loving husband

    they are able to see their children grow

    they are able to fulfill the goal of having a husband & family, & bring up her children

    they can get married & have children & feel as though they achieve something

5. Shaping, molding children's minds; influencing future generations

    their role in society enables them to influence and guide they many people they came in contact with

    we have the opportunity of helping mold the lives of our children

    they are in a position to influence change for the betterment of humanity

6. —they can fulfill several roles (unelaborated) (I-4/5, 3)

    they can be both mothers and career women

    they have a wider choice of roles for their lives

    they can work and have a family too

    they have many ways to fulfill themselves and can combine several worlds

    they can usually choose their future role

they can choose between having a career or working or not
today they can fulfill so many roles: housewife, mother, career,
civic, etc.

7. —they have opportunities to serve; they have privileges in
homemaking and childrearing (I-3/4, 10)
   they have more of an opportunity to see their children go
   through the various stages
   they are many satisfactions and priviledges that she is able to
   share with other people
   they have many privileges in making their home that the hus-
   band does not

8. Responsibilities as privileges
   they may be responsible for their husbands and children
   they, too, have a responsibility to themselves and their families
   when they are married their responsibilities are so big
   their main obligation in life is to make their husbands happy
   they have an important job in life—to raise children
   they are the mainstay of any family—they balance a family—
   and, to be needed and appreciated is essential
   their role is so challenging
   they who give are richer than they who receive

9. —they can lead interesting lives, follow their own interests (I-
3/4, 8)
   they can plan their days to satisfy themselves
   they have the chance to do so many wonderful things, if they
   want to try
   they have a great deal of leisure time during which they can
   increase their knowledge
   they can express their creativity in so many ways
   they don't have specific routines
   they have so many different avenues open to them
   their role can be highly creative

10. —they have opportunities, independence, freedom equal to
men (now)
   they are part of the human race
   they have more freedom and don't feel so regimented, at least
   those in the upper classes
   their opportunities are developing now
   in this age, they have a freedom of activity they have never
   enjoyed before
   they have achieved the respect that wanted years ago

they are not required by our society to fight in wars, however, if they want to, they participate

11. Freedom from responsibilities, pressures (specified) (I-3/4, 11)
they don't have to worry so much about a profession
they are faced with less financial responsibility than men
they don't have to worry as much about the bills as papa does
they do not have to be as security minded as men
they don't have to worry so much about being too feminine or too masculine as the boys do
they can leave the important decisions to the husband

12. —they do not have to compete, be aggressive, take the lead in life
they are the ones that usually get pursued
they bear children and do not necessarily lead as competitive lives as men
they are not expected to be so aggressive as men

13. Emotional differences; special traits (intuition, sensitivity) (I-3, 13)
they can control themselves more than men
they have more tolerance
they usually have the ability to understand peoples feelings
they have a natural creative ability
they express love readily
they always have a bit of strength in reserve for unexpected happenings
small things can make them very happy
they can tolerate many emotional crisis that men cannot bear so well
they seem to have a special warmth, can give freely

14. —they are allowed to show their feelings (I-3, 14)
they can bear children and have or show more sentiment than men
they are more free to show their emotions than men
they are not expected to hide their emotions
they have more emotional outlets than men

15. —they are considered dependent, expected to be weaker (I-3, 15; I-3/4, 6, 9)
they are considered the more fragile sex
their dependency needs are acceptably recognized
they are known to be dependent and can lean on men in time of responsibility

less is expected of them than of men
men think we're frail
men usually think they are helpless

16. —I enjoy being a woman (I-3, 1)
of everything—I love being a woman
they're woman—I guess—I enjoy being a woman—

17. —I don't think either sex is more lucky (I-3/4, 14)
I don't believe in lucky therefore, I have no response to this
no more so than men
they have the opportunity to live. I do not feel either sex is
more lucky than the other
People are not lucky but some people make more of their
opportunities

Unclassified
it is up to them whether a family stays together and is healthy
and happy. Most women have the ability to use their luck
to the best advantage
I think the only lucky women are the ones with good hus-
bands that don't drink

I-4/5

Above I-4 there do not seem to be new themes so much as elaboration and combination of themes present at I-4. Every response rated
above I-4 is unique. Most of the responses above I-4 have at least two
ideas, with at least one of them classifiable at I-4. Where the combination
of ideas is the basis for awarding the I-4/5 rating, a popular response
such as having babies does not count as another thought. Above I-4 the
roles available to women are elaborated beyond simply wife, mother, career. Appearing in several categories at I-4/5 but not at lower levels are
responses bringing out contrasts and contradictions: weak and strong, dependent and independent, "easier" but "dull and boring."

1. Special relations open to women (I-4, 1, 2; I-5, 2)
they are able to birth children and then give themselves com-
pletely to their husband and children
they have the opportunity of bearing children and having the
wonderful relationship of mother and child
Through childbirth they are able to acquire a closeness to
the child no man will ever experience
they get the opportunity to enjoy all that is feminine and
warm without apology

*they can bear children and because They may seek comfort
and solace more easily then may men*

2. —they can perpetuate themselves through their children
   they bear the children to carry on their husband's name
   *they alone carry on the human race and know a tangible
   sense of immortality through their children*

3. Can fill several roles, have wider choice of roles (elaborated)
   (I-4, 6)
   *they generally do not have to bear the sole role of breadwin-
   ner and have more time to develop their artistic and charitable interests*
   *they have the privilege of being both independent and de-
   pendent*
   *they can have children, and can take either a masculine or
   feminine role in society as far as careers go*
   *they have a choice between dependency (upon a husband) or
   their own self assertion*
   *they today live in a world which allows them to get an educa-
   tion and have both a family and career if they are especially talented*
   *they usually have more choice in mapping out their lives than
   men do*
   when the marry, they have freedom to grow in may directions

4. Combination of two ideas, at least one from I-4 level, or
   contrasting ideas (I-5, 1)
   to be cherished is usually easier than to cherish
   *we are the humanizing elements in society and mold the men
   of civilization*
   *they have an easier role in life than men although sometimes
   it is dull and boring*
   *they don't have to face the hardship of life unless they want
   too*
   *in most cases they are not faced with the financial burden of
   supporting a family. Either that is left to the husband or
   they have no family*
   *men treat them with courtesy and respect, and people are
   generally helpful toward them still, even though they feel
   they are equal to men in many fields*
   *since they are considered the "weaker sex" they secretly have
   the advantage of the stronger*
   we can be strong as well as weak

*they enjoy opportunities of fulfillment in the home and out
of it*

*they have more varied choices in their life adjustment and
can choose different avenues more easily without loss of
status*

Unclassified

when they think *they are. (and I* do*)*

*it is not because they are lucky when they are pleased with
this fact*

I-5

In high responses there is an appreciation of the advantages of
being a woman that are subtle yet real. Responses may be deeply serious,
but they may also display a light touch that is rare at lower levels for
this item.

1. Combination of at least three different ideas, at least one at
   I-4 (I-4/5, 4)

   *they have a natural instinct to love—which they should show
   and lead their family by*

   *we are often idealized, catered to, and have so many exciting
   roles to fill*

   *they have great capacity for love, appreciation, and ability to
   help their fellow man*

   *most men respect them, and treat them well. Women have
   equal opportunities, and the added one that they will have
   a family to love and depend on them*

   *they should have the basic role of giving children and sup-
   porting their mate while the husband bears the responsibility of main authority and provider*

2. Unique or deep emotional experiences (I-4, 1; I-4/5, 1)

   *I feel that life offers them deeper emotional experiences than
   men*

   *they can experience the feeling womanhood to its greatest ex-
   tent in many ways*

   *as a broad generality, they seem to be more in touch with the
   realities and eternal verities of life*

3. Existential humor

   *they can flout all sorts of little rules (like being afraid of fa-
   mous men) that men can't. , , ,*

*they are gay, charming, beautiful, witty and on top of all
these things they can become mothers*

I-6

What marks the I-6 level is not absence of themes found at lower
levels (appearance, babies, dependence) but combination of these concerns with I-5 thoughts in an original way.

Unclassified

*they can feel a new life born within them; they are usually
loved and cared for within the haven of a man's gentle
strength*

*they have many roles to play and society allows them wide
choices of creativeness in dress, occupation as well as their
fundamental biological role in the interesting and rewarding experience of dealing with children*

*they can love and be so much more expressive and aesthetic
than men can be. They can legally entertain more whims*

My Father—

Though this unstructured stem lends itself to many possibilities, most subjects just say something nice about father. Alternatively, they may mention something unfavorable about him, give a concrete or neutral fact, or say something about their own relation to their father. High level responses tend to contain several of these facets. One way and another subjects tell us, if not explicitly about their relation to their father, something about their ability to understand relations between people.

At I-3 and below the father is usually described as a stereotyped good or bad figure; at I-4 and higher he usually emerges as a real, complicated figure. Describing directly the relation between father and daughter is uncommon below I-3. At I-3 descriptions are in terms of being close, getting along, loving, or strictness. Increasingly deeper and more complex interpersonal relations are described at higher I levels.

I-2

At this level subject sees father as either completely good or bad. Responses are either unqualified rejections or statements that father is good to me, implying that father does nice things for subject or gives her things.

1. —is good (nice) to me; gives me what I want (Δ, 1; I-3, 1)
    are a good daddy to me
    is very easy to get you what you want

2. —is mean, hateful, hard (unqualified rejection) (I-3, 7)
    is a first class louse
    is a very hateful person

DELTA

At the Delta level there are a few responses expressing typical Delta concerns, such as resentment of control and belief in luck. The category decribing father as married to mother is presumably somewhat sardonic in tone. The one large category here simply says that father is nice or good and presumably belongs here because of its global and undifferentiated tone. In fact it is placed here as compromise; it is relatively more frequent below I-3 but also occurs fairly often at I-3 and even higher.

*1. —is nice, good; is a nice (good) man (I-2, 1; I-3, 1)
    was very nice when he was alive

2. —is the husband of my mother
    is married
    married my mother

3. —is a lucky man

Unclassified
    makes me sick at times
    should tend to his won bissness
    is always lecturing
    is fun but I can't tell when he is serious and I get into lots
    of trouble this way

I-3

The typical I-3 response is a banal and global idealization of the father. He is wonderful, fine, cool, important to me. Comparative versions of the same idea occur at higher levels, for example, "is the greatest man alive" (I-3/4). Many responses at this level are concrete and specific, referring to physical appearance or specific activities. To see the father as having good and bad moods, being nice at some times but not at others, is rated I-3. Although such responses seem to be a recognition of complexity, hence should be rated at I-3/4 or higher, they are more likely a failure to recognize it. They assert rather that father is a good guy and a bad guy alternately. Compare "a strong and determined person, but also kind" (I-4) with "is very nice at time and he has his bad time also" (I-3). These could be two descriptions of the same man.

**1. Banal idealization (I-2, 1; Δ, 1; I-3/4, 1, 6; I-4, 1)
   was a wonderful man
   is a dear
   is a good person
   is a great guy
   is a swell man
   is a sweet man
   was a good father

2. —is easy-going; is easy to get along with (I-4, 5, 13)
   is a easy-going, well-liked person
   never takes anything too serious

3. —is okay
   is cool
   was all right

4. —loves me; I love him (I-3/4, 4; I-4, 1)
   is one whom I love very much
   is very good to me, and most of all he loves me
   was very dear to me

5. —is important to me
   meant a lot to me
   is very important to me because if it wasn't for him I wouldn't be here

6. —and I are (not) close; (don't) get along (I-3/4, 4; I-4, 9)
   and I were never close. I never lived with him
   and I don't get along so hot
   was not to close to me, But was a good worker
   was my buddy

7. —has a temper; has good and bad moods (I-2, 1; I-4, 3)
   is redhead & has a temper
   gets real angry alot of the time

is very nice at time and he has his bad time also
is very mean at times
is a wonderful person to talk with when his is in a good mood

8. —is quiet (I-4, 4)
   is a very silent man

9. Appearance; physical comparisons
   and I look just alike
   is tall, dark, and handsome
   has very pretty blue eyes

*10. —works hard; is a good provider
   works everyday
   worked hard for his family & was kind
   is a hard working man
   has a good job

*11. Occupations
   was a Dentist
   works for the St. Joseph Lead Co.
   is a good businessman
   is retired

12. Concrete activities (I-3/4, 10)
   is going fishing
   is a very good golfer with about a 76 average
   was a good driver
   went to California on a Business trip

13. Shared activities
   and I like to do things together
   and I don't talk together
   and I have fun together

14. —is sick
   has astma attacks
   is going to be operated on
   has been seriously ill recently
   broke his right thumb

15. —is an alcoholic
   is a sweet drunkard

16. —is strict, not strict
   was tough on my older brother & sisters
   was too easy
   spoils me rotten
   is not as strict as my mother

17. —is the head of the family, the man of the house (I-3/4, 3, 11)
    is the head of our household

18. Lack of contact (I-3/4, 13; I-4, 11)
    and mother are apart
    is now so far away from me
    I don't see often enough

*19. —is dead (unelaborated) (I-3/4, 14)
    is deceased

20. —I don't have one; I don't remember (I-3/4, 13)
    I don't know anything of my father

Unclassified
    was a reasonable man
    is so much help to me when I need it
    teases me
    is very old fashions
    is an elderly man

I-3/4

At this level the father is seen as a somewhat more differentiated individual and his relations with the mother and with the subject are described in slightly more differentiated terms. His own feelings are also described here.

*1. —is the most wonderful man in the world; is the best person
    I ever knew (I-3, 1; I-4, 1)
    is the sweetest person I know
    is the greatest in my estimation
    was the finest man I know

2. —was wonderful but not perfect (I-4, 3)
    is a nice, but odd person
    is a wonderful man, although a bit stubborn at times
    is nice but sometimes too overprotective

3. Evaluation of father as parent (elementary role conception)
    (I-3, 17; I-4, 10, 12, 14; I-4/5, 3)
    seems to be quite typical of other fathers
    is not the best
    is a wonderful person & parent
    is not very much of a Father

*is a good provider, he works hard, he's a good husband to my
mother and a good father me my sisters & my brother*
was a very nice man, he treated me like a father should

4. —enjoys, loves, is close to his family (I-3, 4, 6)
   loves my mother very much
   has always adored his family

5. —mistreated my mother; is dominated by my mother (I-4, 13)
   was a yes man to my mother

6. —is a model (I-3, 1)
   though dead, is still an example for some of the things I do
   *is a great person and I hope I can marry someone just like
   him*
   is the greatest in the world—close to my ideal man

7. —is a kind (gentle, considerate) man; likes to help others
   (I-4, 5)
   is a very genorous man
   is a very good hearted man
   was a man who "cared"

*8. —is an understanding man; understands me
   is a person who understands things
   really understands the problems of teens
   and I understand each other pretty well
   was more understanding than my mother

9. —is intelligent, capable (I-4, 6)
   was a great man in his field
   was smart
   was a wonderful, clever and industrious man

10. —is busy, active; enjoys activities (I-3, 12; I-4, 7)
    enjoys his work
    loves to fish
    is very active for his age

11. —is a domineering (aggressive) person (I-3, 17)
    is very outspoken
    is a tyrant
    has control in my house—he has the final decision

12. —is lonely, unhappy, depressed
    I felt sorry for him
    was a very unfortunate and unhappy man

13. —is a stranger; I don't know him (I-3, 18, 20; I-4, 11)
    I don't know very well

is almost a stranger to me
and I never knew each other

14. —died (mention of when) (I-3, 19)
    passed away two years ago
    deceased in my early childhood
    has been dead for eight years
    passed too early for me to remember

Unclassified
    has had many experiences in life
    is a very selfish, inconsiderate person, and I don't like him
    is the conservative, quiet type
    is an introvert
    is mixed up
    is a very complex person

I-4

The trends seen at I-3/4 are expressed more clearly at I-4. The father is presented as a real person with differentiated traits, even contrasting ones, favorable and unfavorable, or traits that are not necessarily either good or bad. At I-3 there are many interchangeable descriptions, while most of the I-4 subjects give a unique flavor to their descriptions. Many of the responses show some distance from and perspective toward the father and his relation to the subject and some capacity to evaluate another's inner life.

1. —is a wonderful man and I love him (I-3, 1, 4; I-3/4, 1)
    was a kind and gentle man whom I loved dearly

2. Devoted, dedicated, sincere, loyal, noble
    was a dedicated family doctor
    is a magnificent man, who is truely a man in the noblest sense

*3. Complex personality (elaborated) (I-3, 7; I-3/4, 2; I-5, 2)
    is a very gentle, yet powerful person
    is a hardworking, competitive, amiable, strong man
    is a well meaning person, but often worries too much
    is a very stern, stubborn, and religious man; but an awful nice guy
    is a sweet but unmature man
    was a very gregarious, but not a very happy man
    is soft under his hard facade

is a beautiful, tragic person
is the boss in our family but not a tyrant
is a happy go lucky sort of man, but is stubborn when comes
to certain things

4. —is reserved; does not express emotions (I-3, 8; I-4/5, 2)
finds it very difficult to show himself freely with other people
is lacking the ability to show any outward signs of affection

5. —is a warm person (I-3, 2; I-3/4, 7; I-4/5, 2)
is a warm friendly, and handsome man
is a very understanding warm individual

6. —is a wise person (I-3/4, 9)
was a fine—wise—generous man
was a wise and humorous business man

7. —enjoys life; cannot enjoy life (I-3/4, 10)
enjoyed beauty
is a very quiet man—oblivious to many enjoyable aspects of
life

8. Appreciation, admiration, respect
is a fine man but a person I'm afraid I haven't appreciated
the way I should
is a respected, devoted, intelligent and successful man
has a very admirable character

9. —and I don't understand each other, have differences of opinion (I-3, 6)
cannot understand women, expecially I
is very kind, understanding but we just don't seem to see eye
to eye on some matters

10. —won't let me grow up; treats me like an adult (I-3/4, 3)
looks upon me as being his "little" girl, who he still somewhat
has to worry about
treats me like a child

11. Description of subject's feelings toward her father despite separation (I-3, 18; I-3/4, 13)
is in the Penetintary, and I don't know him but I would like
to very much
has never lived with me. But I still love him, even though I
hardly know him

12. Father's feelings, attitudes toward the subject (I-3/4, 3; I-4/5, 3)
is often disappointed in me

*is a man who encourages me without smothering my person-
ality*
I love because he treats me like I am, human
did not accept his responsibility for his child

13. Father's relations to others (I-3, 2; I-3/4, 5; I-4/5, 2)
    is interested too much in other women
    *is a very likeable, hardworking person. He appeals to all types
    of people*
    was the kind of man people didn't like to know

14. Father (or subject's relation with father) as changing over
    time (I-3/4, 3)
    is much mellower as an old man
    is a spoiled child but he's being to grow up
    *and I are much closer now that I am in college than when I
    was in high school*
    was very strict, but now that I am a parent I understand him

Unclassified
    is too much like me
    is materialistic
    is very ambitious
    has a delightful, hostile sense of humor
    is a perfectionist
    *is a very fine person, has helped in giving me very high stand-
    ards, and taught me*
    was the most wonderful influence on my life
    an extremely hard-working and self-reliant person
    was a strict disciplenarian

I-4/5

At this level there is a richer, more complex view of interpersonal
relations and a clearer conception of fatherhood as a role.

1. —is a source of concern to me (elaborated)
   *is a source of concern to me because of preoccupation with
   perfection and his desire to control the situation*
   *is a great guy and a hard worker in his profession and I wish
   he wouldn't work so hard—it causes me to worry about him*

2. Complex quality of interpersonal relations (I-4, 4, 5, 13)
   *was a man we loved and respected. He was very firm with us,
   but we always knew he'd stand by us*

*was a gentle man, with narrow horizons but a wealth of love
for others*

*was a brilliant mind, but suffered because he could not share
himself*

*is not easy to understand but yearns for love and companion-
ship*

and I are so much alike we rarely are at ease with each other

*is very mild-mannered, level headed and timid, prefering to
avoid social contacts; he is also a brilliant designer*

*is a thoughtful person but who I sometimes feel I could know
better if he'd let me confide in him directly and not keep
silent when I try to*

*made many sacrifices for his children whom he loved dearly
and gave them many opportunities*

3. Role conception (I-3/4, 3; I-4, 12)

*is a fatherly man. Everyone of my girl freind like him. And
all enjoy his company*

is perfect for the job (of being a father.

Unclassified

is too self-disciplined

is a limited, but good, man

*is a man of rare understanding who helps me see other peo-
ple's view points*

never takes stands on vital issues

*and mother were divorced when I was nine months old;
therefore, I have mixed feelings about him*

*has always been one of the most significant—and at times, the
most significant—persons in my life*

*was wonderful to me and gave us free rein in almost all areas
of life*

*is a remarkable, dignified, reserved, quiet, humorous, hand-
some man. I respect him so much*

I-5

Many of the responses at I-5, including those stressing the father's
love of learning and esteem for education, convey a sense of a long-term
life plan. The composite responses rated here encompass elements of inner
conflict or at least complexity. As compared to the descriptions of a complex personality at I-4, these responses contain ideas (respect, dogmatic,
aspects of personality, self-control) that are rated I-4 singly. They also
combine objective and subjective points of view.

1. Love of learning
    was a man who had a great belief in education, although he himself only went to sixth grade

    is unending in his search for knowledge and his efforts to help others

    gained great satisfaction in his educational and economic progress, entirely self motivated and achieved

    possesses a quick mind, a love of learning, and has high expectations of his family and friends

2. Composite responses, encompassing some conflict or contradiction (I-4 elements) (I-4, 3)
    is a man I admire and respect although there are some aspects of his personality I do not know

    is a brilliant & learned man but often dogmatic and selfish. I am proud of his position & intelligence

    is a strong, self controlled man—a firm disciplinarian whom I did not understand until I became an adult

    is a real man, and I'm lucky, some of my friends fathers aren't I'd never fall in love with him because our personalities are different, but he is a success

I-6

The one response placed at this level conveys gratitude for father being the kind of person he is rather than for things he has done for or to the subject. Contributing to the high rating are time perspective ("my life"), self-fulfillment ("enriching"), indirect influence as compared to love, understanding, or discipline. The two traits ascribed to the father are unique and differ markedly from each other. "Faith in the person" illustrates complex interpersonal interactions.

Unclassified
    has greatly enriched and influenced my life by his immense common sense logic and faith in the person

A Pregnant Woman—

Aspects of response to look for are affect, with a tendency for more positive affects to occur on higher levels; appearance versus feelings, with more stress on appearance at lower levels and feelings at higher levels; idealization, occurring particularly in the middle range; a change from egocentricity at and below I-3 to a child-centered view at I-4; and a progress from a blanket characterization (I-3 and below) to a qualified or contingent one (I-3/4 and I-4), and on to a characterization that unites positive and negative aspects, that unites appearance and feelings, or that contrasts the ideal with reality (above I-4). Contingencies actually appear at all levels. At Delta the concern is "if she's married." This contingency appears also at higher levels with surprising frequency. Although "lucky" and "happy" seem almost synonymous for this item, the Delta subject responds, is lucky if she is married, while the I-3/4 subject states, is happy if she is married. The former response seems to connote that if you get pregnant, you are lucky to be married; the latter, that if you are married, you rejoice at being pregnant. At higher levels other contingencies are mentioned, such as wanting a baby and being able to take care of it.

A few subjects at low levels say that pregnant women are sick, perhaps meaning subject to morning sickness. The I-3 subject may say she is normal, the I-3/4 woman that she is special. Some I-4 subjects say that she is not sick or not different from other women. At higher levels there may be responses that she is different in feelings and reactions. Since this sequence contains possibilities for misclassification, additional cues should be used where they occur in the response. At I-2 and Delta there is a tone of dependent complaining; the I-3 subject is often concerned with ways people are alike; at I-3/4 there may be implied demand for special privilege, but in the context of idealization rather than complaining. The I-4 woman has feelings of responsibility, and above I-4 there is interest in pregnancy as an inner experience.

I-2

At I-2 there is emphasis on sheer physical facts: the tautology "is going to have a baby" and superficial description of physical appearance. Responses distinctive for the I-2 and Delta levels have a negative tone, probably reflecting the inability of subjects at those levels to give without asking anything in return. Two unclassified responses here have overtones of referring to the baby as a gift or source of supplies.

*1. —is going to have a baby (I-3/4, 5)
   has a baby
   is expecting a child
   is a woman bearing a child
   a pregnant woman gets marries have babies

2. —is fat; is big; has a big belly (Δ, 7; I-3, 10)
   has a bulging stomach
   get larger
   is in a bad fit when he belly sticks out

3. —is, gets sick
   is easy to get sick

4. —is miserable, unhappy, pitiful (Δ, 2, 8; I-3, 6, 8; I-4, 5)

Unclassified
   is lucky, becuse she will have someone to keep her happy
   can't wait till she gets her baby
   is sometimes nice

DELTA

There are essentially three themes at the Delta level: she had better be married; she is helpless and should avoid work; and she is grouchy and looks clumsy. Altogether this makes for an unsympathetic portrait of the pregnant woman. The most surprising category is the one that implies that the term "pregnant woman" applies only to unmarried ones.

1. —should not do hard work; should take it easy (I-3, 2, 1)
   shouldn't have to work

2. —has a hard time (I-2, 4; I-3/4, 10)
   goes through a lot of trouble
   has it kind of bad. Because it is complicated having a baby
   can get into a lot of trouble

3. —is helpless; needs help
   is a helpless soul
   be helped all she can be

4. —should be married
   should be married or engaged

5. —is lucky if she's married (I-3/4, 6; I-4/5, 3)
   is O.K. as long as she is married
   is the lukiest girl in the world if she's married

6. —is usually not married; better get married
   should get married or put the baby up for adoption
   should know who the baby is and who gave it to her
   is one who don't have a husband

7. —looks clumsy, awkward, ridiculous (I-2, 2; I-3, 10)
   is funny look to kids
   is a clumsy woman

8. —is grouchy, hard to get along with (I-2, 4; I-3, 8; I-4, 5)
   can be mean at times
   is sometimes evil while pregnant
   sometimes is very crabby
   is usually cranky

I-3

It appears to be more true for this item than for some others that the frequency and location of a category depends on the sample used.

Of course many I-3 subjects say that pregnant women are pretty; none-theless, the distribution for the category centers at I-3/4. Unlike responses concerning appearance for other items, this response category rarely appears on protocols rated below I-3. Other remarks concerning appearance do occur at I-3 and below, particularly those referring to changes in size and shape. The conformist attitude is displayed in a large preponderance of stereotyped references to positive feelings ("is happy") plus an emphasis on rules for the pregnant woman to follow. The "happy" category is found at all levels but mostly at I-3, I-3/4, and I-4. Although it is somewhat arbitrary, we class at Delta descriptions of poor disposition, at I-3 unhappy or demanding behavior that seems to imply a change from her prepregnancy behavior, while at I-4 the corresponding category describes mood swings during pregnancy.

**1. —is, looks, should be happy, lucky, proud (I-4, 3, 4)
  should try to be happy
  is very fortunate
  can be happy if she try
  is the luckiest person alive

 *2. —should be careful; should take care of herself (Δ, 1; I-3/4, 8; I-4, 9)

 3. —should always keep her appearance up
  should stay neat and clean
  should dress modestly

 4. —needs care, love, understanding (I-4, 6)
  is to be pampered
  should be treated with kindness
  is to be took care of

 5. —is respected
  is a woman to look up to
  deserves respect

 6. —is tired, uncomfortable (I-2, 4)
  looks very uncomfortable
  really bears alot of pain
  is slowed down
  sometimes suffers quite a bit during her pregnancy
  is uncomfortable during her last months
  will have a lot of pain during delivery

 7. Specific prohibitions or rules (Δ, 1; I-3/4, 8)
  must cut down her activities
  should not gain too much weight

> *shouldn't wear shorts or tight clothes*
> *should not lift anything to heave because she might lose the*
> *baby*

8. Emotional change (I-2, 4; Δ, 8; I-3/4, 4; I-4, 5)
   is sometimes moody
   Is very upset most of the time
   feels that she should have pity most of the time
   is sometimes more demanding for attention
   are some times hard to please
   cries easily

9. Banal or broad description of pregnant condition
   usually has morning sickness
   is usually married
   is often seen in the hospital
   may have a craving for strawberries
   could expect to be in that condition for 9 months
   wears maternity clothes

10. Changes in size, shape, appearance, bearing (I-2, 2; Δ, 7)
    is out of shape
    waddles
    cannot touch her toes
    usually has a nice skin and complexion
    is not very neat looking
    is an unpleasant sight
    looks like Humptey Dumptey
    becomes ungainly

11. —is normal; is a commonplace sight (I-4, 10)
    can be as any other normal woman
    is seen everywhere
    is a part of the community
    isn't unusual

Unclassified
   is happy when her baby arrives

I-3/4

In general, in going from I-3 to I-3/4 there is a change from concern with appearances to concern for feelings. While a number of categories for this item follow that rule, the most frequent responses appear to reverse it, with feelings ("happy") at I-3 and appearance ("beautiful") at I-3/4. The following explanation is admittedly *ex post facto*.

Probably stating that a pregnant woman is happy is more a statement of a norm than a perceptive remark about feelings, while to state that she is beautiful is not so much a description of appearance as an interpretation or feeling about her appearance. Anxiety, embarrassment, anticipation, problems, and health are other typical I-3/4 themes found here. For the subject simply to state her own feelings or reactions toward pregnant women, regardless of what those feelings may be, makes a quite discriminating category at this level.

*1. —is beautiful, attractive, a lovely sight (I-4, 1)
    is sometimes cute
    has an attractive quality about her
    is graceful and happy looking
    looks her best
    is a wonderful sight
    is the most beautiful thing alive
    is always beautiful, in my eyes

2. —can be attractive (if she tries)
    can be just as stylish and attractive as an unpregnant woman
    can look neat and pretty or slopy and unattractive
    can be beautiful
    need not resemble a hag!

3. Feelings about her appearance; embarrassment; attracts attention
    is usually concerned about her appearance
    should never feel ashamed of her appearance
    sometimes feels funny in a crowd
    often feels unattractive
    is a person who is insecure due to the feeling of being unattractive

4. —is anxious, nervous (I-3, 8; I-4, 5)
    has a lot on her mind
    often times has fears
    sometimes has a hard time because of false information
    will sometimes worry if her baby will come out OK or deformed in some way
    is nervous I suppose because she is going through a physical change

5. —looks forward to having a baby, being a mother (I-2, 1; I-4, 9)
    has alot to look forward to

hopes to have a normal child
generally hopes for the day of delivery to see what she has
has a feeling of suspense. Boy? girl? When?
has something to live for
usually anticipates motherhood

6. —is happy if she is married, wants the child; is sometimes happy, sometimes not (Δ, 5; I-4/5, 3; I-5, 1)
if married must feel great
is very fortunate if she really wants the child
is fortunate if she's happy with the situation

7. —is happy even though uncomfortable (I-4, 4)
feels awkward sometimes and wonderful the other times

8. —should have good prenatal care (I-3, 2, 7)
should follow Doctor's orders
must be careful of her health
should keep up their nutritional needs
must have a special diet

9. —is special; is a symbol; is blessed (I-4, 7)
must feel pretty special
to me represents that a wonderful event will take place
is a person who God has blessed
is a blessing
carries a blessing
is a symbol of fertility

10. —has problems; has my sympathy (Δ, 2)
arouses my sympathy in the summer time
problem is just beginning
presents a problem
has a complicated nine months
Ive never had the pleasure but I sympathy with them

11. —makes me feel . . .
nauseates me
fascinates me
sometimes bores me
makes me feel unconfortable
makes me wonder what its like to carry & have a baby
to me looks beautiful, but upsets me inwardly
is one I (for no reason) do not especially like to look at

12. —is what I'd (not) like to be, have never been
is beautiful as long as it is not me

is fat and beautiful and something I hope to be soon
When I look at a pregnant woman I am glad I am not her—
  I have six already
can't relate it because Ive never be a pregnant woman

Unclassified

should have danced all night
should not take advantage of her condition

I-4

Here one finds a clear distinction between appearance and feelings. They may be contrasted ("is physically ugly but spiritually beautiful") or seen as interrelated ("seems to have a radiant look"). Other manifestations of the more differentiated inner life at this level are the description of a sense of contentment and joy, stated more intensely and less banally than "happy"; giving a combination of feelings, such as proud and happy; and description in terms of a miracle or a gift from God. Distinctive of the I-4 level are references to husband's feelings toward her and to responsibility and preparation for the coming child. Not obvious is why some I-4 subjects state that the pregnant woman is not sick or an invalid; however, in connection with the emphasis here on duties and responsibilities, we may guess that the I-4 subject is objecting to pregnant women using their condition to get out of the ordinary obligations of life.

*1. —has an inner glow; is radiant; is prettier than before (I-3/4, 1)
    should be radiant
    frequently has a rare facial expression of happiness
    is usually beautiful in a way a woman who is not preg. is not
    has joyful look in her eyes

2. Distinction between feeling and appearance (I-4/5, 4)
    is awkward-looking figurtively but she really is the happiest
    looks and feels like a mother
    is beautiful when she is happy about the expected child
    always looks very happy and beautiful, even if she is uncomfortable and ugly
    is physically ugly but spiritually beautiful

3. Finds joy, contentment, satisfaction, well-being (I-3, 1)
    finds peace
    usually is joyful all the time, even when she does not feel good, in her heart she is still happy
    usually wears a look of well-being

4. Combination of different feelings (I-3, 1; I-3/4, 7)
   is usually a very happy and proud woman
   should feel proud and priveledged of her condition
   is a person that should be thankful to God and she should be
     as calm as possible
   is usually more apprehensive than happy
   I've heard is happy and feels fulfilled

5. —is emotional, unstable; has emotional problems (I-2, 4; Δ, 8; I-3, 8; I-3/4, 4)
   is often ambivalent about her status
   is happy at times and moody at times
   is unpredictable
   is likely to have emotional extremes
   gets the blues very easily
   may have many physical and emotional problems

6. —needs special consideration (from her husband); is loved by her husband (I-3, 4)
   should be shown all the courtesy possible
   is beautiful as she has the gift of a loving husband
   is often loved more than when not. Also cared for in the ex-
     treme
   with a loving husband is a very privileged person
   needs special understanding from her family

7. —is part of a miracle (I-3/4, 9; I-4/5, 1)
   is a marvel of nature & God
   should enjoy this miracle and thank G-o-d
   is blessed and closer to God and life
   carries a burden yet it is a wondrous gift from God

8. —is fulfilling her purpose (I-4/5, 1)
   is fulfilling her duty to the world
   should always feel thankful to be bringing another birth onto
     the world for thats why she was put here
   feels her goal is being fulfilled

9. —has a responsibility, duty to her child; should prepare for her child (I-3, 2; I-3/4, 5)
   has a great obligation to fulfill toward someone besides her-
     self
   is blessed with one of the most important duties in life
   is a wonderful woman and will have a person's whole life in
     her hand

has quite a blessed event to prepare for
needs to take care of herself for her babies' sake

10. —is not sick; is not different from other women (I-3, 11)
    isn't sick but she isn't a normal person
    is not necessarily an invalid and can lead a normal life
    seldom views herself as "sick"
    should continue normal activities as much as is medically
        advisable
    should feel just like any other woman

Unclassified
    if married very beautiful if unmarried—very pittiable

I-4/5

Most responses classed at I-4/5 are significant elaborations of
themes at lower levels, requiring higher ratings because of the greater
conceptual complexity. The notion that appearance reflects attitudes
probably is anticipated in saying that a pregnant woman is beautiful
(I-3/4); it is expressed clearly in saying she has an inner glow (I-4). At
I-4/5 it is carried further in the statement that attitudes determine appearance. Other reflections of psychological causation are statements that
one person's attitudes affect those of other family members and that the
attitudes and feelings are themselves dependent on circumstances. New
themes at I-4/5 are the appreciation of pregnancy as an experience in
itself and thinking of pregnancy as creation of new life. The latter puts
the experience in broad and abstract terms, comparable to putting it into
social perspective.

1. —is creating new life; has life within her (I-4, 7, 8)
   must find much joy in playing a role in the creation process
   is a living portrait of God's creative power
   is a woman in a position of creation and a resource of love
       and of vitality
   should be happy because she is blessed with the ability to creat
       a new life
   is lucky because she holds the precious body of another human
       being within her body
   is beautiful in a way no other woman is because of this extra
       life generated within

2. Appreciation of pregnancy and motherhood as experiences
   has new and wonderful experiences awaiting her

is experiencing the most wonderful thing that can happen to a woman

should be the happiest person in the world each time she feels her baby move

is someone never realy understood by anyone. Her feelings and way of thinking are entirely different

is going through an experience which may be painful, but is always rewarding

has an enormous amount of ideas and feelings on her mind

should pamper herself & enjoy every minute of her condition

3. Attitude and feelings are dependent upon the circumstances of the pregnancy (Δ, 5; I-3/4, 6; I-5, 1)

should be happy if the pregnancy was bought on in the right way

is a lucky woman if she can care for her child

is happy I hope—she should be. If she isn't it's her fault, she didn't plan

is the luckiest woman in the world if her circumstances are such that the baby will be well taken care of and will be loved and wanted

4. Complex causation (I-4, 2)

should be happy and contented because I feel her attitude, from the time, she conceives, is a determing factor in whether her baby is happy or unhappy

can be beautiful. and to her husband is beautiful. She is also very happy—if her husband is happy

is only as healthy and lovely in appearance as her attitudes towards her unborn child are healthy and lovely

5. Contrast of inward and outward orientation

can be a sweet and lively person, if she will concentrate on others as well as herself

should relax and try to be more outwardly directed during pregnancy

Unclassified

shouldn't bemoan the fact & make everyone else wish she weren't

Imagines things about her expected child

is the sign of a fulfilled love

is still the object of some self-consciousness or curiosity in our society

has her hard moments but she always looks into the future
has many advantages within recent years being able to work,
to continue social life, with excellent pre-natal medical care

I-5

New themes at I-5 are that appearance and actions are ways to communicate feelings; that the stereotyped idealization is different from the reality; and the juxtaposition of conflicting aspects or possibilities. In the last category the responses are all original and all contain some contrast other than the type "if married very beautiful if unmarried—very pittiable" (I-4). The theme of finding one's identity as a woman may appear here, but a well-elaborated response of that type would be rated I-6.

1. Reconciliation of conflicting possibilities (I-3/4, 6; I-4/5, 3)
    is a contradiction of unattractive bulk and vast femininity and womanliness
    feels alternately supremely beautiful and clever and huge and lumpy
    can be a joy or a tiresome neurotic
    can either glow with an inner light or look abused beyond salvation
    has a wonderful burden
    may be beautiful or tragic
    can be extremely happy and beautiful or terribly despondent, depending on her desire for motherhood

2. Concern with communicating feelings—specified
    should be proud of her status and show her feelings in dress and actions
    is attractive if her husband conveys this feeling to her both in words and deeds
    conveys her inner feelings in accentuation, it seems to me; she radiates a happiness or depression without speaking
    should show the world that she is proud to become a mother by dressing neatly & taking good care of her health

3. Distinction of stereotype or idealization from real woman
    should feel like a miracle has happened to her, but most women don't feel like that
    is a happy woman—supposedly
    is often idealized by everyone except herself
    should be a happy woman but too often is not—it's rather sad when they're not happy about life

Unclassified

> *can stimulate a variety of feelings in me—sympathy, envy, disgust, anxiety—according to how I perceive the circumstances and meaning of her condition*
> *is blessed and in a position of better understanding her identity as a woman*
> *carries burdens of all sorts, weight, problems, fears and doubts and speculation*

I-6

The response classed here has more than one aspect that could be rated I-5. It also summarizes the views expressed by many women at other levels.

Unclassified

> *is often beautiful, somewhat anxious but usually quite healthy woman looking forward to the fulfillment of her role as a women and quite secure in her husband's love*

When My Mother Spanked Me, I–

Owing to typing errors, this stem has sometimes appeared with a final "I," sometimes without. Greater variability of response might result from omitting the final "I." One might expect the stem to elicit regressive responses at I-2, expressions of obedience at I-3, of hurt feelings at I-3/4, concern for justice at I-4, and inner conflict above I-4. Such responses occur at the appropriate levels, but they are a small proportion of the total. By far the most common response is "cried" and its minor variations. It occurs at all levels; some of the small variations are scorable, however. Having such a popular response is one factor in decreasing the discriminating power of the item, but the test may be easier for the subject to take for the presence of a few such easy answers.

The chief clue to I-level is some way of showing distance from the situation; the greater the distance, generally the higher the level. Least distance is shown by responses in present tense. In the absence of some other indication of perspective or distantiation, such responses are scored at I-2 or Delta. The stem tends to elicit a narrative style, with two or three aspects often mentioned. This may occur at any level; hence compound responses are usually scored at their highest level. Of course some compound responses do show a real conceptual complexity, and are scored accordingly. The item does not seem to elicit as many distinguishable high-level responses as do many others. No responses are listed at I-6 because we could not distinguish the responses given by I-6 subjects from those of subjects at lower levels.

I-2

The only frequent I-2 category is "cry, get mad, leave" in the present tense and including combinations. We do not know what accounts for this category, whether subjects that give such responses are younger and their mothers do indeed still spank them; whether inappropriate use of present tense is indicative of low intelligence and only indirectly indicative of I-level; whether it is a social class difference in language usage, again only indirectly indicative of level; or whether I-2 subjects are more responsive to the regressive pull of the stem. In any case there is a literal immediacy in the category, as opposed to distance in time at higher levels.

*1. —cry; get mad; leave (present tense) (Δ, 3; I-3, 1; I-3/4, 6, 12)
   get mad and I go outside and cool off
   get real mad and leave the house
   get mad and start crying
   cry for a long time

Unclassified
   could murder her
   say Yes Mother
   pet me
   she spanked me good

DELTA

At this level responses show one or more of the following signs: impulsivity; callousness; immediacy; opportunism. Classed here somewhat as a compromise are responses that show simple feelings, or responses more complex than crying, of sorts that are found at I-3 and I-3/4, yet are expressed in present tense.

1. —hit her back (I-3, 6)
   spank her back
   kicked her
   hit her back and ran away for 1—for 2 nights of fun!

2. —laughed
   tried not to laugh
   laughed cause she can't hit worth beans!

3. Simple feelings, present tense (I-2, 1; I-3, 5, 7; I-3/4, 2)
   feel a shame
   feel like a hate her
   feel sorry for myself
   need it
   cry & pout

4. —felt like running away (I-3/4, 12; I-4, 5)
   cried and tried to run away

Unclassified
   she doesn't anymore
   never gave her a chance to
   cried, not because it hurt, because I thought I could get away with it
   cryed and promised not to do that any more

I-3

Most of the responses classed here refer to actions, banal feelings, or acceptance of authority. References to physical pain have an outward rather than an inward orientation in a somewhat different sense. Even the rejection of the stem has an outward rather than an inward focus: Mother never spanked me, contrasted with "I don't remember" (I-4), which is more frequent at higher levels and implicitly more self-critical.

**1. —cried, screamed, yelled (I-2, 1; I-3/4, 1)
   squalled
   would cry all day

2. —never cried; tried not to cry (I-3/4, 1)
   did not cry
   refused to cry

3. Reference to physical pain
didn't care because I knew it really didn't hurt
squirmed and usually didn't suffer much
cried because she used a switch
vowed never to be bad again around her. She hurt worse
than my grandmother

4. —didn't like it (I-3/4, 7; I-4, 3)

5. —was sad, unhappy; felt bad; felt sorry for myself (Δ, 3; I-3/4, 4)

6. Expression of anger (not hitting or kicking) (Δ, 1; I-3/4, 6)
stuck my tongue out at her
started to cry and call her names
felt like swearing at her

7. —felt ashamed (Δ, 3; I-3/4, 5)
felt sorry for myself, and then ashamed
would be ashamed, if I had one

8. —needed it (I-4, 1; I-4/5, 1)
felt that I needed it
usually asked for it

9. —knew I had done something wrong (I-3/4, 11; I-4, 1)
must have done something wrong
was doing something I shouldn't have been doing

10. —learned my lesson; learned right from wrong; it was for my own good (I-3/4, 11; I-4, 11)
know not to do wrong again
think it is to show me I've done wrong
remembered not to cross the street again
Gets mad but still it was for my own good

11. —obeyed
felt it & minded

12. Went to someone else (I-3/4, 12)
cried for "daddy"
ran to my brothers for protection
ran to my grandmother

13. —just took it; said nothing
didn't do a thing
remained silent

14. —she didn't spank me (I-4, 14, 16)
    she never did it, my father did
    (my parents have never spanked me.)

15. —don't have one; don't remember my mother (I-4, 16)

I-3/4

Responses referring to crying at this level must have some qualification or modifier indicating some distance from the event. Classed here also are partly differentiated feelings, such as hurt and lonely, guilt feelings, and the first intimations of search for reasons.

*1. —usually cried; cried when I was younger (I-3, 1, 2)
    probably cried
    cried—but I'll probably spank my own
    cried, of course, but that was a long time ago
    cried—natch
    often refused to cry

*2. —pouted; sulked (Δ, 3)
    pouted and wouldn't speak to her

3. Exaggerated or intense response, with perspective
    used to throw a temper
    I thought it would surely kill me
    often got mad and tried to fight back
    was heart broken
    felt like crawling into a hole

4. —felt hurt, lonely, unwanted; felt she didn't love me (I-3, 5; I-4, 13)
    cried and was hurt
    grew very depressed
    felt hurt and abused

5. —was sorry; felt guilty, embarrassed (I-3, 7)
    was sorry for what I had done
    was usually sorry I had upset her
    cried and was sorry for what I did wrong

6. —was angry; got mad (I-2, 1; I-3, 6)
    would become very angry
    was mad at first
    cried and got mad

7. —hated, disliked her (I-3, 4; I-4, 3, 7)
    think I didn't like her

8. Wanted her to feel sorry (I-4, 5)
  wanted it to stay red for a long time and make her sorry

9. Denial of hurt feelings or resentment (I-4, 12)
  liked her even more
  had respect for her

10. —knew there was a reason; wanted to know why (I-4, 10)
  know now there must have been a reason
  understood why she did it
  sometimes understood why
  couldn't understand why
  was puzzled because she then kissed me

11. —realized I was wrong, mother was right (I-3, 9, 10)
  did not become angry because I realized I was in the wrong
  was angry but I knew she knew best
  understood that I had done something wrong

12. —went to my room; avoided her (I-2, 1; Δ, 4; I-3, 12)
  ran to my room and cried
  went off by myself & talked to no one for 2 or 3 hours

I-4

Most characteristic for this level are responses bringing in a notion of justice or injustice, or those with a "but" clause, where the second half represents an alleviation of hurt feelings, or change over time, or acceptance of responsibility. There are also other ways of showing increased distance from the event, such as describing exaggerated feelings or plans for revenge. The notions of being stubborn and rebellious are classed here empirically; while we know nothing of actual behavioral correlates of such responses, their occurrence at this level may give comfort to some parents faced with corresponding conduct. That the subject was surprised at being spanked is also classed here empirically; however, it is consistent with the frequency of responses at this level and particularly at higher levels that mention that spanking was an infrequent event.

*1. —deserved it (I-3, 8, 9; I-4/5, 1)
  knew I had it coming
  I accepted it as earned
  didn't like it but I probably had it coming to me

2. —thought she was unfair; felt mistreated
  hated her because it was mostly for something I did not do

*3. —resented it; felt resentful (I-3, 4; I-3/4, 7)
  was very resentful to her for days to follow
  felt a deep resentment and no justice
  resented it more than when my dad spanked me
  resented her

4. —became stubborn
  still didn't give in
  would never cry a bit stubborn I suppose
  either was to stuborn to cry or threw a fit
  resented it with loud crying—she said I was a stubborn one

5. Wish for revenge (wish or plan distinct from act) (Δ, 4; I-3/4, 8)
  resented it and vowed to hate her forever
  got angry and wanted to hit her back (but didn't)
  use to plan what I was going to do to her when I got grown

6. —rebelled; felt belligerent
  felt rebellious

7. Feelings of hatred (I-3/4, 7)
  hated her for that one minute
  felt that she was the most horribly mean and hateful person there was

8. Crying, anger, and so on, followed by alleviation
  felt kind of unwanted at the time but soon got over it
  resented it for awhile, but soon forgot about it
  would sit and pout for hours but after a while I would be myself again

9. Feelings then versus feelings now (I-4/5, 3)
  was mad then, but glad for all the spankings I got, now
  hated her at the time, but in the long run I was better off and I respected her more

10. Reaction alleviated by understanding reason, accepting blame (I-3/4, 10)
  resented her until I figured out it was only my fault that I got spanked
  was mad because I didn't think I did wrong. But upon consideration I knew I was
  used to feel sorry for myself especially if it was not explaine to me clearly what I did wrong
  was angry unless I definitely knew the reason

11. —knew she meant it; got the message; tried to avoid a repetition (no mention of right or wrong) (I-3, 10)

was impressed with need for change in behavior or attitude
usually remembered what not to do again
cried and tried not to be spanked for the same thing again
knew that her authority was real and that misbehavior would
not be tolerated

12. —knew she still loved me, that she cared (I-3/4, 9; I-4/5, 4)
it was because I had it coming. And that she cared. Not dis-
like
was able to accept it because I thought she loved me
cried and loved her for it for letting me know that she cared

13. Contrast of physical and emotional hurt (I-3/4, 4)
was hurt not physically, but mentally
was deeply hurt, but not physically
cried not because she spanked me but because I was hurt
inside

14. Comparison with scoldings, other methods of discipline (I-3, 14)
accepted it, but when she scolded me, I cried
(I can't remember her spanking—she reasoned things out
with me.) My dad spanked but rarely
raised cane. I'm not spoiled now. I was punished in differ-
ent ways

15. —was surprised, amazed

16. No memory of spanking or reactions (I-3, 14, 15; I-4/5, 2)
don't recall
can't remember. It was too long ago
don't remember what I did or thought
cannot imagine this

I-4/5

Many responses above I-4 specify whether the spanking was a rare event or an often repeated one. All of them contain some kind of conceptual complexity.

1. Spanking an indication that subject deserved it (I-3, 8; I-4, 1)
would know that I had deserved it or she wouldn't have
spanked me, but some families are different
felt like I really needed it, as I seldom got a spanking
deserved it as she seldom spanked me
felt that I had done something really asocial, as she spanked
me rarely

*must have felt it was a natural consequence of my behavior,
for I don not even recall it*

2. Felt spanking was inappropriate (I-4, 16)
   was mad because I think I am too old to be spanked
   usually knew why, but didn't agree with her reasoning
   *My mother never spanked. (Neither do I and I feel very
   strongly about this.)*
   usually felt the discipline was excessive
   *(I can't remember having been spanked) my parents raised
   me to be respectful and I would be shown the same courtesy*

3. Contrasting or conflicting emotions (I-4, 9)
   was usually either mad or embarrassed
   felt rebellious and also ashamed
   rebelled, but later felt contrite
   was both angry and hurt
   *hated her for a whole half an hour, and then we made up in
   each other's arms*

4. Concern with mother's (differentiated) traits or feelings (I-4,
   12)
   became furiously angry at her insensitivity
   *got repulsed, because it was more nervous anger than actual
   discipline*
   she didn't, except once in violent anger
   *felt very hurt not because I was hit but because I realized I
   did something I shouldn't have done and that it hurt her*
   knew I had really distressed her
   *I was angry at her. But, now I see that I deserved the spank-
   ings I remember the most. I don't feel that she was being
   cross or unloving at all*

Unclassified
   *I have never been spanked, but when disciplined, I have felt
   grateful because I always understood the cause of the punishment*
   *screamed as though she was killing me, but I also learned my
   lesson for a while*
   didn't mind it as much as when she spanked someone else
   no longer felt guilty

I-5

Many of the responses at this level show an appreciation of paradox, a touch of existential humor.

1. Spanking did not prevent more misbehavior

   usually forgot it in no time and a couple of more before the day was over

   accepted it for the wrong I had done. Sometimes repeating the wrong. I'd get another

   felt ashamed, but I never hesitated to go do the very same thing behind her back

2. Vivid evocation of a unique episode or feeling

   had thrown up all over my new silk dress at the age of 3 and we were ready to go out

   I can only remember being slapped across the face just once for a fresh remark—I took it—for I knew the slap was coming!

   used to think she was a giant—but then I realized she wasn't that strong

Unclassified

   can't remember my mother spanking me—but her strong scouldings always made me mad, then disappointed with myself

   cried at age 5, yelled at 10, screamed at 15, and now I clench my fists if she smacks me

A Wife Should—

This stem has a high pull, since wife is a role. Some sociologists prefer the term office, since it permits one to distinguish the office from the program for the office, which role does not. The evolution of the notion of office can itself be traced in the responses: "be a good wife to her husband" (I-2); act like or be a wife (I-3); "be all that the word implies" (I-4). Compound responses are common for this stem for all levels except I-2. Most compound responses consist of two clauses that would separately be rated at the same level; the compound is rated at the same level as the separate clauses. However, examples at Delta and Delta/3 include some for which one clause is a fairly common response at I-3 or I-3/4. That the office of wife comprises other offices, typically homemaker or mother or cook or any two or all three, has become a banality and is rated I-3, even though the combination of three offices sounds much like responses above the I-4 level for other items. Such responses are rare below I-3. Rather than merely listing, at I-4 and higher one finds comparing, proscribing, and assigning priorities to offices. Exclusive concern for the wife's sexual office can be expressed in terms of sleeping with her husband (I-2) or being mistress or lover (I-3). Listing mistress alongside being mother or carrying out housewifely functions carries connotations of the contrast of the sexual aspect with other aspects of the wife's place and occurs typically at I-4 or I-4/5. The pejorative view of the sexual function is clearest in use of the term "whore," not uncommon at I-4 but incompatible with the integration of sex into a broader human relation characteristic of levels above I-4.

The majority of responses prescribe the program for the office rather than naming the office. The program comprises rights, duties, and even cautions. Although the grammatical form is as suited to one as to another, most responses concern duties. An example of a caution is "watch herself" (Delta). Examples of rights or expectations are "be happy" (I-2), "enjoy her husband" (I-3), and "not be expected to support the family" (I-4). At I-4 the norm of reciprocity may appear; in such responses rights and duties are in balance. Above I-4 rights such as individuality and independence are mentioned more frequently than at lower levels, but they are not presented in terms of self-interest alone but in context of the interrelatedness of rights and virtues. The highest responses are in terms of identity, self-fulfillment, and philosophy of life. Work has onerous overtones at low levels and overtones of fulfillment at high levels. The conventional social role tends to be prominent at low levels, but at high levels one finds both responses that stress primary obligation to family and ones that say she should maintain a broad outlook and invest in the world as well as her family. A few subjects suggest that the program should depend on the office-holder: "be what she is and not what a neighbor or book says she should be" (I-4/5).

Many subjects, primarily at I-3 and below, respond to the stem as if "mother" were substituted for "wife," indicating a lack of differentiation between these offices: "always treat each child equally" (I-3/4) ; "be at home with the children" (Delta/3).

I-2

Placed here are responses that say a wife should "be good to her husband" or "be a good wife"; they indicate a dichotomization of behavior into good-bad without awareness of the more differentiated social virtues mentioned at I-3. "Be a wife" and "try her best to be a good wife," classed at I-3 empirically, show a glimmer of what later becomes the notion of role or office.

*1. —be good, nice, kind; be good to her husband; be a good
    wife (I-3, 2, 5)
    be a good woman to he husband
    treat her husband good
    be good to her husband and children
    be kind to her love one
    make a good wife to her husband
    be nice to her family

2. —keep the house clean (Delta/3, 1)
   clean up around the house
   clean house watch chindlren
   do her house jobs

3. —be happy (I-3, 10)
   feel very happy to raise a fine child
   be happy to have a husband

Unclassified
    have everything she wants
    al whife should sleep with her husband
    be able to get pregant

DELTA

The chief preoccupation distinctive of the Delta level is prohibi-
tion of transgression, particularly lying and going out with other men.
Responses stating that a wife should work, with no indication of the kind
of work, are classed here empirically. Some of the responses in the unclassified group have clauses that would by themselves be rated higher; in
these cases the remainder of the response appears to negate the high
implications.

1. —not go out with other men

2. —never lie to her husband (I-3, 4)
   be truthful to her husband
   never lie to her husband or doing anything behind his back
   that isn't nice

3. —work (kind of work not specified)
   work like a wife at home
   work and also husband should work to feed the children if
   any
   have a job

Unclassified
be married
watch herself
wait on her husband he thinks
respect her husband and make him feel he is the King of his
Castle and she can always have her way
respect her husband's wishes, and not be an old bitch

DELTA/3

The theme of staying home and keeping house at this level is less primitive than simply keeping the house clean (I-2). Keeping the house neat rather than merely clean, as well as mention of other simple chores, raises the response to Delta/3. To be a good cook or good housekeeper (I-3) implies a standard of achievement, unlike "be good to her husband" (I-2), and raises the response to I-3. Naturally these categories cannot be sharply discriminated.

1. —take good care of the house; keep house (I-2, 2; I-3, 7, 11)
   always have the house very neat
   always keep her husband cloths clean and house work done

2. —stay at home; be home (I-3, 11)
   stay at home and take care of the house & children
   stay home and have meals at the table
   be home with her children
   stay home with her family and not run around
   be a housewife, not to get out working
   not work

I-3

The most common responses at I-3 mention qualities or virtues that are general, social, and not specific to marriage (pleasant, gentle) or that are taken from the marriage contract (faithful, true, love, honor, obey). Responses emphasizing striving for rather than possession of the former virtues are classed I-3/4. Most responses at I-3 are either vague and general (do her duty, do her best, be helpful) or specific and concrete (fix meals, listen to her husband, be neat and clean). At higher levels the functions described at I-3 are elaborated, stated in less banal and more differentiated terms, or given a more interpersonal and affectional expression.

**1. —love, honor, obey her husband (I-3/4, 1, 10; I-4, 11)
   love her family and home

> *love and obey her husband and never get a divorce*
> *be obendient*
> love
> *be very respectful to her husband*

*2. —be loving, understanding, considerate, gentle, pleasant (I-2, 1; I-3/4, 5)
>   *be kind and conciderate*
>   *be loving, kind and honest to her husband. Also she should be neat*
>   *be loving and cheerful and a good homemaker*

*3. —be helpful; help her husband (I-3/4, 7, 9; I-4, 4)
>   *try to help her Husbond*
>   *help her husband and family*
>   *help her husband in any way possible*
>   *always be there to help*

*4. —be faithful, loyal, true (Δ, 2)
>   *loyal and truthful*
>   *be loyal to her husband at all times*
>   *be true to her husband and a good housekeeper*

5. —be, act like a wife; try to be a good wife (I-2, 1; I-4, 13)
>   *act like a wife in all respects*
>   *be a wife first*
>   *act like one*

6. —do her duty; accept her responsibilities (I-4, 6, 8)
>   *live up to her duties*
>   *take main responsibility in housekeeping*
>   *carry her own burdens*
>   *be a very responsible person*
>   *do all her duties to and for her husband and children*

7. —take care of her husband, family (Δ/3, 1; I-3/4, 2)
>   *take care of her home and family*
>   *care for her husband & children*

8. —be a good mother, homemaker; be a mistress (I-3/4, 7; I-4, 15)
>   *be a nice house wife*
>   *also be a lover*
>   *be a good mother good cook & keep house clean*

9. —do her best
>   *do the best she can for her family*
>   *do as good a job as she can*

raise her children as best she can
do as much as she can
always look and act her best

10. Enjoy being one (I-2, 3)
    try to enjoy homelife
    be happy & love being a homemaker
    love to take care of her family
    enjoy her husband

11. —know how to cook; fix her husband's meals (Δ/3, 1, 2)
    always get her husband's breakfast
    keep her home neat, and have meals on time

12. —always be neat and clean
    not become a slob
    remember to look decent (if not pretty) especially when near her husband
    be neat, good cook, and appealing

13. —listen to her husband
    respond to her husband
    always be ready to listen to her husband

14. —stand for her rights
    nag at her husband if he's late from work
    make the husband help her do the dishes, and help work
    not have to cut the grass or do heavy work but try to help
    have her say

I-3/4

At I-3 and lower husband is just there to have things done for him. At I-3/4 he can be pleased, satisfied, and made happy; he is a companion with his own interests. At I-3 the wife is understanding, considerate, as if that could be accomplished once and for all; at I-3/4 she must try to achieve those qualities. While the wife is seen as a more differentiated person at I-3/4 than at I-3, at I-4 the husband is also more differentiated. At I-4 husband has wishes and needs to be respected, sorrows to be shared, faults to be forgiven. Where the I-3 mentions "love her husband," at I-3/4 this becomes to give or show her love, implying a difference between feeling and expression. Rather than taking care of home (Delta/3) or family (I-3), at I-3/4 one finds "make a home for her family," which implies the addition of affectional qualities to household duties, but is not as explicit as "be concerned with creating a loving home for her husband and family" (I-4).

*1. —please, satisfy her husband; do what her husband wants
      (I-3, 1; I-4, 11)
      try to please her husband
      know how to please her husband
      take care of her family and satisfy her husband in as many
        ways as she can
      go along with her husbands plans

*2. —make her husband, family happy (I-3, 7)
      do the utmost to keep her husband happy
      love her husband and children and try to do whatever she
        can in order to make them happy
      do her best to make her husband happy and comfortable

3. —make a happy (good, pleasant) home for her family (I-4, 5)
      fun and happy and not keep the house so clean you don't
        want to walk into it
      try to make a good home—one that is attractive, clean, etc.
      make a comfortable home for her husband
      concentrate on making her husband a happy home life
      maintain home life for husband and children

4. —be devoted, unselfish
      give of herself freely
      not be self-centered
      be dedicated
      devote herself to her husband
      be devoted to her family and her husband and her home

5. —try to be understanding, considerate; be patient (I-3, 2;
      I-4, 3)
      as considerate as she can
      try to understand and sympathize
      be patient and faithful

6. —put her family first (I-4, 9, 10)
      think first of husband & children
      consider her family before others

7. —be a companion, friend, helpmate (I-3, 3, 8)
      be a helpmeet for her husband
      be a companion to her husband as well as a wife

8. —be intellectually equal; take an interest in her husband's
      work (I-4, 3)
      be an intellectual companion to her husband
      consider herself equal to her husband

try to help and understand her husbands problems in the profession

9. —stand by her husband; be there when her husband needs her (I-3, 3; I-4, 4)
   always be by her husband
   go wherever her husbands work is

10. —give, show her love (I-3, 1)
    love her husband and show that she loves him
    keep house and show love and respect for her children

11. —respect her husband; trust her husband; be trusted (I-4, 3)
    love & respect her husband
    believe in her husband and enjoy things with him
    trust

12. Be impartial
    love her husband and children equally
    always treat each child equally
    be considerate to her husband's family as well as her own
    be fair to her husband

13. —I don't know because I'm not married

Unclassified
    love, honor, but not obey her husband

I-4

At the I-4 level are responses that view marriage as a cooperative endeavor with mutual responsibilities, satisfactions, and problems. Subjects at this level aspire to be confidantes and sources of comfort and encouragement, and they elaborate on these topics. Where the I-3/4 woman speaks of respecting her husband or taking an interest in his business, the I-4 woman's concern is with the more intangible ideas, moods, and feelings of the husband; she tries to understand his point of view. She is concerned with priorities and choices. Her sense of choice may be evident even when describing submission to her husband: "try not to dominate decision-making." The notion of role or life-pattern, found at higher levels on other items, is clear at I-4 for this item. Although the negative or dissociated view of sex implied in the response, "be a lady in the 'living room' and a whore in the bedroom" is not common, it does illustrate a kind of moral dichotomizing typical at I-4 and rare at higher levels.

*1. —cooperate, share responsibility, communicate, work with her husband
   be cooperative

be willing to talk things over with her husband and be understanding

understand her children and have a very good understanding with her husband

share problems as well as be considerate

help her husband make the best of their marriage

enjoy her family and learn to devide responsibilities so she doesn't feel like a slave

be consulted on any relatively major decision concerning the family

have an equal partner relationship with her husband

2. Reciprocity with husband

   Have respect for her mate, also should he for her

   love, respect and admire her husband and expect the same in return

   meet her husband half way

   put her husband first and make him happy, then she will be happy too

   do things for her husband & not always take things from him

   do as much as possible to please, but in return should receive great cooperation and gratitude

3. —consider (respect, understand) her husband's feelings, opinions, needs, problems (I-3/4, 5, 8, 11)

   try to understand her husband and be considerate of how he feels after working all day

   respond to needs of husband and self

   always consider her husband's needs and desires in making any decision

   be the person who stands in back of her husband, supports his ideas & views & believes in him

   never stop her husband from doing what he feels is right

   compromise with her husband and recognize his personal needs as well as her own

4. —comfort, support, encourage her husband (I-3, 3; I-3/4, 9)

   comfort her husband when he is in pain

   be a positive and encouraging source of help for her husband

   be willing to support her husband emotionally

   stand back of her husband during all times of stress and strain

   encourage her family

   assist her husband in his adjustment to life, work etc.

5. —make a warm, loving home (I-3/4, 3)
   be capable to provide a warm atmosphere to the family
   provide a warm, well-organized home atmosphere for her husband

6. Combination of love and duties (I-3, 6)
   be loyal, loving, kind, faithful and strong
   love and care for her husband in every possible way
   do her duty and love her family
   be loving and strive to do the most for her family

7. Idealization of role
   be the inspiration to her husband
   be loving. She should always be a guiding light for her husband as well as for her children
   be the foundation rock which a family can lean on

8. —fulfill her vows (I-3, 6)
   always try to carry out her marriage vows especially in making as successful marriage

9. —put her husband first, before the children; not neglect her husband (I-3/4, 6; I-4/5, 4)
   take good careful of her children, but should not fail to notice her husband
   be first a wife, then a mother
   place her husbands interests first
   always considered her husband most important
   devote herself to her family, but mainly to her husband
   be a good home maker and very considerate of all members of the family, but not put the children ahead of her husband
   devote all her time to her husband, family, & house, in that order

10. —place her husband, family before outside interests (I-3/4, 6)
    be a wife & not a career woman
    devote as much time as possible to her husband, children and then map her outside activities
    put her home and family first, tho she may well hold a job
    put her husband and family before social activities

11. —submit to her husband; consider her husband the dominant partner (I-3, 1; I-3/4, 1)
    be subject to her mate
    be subservient to her husband at times
    try not to dominate decision-making

12. Minimize or cope with her own emotions
    disregard her ill feelings to keep peace in the family
    *always have a smile for her husband after a days work no
    matter how the day has been with her*
    *never go to bed angry nor leave for any place with any dis-
    agreement between husband and wife*
    never hen-peck her husband, and try not to lose her temper

13. Recognition that "wife" implies a role; pattern or focus of
    life (I-3, 5; I-5, 3)
    be all that the word implies
    concentrate on being exactly that
    *be a wife, that include not working, having children and tak-
    ing care of theirself. Cooking (etc) just taking care of home
    while Dad work*
    *work for the happiness of her family & it should pattern her
    whole life*
    concentrate her talents on being the best wife she can be
    make her marriage her life's primary focus
    *be at home, and should have her life really centered in the
    home*
    make her family her vocation

14. —be versatile (I-5, 4)
    be able to perform many roles well if she is to be a good wife
    *be able to do every thing cook, sew clean help her children
    with their school work, and help her husband save money*
    be all things to her husband and family

15. —be a lady in the parlor and a whore in the bedroom (I-3,
    8; I-4/5, 3)
    be a whore, a hostess and a cook
    *be the best hostess in the living room, the best cook in the
    kitchen & the biggest whore in the bedroom*

16. Concern with expectations of self and others
    not expect too much of herself or her husband
    always be what her husband thinks she is
    *try to make her husband happy by trying to continue to be
    the person he married*
    *have a good understanding of what is expected by her hus-
    band and agree with it*
    be a good wife and expect fidelity from her husband
    look to her husband for security and dependency

17. Sense of choice or decision
   consider many things when making decisions that will affect
   others than herself
   love and respect her husband and know whether or not she
   can before she marries him. If not don't

18. —be an asset to her husband
   make her husband proud of her

Unclassified
   never use sex as a weapon against her husband
   not be expected to support the family

I-4/5

At I-4/5 the leading category concerns the wife retaining her individuality and independence, which are somewhat different matters, but not necessarily distinguished in the language of our subjects. Most responses saying that she should not be a maid, slave, or servant belong here, but there are exceptions: "enjoy her family and learn to devide responsibilities so that she doesn't feel like a slave" is classed at I-4; "not be a slave to her husband, but have her own self-identity" is classed I-5. Note that all the examples given have a second clause. The remaining categories at I-4/5 concern interpersonal relations seen as themselves the central focus and sexuality as an accepted part of a multi-faceted human relation.

1. Keep her individuality and independence (I-5, 2)
   respect her husbands opinion and maintain her opinions too
   when she feels she is right
   meet her husband halfway and the same—be understanding
   and patient but should also be respected, have her own due
   be what she is and not what a neighbor or book says she
   should be
   love her husband and family more than anything else in the
   world. She should respect her husband's wishes, but not be
   a servant
   be thoughtful, considerate of her husbands welfare, but not
   submissive
   fulfill herself as well as care for husband and family
   try to live her life and to help her husband live his and to-
   gather

2. Concern with continuing relation with husband
   never stop trying to "catch" her husband!

*never forget she is in love with her husband and he comes
before anything*

*be close to her husband in thought and relations every day.
Once in a while doesn't work out*

*be loving, understanding, & try not to be excessively control-
ling & competitive with her spouse*

*always encourage her husband and let him know how impor-
tant he is to her*

3. Sexual role as part of a human relation (I-4, 15)

*be a helpmate, lover, supporter, companion, hostess, etc., to
her husband*

*above all things, love her husband with her heart, mind and
body*

be a companion, mistress and good housekeeper

*first of all be very understanding of her husband as well as a
companion and lover*

*be as much her husband's mistress as his home manager—in
fact more of his "date" than cook!*

*be able to be homemaker, companion, nurse and dream girl
to her husband*

*love her husband, try to understand his needs & fulfill them—
including mental as well as physical*

4. Recognition that husband-wife relation affects or is affected
by children (I-4, 9)

*always keep her husband first, not letting the children change
their relationship*

*put her husband first because if the marriage is right children
can glean much from this*

Unclassified

be proud of her husband and help him toward his goals

*be a woman mainly in the sense that she regards her husband
as the chief boss and authority*

*be understanding and view her husband's actions as objec-
tively as possible*

*always make it a point to listen to her husband no matter
how insignificant or personally uninteresting his conversation seems to be*

I-5

At I-5 appear the familiar themes of personal growth, identity,
and a sophisticated version of role conceptualization. The responses con-

trasting the various facets of the husband-wife relation are more original than at I-4/5, and sometimes humorous; inclusion of the sexual aspect does not necessarily occur but certainly does not contraindicate classing at I-5.

1. Personal growth and philosophy of life

   try to help her husband achieve his self-fulfillment but at the same time should try to achieve her own "growth" too

   be someone whose interest and philosophy of life are similar of her husband's

   fulfill her marital obligations with love and affection, encouragement, and personal growth and development

   try to understand her husband and develop some interests so that she can talk to her husband

   have interests outside the home as well in order to maintain contact with the world of ideas and current events

   be loving, helpful, honest, good housekeeper, good companion, understandable, and continue to develop in her profession or in her other recriational or scientific goals

2. —maintain her own identity (I-4/5, 1)

   maintain her distinct identity, as that's probably what attracted her spouce, if she wants to keep him

   be a good wife, and mother, but still have an identity of her own

   not be a slave to her husband, but have her own self-identity

3. Define her own role (I-4, 13)

   define her role as she and her husband perceive it and not necessarily according to the dictates of their society

   do whatever is required to be a good wife, within her own frame of reference for "good wife"

4. Original responses, contrasting several facets (at least 1 at I-4) (I-4, 14)

   love, honor, obey, pardon, look up to, and laugh with her husband

   devote her life to her husband primarily, her children secondarily, She should also be an informed intellectual companion and a "lover" too

   be a companion, a friend, a mother, a psychiatrist, a washing machine, a dish-washer, an alarm clock, & a vacum cleaner among other things

   always stand by her husband, give herself completely to him, never nag and never deceive. She should always keep her feminity and encourage his masculinity

Unclassified
> *consider her husband her her children's welfare equal to her*
> *own and at times above it unless the sacrifice is too great*

I-6

This stem does not seem to draw different responses from I-5 than from I-6 subjects. The single I-6 example contains the following elements: social reference, role conception, search for identity, complex psychological causation, and probably also fitting the program to the office holder.

Unclassified
> *try to make some sense for herself out of the strange dual role*
> *the modern world has placed her in . . . so that she is*
> *free to make her husband happy*

I Feel Sorry—

T his stem was included on the presumption that pity for others would be expressed at I-3 and lower, in terms of phrases and clauses beginning with *for;* guilt or regret for mistakes would be expressed at I-4, in terms of phrases and clauses beginning with *about, because,* or *when;* and concern for larger social issues would be expressed above I-4, in terms of phrases and clauses beginning with *that* or *about.* The majority of subjects at all levels begin with *for,* and there is not a close connection between word choice or grammar and the thought expressed. The grammatical form is not crucial in deciding whether a response belongs in a given category. On the whole, this is a good item, affording valuable discriminations at both extremes as well as between I-3 and I-4, but it is not as easy to score as had been hoped. Guilt and regret are not frequent at any level.

Expressions of pity, being sorry for groups of people defined in terms of external, superficial characteristics, make up the largest group

185

of categories and are classed I-3. At Delta pity is expressed for particular individuals. The Delta category expressing resentment of the test illustrates the failure of grammar as a cue, since it includes "for whoever is grading this test" and "I came today." At I-4 pity is expressed for persons defined in terms of inner states such as loss of ambition.

Expressions of concern and regret about social issues do occur at high levels. The same grammatical form may be used to express self-pity: "about my baby that I lost" (I-3). The first expression of social concern takes the form of worrying about the state of the world in general at I-3/4. At I-4 it is stated more abstractly: "when I see prejudice." At I-4/5 the statement is more vivid and explicit: "that there is poverty, illiteracy, crime, war, etc."

I-2

Many I-2 subjects name a specific person, but so do many subjects at the Delta and I-3 levels. Most such responses are classed at Delta. Responses such as "for myself" also occur on higher protocols, but there they usually are qualified in some way that implies some distance from self. The examples classed at I-2 seem completely self-centered and in some cases seem to mean "sad" rather than "sorry." The unclassified examples illustrate the concreteness of the situations that elicit pity at this level.

1. —for myself (I-3, 12; I-3/4, 21)
   for me
   for myself when I am sad
   for my self when I get big
   because I am tall
   for myself when cannot have something I want

Unclassified
   when people get hit by cars
   if someon fell in the mud

DELTA

Responses at this level designating specific persons show a failure to generalize the reaction to a group or category, as do most subjects. The Delta concern for getting in trouble also appears; it is not the same as concern for people who have troubles, though of course the distinction can be difficult. Responses in the category "when I have done something wrong" occur on I-3 and I-3/4 protocols as well. As the unclassified examples illustrate, mention of concrete acts is indicative of low ego level.

We differentiate expressions of hostility toward the test or the testers from those classed at I-3/4 that complain of taking the test in lieu of doing something else. This item offers a logical opportunity to express resentment toward the test (unlike, for example, "My conscience bothers me if—I waste precious time taking a test like this"); dislike of the test by itself does not require a Delta rating.

*1. For specific people (I-3, 10)
   for my mother
   for my children
   for Lynn
   for the little girl who got hurt in the street

2. Personal pronouns
   for you
   for her because of her brother

3. —for the guy that marries me
   for the guy that likes my sister

4. —for people who get in trouble (I-3/4, 2)
   when someone gets in trouble
   for girls who get in trouble

5. Hostility toward test or testers (I-3/4, 23)
   I came today
   that I got up at 7:00 a. m. for this class
   who whoever is grading this test

6. —when I have done something wrong (I-3/4, 18)
   when I do things wrong
   for the things I've done

Unclassified
   when a man jump on a woman
   after I beat my kitty and it looks at me with its big blue eyes
   for my brother is going to get a beating from saying bad words
   when some one dies
   for people who get killed

I-3

The typical I-3 response is mention of a specific group of unfortunates, persons suffering from social or physical ills, people who are sick, mentally retarded, poor, in prison, or groups defined by marital or geographic status. Such superficial categorization is distinguished from groups similar in terms of inner feelings (usually I-3/4) and those similar in traits and life style (usually I-4 or higher).

**1. —for the sick, crippled, handicapped (I-3/4, 2, 5)
for mentally ill people
for people who have had a lot of sickness and trouble
for the people who are in the Hospital unable to get out

*2. —for poor, underprivileged people (I-3/4, 1)
people dying of starvation
for people in need
for unfortunate children

*3. Specific groups of people (demographic, physical variables)
for the people in Viet Nam
for old maids
for people in prison
for people who live in the slums
for fat people
for the new freshmen
for women who can't have babies

4. —for orphans, homeless children (I-3/4, 3)
for children of divorced parents
for unwanted children
for kids who don't have a family

5. —for unmarried pregnant women
for unmarried women who are bringing children in the world
for women who are pregnant and the guy took off and left
  her alone in the world

*6. —for some, many people (I-3/4, 16)
for others
for a great deal of the human race

*7. —for helpless people, people who can't help themselves (I-4, 8)
for my children and anyone needing help
for helpless poeple and animals

8. Animals (I-3/4, 22)
for homeless animals
when I see an animal sick or injured
for a little dog Dutchess

9. —for snobbish people (I-3/4, 12)
for people who think they are better than anyone else

10. Specific family situations (Δ, 1; I-3/4, 3, 15, 20)
for my mother when she's sick
that my aunt is driving her 3rd daughter crazy
when my borther & sister get spanked
when my daughter act up in School

11. Because I miss, don't have certain things
   about my baby that I lost
   I feel sorry because I miss my family
   because I don't have a house of my
   Because I am single
   that I never had more children
   When their is not money in my house and my Bill are not
   pade

12. —for myself sometimes (I-2, 1; I-3/4, 21)
   for myself, at times
   for myself, mostly

13. Frequency
   sometime
   for people easily
   very seldom
   I never have time to feel sorry

Unclassified
   for people who have nothing to do

I-3/4

As compared to responses at I-3 and lower, those classed I-3/4 are more abstract, more interpersonal, more self-critical, and more descriptive of a process rather than a result. The last point is illustrated by mention of orphans at I-3 compared to neglected children at I-3/4. At I-3/4 the subject is more likely to mention inner feelings, such as suffering or love, while at I-3 and lower she is more likely to mention observable ills such as being crippled. Feeling sorry for bad deeds may occur at any level, contrary to our initial expectations. While bad deeds at Delta tend to be concrete, like "saying bad words" or beating kitty, at I-3/4 they are evaluated in terms of consequences, particularly hurting other people's feelings. Feeling sorry because of failure to do something positive (in contrast to feeling sorry for having done bad things) is a new theme at I-3/4. Social conscience is displayed in only rudimentary form at this level. Self-criticism has a more genuine ring at this level than at lower levels. For example, "for myself too much of the time" is self-critical, compared with "for myself at times" (I-3), which is more likely self-indulgent.

*1. —for those less fortunate than myself (I-3, 2; I-4, 9)
   others cannot be as happy as I
   for others who haven't had a chance like me

2. —for people with problems, troubles, misfortunes (Δ, 4; I-3, 1; I-4, 11)

for anybody that is having a rough time
when I hear of someones misfortune
for people who are in distress, due to fincial difficulties or who
*   have many trials*
that there are so many youths droping out of school

3. —for children whose parents neglect them; for children
   brought up in unhappy homes (I-3, 4, 10)
   for dependent and neglected children
   for children whose fathers forsake them
   for families which are broken up

4. —when I cannot help someone in trouble
   for those I can Not Help
   when I don't spend more time helping my boy with school
   work

*5. —for people who are unhappy, suffering, hurt (I-3, 1)
   for unhappy children
   when a child gets hurt
   for people when they are hurt
   when I see people suffer
   when I see someone depressed

6. —for people who are lonely, alone
   for people who are old and have no family
   for those who have no friends
   for very old people who have lost the feeling of belonging
   for persons without families

7. —for girls who don't have dates

8. —for people who are not loved (I-4, 10; I-4/5, 1)
   for people without true *friends*
   for children whose parents don't seem to care
   for those who have never loved or been loved
   for people who aren't in love
   for people who do not believe in love

9. —for people who lose loved ones
   for bereaved families
   when I think about the loss of my husband
   about the death of our young neighbor's husband

10. —for people who are embarrassed, don't have confidence in
    themselves
    for people who make fools of themselves
    for people who are placed in awkward situations
    for people that is made in fun of, which is wrong

11. —for people who feel sorry for themselves
for people who want pity

12. —for selfish people (I-3, 9; I-4, 7)
for anyone who is never grateful

13. —for those who are ignorant; for sinners (I-4, 12)
for the people can not say no to the things they know is wrong

14. —for people without faith
for those who do not know God

15. —for people who have bad marriages (I-3, 10)
for people who can't make a go of their marriage
for two people who are married but don't love each other
for myself because my husband and i couldn't get along

16. —about the state of the world (I-3, 6; I-4, 11, 12)
the world in general
for most of mankind
for so many things my child because he can't read & the mess the world is in
for suffering humanity

*17. —when I have hurt someone; been unfair to others (I-4/5, 4)
when I forget other people's feelings
when I say something to someone and don't really mean it
when I have treated someone badly
for the way I have treated my grandmother

18. —immediately after I do something wrong; when I know I have done something wrong (Δ, 6)
when I've made a mistake

19. —when I don't do my best (I-4, 2)
when I have ruined a test or something similar because of negligence on my part
at times when I realize I could have done better
for not being as understanding as I should
when I get into trouble or fusses, not for myself but the person to whom I acted nasty toward

20. —when I get angry, am cross with my family (I-3, 10)
when I lose my temper
when I have quarreled with my husband
for my family when I am nervous because I scream my head off

21. —for myself (elaborated, self-critical) (I-2, 1; I-3, 12)
    for my self if I cant improve
    *for myself I try to think about other people and their prob-
    lems*
    for myself at times, which is a mistake I realize
    for myself too much of the time

22. —for mistreated animals (I-3, 8)

23. Taking the test instead of doing something else (Δ, 5)
    *that I came to [deleted] today, and have to take this test in-
    stead of learning something*
    *that I have to be subjected to this when we are supposed to
    be having class*

Unclassified
    about many things
    for anyone that needs help and can't get it

I-4

Many subjects at the I-4 level couch their responses in terms of a
broad view of life. Ideas such as purpose, direction, goals, and ideals are
introduced. The question of having or not having choice or control over
one's destiny appears in some responses. A sense of responsibility is clearer
than at lower levels, but regret for past mistakes is classed I-4/5. Concern
for social issues is more explicit. The concepts employed are more differentiated, a particularly clear example being the contrast between the
physical or material and the mental or emotional aspects of life.

1. —for people without purpose, direction, goals in life (I-5, 2)
    for people who have no real drive
    for people who don't know what they want from life
    for people who have lost all ambition
    for teenagers who feel life is nothing but a good time
    for people that cannot "find" themselves
    for the sick, homeless, and unresponsible

2. Failure to achieve goals, duties, ideals (I-3/4, 19)
    when I don't fulfill all my duties
    *for people who try terribly hard at something but still don't
    succeed*
    *for people who don't ever rise above their shortcomings and
    attain their life goals*
    *for girls who marry men whose standards & values are lower
    than theirs*

*because I am often not the kindly sort of person I would wish
to be*

when I realize how absolutely "vile" I can be at times

3. —for people who do not enjoy life (in general terms) (I-5, 3)

   for people who do not know how to be happy

   *for those not able to see the good things in life & must con-
   stantly complain even tho' they are richly blessed*

4. —for people who can't adjust to life

   *when I see the enormous amount of people who have been
   unable to adjust to life and its many complexities*

5. Contrast of physical and mental (I-5, 2)

   *for someone with material goods, but not an equal amount of
   personal maturity*

   *for people who are prevented physically or mentally from
   achieving their goals*

   *for people who think the most important thing in the world
   is earning money or status*

   when others are in pain physical or emotional

   for those who have less than I (and I don't me materially)

   *for those who can't find beauty in immaterial things as well
   as those less fortunate than we are*

6. —for those unable to be honest with themselves (I-5, 1)

   persons who have problems and are unable to recognize them

   *for people who delude themselves and unhappily confront
   reality*

   those who can't face themselves and the wrong the do

7. Characterological descriptions: narrow-minded people (I-3/4,
   12; I-4/5, 2)

   for people who lead very restricted lives

   for strict conformists

   for "hard-shell" people

   for narrow-minded, shallow persons

   *for people who hate esp. Negroes, they have such a narrow
   scope*

   for people who think only of themselves

8. —for those who do not help themselves (sense of choice implied) (I-3, 7)

   for people that won't try and make anything of themselves

   for people who believe they are unable to help themselves

   *for nobody, I think people should get off of their behinds
   and work for what they want, and not cry about what they
   are not getting*

9. Lack of opportunities; controlled by circumstances (I-3/4, 1)
   for people who have few opportunities to make the most of
   their lives
   for sick or underpriviledged children who will never have the
   opportunity to have a good life
   when I see people who have no opportunity to go to school
   to see so many people controlled by circumstances while being
   blamed for inadequacy by society
   for people who seem trapped in situations beyond their con-
   trol
   for those people who have a problem or phys. condition they
   cannot help
   when people are rejected by a group for a fault which they
   cannot help

10. Unkindness, hate, lack of trust between people (I-3/4, 8;
    I-4/5, 1)
    when people are unkind to each other
    that people distrust each other
    for people who mistrust other individuals & every new person
    he meets
    when people take advantage of others
    for people with bad attitudes and little compassion for their
    fellow man
    for people that don't like people

11. —for the mistreated, the underdog (I-3/4, 2, 16)
    for children who are pushed around or ignored
    for those who are persecuted as were the Jews during W.
    W. II

12. Ignorance, prejudice, injustice as social issues (I-3/4, 13, 16;
    I-4/5, 3)
    when I see prejudice
    when I think of the degree of public apathy
    for the ignorance which prevails in some of our states
    when I observe some of the injustices existing in the present
    day world

13. —that I don't have enough time
    that I don't have time-to keep a better home for my husband
    that I don't have time to do more interesting things
    when I don't get everything done on time
    that I have not left more time for friendships

14. Lost opportunities (I-4/5, 4)

that I have not made better use of earlier opportunities

that my childhood has been so sheltered

when I look back on all the things in my past that could have been different

Unclassified

when I have scoled my children before I have gathered all the facts

if I let my feelings get the upper hand of my self control

for the individual who cannot pity his fellow man

for those who cannot look beyond themselves for a source of strength

I-4/5

Categories at the I-4/5 level represent elaborations of themes found at the I-4 level. There is interest in interpersonal relations as such. Above the I-4 level answers are unique and generally vivid and full of feeling. Many responses include a reference to causes or consequences of behavior; in doubtful cases this can serve as a criterion for I-4/5 rather than I-4 rating.

1. —for people who have poor relations with most other people (I-3/4, 8; I-4, 10)

for people who have hollow & mechanical relationships

for people who are always scheming to use other people to get their own way, and for people who are revengeful, because they are lonely people

for girls who feel that they only way they can interest the opposite sex is to be free with themselves

for people who are so intelligent they can't relate or accept others who are less intelligent

2. Characterological limitations (original, nonstereotyped) (I-4, 7; I-5, 1, 2)

for people who despair

for people who live in a tunnel rather in the open world

for anyone who lacks understanding and tolerance

for people who are afraid—afraid of what people think; of getting old; of getting sick; meeting new people, etc.

when I see people not even bothering to see another's position

3. Social issues, elaborated (I-4, 12)

that there is poverty, illiteracy, crime, war, etc.

and want to help in the Negro situation, esp. in the South for
the biggest advances need to be made there
for the aged who are misfits in our society
that the people of the world have not learned to live together
in peace
for the people in this world who do not have the ability to
maintain a minimum income and thus are deprived of the
necessary wants
that there are many human beings are in distress and there is
such limited understanding of them

4. Personal shortcomings, elaborated (I-3/4, 17; I-4, 14)
   for myself when I think of the mistakes I've made of a major
   nature which were unnecessary
   that I have made life difficult for some of the people I lived
   with
   when I cause people to be hurt either by something I have
   said or done

Unclassified
   for engaged women or newly wed women whose husbands
   die. I can't think of anything worse than to lose the man
   you love
   that I can't do more to help—both myself and those I know—
   or don't know

I-5

All the categories classed at the I-5 level are in a sense elaborations of the theme of characterological limitations: lack of objectivity or
of zest and loss of purpose or of values. Some of the responses also convey concern for social issues. There is no exclusion in principle of other
topics at this level, however, especially since all responses are unique. The
category concerning loss of purpose or values is somewhat difficult to distinguish from a category concerning lack of purpose at I-4. The responses
classed I-4 seem to imply that if people would just try, that is, had drive
or ambition, ... All the responses in the I-5 category are a little more
complex, or subtler, or more original.

1. Lack of objectivity or perspective (I-4, 6; I-4/5, 2)
   for those who can never be objective toward their problems
   for people who are blinded by prejudices
   for the man who cannot see above present small difficulties
   for all who loose sight for the shortness of life on earth

2. Loss of purpose or values in life (I-4, 1, 5; I-4/5, 2)
  for those who have rejected any hope of finding life purposeful and enlivening
  for people who have no dreams or aspirations
  for people who are lost and do not know their purpose in life
  for people who work all their lives for money only to find out money alone will not bring them happiness
  for people who do not know what they want from life or what makes them happy
  for one who loses his sense of value

3. Lack of zest for life (I-4, 3)
  when I let things pass unnoticed or unappreciated
  for people who don't enjoy the solitude and wonderfulness of a camping trip in a sleeping bag under the stars
  for those who have not learned how to appreciate the good & bad experiences in life & look forward to each day of life with the feeling that it is wonderful to be alive
  for anyone who has lost hope and enthusiasm for life
  for those who do not appreciate the beauty of nature
  for people who can't see any humor in life, or people who have no imagination
  for those people not equipped to grow and discover the world around them

I-6

All the responses classed here are complex and contain, among other high elements, an unusual degree of distance from self or of concern for self-perspective. Explicit expressions of inner conflict, paradox or contradiction are rarer on this item than on most others.

1. Coping with inner conflict or contradiction
  that I can't do more for people and places and things, but refuse to try when I know it is futile
  if I see someone in pain or trouble or have to discipline the children. Never the less I do so
  for the disadvantaged and particularly the negro to the point that I am outraged and intolerant of prejudiced people

Unclassified
  for people who are imprisoned in their worlds of ignorance and prejudice and for those who do not attempt to know themselves

When I Am
Nervous, I—

In general, answers to this stem fall into three broad classes: symptoms, translation of the fact of being nervous into other terms; results, statements about oneself that are consequences different in kind from the fact of being nervous; and methods of coping. Physical symptoms of being nervous, for example, trembling, perspiring, feeling nauseated, constitute the most common type of response to this stem and are given by subjects at all levels. Though the placement of these responses into categories at I-2, I-3 and I-3/4 respectively reflects primarily an attempt to achieve some discrimination in the ratings, these symptoms can be seen as forming a progression from the primitive, external "shake" at I-2 to the differentiated inner feelings such as "depressed" at I-4.

A common result of nervousness at all levels is hostility to other people. At Delta the hostility is a deliberate strategy: "stare at a person in the eyes and mock them." At I-3 it is reported as a concrete action not evaluated: "yell." At I-3/4 it is reported as a cross or angry mood. The I-4 subject criticizes herself or sees the bad effect on others, a type of response further elaborated at I-5.

Coping as reported at I-2 is essentially doing nothing, "sit down." The I-3 subject looks for external sources of relief, drinking, taking medicine, praying, or in some unstated way she relaxes. It is not until I-3/4 that coping becomes a personal effort reflecting a conception of nervousness as a psychological state, a transitory part of oneself. At I-3/4 the most common means of dealing with this state is a sort of occupational therapy, keeping busy, reading, taking walks. At I-4 there is less emphasis on physical activity, per se, and more on its mental effects and on introspection: searching for the cause or reason, discussing the problem with others, taking one's mind off of being nervous. Responses that combine several of these means of coping are placed at I-5.

I-2

The I-2 is most likely to respond to this stem in terms of a physical reaction to nervousness or some sort of symptomatic behavior. Many of these responses, for example, "eat," are classed higher because they cannot be discriminated from those given by higher level subjects. Classed here are the rather primitive, physical responses to nervousness, "shake," "get sick," along with the actions "sit down," "go to bed." The latter is contrasted with "rest" and "relax," classed at I-3, in that at I-2 are placed actions and at I-3 the results of these actions.

*1. —shake, tremble (I-3, 1; I-3/4, 1)
   shake and sometimes my mother gets nervous too

2. —am sick, get sick (I-3, 9; I-3/4, 1)

3. —sit down, go to bed (I-3, 7; I-3/4, 11)
   Lie down
   sit down for a little while

Unclassified
   want to die
   am very evil

DELTA

Most of the responses classed at this level are unmodulated expressions of hostility. At I-3/4 are classed responses similar to "lose my temper" (Delta), but they either indicate that such an outburst does not always follow getting nervous, "generally go into a tantrum which only makes it worse" (I-3/4), or speak of tendencies rather than actual behavior, "am short tempered," "am more likely to get angry" (I-3/4). "Like to kill someone" should be contrasted with the report of feelings as feelings, "feel like screaming. Or want to hit something" (I-3/4). Also classed here are responses that state or imply that the subject gets into trouble, a concern common at this level.

1. —lose my temper, get mad (I-3/4, 12, 14)

2. Unmodulated hostility toward others (I-3/4, 15)
    stare at a person in the eyes and mock them
    like to kill someone

3. —get into trouble (I-3/4, 4)
    get in all kinds of trouble
    do thinks I not suppose to do

Unclassified
tell lies

DELTA/3

Placed at Delta/3 is one category, "get upset," a rather global reaction given by subjects ranging from I-2 to I-4. It may be that at the lower levels the word "upset" has physical connotations and at higher levels emotional connotations. Whatever the meaning, it is more likely to be given by subjects below I-3 than above.

1. —get upset (I-3, 10)
    become upset
    get upset if something happens to the Kids

I-3

Most of the categories at this level describe concrete actions. Most of these responses have two things in common, they are nonevaluative and they are egocentric rather than interpersonal, that is, they mention actions that can be performed alone. Thus at I-3 are found responses like "chain smoke" or "talk alot," rather than the more evaluative "smoke too much" or "talk more than usual" (both I-3/4). Concrete actions are also used to describe causative situations ("am waiting for someone") or attempts to cope ("take a pill," "pray"). Some categories also include the negative of actions: don't sleep, don't know what to do. The physical symptoms of nervousness classed at this level are more concrete than those at I-3/4 in that they are external and observable. Feelings and emotions classed I-3 are either the physical "feel sick," or the global "feel bad." Confused, scared, and excited are empirically classed here but are less differentiated than emotions classed at I-4. Evasive answers and denials of nervousness are also classed here.

*1. Physical symptoms—external, observable (I-2, 1; I-3/4, 1)
   blush easily
   perspire more
   break out on my hands
   flush
   perspire, my hands get wet
   tremors of the lips
   cough

*2. —smoke, eat (a lot) (I-3/4, 8)
   chain smoke
   smoke like mad
   crave cigarrettes and coffee
   usually eat something
   like to nibble

*3. —bite my fingernails; chew things (I-3/4, 3)
   just eat my fingernails
   chew my fingers
   chew a pencil
   chew gum

4. —take medicine; drink
   take a nerve pill
   take a laxative
   have a tendency to mix myself a good cocktail

*5. —talk, laugh, get loud (I-3/4, 9, 13; I-4, 13)
   talk alot
   yell
   scream
   talk very fast
   chatter

*6. —cry (I-3/4, 12)
   want to cry
   start to cry

always end up crying
cry a lot
sometimes cry

*7. —sleep, rest, relax, calm down (I-2, 3; I-3/4, 11; I-4, 10, 12, 14)
usually go to sleep
try to lie down and rest
try to calm myself by relaxing
take a nap
am in need of rest

8. —don't sleep, eat (I-3/4, 6)
do not sleep well

9. —feel sick, bad (I-2, 2; I-3/4, 1)
feel terrible
feel real weak
'm miserable

10. —get scared, excited; am easily upset (Δ/3, 1; I-3/4, 2, 14; I-4, 4)
am very excitiable
am scared too

11. —am confused, flustered; don't know what to do (I-3/4, 7; I-4, 4, 5)
get all flustered and flushed
don't know what to do with myself
get very confused

12. —pray (I-3/4, 11)
pray and sing hyms
pray for the strength to endure

13. Concrete situations
am waiting for some one
have to give a report or sing in class
When I am at Work
am taking a test

14. —I am not nervous (I-4, 16)
(don't effect me)
am unaware of it

15. Evasion
I don't know

I-3/4

At this level the emphasis shifts from what one does to how one feels, either emotionally—grouchy, crabby, moody—or physically—tense, jittery, uncomfortable. Symptoms are described as physical feelings and thus internal rather than as external actions or signs. While the I-3 subject gives symptomatic actions, the I-4 may say she cannot relax or be quiet, must be doing things. We class at I-3/4 an intermediate category of activities described as repeated or nervous or more or less compulsory movements, for example, pace, fidget, "eat, eat, eat." Other actions classed at this level are similar to those seen at I-3 or below but are either evaluated ("eat too much") or placed in an interpersonal context ("get mad and start picking on people"). "Want to be alone" is perhaps a means of coping with or avoiding such behavior. This is specified at I-4, "try and stay away from people so I won't yell at them." The interpersonal reference is also evident in the response, "show it," or "try to hide it." Results of nervousness at this level are concerned with thinking, "cannot concentrate," or with productivity, "can't do a thing." Compare the latter response with the vague, "don't know what to do" (I-3) or with the comparative, "cannot do my best" (I-4).

*1. Physical symptoms—internal, not necessarily observable (I-2, 1, 2; I-3, 1, 9)
   usually feel sick to my stomach
   get diarrhea
   have to go to the bathroom
   get short of breath and perspire
   get indigestion
   get butterflies in my stomach
   get a dry mouth
   get a headache
   loose my appitite
   tremble inside
   itch

2. —get tense, jittery, uncomfortable (I-3, 10; I-4, 4)
   feel tied up in Knots
   get jumpy, and bite the nail polish off my nails
   feel all mixed up inside

*3. —pace, fidget; nervous movements (I-3, 3; I-4, 1)
   move my fingers around
   curl up my toes

eat, eat, eat
fumble with objects with my fingers
do something with my hands or take a walk
doodle
bite my lip
pick at the pimples on my face
get restless

4. —can't do anything; am clumsy, make mistakes (Δ, 3; I-4, 2)
   do everything wrong
   usually break things
   can't do a thing
   can't get things done
   am spastic
   cannot do my work

5. —can't talk, say what I want to say; say things I don't mean
   (I-4, 14; I-4/5, 2)
   can't talk too, well
   say many things I can't remember after my rage is over
   laugh at things I shouldn't
   say and do things that I am sorry for later
   talk nonsense

6. —can't eat, sleep (I-3, 8)

7. —can't concentrate, think clearly (I-3, 11; I-4, 4)
   can think straight
   do not function too well mentally
   can't think logically
   am not able to comprehend the lecture

8. —smoke, eat too much, more than usual (I-3, 2)
   tend to smoke too much
   indulge in eating and smoking too much
   eat more than usual
   smoke more

9. —talk too much, too loud, more than usual (I-3, 5)
   talk to loud and long
   speak too rapidly
   tend to laugh too much

10. —try to keep busy, find something to occupy my time (I-4, 9)
    keep myself busy
    get real busy at some task
    try to find something to do to take up the time

*11. Concrete activities (I-2, 3; I-3, 7, 12)
write
like to swim
play the piano
take a hot bath and try to relax
work it off
play solitare

12. —cry, lose temper, get angry easily, usually (Δ, 1; I-3, 6; I-4, 8)
usually cry at the slightest provocation
generally go into a tantrum which only makes it worse
get mad very easily
am more likely to get angry
am short tempered

13. —feel like screaming, yelling, etc. (I-3, 5)
feel that I could just scream
usually want to tear up a storm
could just scream but run the halls instead

*14. —am irritable, cross, moody, hard to get along with (Δ, 1; I-3, 10; I-4, 6, 7)
am an absolute bear
am in a bad mood
get very emotional
fly off the handle to much
am no person to be around
am difficult to live with
make it hard on everyone around me

15. Mean, hostile behavior toward others (Δ, 2; I-4, 6, 7)
act mean toward others
snap at people
get mad and start picking on people
usually get into an arguement with my husband or fix something to eat, sometimes both

16. —want to be alone; need peace and quiet (I-4, 14, 15)
usually sit down somewhere alone
would like to take a walk by myself
lik to get away from people
I would rather be alone
try to isolate myself
like to go to a place where it is quiet

17. —try to get out and be with people (I-4, 13)
    go shopping or to some one's house
    like friends to call
    see my psychiatrist

18. —show it; don't, try not to show it (I-4, 16; I-5, 1)
    keep all my feelings inside
    try to hide it
    usually do not show it

I-4

At this level symptoms are described as psychological rather than physical feelings: anxious, afraid, depressed (I-4) rather than tense, jittery, uncomfortable (I-3/4). Differences in behavior or performance are specified, for example, "don't study as well as I otherwise might." Symptomatic actions are described not as something one does (I-3 and I-3/4) but as something one is compelled to do, "can't stay in one place long enough," "cannot sleep," and thus they become results rather than mere signs of being nervous. Related to these responses is a concern for being in control of one's own behavior. The interpersonal consequences of one's nervousness are more clearly specified at this level. Empirically classed at this level is "worry," which may be either cause, "usually am worried about something," or effect, "worry a lot." Related to these responses is one method of coping classed I-4, "try not to let it bother me." Other methods are a search for causes and discussing the problem with others.

1. —can't relax, be quiet; have to be doing things (I-3/4, 3)
   have to be doing something with my hands
   can't stay in one place long enough
   can't sit still

2. —can't perform properly, efficiently (I-3/4, 4)
   can not do things as well as they should be done
   get disorganized
   can't perform very well

3. Actions, mood compared with non-nervous state
   get more irritable than usual
   think I do some of my best work but I feel that it is the worse
   sometime perform better
   do anything I do much more rapidly
   do things and say things I normally would not think of doing
   don't make as good grades

talk faster
become more cautious than usual

4. Psychological consequences: afraid, depressed, less confident, and so on (I-3, 10, 11; I-3/4, 2, 7; I-4/5, 1)
   get irratated or shy
   become anxious and compulsive
   sometimes feel insecure about myself
   get perspirous and doubtful and afraid
   lose all my self-confidence
   either talk a lot or become depressed

5. —worry (I-3, 11)
   worry a lot
   get very upset and I worry about every little thing
   usually am worried about something
   worry & fret about trivialities

6. —get cross, irritable toward others; take it out on them (I-3/4, 14, 15)
   get out of sorts with people too easily
   take it out on my children and husband
   have a terribel habit of biting my nails and I also take it out on my parents

7. Concern with bothering, hurting others (I-3/4, 14, 15; I-5, 2)
   am irritable, cross, and should be separated from my family
   bit my nails and try not to get on other people nerves
   try and stay away from other people so I won't yell at anyone
   don't want to be around people because I could make them nervous
   often give sharp answers which hurt others
   become emotionlly upset and act from nerves I don't think if the way I act hurts others

8. Concern with loss of control, effort for control (I-3/4, 12; I-4/5, 2)
   find it hard to control the tears
   lose my composure and scream
   become excited and speak and act thoughtlessly
   get disgusted with myself and my inability to control my nervous behavior
   have a very hard time to keep from crying it out by myself

9. —try to keep my mind busy, think of other things (I-3/4, 10)
   try to think of something pleasant

*try to overcome this, by doing other things to take my mind
    off what is making me so nervous*
find work for my hands, as well as my mind

10. —try not to let it bother me (I-3, 7)
    don't let it bother me too much
    try to forget about the experience
    try to ignore it
    bite my nails, twirl my ring, or just try to grin and bear it
    *go lock myself in my room, take a deep breath, and then con-
        tinue what I was doing*

11. —try to find out the cause
    *make a conscious effort to determine the cause and to remedy
        or control the situation*
    eat too much and wonder why
    strive to analyze the reason
    try to figure out why and get over it
    think it through and work out the reasons
    try to sort out what is troubling me

12. —try to relieve the tension (I-3, 7)
    let off steam physically
    try to talk myself out of it
    try to release my emotions
    *become tense and must find some outlet, playing the piano,
        etc.*
    have to cry and get it out of my system
    would find some way to relieve the tension

13. —talk to others (I-3, 5; I-3/4, 17)
    *find that discussing the source of difficulty with my husband
        is very helpful*
    would like to talk to someone who could help me
    talk to a friend and tell them my trouble
    need someone to tell my worries to

14. —become quiet (I-3, 7; I-3/4, 5, 16)
    become silent
    are either very quiet or chatter
    sit somewhere quietly until I feel better

15. —withdraw, escape (I-3/4, 16)
    sometimes turn to people, sometimes withdraw
    usually escape by means of an absorbing book

I want to escape
feel like hiding

16. —recognize it, realize it (I-3, 14; I-3/4, 18)
     recognize it and lay down or try to get done what is making
     me nervous
     usually am aware of it
     usually realize I am

I-4/5

Two categories are placed at I-4/5. Both deal with the results of nervousness by evaluating oneself in an interpersonal context. One, becoming self-centered, is concerned with an overall change in interpersonal orientation rather than specific actions or mood states. The other, finding it hard to express oneself, appears to be achievement-oriented.

1. —become self-centered (I-4, 4)
    tend to think only of myself
    perspire readily and become too self oriented
    tend to become self-centered and over look the needs and de-
    sires of others
    tend to take myself and the particular problem too seriously

2. Concern with expression (I-3/4, 5; I-4, 8)
    have speech flow that is not as smooth as I would like
    find it hard to express myself clearly
    cannot communicate effectively with others
    have trouble expressing myself

Unclassified
    get a funny feeling in my stomach. When I was younger I
    would bite my nails
    can't sit still and I find that sometimes I am getting sick (the
    flu or something) and don't know it yet
    am a pacer, but I trust in my faith and prayers to see me thru

I-5

Classed I-5 are responses that differentiate appearance and actions from feelings, that contain awareness of one's social impact, and unique responses concerning alternative high-level methods of coping, and self-criticism of high-level methods of coping.

1. Differentiation of feelings and appearance (I-3/4, 18)

    try to cover up by being funny

    am able to hide the feelings to the extent people invariably consider me calm

    become very quiet, but I always feel as if I am about to burst from within

    try to relieve some of these feelings through humor

    feel myself going to pieces inside—can't eat—

2. Statement of subject's effect on others (more differentiated than nervous, hurt, or bother) (I-4, 7)

    tend to be irritable and disrupt other people and their activities

    talk very fast and make the people around me uncomfortable

    have to watch carefully my reactions to others and exert more self control

    am usually tense and anxious and try hard to avoid any conflicts as far as possible. Quiet seems to right things in short order

3. Methods of coping: alternatives or evaluated

    sometimes I shut it all within myself—It is wrong but nevertheless—I do

    seek physical activity, or solitude, or a novel

    swing my feet, day-dream, worry, think of happy times, think about when the situation is over

    seek another type of activity if continued effort at the one in hand is reaching the point of diminishing return

    smoke too much, scrub a floor or read a technical book

    want to take a long walk alone, or do some strenuous exercise. I want to be alone

    take along walk, a hot bath, or clean house

ITEM **18**

A Woman's Body—

This stem has a low pull since it elicits concern for the physical rather than the emotional or interpersonal aspects of the person from subjects at all I-levels. Though there is no sharp dividing line, virtually all subjects at the I-3 level or lower construe the stem as referring to the body as an object, evoking descriptive responses, or as a possession ("is good to have," Delta; "is her most valuable thing," I-3), while many high-level subjects view the body as one aspect of the person ("is a projection of her personality," I-4; "is only one facet of what and who she really is," I-5) with interpersonal implications ("commands respect," I-4; "is a different image to everyone," I-4/5).

Although crude references to sexual functioning might be expected at the I-2 or Delta levels, we have not seen any. Both covert and obvious references to the body as a source of sexual gratification are found at the I-4/5 and I-5 levels. They belong there both empirically and because the concepts implied—fulfillment, interaction of physical and psychological factors—are high level concepts.

I-2

Most I-2 subjects give descriptive responses which cannot be distinguished from those also popular at higher levels. The concern for cleanliness and dirtiness, distinctive of the I-2 level on other stems, is frequent enough at higher levels on this item to be given a Delta/3 rating as a compromise. The declaration, "is clean," however, is placed at I-2 empirically. Though this may be an artificial distinction on the basis of grammar, the response suggests a global evaluation similar to "is good" or "is pure," also classed here. Other responses placed at this level apparently reflect a primitive sensuality, soft, smooth, tender in different parts.

1. —is soft (I-3, 2, 4)
   is usually soft
   is very tender in different parts

2. —is weak, vulnerable (I-3, 4)
   is very easy to hurt

3. —is clean, pure, good, nice (Δ, 1; Δ/3, 1)

Unclassified
   is a mess
   should be keep nice and smooth because when she went to touch a baby she would scratch him or her

DELTA

The categories placed at Delta refer to the body as a thing, an object someone has or uses. These responses are distinguished from those at higher levels which are either more idealized, "a prized possession" (I-3), or imply personal responsibility and control, "is her personal property" (I-3/4). Our sickest example of sick humor, "should be placed in a casket when dead," also occurred on this item.

1. —is good to have (I-2, 3)
   is a very good thing to have

2. —is made for, belongs to men (I-3/4, 10)
   is made for the enjoyment of men
   belongs to a man

Unclassified
> *should be placed in a casket when dead*
> *can be a very dangerous weapon*
> *is full of temptations*
> *can get her into trouble*
> *is always painted and made fun of*

DELTA/3

The category "should be clean" is placed at this level; it occurs frequently at the Delta level but also at higher levels. Where another idea is included, such as attractiveness or neatness, it governs the rating. For example, "should be kept clean, neat, and presentable," is rated I-3/4.

*1. —should be clean (I-2, 3; I-3, 1)
> *should always be kept clean*
> *should be clean at all times*
> *must be clean*
> *should always fresh & clean*

I-3

Most categories placed at I-3 are descriptive, including the responses saying that a woman's body is not beautiful. Standards evident at I-3 are banal, idealized, and general, "should be beautiful," "should be her pride and joy." Morality is expressed in terms of modesty, that the body should be covered, not displayed.

*1. —is, should be neat, beautiful, attractive, lovely (Δ/3, 1; I-3/4, 1, 2; I-4, 1)
> *is usually something of beauty*
> *is the most beautiful thing on earth*
> *should be attractive as possible*
> *should always be kept clean and attractive*
> *is beautiful and should be kept clean*

2. Physical description (I-2, 1; I-3/4, 14)
> *is fat*
> *usually has curves*
> *will enlarge if she is pregnant*
> *is usually soft and rounded*
> *is shapely*

is very strong
should have a nice figure (36, 24, 36)

3. Clothes, weight, food (I-3/4, 1; I-4, 2)
   I don't pay that much attendition to it except my weight
   tells a lot about the food she eats
   was never designed for high fashion
   needs lots of clothes

4. —is sensitive, fragile, delicate (I-2, 1, 2)

5. —is graceful, feminine
   should be very feminine
   is graceful and should be kept that way

6. —is important, an asset (I-4, 1)
   is important to her
   is the most impoting thing of all
   is very important to her family
   is important to a man
   is an asset or can be an asset
   can be her most powerful asset

*7. —is precious, special, her pride and joy, a prized possession
   (I-3/4, 9; I-4/5, 1)
   is something she can be proud of
   should be her pride and joy
   should be something very special to her
   is her pride
   is her most valuable thing
   is her greatest teasure
   one of her greatest gifts

8. —is OK, all right

9. —is not beautiful, nothing special (I-4, 15)
   is to me unglamorous
   is very ugly in the nude
   is only pretty in youth
   is just a body
   is like any other woman's body

10. —is different from a man's (unelaborated) (I-3/4, 15)
    difference from the man body
    is anathomically different
    consists of parts that a man's body dosn't

11. —should be covered; should not be displayed (I-3/4, 1, 10)

shouldn't be showed off
is nice if they don't show it off in front of men
is to be adorned with clothes
should never be seen by anyone other than her mate

12. —don't know; none of your business
    cannot answer
    doesn't bring any particular thought or impression to my mind
    what do you mean by that?

Unclassified
    is pure and should not have impure touches or move it around
    in impure ways

I-3/4

Where I-3 subjects give responses describing the body as beautiful or attractive, I-3/4 subjects give responses suggesting how this may be achieved, "should be thin," "needs constant care," or recognizing that a woman's body is not necessarily attractive, "can be a beautiful thing." Thus the I-3/4 subject recognizes process and diversity. Other kinds of responses placed here view the body in the context of interpersonal relations; it is not merely attractive (I-3), but attractive to men (I-3/4), to be loved and admired. The notion of personal responsibility for her actions, explicitly stated at I-4, is implied in responses saying that it is her own business and should be saved until marriage. The responses, sacred, holy, classed here, appear to be similar to those saying that a woman's body is personal in that they imply that it should not be misused. This is stated clearly in one response, "is holy, not a toy."

*1. —should be kept in shape; should be attractively, appropriately attired (I-3, 1, 3, 11)
    should be kept carefully and nicely groomed
    should be kept clean, neat, and presentable
    should be clothed femininely
    should be clothed in proper fitting wearing apparel
    should be kept clean & sweet smelling & modestly covered!
    should be well propotioned
    should be neat and trim
    should be clean and not flabby

*2. —can be beautiful, attractive (I-3, 1; I-4, 1)
    can be a beautiful thing
    can be very lovely but usually isn't

can be very pretty
can be lovely or obnoxious

*3. —should be cared for (I-4, 2)
  is meant to be cared for tenderly
  should be kept up
  needs constant care
  should be protected

4. —should not be abused, misused (I-4, 9, 12)
  is sometimes misused
  should not be hurt

*5. —is sacred, holy; is God's gift; is a creation of God (I-4, 6)
  is a beautiful thing in the eye's of God
  is the temple of her soul
  is holy, not a toy
  is a thing of God, not of man
  is a wonderful gift from God

6. —is a work of art (unelaborated) (I-4, 4)
  is a piece of art

7. —is wonderful, marvelous (I-4, 6)
  is a wonderful thing
  is a thing to marvel at
  can do marvelous things
  is a wonderful thing, men think
  is a marvelous wonder

8. —is serviceable, functional, useful (I-4/5, 4)
  is something to be enjoyed, also useful to her
  is a thing of beauty and service
  is useful & has its purpose like any other body
  is made for many things

9. —is personal, her own (I-3, 7; I-4, 10, 14)
  should be her personal pride
  is her personal property
  is hers
  is her own buisness
  is her business (& her husbands)
  is her own and should be kept that way unless she marries

10. —is for her husband (Δ, 2; I-3, 11)
  is one of the things she can give to her husband
  is something to save for her husband

is a great gift to her husband and it should be taken care of
belongs to herself and her husband
is to be shared with her husband

11. —attracts, is appealing to men
    is something that almost all men notice
    is an object of desire to men
    is desired by her husband
    is what men admire

12. —is to be loved, cherished, admired (I-4, 11)
    is to be loved by a man's
    should be cherished by her husband
    is to be admired at all times
    is as god planned, a thing to be adored by men

13. —is a problem, a source of trouble (I-4, 3)
    is usually a problem to her
    could be miserable or tired
    sure takes a beating sometimes
    goes through a rough life

14. —can vary; changes through the years (I-3, 2)
    comes in many shapes & sizes
    changes many times
    shows depreciation rapidly at my age
    begins to be a maintenance problem after 30
    disintegrates with age! Ugh!

15. Specific comparison with man's (I-3, 10)
    is heavier than a man's
    is fuller than a man's
    is softer than a man's
    has more structural and functional advantages than men's
    is biologically different from a man's

I-4

Some responses at I-4 refer to the body as a physical object, but the concern is with health and stamina rather than with attractiveness. This does not mean that the I-4 woman cares little about beauty, but that she recognizes contingencies and distinguishes beauty from physical attractiveness: "can be a beautiful object in an esthetic sense," "is beautiful in that it is a miracle." The greater conceptual complexity at I-4 may be shown by recognizing the complexity and mystery of the body, particularly in relation to reproduction. Another kind of complexity is shown in responses saying that the body is expressive or a part of her. When the interaction of physical and psychological functioning is clearly evident, the rating is I-4/5. The contrast of body with mind, personality, or soul is a typical I-4 dichotomy, similar to love versus lust. These dichotomies are of interest despite the fact that they are infrequently made explicit because they contrast with ideas both at lower and at higher levels. At I-3 and below moral dichotomies tend to be expressed in terms of clean-dirty and pure-impure; body almost always means torso or figure rather than being contrasted with mind. Above I-4 moral dichotomies are not characteristic, and body and mind are seen as interrelated. Thus the response, "is a precious possession, not to be used promiscously, kept clean, and not expose herself," although it combines a number of different ideas, could not be rated higher than I-4 and actually comes from an I-3/4 protocol.

1. Wonderful, attractive, and the like, contingent on care, shape, how used (I-3, 1, 6; I-3/4, 2)

    is a thing of beauty when properly cared for
    is beautiful when fully developed
    can be beautiful depending on the woman and how she "wears it"
    is beautiful if thy don't get too fat
    can be an asset if she takes the proper care of it
    a wonderful thing if she uses it for righteous things
    is a wonderful thing if it is kept respectable

*2. —should be kept healthy, given the proper diet (I-3, 3; I-3/4, 3)

    should be kept healthy and strong in order to be beautiful
    should reflect a picture of health, exercise and proper rest and diet
    is something to take care of. (diet, exercise, comfortable clothes, etc.)
    should be taken care of by proper exercise, nutrition, etc.

3. —is capable of great endurance (I-3/4, 13)

    has less physical strength but more stamina than a man's
    can endure a lot
    is built to withstand many changes
    has to be stronge, well builded to take this world of to day

4. —is an artistic, esthetic object (elaborated) (I-3/4, 6)

    is a beautiful piece of work that God has made
    is often used as a model by artists

*is an artistic model; for example, many paintings are of a
woman's body*
can be a beautiful object in an esthetic sense
is a beautiful creation of God, but only for her husband to see

5. —is complex, intricate (I-4/5, 3)
   is a complex but wonderful thing
   has many interesting facets
   is an intricate & marvelous creation
   is a very complex structure

6. —is mysterious, miraculous (I-3/4, 5, 7; I-4/5, 3)
   is really a beautiful and also a mysterious part of the woman
   is beautiful in that it's a miracle
   is a mysterious but wonderful creation
   is an amazing machine

7. Reproduction as miraculous
   has within the marvelous parts necessary for reproduction
   is quite a miraculous thing, reproductively speaking
   *is amazing. The ability to conceive and bear children is un-
   believable*
   *Should be looked upon as something immaculate, as it seems
   like a miracle the way this body can nourish a cell into being*

8. —is designed for a purpose, for bearing children
   is God's creation to fulfill a needed purpose
   is intended to be fruitful
   is cleverly designed for pregnancy
   derives its main purpose in bearing children
   gives life

9. Concern with how used (I-3/4, 4)
   should be used for the purposes for which God made it
   can be used in both good and bad ways
   can be used to her advantage or disadvantage
   should be to please a man, in love, not disgust him, in lust

10. —is her responsibility (I-3/4, 9)
    is as attractive as a woman makes it
    is what she makes it
    is hers so its up to her to take care of it
    is the only thing she has complete say over
    Is hers and she can share it with anyone she wants
    belongs to her and she alone should have control over it

11. —should be respected (I-3/4, 12)
    is to be admired but respected
    should always be respected by her husband
    commands respect

12. —should be treated with respect, not exploited (by herself or others) (I-3/4, 4)
    should be treated in a very special way
    should not be treated like a toy
    is a wonderful thing, not a playtoy be bee used or disrespected by anyone
    is not to be given cheaply
    is not something to be just handled and thrown away
    should not be used for her own gain

13. —is nothing to be ashamed of
    should be something of pride, not something shameful to hide

14. —is expressive; a part of her (I-3/4, 9; I-5, 2)
    can tell alot about her
    is a projection of her personality
    is an important aspect of her total self
    is part of her attractiveness
    is the most important thing about her
    is to be used to express her love

15. —is not most important; is overrated (I-3, 9)
    is not as important as her mind
    should not be as important as other things
    shouldn't be the most important thing in her life (emphasis on developing it, I mean)
    isn't her greatest asset
    is not as important as her "personality"
    is her second greatest attraction

Unclassified
    should be a beautiful wrapping for a good and happy soul

I-4/5

The appreciation for complexity expressed at I-4 is elaborated at I-4/5 in responses that explicitly recognize the interaction between physical and psychological functioning. Responses stating that the body is a source of pride can perhaps also be interpreted that way. They are distinguished from those that say that the body is a source of pleasure (I-5); some subjects use phrases or terms, such as satisfaction, that can be interpreted in terms of either pride (I-4/5) or pleasure (I-5). Doubtful responses should be classed I-4/5. Related ideas classed at this level are elaborations of the notion of the body as functional and elaborations of the notion of the body as a creation of God or nature in terms of its complexity or in comparison with man's body.

1. —is, should be a source of pride, satisfaction (I-3, 7; I-5, 1)
   should be a source of pride for her and cared for and "guarded" accordingly

2. Interaction of physical and psychological functioning
   is one thing she should take care of not only for health reasons but because it gives her self-confidence
   needs training to prepare for marriage. Men need to realize their wives aren't like some animal the moment they're ready
   often determines her feminine qualities. Beauty is important —more than I have ever given cognizance to
   is meant to be beautiful, reflecting by its posture and carriage her pride (or lack of it) in being a woman
   is beautiful only if her mind is the same
   houses a mind, a spirit and a heart and can be creative in many ways

3. A creation of God or nature, elaborated in terms of complexity or comparison with man's (I-4, 5, 6)
   is any human body an exquisite, intricate and detailed display of the omniscient power of God
   is a beautiful and intricate structure, one of nature's masterpieces to be respected
   is reserved to be beheld by the man she loves. A woman's body represents the intricate machine of reproduction produced by God
   as well as a man's are the two most beautiful and perfect objects G-d has created
   is a gift from God—the most beautiful of God's creations
   equal only to a man's body. It should be cherished and given to only one man
   is a sacred masterpiece made to compliment the nature of man

4. —is functional (elaborated) (I-3/4, 8)
   is wonderfully designed for its functions
   is a beautiful structure of symmetry and practical arrangement

is beautiful and functional and should be kept in good "order" by habits of living that tend to help it function properly

depends on the woman. I consider mine merely functional
is ethical and functional. Both should be taken care of

Unclassified
should be treated with dignity by herself as well as others
met to discuss the problems of todays children
is a different image to everyone
is sacred to herself just as life is sacred to man

I-5

Somewhat surprisingly, responses that refer to a woman's body as a source of fulfillment or of physical pleasure come exclusively from high-level protocols in our experience. (It is conceivable, however, that much cruder responses with this content could appear in other samples at lower I-levels.) Other categories here refer to her identity and to acceptance of her destiny.

1. A source of pleasure or fulfillment (I-4/5, 1)
   is a miraculous machine capable of producing and experiencing the most thrilling things in life
   was designed to meet her needs
   is a delight to her in many ways
   should always be will cared for; is a beautiful thing; should not be too fat or too lean; should be a source of enjoyment
   can be a source of pleasure, of vanity & unattractive when overweight
   is a joy—a gift, a happy place, and something to be saved for her husband
   is a source of satisfaction and joy if she is healthy
   can be delightfully pleasing both to herself and to her man

2. An aspect of her identity (I-4, 14)
   is only one facet of what and who she really is
   is often very much a part of her self-concept, fortunately or unfortunately as the case may be

3. Part of her destiny
   is what she must learn to live within
   if well-shaped is beautiful. I've always envied those with perfect figures & find it hard to accept my own at times

I-6

The response placed here obviously contains several I-4 themes and implicitly possibly the notion of identity or destiny. What determines the high rating is not only the balancing of diverse ideas but also conveying the idea of woman's need to find inner balance.

Unclassified

is a part of her. It shouldn't dominate her. I believe personality and intellect are more important, but neither should it be abused

When a Child
Won't Join in
Group Activities—

Since some subjects apparently misread "won't" as "want," we now use the form, "When a child will not join in group activities—." We anticipate that most responses will be unaltered.

This stem presents a more structured situation than most, and while some subjects at low levels have trouble with spelling and grammar in their responses, the responses are mostly germane. The content of the

224

responses is an important clue to I-level, rather than, as with many other items, mainly the formal aspects of response. Responses concern three broad topics, what to do for the child, why he acts as he does, and, infrequently, the possible results.

At I-2 the idea of psychological causation is missing or shaky; hence one finds either a physical cause, he is sick, or a misunderstanding of the stem, he is excluded. At Delta, the subject prescribes force or punishment; correspondingly, the child is suspected of bad motives, "spoiled" or planning to run away. In the I-3 through I-4 range the view by far predominates that something is wrong, the child has a problem, he should not be forced, but he should be helped. Not joining in group activities is a psychological problem. Results of not joining are that he is not "in" (Delta), that he is missing fun (I-3), or that unfortunate consequences may follow at a later time (I-4). A minority view, however, sides with the child and his rights: not only should he not be forced, but let him do what he wants (I-3), he may want to be alone (I-3/4), or have a good reason (I-4), for example, other interests (I-3/4). Above I-4 there is explicit recognition that there are many possible reasons, some of them perfectly healthy ones, and that what one does is contingent on the child's reason for not joining. Almost all subjects above I-4 make a response that is in some way tentative ("it may indicate"), qualified ("usually"), or contingent; almost all subjects below I-3 make positive statements about cause ("he's shy," scored I-3) or what should be done ("he has to play alone," Delta).

I-2

The category "he is sick" at I-2 contains positive statements and is separated empirically from the similar but speculative statements at Delta/3. Though this category does provide a cause for volitional behavior, the cause is physical rather than psychological; the latter is seen at higher levels.

1. —he is sick (Δ/3, 2)
   she doesn't feel well

2. "Won't" misread as "want"
   he ask's can I do that
   LET IT JOIN
   he sure aske to join the group
   she signs up for it

Unclassified
he is bad
I think they aren't good

DELTA

Use of force or punishment, the solution typical for the Delta level, is specifically proscribed at higher levels. Where motives or causes are assigned, they are rendered unsympathetically: he is spoiled or planning to run away. Where results or consequences of not joining are mentioned at the Delta level, they are not long-term effects but rather so tied to the immediate situation as to be almost restatements of the stem: "he has to play alone."

1. —force him; punish him (I-3, 1)
   make him
   he should be prodded
   he should be put in a corner
   you should force her to for her own good
   kick him in the ass and ignore him

2. Bad motives (I-3, 7, 8)
   they are stuck up
   he is either a spoiled brat or shy
   they must be crazy
   she feeling sorry for herself
   she is paining a runaway
   he is stubern and need a spanken or he or she could be sick too
   is silly
   he is anti-social

3. Immediate results (I-3, 10)
   he has to play alone
   he's not "in"
   he won't learn
   he is by himself
   he becomes idol

4. External or physical cause
   they don't have all the materials needed, skate, bathing suits, etc.
   it is usually because there is someone they do not know or don't know the game

> *either his parents can't afford it or he isn't liked by anyone of his age*
> *sometimes it is because they are not allowed to*

Unclassified
> *you tell me*
> *you should always try to talk to her so she don't get into trouble?*

DELTA/3

Causes seen in responses classed at the Delta level tend to be physical rather than psychological and external rather than internal. The category "something is wrong" is ambiguous with respect to such distinctions; it occurs on many I-3 protocols, rarely on higher protocols, and proportionately more often on protocols below I-3.

*1. —something is wrong (I-3, 9; I-3/4, 3)
> *something must be the matter*
> *there is something troubling usually*
> *something is wrong with him or his parnets think he's too good*

2. —he may be ill; he must be sick (I-2, 1)
> *he could be sick and not always shy*
> *she or he might not feel to good*
> *He must be tired or sick*

I-3

The shift from physical to psychological causation and from an unsympathetic to a partly sympathetic view of the child's motivation at I-3 is more striking here than for some other stems. At I-3 and higher force is taboo and bad motives are not ascribed, unless one counts "lazy" and "poor sport" at I-3. Illness may be mentioned as one possible cause. Though a few I-3 subjects assert the child should be allowed to do as he pleases, the pervading idea at this level is that the child has a problem and he needs to be helped to join the activities. When force is proscribed, it is stated as a command: "don't force him." The command is in fact often paradoxical: don't force him, but coax him or talk him into it. The I-3 tends to see just one type of child as involved and to seek a single solution for the situation. Where the I-3 presents alternatives, they are stated in a manner that excludes further possibilities: "he's either shy or he just doesn't want to." "Shy" is frequent and nondiscriminating; when it occurs with another alternative, the response should be rated according to the other alternative. That the child does not want to is also undiscriminating, though infrequent. "Because he don't want to" occurred on an I-2 protocol; "he may not really want to" occurred on an I-5 protocol. One notes that the latter is both more germane and more tentative, but there still is a wide range for what is essentially the same thought. Reasons seen by the I-3 person tend to be long-term traits or feeling states (shy, lonely), while subjects at higher levels tend to mention feelings elicited by the group activity (scared at I-3/4, insecure at I-4).

*1. —he should be helped, encouraged, asked to join (Δ, 1)
   try and talk them into it
   they should be coaxed into participating
   you have to help him to join
   I try to encourage him or her
   he needs friendship

*2. —don't force him; leave him alone; encourage but do not force him (commands) (I-3/4, 9; I-4, 6)
   don't push him, but rather let him do as he pleases
   don't try and make him
   do not neglect, neither should you use force
   he should not be scolded

3. —I don't force him

4. —let him do something else, what he wants (I-3/4, 9)
   he should be encouraged to do something else
   you should find something for him to do

5. —he doesn't like that activity (I-3/4, 10, 11, 12)
   he must not like to play
   he may not like the activity or the people involved
   that means they don't like group activities
   he must have other ideas of fun

6. —he may not want to; he isn't sociable (unelaborated)
   (I-3/4, 12)
   he's either shy or he just doesn't want to
   he doesn't want to be bothered
   he most don't like to be with people

*7. —he may be shy, lonely, an introvert (Δ, 2; I-3/4, 5, 6, 7, 8)
   it is bashful or retarded
   the child is very lonely and needs friends

8. —he is lazy, dull, a poor sport (Δ, 2)
   is lazy or don't care

9. —he needs help; he has a problem (Δ/3, 1; I-3/4, 4, 5; I-4, 4)
   he needs training
   they have problems
   he or she has problem in making friend

10. —he is missing fun (Δ, 3; I-4, 10)
    they are missing alot out of life
    he loses out in much

11. —I feel sorry for him

12. —he is unhappy

13. —it is all right; it is too bad
    its sad
    it is a shame

Unclassified
    , Try to get the group to join him
    he should all ways have something to do
    I think they're trying to get attention
    let him alone he will

I-3/4

As one proceeds from the I-3 to the I-4 level, the problem is seen as more an inward than an external problem; it is also seen in more differentiated and less banal terms. Ambiguous categories receive I-3/4 ratings. That the child has a problem is rated I-3, that he has a reason, I-4. "Try to find out why" is an intermediate thought and rated I-3/4. Of course these categories are not sharply discriminating at the respective levels. On our evidence, saying that the child is an "introvert" is as banal and stereotyped as saying he is shy; it occurs typically at I-3. There are more specific words for what may be the same thought at I-3/4, such as afraid, self-conscious, feels unwanted. A somewhat exaggerated view of the child's problem is expressed by those subjects at I-3/4 who see him as abnormal or as having a complex. A more benign view of his behavior is also made explicit at this level, in terms of the child's interests. Among the unclassified responses at this level are some that come under contradictory rules. "You should try to force him because he might become too much of an intrevert" concerns long-term effects (1-4) but prescribes force (Delta). "He's either spoiled or mentally unbalanced or feels unacceptable" has three distinct, contrasted thoughts (I-4/5) but takes a more disparaging view than is likely at levels over I-4.

*1. —try to find out why (unelaborated) (I-4, 1, 2)
someone should find out why
I try to find out what is wrong
you ask why
the matter should be looked into

2. —I wonder why; I worry about him
I wonder about him
it makes one wonder why
it worries me why she doesn't want to

3. —something is bothering him (Δ/3, 1; I-4, 1)
something is greatly disturbing him
he is disturbed

4. —he needs guidance, special attention, professional help (I-3, 9; I-4, 3)
one needs medical att.

5. —he is (is not) abnormal, maladjusted; he may have a complex (I-3, 7, 9; I-4, 4; I-5, 1)
he may not be socially maladjusted
there is something wrong with its personality development
he may not be abnormal—just want to be alone
he is very shy or has an inferiorty complex

6. —he is afraid, scared, timid (I-3, 7; I-4, 5)
it is probably because he is scared of people
you should usually leave it alone, for you might scare them even more

7. —he feels unwanted, not accepted (I-3, 7; I-4, 5)
he feels the group will not accept him

8. —he is embarrassed, self-conscious (I-3, 7)

9. —he should be left alone, not forced (I-3, 2, 4; I-4, 6)
he shouldn't be pushed
he should not be pressured to join
I guess it best to leave them alone
he should be allowed to play alone

10. —he may prefer to be alone (I-3, 5; I-4, 9)
perhaps he likes to have a few minutes to himself

11. —it's his business, his decision (I-3, 5; I-4, 8)
I think that it is up to her to decide

12. —he is not interested; he has other interests (I-3, 5, 6; I-4/5, 3)
he would rather do something else
his interests may be elsewhere

*perhaps it is because he has individual interests which should
be encouraged
he should be let alone to enjoy his own interests*

13. —try to get him interested (in something else) (I-4/5, 3)
*you should try to motivate through individual activities
the parents shoud try to get him to mix with other children
around home
try to find their interests*

Unclassified
*you should try to force him because he might become too
much of an intrevert
he's either spoiled or mentally unbalanced or feels unacceptable
he may be unhappy*

I-4

Solutions classed at this level never imply forcing the child to participate. The conception of and respect for the child's inner life is clearer
than at lower levels. The child has his reasons and his pace. If the child
is seen as having a problem, it is explicitly an emotional or psychological
one. He should be helped tactfully and gradually. Psychological causation, in terms of both causes and effects of the given situation, is mentioned. These ideas are made clearer and combined at higher levels.

*1. —there is, must be a reason (I-3/4, 1, 3; I-4/5, 1)
*there could be many reasons for this behavior
he usually has a good reason and this should be understood
there could be several factors involved*

*2. —try to find the reason, cause, source (I-3/4, 1)
*one should attempt to find out the reason
, I am drawn to him to discover his feelings
his reasons should be analyzed*

3. —he needs understanding (I-3/4, 4)
*, don't try to force him, just understand
, he needs guidance and understanding*

4. —he may have an emotional (psychological) problem (I-3, 9;
I-3/4, 5)
*I would think something emotionally is bothering him
something may be wrong psychologically with the child
it could be a sign of emotional disturbance*

their is something missing in his emotional make up or personal life

there is usually a family or mental problem

*5. —he feels insecure, unsure of himself, inadequate (I-3/4, 6, 7)

I feel that it is due to fear of failure

I often feel he is not at ease with himself

it is often because he feels inferior

, he is an unhappy child—he lacks assurance in some way

6. —he should be encouraged but not forced; he should be gently encouraged (I-3, 2; I-3/4, 9)

he should be made to feel welcome but not hounded

he should be invited and coaxed, but never pressured to join

it's best to leave them alone because they shouldn't be made to participate

it's best to ask gently and once only if he would care to join

7. He should be brought in gradually, unobtrusively (I-4/5, 5)

it is best to move slowly, allowing him to move into them at a comfortable pace

I wouldn't be too obvious in encouraging his joining

he must have a good group experience gradually to join in with the others

he may do better starting on a one to one basis

I will try to give him special attention but not the point of embarrassing him

he must be gone to individually & figure out the reason privately

8. —he will join when he is ready, on his own (I-3/4, 11; I-4/5, 5)

he should be left alone, because eventually he will come to a group by himself and enter into an activity

let him watch for awhile. Don't beg or push him & usually he will join in of his own accord

don't push them into it, let him make the first step

9. —respect his wishes (I-3/4, 10; I-4/5, 2)

his wishes should be deferred to

it does not mean that he is unsociable. If he doesn't want to join in, the others should respect his feelings

10. He needs to learn about the pleasures of group activity (I-3, 10)

> *he probably does not enjoy the pleasure of the activities be-
> cause he has not learned how*
>
> *an adult should try to help the child by showing him all the
> fun he can have with a group*
>
> *she doesn't know just how much fun it is and she could be
> just too shy*
>
> *some one should try to show him the interesting points of the
> activity*

11. Unfortunate long-term future results
    > *it can lead to trouble or broken friendship*
    >
    > *he will probably be a very unhappy adolescent*
    >
    > *it is important to try to get them to because growing up feel-
    > ing lonely is very sad*

Unclassified
> *usually he doesn't feel well or just not in the mood*

I-4/5

Responses above the I-4 level tend to have a tentative tone and
to envisage more than one possibility. Taken together, they reveal a deep-
ened respect for the child's reasons, his interests, and his tempo that goes
beyond merely respecting his wishes (I-4) or letting him do what he
wants (I-3). The idea that he is abnormal (I-3/4) is not characteristic,
although physical illness and emotional problems may be acknowledged
as possibilities.

1. Three contrasting reasons (I-4, 1)
   > *he may not feel wanted. He may be shy. He may be ill*
   >
   > *he may be shy, sick, or just getting a "feel" of the situation
   > first!*
   >
   > *he is usually shy and afraid or wants to be the leader and
   > can't co-operate with other children*
   >
   > *he may be shy, feel uninvited, or not interested in groups*

2. Individuality as a positive value (I-4, 9; I-5, 1)
   > *one can be thankful because he may be an individual*
   >
   > *respect his wishes—I hate groups. Beat him to death?*
   >
   > *I won't make him. A lot of people, adults, teens and children
   > prefer to be by themselves than be in group activities. You
   > can hurt (mentally) a person by making them join*
   >
   > *they should be encouraged to do so—but only along their in-
   > terest lines. I do not like a "joiner."*

3. —observe what he is interested in (I-3/4, 12, 13; I-5, 2)

*care should be taken that he wont be lonely, or trying to lo-
cate his interests and get him to join activities he likes*

*exposure to a group and subtle approaches through his known
interests might be attempted (depending on the age, reason, etc.)*

*talk to him and find out why. Discover what he would join if
given the opportunity*

4. Response or value as contingent (I-5, 1)

it is okay as long as it isn't an all-the-time choice

*depending on the frequency and situations, he might need
counseling*

*he should not be forced to do so without any consideration of
why he refused to participate*

*the cause for his retisence should be discovered, and he should
patiently be helped to participate, except for special reasons*

*he should be helped in whatever way is appropriate to find
enjoyment in such activities*

5. —give him time (elaborated) (I-4, 7, 8; I-5, 2)

*it is wise to give him time to watch others, and to cautiously
build up a feeling of trust in him*

*don't push! Try to find out why. But give the child time, be-
cause some socialize slowly*

*he should be left alone until he is ready or encouraged by a
peer to participate*

Unclassified

*the causes may be temporary, or they may have profound sig-
nificance. If it persists, the teacher or mother should try to
discover the cause*

I-5

The two categories at this level involve not only alternative constructions but both favorable and unfavorable ones. In one category both
healthy and unhealthy interpretations of the refusal are specifically recognized. The other category moves toward a truly autonomous point of
view, with recognition of the value of both group and individual activity.

1. It may be a healthy thing or not (I-3/4, 5; I-4/5, 2, 4)

he may be shy and need help, or he may be self-sufficient

he shouldn't be forced; but one should seek out the reason and give help if necessary. It is not unhealthy to want to do things individually

, he may have a problem although this is not necessarily the case

2. Respect for autonomy (implicit recognition of value for group and solo activities) (I-4/5, 3, 5)

he must continue to enjoy his interests and be permitted to activate any later interest for companionship

, he should be encouraged to join if he is doing nothing else really interesting or profitable to him, but he should never be forced

I try not to force realizing all of us need some time alone

I-6

The response classed here shows three alternative possibilities, healthy and mildly unfavorable possibilities, and the concept of identity.

Unclassified

it may be because he feels no identity with the group, is too self-conscious, or has no real interest in the activity

Men Are Lucky Because—

This stem has a strong Delta pull and does not discriminate well at the extreme I-levels. It elicits responses concerning dominance-submission, getting away with things, doing as one pleases, and protecting oneself in a hostile world that would be scored Delta if offered spontaneously to another stem. Some Delta individuals make such responses, but so do women at higher levels. It is somewhat arbitrary whether the rating is Delta with a note indicating that others also give the response or whether the category is given a higher rating. In either case, one cannot extract information that is not there—that is, one cannot disentangle the Delta responses indistinguishable from ones of higher level subjects.

Many of the responses to this stem are concerned with the freedom or opportunities more available to men than to women. In general,
at lower levels one is lucky to have freedom *from,* at higher levels, freedom *to* (as Erich Fromm has pointed out). Some examples of the kinds
of freedom valued are getting away with things (Delta), avoiding housework (I-3), obtaining challenging and interesting jobs (I-4), developing
one's capabilities (I-5).

Astonishing for its virtual absence is the psychiatrist's concern for
the more problematic sexual responsiveness of some women. The only
respondent who mentioned it was I-4 and appended it as an afterthought.
("They don't have to worry as much about conception. This is a constant
worry for me. I have 3 children and think this is enough. Sex is probably
more enjoyable and relaxed for them.") Of course this problem may be
implied in the response "they are men," or "they can do anything they
please."

I-2

There are only a few small categories of response that can be
placed at I-2, all seeming to reflect a confusion of cause and consequence,
or failure to understand "because." Responses such as "they are cute,"
"they are clever," or "they are working" almost certainly do not mean
that all men have those attributes. They make sense only if inverted: "If
men happen to be cute, they are lucky."

1. —they are good to look at
   they are cute
   they are hasom

2. —they are clever, smart
   they no more
   Some are very clever mens

3. —they work, have good jobs (I-3, 8, 19)
   They are working & have a Job
   he can get a good job
   they can work
   if they have a job

Unclassified
   there happy
   they wants something
   of his Wife
   they have a lot of money

DELTA

The Delta subject considers men lucky because they are better able to do what she would like to do, control or take advantage of others, get one's own way, and stay out of trouble, including the prototypic "trouble," an unwanted pregnancy. Responses similar in content to those classed here are found at almost all higher levels, reflecting the actual or perceived advantages of men in our culture due in part to the double standard.

1. Avoidance of responsibility for unwanted pregnancy
   they aren't the ones that have the baby
   if they aren't married to a woman, but they get her P.G. they can say prove it and won't be in any trouble because they can't prove it

2. —they can get out of trouble easier than women (I-3, 14)
   they don't have to worry as much as women when they go out to have fun & get into trouble
   they can walk out when they feel like it

3. —they control women, get what they want (I-3, 13; I-4, 1, 4)

Unclassified
   they dont no what its all about
   they like women who are superior to them

DELTA/3

Responses classed at this level are given by a number of low level persons but are indistinguishable from those given by 1-3/4 and I-4 subjects, so are placed here as a compromise rating. The implication of "they don't have to have babies" for the I-2 and Delta subject may be that having a baby is due to fate and an inescapable part of being a woman. "They can't have babies" may be similar in meaning to avoiding responsibility for unwanted pregnancy (Delta). The second category placed here is similar to several placed at higher levels. That men can marry or fall in love focuses on the action of dating, marrying, rather than the different options open to men and women (I-3/4 and I-4).

1. —they don't have to have, can't have babies (I-3, 17)

2. —they can date, marry, fall in love with women (I-3, 3; I-3/4, 3)
   they can fall in love with buitiful women

they get to marry women
they can easily find wives
they get to date gorgeous girls and don't have to pay for the
    wedding

I-3

Two large categories placed at this level, "they are men," "they have women," appear to be clichés, the easy answer to this stem coming from subjects at all I-levels. Typically I-3 are the responses concerned with appearance or concrete male prerogatives. One I-3 category refers to man's contribution to his family, but it is in terms of his financial support or simply that he can take care of his family rather than his emotional support (I-4/5) or his responsibilities to his family (I-4). Most of the other responses classed here define men's luck in terms of escape from woman's lot. Many of these responses are essentially things men do or do not do: they can get out, not mind the children, not have to iron, get away with bad behavior. At higher levels responses in a similar vein either make explicit comparisons, "they can be out among people more" (I-3/4) or are concerned with differing responsibilities, restrictions and opportunities—in other words, the differing expectations and standards set by society that to a great extent determine behavior. The responses placed at I-3 that are on a more abstract level are essentially blanket statements or generalizations, "they have fewer problems," "they are independent." Subjects at higher levels tend to state which problems men are free of or what kind of independence men have. "They can leave a pregnant woman and have no sigma [stigma]" is classed I-3 as a compromise; the first half alone would be classed Delta, but the notion of social stigma is more characteristic of levels above I-3.

*1. —they are men, fathers, not women (I-3/4, 1)
    they can be fathers
    they are the fathers of the world

*2. —they have women; there are women (I-3/4, 2)
    they have us
    the opposite sex are around
    women exist

3. —they have good, nice, wonderful wives (Δ/3, 2)
    they have thoughtful wives
    When they get a good wife
    some of them get very nice wife

4. —they have women for companions, to come home to
   they have a wife to come home to at nights

*5. Appearance, clothes
   they don't have to worry about their hair
   they don't fuss over themselves like women
   they can grow beards and mustaches
   they can wear topless bathing suits

6. —they don't have pain, physical discomforts
   they don't have menstrual periods
   they don't have to bear the pains of child birth
   they are not subject to cancer of the breast!

7. Special (superficial, concrete) prerogatives
   they have cars
   because they can go to stag parties
   they can participate in all sports
   they can smoke pipes

8. —they get better, higher paying jobs (I-2, 3; I-4, 10)
   they recive better jobs
   they can usually get a better job than a woman can
   they can make more money

*9. —they have an easy life, fewer problems, less worries (unspeci-
   fied) (I-3/4, 7; I-4, 7)
   they get all the "breaks"
   have an easy way to go
   their lifes don't seem so complicated
   they don't have much to worrie about
   a women has all the worries
   they don't have as rough a time as a woman does

*10. —they don't have to mind the children, do the housework
   (I-4, 7)
   they usually don't have to wash dishes
   they do not have to cook
   they don't have to listen to kids fight all day

*11. —they don't have to stay home; they can get out, away from
   children (I-3/4, 4; I-4, 7, 11)
   they get out to work
   they can be out for a while
   they aren't cooped up at home all day
   they're at work all day

they can get away and forget somethings
they are not tied down with kids

12. —they are free, independent (unelaborated) (I-3/4, 5; I-4, 5, 6; I-4/5, 2)
     they have there own Freedom
     of their freedom
     they are rather independent
     they are subject to no one
     they can be so damned independet

13. —they can do what they want; they can go where they please (Δ, 3; I-4, 5)
     they are so free to do as they choose
     they get to go all most any place they want
     they come and go as they please
     they can go what they want with whomever they please

14. —they can get by with bad behavior (Δ, 2; I-4, 8)
     they can mess around more
     they get by with so much that a woman can't
     they can leave a pregnant woman & have no sigma

15. —they are brave, daring; they take chances
     they are the braver of the two sexes
     they are gamblers
     they don't have to be as careful as women

16. —they are able to protect themselves
     they can go out and feel fairly safe
     they don't have to worry about so many thing, such as being out after dark, etc.

17. —they do not have babies (Δ/3, 1)
     they never become pregnant
     don't give birth

18. —they care for, give financial support to wife and family (I-4, 1; I-4/5, 3)
     they can support a wife and are usually the background of the family
     they have a family to care for
     They can get married & support a family
     they have women to look after
     they get to work for their family

19. —they work hard, harder than women, not as hard (I-2, 3; I-3/4, 8)

they have plenty of work
they can do a hard days work
they don't have as much to do

20. —of a lot of things

21. Evasion of stem (I-4, 17)
    no opinion on this
    don't know
    ?

I-3/4

The response "they have women" (I-3) is explained at I-3/4 in terms of interpersonal actions, women take care of them, where at I-4 the emotional aspects of the relation may be specified, women love and admire them. A rudimentary role conception is shown in responses referring to being head of the family, as compared to the I-3 version of father. Other responses scored at this level reflect a change, one which is more apparent at I-4 and above, from the I-3 concern for escaping a woman's lot to the positive advantages of man's lot. Man is seen as being more independent, having more opportunities, and being able to do more. That "they still do the asking" and do not have to wait for dates also reflect a change in the direction of "freedom to" from "freedom from."

1. —they are the head of the house (I-3, 1; I-4, 1)
   they have the distinction of being head of the family

2. —they have women to take care of, help them (I-3, 2; I-4, 3)
   they have women to wait on them
   their wives do everything for them
   they have women to look after them
   some Women spoil them
   they have women to fall back on
   they have women to turn to

3. —they can propose, date whom and when they please; don't have to wait to be asked (Δ/3, 2; I-4, 4)
   they do the asking
   they can ask girls out
   they are able to ask any girl they like for dates
   they can date whenever they choose
   they don't have to wait around for dates; they can ask

4. —they can get out, be with people more than women (I-3, 11; I-4, 5, 11)

they get to go out more than their wife
because they are out of the house more
they get to get out and meet more people on a whole than
   do women
they can be out among people more

5. —they are more independent, freer than women (I-3, 12; I-4, 5, 6)
they have more freedom
you have more freedom or free time
they seem to have more freedom in certain areas
they are or can be more independent
they are allowed more freedom than women

6. —they can be aggressive, demanding, assertive (I-4, 9; I-4/5, 4)
they can assert
they can be sexually agressive
they are "the bosses"

7. —they are carefree (I-3, 9)
they just seem more carefree

8. —they work only eight hours (I-3, 19)
they don't have to use every waking minute for work—they
   can relax
when their work day is over they can stop for the day! (or at
   least stop their job)
they go to work 5 days and have 2 days off

9. —they have less responsibility; can avoid responsibility, blame
   (I-4, 7)
women take on much of the responsibility
of freedom from responsibilities
it is easier for them to shun their responsibilities
they can avoid responsibility where most women won't
they can blame their mistakes on women

10. —they have more opportunities, privileges (unelaborated)
   (I-4, 10, 12)

11. —they can do more things (general)
they can do things women can't
they can do a lot more than a woman
they are permitted to do more than women

12. —they are strong, have more physical ability
they have the strength to do many things women cannot do

they are strong, virile and desirable
they have greater endurance

13. —they are here; for no special reason
their living
just plain lucky
they are

Unclassified
they always can come home to a happy home after a hard
days work with tension

I-4

At this level men are considered lucky because they have opportunities for achievement and responsibility and leadership. On the other hand, they have fewer responsibilities in relation to home and children, and women love, admire, and support them. The I-4 subject mentions the interesting and challenging experiences and opportunities for achievement open to men outside the home. Where the I-3 woman may state that men "get by with so much a woman can't," the I-4 woman mentions differences in social restrictions, standards, and freedom allowed the two sexes. Several categories placed at this level are concerned with men's roles, explicitly that their roles are clearly defined and that they can be leaders and have authority, implicitly that theirs is the dominant role in dating and marriage. Where physical differences are of primary importance at I-3 and below, social expectations are of central importance at I-4 and above.

1. —they are leaders, have authority, make decisions, take responsibility (Δ, 3; I-3, 18; I-3/4, 1)
they seem to rule the world
they can be community leaders
they are by nature endowed with a measure of authority
they are dominant
they are the head of the household and most important decisisions are up to them
they have a great responsible
they have the responsibility for establishing a home and providing for their families

2. —it's a man's world
they belong in a mans world
it still is a man's world

the world is in their favor
they make most of the rules

3. —women admire, love, support them; share their lives (I-3/4, 2; I-4/5, 3)
   women love them
   women will give them attention & encouragement
   women usually help build up there ego & it makes them feel important
   they are respected and loved by their families
   they generally come first in a woman's life
   they have women to interest them, share their hopes and dreams

4. —they have the choice, the initiative, the advantage in dating (Δ, 3; I-3/4, 3)
   they can choose the girls they want, but many times they can't get them
   they can pick and choose
   in courtship they do not have to sit back and wait for the other person to take the initiative
   they can make the first step in starting a romance
   it is their place to take the initiative in any relationship with a woman
   they have the upper hand in chosing dates
   they have the advantage in the dating game

5. —they have freedom of action, more social freedom (I-3, 12, 13; I-3/4, 4, 5)
   they can travel anywhere, anytime
   they are freer to move about in the social and business world
   they can travel alone go places without an escort
   they have more freedom than women to experience adventure and excitement
   they have more freedom in society
   they can be more socially mobile than woman
   they are under less pressure to conform
   they are easier able to choose their social activities

6. —their independence, freedom is different from women's (I-3, 12; I-3/4, 5; I-4/5, 1)
   they have an independence and freedom a woman can never achive
   they have freedoms that women do not have
   they have a type of independence which is different from that of a woman

*they have a degree of independence, even when married, that
is unknown to a woman*

7. —they are free of household, child responsibilities, worries
   (I-3, 9, 10, 11; I-3/4, 9)
   *they dont have to worries as much about family affair as
   women*
   they need not worry about housework
   *—The only worry they have is making money to support his
   family*
   *they don't always have to worry about running the house and
   paying all the bills*
   they have less responsibility in housekeeping

8. —they have fewer restrictions, are not as apt to be judged by
   others (I-3, 14)
   they do not have so many restrictions
   in many ways they lack the restrictions placed on girls
   the double standard favors them
   no matter what they do they still have a good reputation
   they are never disgraced
   *they do not have to answer to anyone they do what they
   want to*

9. —they are more stable, stronger emotionally, can blow off
   steam (I-3/4, 6; I-4/5, 3, 4; I-5, 1)
   they take hardships easier than most women
   *they are usually more able to be brave in unfortunate situ-
   ations*
   they have more even emotional systems
   they are just men! and are able to shrug things off
   they have more outlet for excess energy

10. —they can pursue a larger variety, more interesting careers;
    they gain more satisfaction in their work (I-3, 8; I-3/4, 10;
    I-4/5, 6; I-5, 2)
    there are wider fields open to them than those open to women
    *they are more often positioned in occupations which are the
    most challenging and interesting*
    their jobs are so meaningful
    they can often find interesting work and can do it well
    they have more freedom occupation wise

11. —they have wider interests; they can be with different, more
    interesting people; they are not tied to routine (I-3, 11;
    I-3/4, 4)

they have variety in their life
they are not expected to have limited interests
there are so many vistas open to them
they meet many interesting people
they are not in the same rut as women
they get out and meet more people and have a change of
routine
they can have an independent life outside the home

12. —they are better able to get ahead, achieve more, shape their own lives (I-3/4, 10; I-5, 2)
they have the ability to get ahead and do more things than
women
they can rise in their field of business and achieve fame
any height can be reached if ambition is present
they have less trouble in proving their ability in any particu-
lar area
they can strive toward more intensified educational goals
they can make the most of life as can women
, it is easier for them to find a place in life
they can do so many things with their lives

13. Advantages given men by social mores
they are given more freedom in this society—they are not ex-
pected to conform as much as women
different and more liberal standards are allowed them
they can experience so many things that are taboo for women
they have a less rigid code than women
they are allowed more freedom in our society than are women

14. —their roles are clearly defined (I-4/5, 5)
their role in life is more easily defined
their role in society is defined—which sometimes is a detre-
ment

15. —they are part of the human race
they were made in the image of God
they are able to take part in giving life to another
they too are rational animals with a soul and free will

16. —they think they are

17. —they are not luckier than women (I-3, 21)
again, I don't know if they are
I disagree. I think they live hard lifes

Unclassified
they do not have to dependent as long as women

I-4/5

A new idea expressed at this level is that man's behavior is less determined by his emotional makeup than is woman's. At lower levels such differences are implicitly or explicitly attributed to differing social standards. To say that men are lucky because their families depend on them is a reversal of the stem pull; it gives duties the status of privileges. Several categories placed at I-4/5 are variations on themes found at lower levels. At I-4/5 the appearance of independence is differentiated from reality. Instead of freedom from household and family responsibilities (I-4), freedom from conflicting career-family demands may be mentioned. Where the I-4 subject values freedom of action and social freedom, the I-4/5 subject values freedom of expression. Other responses placed here as examples are either elaborations of I-4 themes or responses with a light touch, "they know that they are gay, charming, handsome and wonderful."

1. Emotional independence (I-4, 6)
   they have always enjoyed a sense of independence and have not been weighed down by affections
   they can be just friends with other men, without forming attachments the way women are thought to (Remember I'm in high school)
   they can isolate sexual involvement from other areas of life more easily than women
   love isn't their entire life or as great a part of life
   they are not so dependent on others for their love

2. —they give the appearance of independence, self-confidence (I-3, 12)
   they can appear to be very independent of others
   they seem so independent
   the are able to give the appearance of great self-confidence
   they usually seem less insecure & more self confident of finding a mate

3. —they are the object of dependence; give strength, protection (I-3, 18; I-4, 3, 9)
   they are the object of great dependence in marriage
   women often look to them for support
   they can give support and strength in a crisis and in everyday living
   they are the stronger sex and must supply strength and comfort for the women

they can raise and protect a family

they are capable of earning a living and I, as a wife, am really dependent upon my husband because I have never really earned a living

4. —they can express themselves openly (I-3/4, 6; I-4, 9)

they are allowed, in their relationships w each other to be more open

they are more free to overtly express their feelings

they are less frowned upon when they express their feelings overtly

5. Freedom from career-family conflicts (I-4, 14)

they are not as torn between career-family and social-domestic pressures as are women

their role in life is not so seriously divided between a vocation and a family

it is easier and more acceptable for them to become successful in their chosen careers

6. —they can use their knowledge, express their talents (I-4, 10; I-5, 2)

if they have chosen the right profession they can never be bored. If they spend a lot on education it is worth it as they use their knowledge

Unclassified

they have the opportunity to win the respect and admiration of others for success in jobs and providing for a sound home

women usually love men more fiercely & wholly than men love women

they are less prone to self-evaluation than women

they can void with less fuss and bother (especially handy for travelling!)

they know that they are gay, charming, handsome and wonderful

they have self knowledge that they are boss. If they are real men they are boss

lets face it is still a man's world, more specifically, the white man, although it is gradually changing

I-5

Classed I-5 are the familiar themes of self-realization, concern for the meaningfulness of one's goals, and conceptual complexity. To say that men are lucky because they are less subject to trivial problems is to evaluate or take a distance from the familiar problems of women, which at I-4 are seen as worries and responsibilities.

1. Less subject to trivial problems and worries (I-4, 9)

> *they do have more outlets than women and because many of them don't seem to worry about little things*
>
> *many of them seem to have a knack for shutting out trivial things and concentrating on the central issue*
>
> *they are less troubled by the vanities women subject themselves to*

2. Self-realization, self-development (I-4, 10, 12; I-4/5, 6)

> *they have more opportunities to practice and develop their intellectual capabilities and interests*
>
> *they are more readily accepted as having worth (very generally speaking) proving themselves comes second not first as in the case of women*

3. Three contrasting facets of an I-4 idea

> *they get to make all the important decisions, of state family, and religion*

Unclassified

> *when they are "loved" all the way their goals become more meaningful*
>
> *as the aggressor, they are not so restricted as are women in taking the initiative in in forming and maintaining and determining relationships with women*
>
> *they think, and woman think that the world is more open to them and I do think they are more free*

I-6

The one example placed at this level not only combines the contrasting ideas of choices, roles, and demands, but goes beyond the I-5 level in weighing and evaluating differing role expectations.

Unclassified

> *they have many choices, as do women, of occupational roles and there is not the necessity to conform to the "good housekeeper, etc. complex" but on the other hand the demands of the economic world probably outweigh this*

When They Talked About Sex, I—

The most frequent categories of response to this stem are "listened" and "joined in." Both occur at all I-levels and are frequent at the I-3 level, hence are classed there. Since they describe a social interaction in terms of behavior and a feeling-provoking subject without feeling, they also belong at this level theoretically. Seeing oneself as simultaneously listening and joining in, however, does not occur below I-3 and is somewhat more frequent at I-4. "Joined in" is more frequently expressed as "participated," "discussed with them," or "contributed" at I-3/4. At higher levels a more genuine sense of participation is evident. Because of the subtle changes in responses as one goes up the scale, discriminations may be hard to make, especially between I-3/4 and I-4.

251

Most categories below I-3 concern simple evasion of the topic or direct expression of impulse, such as sex, anger, or fear. The I-3 subject tends to describe what is happening in terms of behavior; the I-3/4 tends to describe what is happening in terms of interest and of feelings, particularly embarrassment and discomfort, or the denial that they are being experienced. Many responses at the I-4 level reflect perspective—a sense of purpose and an increased sense of choice and participation, both in relation to the group and to one self. Whether one listens or joins in depends on the appropriateness of time, place, company. Similar ideas are expressed at the I-4/5 level, but with increased time perspective or with greater abstraction. At the I-5 level there is concern for causation of one's own and others' attitudes and for deeper meanings or philosophy about sex. Note that though in the past tense, the stem does not indicate how far in the past it refers to. Most persons seem to interpret it with reference to the immediate past.

I-2

Most I-2 subjects give responses to this stem that cannot be distinguished from those given by subjects at higher levels. The classifiable responses describe a negative or an impulsive reaction to the situation. "Agree" is placed at this level because of its indiscriminate quality.

1. —get sick; get mad
   could kick them in the pants
   they make me sick

2. —go home (Δ/3, 1)

3. —think it's bad, nasty (I-3, 7; I-3/4, 14)

4. —think of boys and girls
   say you are talking about Johnny and Diane

Unclassified
   agree
   hell

DELTA

While there are few characteristic Delta responses to this item, those that do occur either reflect a need for maintaining the appearance of invulnerability or admit sexual desire. Sexual desire is seen as a physiological response rather than an interpersonal relation.

1. —ignore them; avoid the question ($\Delta/3$, 1, 2; I-3, 4)
   disappear from anyone who is saying it

2. —laughed

3. Direct expression of sexual thoughts or desire
   get the urge to be loved
   pitched in my feelings I love sex can't live without it
   get very hot blooded

4. —try to control myself
   listen, cause I wont get in trouble, also I know what I'll be doing
   leave the room for I don't know that much about it, and I wouldn't want to make a fool of myself

Unclassified
ll leve that to your thought

DELTA/3

Four categories are placed at this level, somewhat arbitrarily. Responses such as "leave" occur at I-2, but are more frequent at Delta/3 and I-3. The responses in this category are quite similar to "avoid the question" at Delta; the difference is in the specific reference at Delta ("disappear from anyone who is saying it"), which is lacking in the Delta/3 responses. They are rare above I-3. Phrasing of this response in the past tense or qualifying it is enough to raise the rating to I-3. "Got scared" is suggestive of concern for impulse control in a form theoretically compatible with the Delta/3 transition. The response is too rare to confirm this rating empirically. "Kept quiet" may also be indicative of concern for impulse control. "Enjoy it, like it" are responses that occur at the lowest levels and also, but rarely, in the I-3 to I-4 range. In this case the Delta/3 rating is a compromise for a category that seems both empirically and theoretically compatible with either a higher (probably I-3/4) or lower (probably 1-2) rating.

1. —leave; go out of the room (I-2, 2; Δ, 1; I-3, 3)
   walk out door

2. —kept quiet (Δ, 1; I-3, 2; I-3/4, 13)
   had nothing to say
   never talk along with them

3. —enjoy it, like it
   joined in an enjoyed it

4. —got scared (I-3/4, 1)

I-3

Although the range of reactions reported in answer to this item is not much different at I-3 than at I-4 and higher, the way of expressing them shifts. Rather than expressing interest, the I-3 subject "listened" or "joins in." Although she may say she "didn't like it," the I-3 is more apt to say she "decided to leave" or "changed the subject." Actions are the overriding theme at this level.

**1. —joined in; talk with them (I-3/4, 10, 11, 12; I-4, 5)
   do too
   general put my two cents in
   usually have something to say about the subject
   enter into the conversation
   usually ask questions

**2. —listened; learned a lot (Δ/3, 2; I-3/4, 5, 6, 7; I-4, 2, 4, 5, 6)
   usually listen
   thought it was educational

3. —left; like to leave (Δ/3, 1)
   walked away
   withdrew
   excuse my self

4. —change the subject (Δ, 1)
   usually change the topic
   try to change the subject

5. —blushed (I-3/4, 2)

6. —thought it natural, a normal thing

7. —don't like it (I-2, 3; I-3/4, 14)
   don't care for that
   don't like in mixed group
   didn't in my home

Unclassified
   turned my ear away

I-3/4

The most frequent I-3/4 reactions are to report uncomfortable feelings, especially embarrassment, or to deny them. Rather than simply listening, the I-3/4 subject listens with interest. Rather than simply joining in, she participates in or contributes to the discussion. Thus this level is manifest chiefly by greater awareness of her feelings or by a more differentiated notion of what she is doing. Emphasis is also given to learning about and understanding sex.

1. Uncomfortable feelings (Δ/3, 4)
   feel self-conscious
   felt a little funny
   felt a little on edge
   usually felt kind of shy
   felt afraid to express my own feelings

2. —was embarrassed (I-3, 5; I-4, 9)
   was embarrassed at first
   sometimes feel embarrassed
   got so embarrassed I wanted to hide

3. —was not embarrassed, shocked
   took it in it's stride
   talked right along without feeling funny at all
   when they talk about sex it dosent Bother me

4. —was bored; was not interested
   listened without paying much attention
   don't have too much opinion one way or another

*5. —was interested; listened carefully (I-3, 2; I-4, 1, 9)
   was all ears
   wanted to talk with them
   am always interested because it is a natural thing
   joined in as it was interesting

6. —listen and learn; learn something; was curious (I-3, 2; I-4, 2; I-5, 2)
   listened and many of my questions were answered
   listen, because you learn my listening

7. —listen for their viewpoint (I-3, 2; I-4, 3; I-4/5, 3)
   listened because I wanted to know their views
   listened to find out what other people felt about it
   usually listen to see how much they really know

8. —did not understand; tried to understand (I-4, 9; I-4/5, 1)
   didn't know what I was talking about
   wasn't aware of what they were talking about
   didn't know the meaning of their jokes
   was pretty naive

9. Try to be mature, intelligent, objective
   try to be liberal & educated at the same time
   viewed the whole thing objectively
   was clear minded
   try to hold a mature attitute toward the conversation
   try to discuss it in an intelligent way

10. —gave my opinion, point of view (I-3, 1; I-4, 4, 5)
    say what I think
    contributed my ideas
    engage in the conversation to present my views
    should join in & discuss my point of view on the subject

11. —tried to explain; answer sensibly (I-3, 1; I-4, 4, 5)
    tried to explain all of the questions
    explained what they wanted to know
    join in if there is some information I can give

12. —participated; discussed it with them; contributed (I-3, 1; I-4, 5)
    became involved in the conversation
    was able to discuss it freely with them
    add to the conversation
    helped the discussion along with ease

13. —sometimes participate; don't say much (Δ/3, 2)
    may or may not joint
    rarely participated
    didn't have too much to add to the conversation

14. Subject discussed in wrong way, too much, not seriously enough (I-2, 3; I-3, 7; I-4, 2, 7; I-4/5, 4)
    feel they sometimes make a game of it
    was somewhat annoyed because they made it sound dirty
    think it not right to talk about it
    listened—unless "too nasty"

15. Concern with privacy of the matter (I-4, 7)
    think that is a subject to talk about private
    said sex is too personal to discuss

feel there is a time and place for everything
believe that sould be discuss between man & wife no one else

I-4

I-4 subjects are interested in knowledge, information, and misinformation. Comparison of one's own with others' opinions is another recurrent I-4 theme, comparisons being rare at lower levels. Inner standards of propriety are shown in stating that participation is contingent on time, place, other participants. While a feeling that the discussion was wrong—or all right—may be expressed occasionally at a lower level (I-3/4), the idea that the rightness or wrongness is contingent is characteristic at I-4.

1. —was interested (elaborated) (I-3/4, 5; I-4/5, 3, 4)
   was interested but at the same time, embarrassed
   was usually very interested, for it is nothing to be ashamed of and should not be feared or shamed
   usually was very interested and sometimes amused
   was interested but felt they treated it wrongly

2. Evaluation of information (I-3, 2; I-3/4, 6, 14; I-4/5, 2, 3)
   learned something true, but other things they just made up
   knew they had not been instructed at home
   felt they had a very wrong concept
   began to wondered if they really understood it
   found it informative, & helpful

3. Comparison with others' opinions, views, ideas, attitudes (I-3/4, 7; I-4/5, 3)
   found that others had similar questions
   found that I had definite views which differed from most

4. —listened and gave my opinion, ideas, point of view (I-3, 2; I-3/4, 10, 11)
   listened too and maybe would add my point of view
   asked questions and contributed my opinions

5. —listen and join in; listened and participated (I-3, 1, 2; I-3/4, 10, 11, 12)
   listened and discussed it, too
   listened and contributed

6. —listened but said nothing, little (I-3, 2)
   usually would rather listen than to participate in discussion

Was always eager to listen but I never replied to any questions asked

*7. Participation contingent upon how subject is handled, with whom it is discussed (I-3/4, 14, 15; I-4/5, 4)

do not avoid it, if they do not get inhuman about it

listened unless it became vulgar

shyed away at first because there is a time and place for everything

try to change the subject, unless it should be a serious conversation

never liked it, but I talk·to my daughter about it

Listen if educational, otherwise No

8. Participation contingent upon own feelings, knowledge

listen and sometimes join provided I have something pertinent to say

clam up because I know so little as for a correct names, etc.

enjoyed it because I think sex is one of the most wonderful things God created

listen and make sure I know what they are talking about before answering

9. Description of former feelings and reactions (I-3/4, 2, 5, 8; I-4/5, 1)

was interested and respected what they said

was as interested as any other child was

used to get embarassed, but I don't any more unless people use it to be dirty

felt as though I could not fully understand it until I experienced it myself

listened. That is, when I was ten

wasn't really astounded having discussed it with Mother and elder sisters

Unclassified

was careful not to get too involved

felt it was a good general topic if kept impersonal

tried to make them view it in a more mature manner

I-4/5

Responses at the I-4/5 level involve an ability to evaluate and place in perspective sexual discussions, which is absent at lower levels. One such category concerns evaluation of past knowledge and feelings in terms of one's immaturity. Another category concerns evaluation of the interpersonal relationship within which a sexual discussion may take place. Discussion of sex may even be viewed as a means of understanding and communicating with others rather than as an end in itself. Like the I-4 subject, the I-4/5 woman may see participation as contingent on the circumstances, but unlike the I-4 subject she can express the general principle as well as the concrete contingency. Her more abstract orientation is also reflected in seeing sex as a "universal language." Each of the responses in the compound category contains an observation of the subject's feelings as well as actions.

1. Evaluation of past understanding (I-3/4, 8; I-4, 9)
    listened, giggled as a girl, thought immoral, was naive
    was confused as my friends were two years older than I at the time. I was 10 and very immature
    was only 11 and hadn't grown up but I told them I knew all about it and that it meant having babies and things and I was so shy
    as a youngster often cringed thinking it to be something dark and sinister

2. Evaluation of or concern with another's reaction (I-4, 2; I-5, 1)
    recalled my parents' reluctants to discuss such with me
    realized that that they were trying to appear "in the know"
    usually join in the discussion & shock others with my frankness
    felt they weren't entirely happy in their relationship
    always listened because my parents said little and the school pretended it didn't exist
    usually listened eagerly because my mother never would talk about it, she treated it a something bad

3. Source of information about or means of communication with others (I-3/4, 7; I-4, 1, 2, 3; I-5, 1)
    always joined in, because it's a universal language
    was sometimes amazed at the different aspect sex play's in their lives
    was interested in their widely different attitudes toward it
    can really tell how or what a person is. Sex is what you make it!

4. High-level moral dichotomy (I-3/4, 14; I-4, 1, 7)
    was interested if it was a mature discussion—then I participated too. If it was dirty, I showed my disgust

*did not feel embarrassed because they were being sensible
about it & not acting like children*

*get interested, as long as it is educational or "cute" but not
vulgar*

*was interested if it was treated with respect; repelled when it
was vulgar or ignorant*

*listened or joined in the discussion, if it was sensible and
in good taste, otherwise I was indifferent or changed the
subject*

*was not embarased because there discussion was very educa-
tional and not vulgar in any way*

5. Compound response, at least three elements, feelings and actions

*respected their remarks and contributed my ideas but did not
prolong the subject*

*felt uneasy, but joined in, and then tried to change the sub-
ject*

*listened, laughed if the point was told in joke fashion, con-
tributed a bit, and wasn't bothered by the topic of conversation*

Unclassified

was avid for information

*It depends on the frame of reference. If its being taken as a
joke i don't listen, I may leave*

*was not in a particularly good position to offer much that
was constructive from experience gained first-hand*

I-5

The I-5 subject sees sex not just as a topic involving right and
wrong information to be learned and evaluated, but a topic with deeper
meanings in relation to life as a whole. People discuss the subject for varying reasons and motivations that are not always discernible. One's current feelings and reactions result from past experiences. The response
"usually took a righteous stand of some sort" is classed as concern with
motivation, but it also shows humor and an unusual degree of self-
criticism.

1. Concern with reasons, motivations (I-4/5, 2, 3)

usually took a righteous stand of some sort

wondered what their real motivation was

wondered why they were so reluctant to say what they meant feel old fashioned and out of date because I was taught not to talk about it

am very interested in how others feel because I don't feel I have the right feeling

try to listen to discover whether they are being serious or making light of a subject not to be taken unseriously

2. Concern for deeper meanings (I-3/4, 6)

listened so I could know of its real meaning

could clarify my philosophy on the subject

Unclassified

felt they did not always consider the feeling which followed this subject

accept well any scientific, medical or moral aspects, but can not be patient with the flippancy

At Times She Worried About—

The word "she" in this stem is obviously ambiguous. To judge by the answers, it is almost always taken to mean either subject or Mother. There are two ways to make a self-centered response, to assume that "she" refers to oneself, or to assume that "she" means Mother but that Mother worries about subject. Most subjects interpret the stem in one of these two ways.

Clear differences in content between lower and higher level responses are not to be found. Worry about oneself, family, life, the future, others' opinions, as well as belittling of worry itself, occur at all levels. More helpful in making discriminations is capacity for attaining some distance from problems of the moment: discriminating important from un-

262

important worries; conceiving them as "problems" or as "issues" rather than "things"; time perspective; and distinguishing one's own view from someone else's. The inadequacy of abstractness-concreteness as a measure of ego level is well illustrated by this item. In some respects the progress from I-3 to I-4 is one of increasing abstractness, from "money" to "financial problems"; in other respects progress is in terms of increasing concreteness, from "my sister" to "my sister on dates."

There are few pathognomonically low-level responses. The distinguishable categories seem to indicate complete submersion in problems of the moment, whether "little things," struggle with Mother or husband, or fear of pregnancy. The most characteristically low concern is sex, whether in terms of getting in trouble or of "sex appeal." At the I-3 level the worries are about concrete things, looks, job, money, and so on. There is a glimmer that some problems are not worth worrying about ("littlest things"), but time perspective is rare and comparison of one's own view of a problem with someone else's view is virtually absent prior to I-4. Responses at the I-3/4 level are predominantly concerned with one's social behavior: "how she looks to others," "how she gets along with others," or "doing the right thing." Prominent at I-4 are a longer time perspective ("growing up") and self-evaluation ("foolish fancies," "not being able to play the cello well"). Above I-4 there is characteristically some distance from one's worries and comparison of two points of view or two points in time.

I-2

Many I-2 subjects give responses beginning with or consisting of "me"; however, these are classed at Delta/3 because they occur as frequently at I-3 and I-3/4, and occasionally are seen at higher levels. The only category at I-2 is a kind of put-off, "things."

1. —things (I-3, 9, 10; I-4, 1; I-5, 1)
   other things
   something
   different things
   little thing

DELTA

The predominant concern at the Delta level is sex, though not all such responses are classed here. Many of the responses here have overtones of trouble or of competition.

1. —getting pregnant; if she was pregnant (I-3/4, 6; I-4, 9)
   my period
   having a baby which had no father

2. —boys; men (I-3, 2)
   sometimes I worried about Chuck, especially when I thought
   he ran away

3. —her sex life (I-3/4, 4)
   if she had any sex appeal
   her reputation as a slut. She didn't know if she was known
   enough

4. —her husband going out on her (I-3, 1; I-4, 10)
   her husband dating other women when he came in at 2:00 in
   the morning

Unclassified
   competition

DELTA/3

The categories at this level are compromises. In each case there are proportionately more responses below I-3, but the range is from I-2 or Delta to I-4 or I-4/5. On other stems emphasis on getting into trouble is characteristic of the Delta subject. A good many of such responses on this stem, however, come from adolescent protocols which range in ego level from Delta to I-4. Mother worrying about her daughter getting into trouble or going on dates (basically identical worries) and daughter resenting such concern are probably more related to age than to ego level. Similarly, "B.O." can be the kind of hostile humor typical of a Delta subject, but it is also a prevalent worry of teenagers. Again, most of these responses came from adolescent protocols varying in ego level.

*1. —me (I-3, 3, 6)
   me outside playing
   me being away from home
   me, more than anyone else
   She always worries about me
   me too much

2. —me getting into trouble; me when I go out (I-3/4, 6)
   me, thinking I might get into trouble
   where I was and what I was doing
   me going with the wrong kind of boys
   her mother seeing her with a boy

*what was happening when I sat in front of the house with my
boyfriend*

3. —bad breath; perspiration (I-3, 4)
   B.O.

I-3

The I-3 subject states rather than evaluates, and sees in concrete terms what the I-4 subject sees more abstractly. Thus she worries about "money" rather than "financial problems" (I-4), about "her job" rather than "doing a good job" (I-4), and about "her children" rather than "her children's problems and happiness" (I-4).

The I-3 subject may deny worries, "nothing," or be very general, "everything." The "little things" which some I-2 subjects mention are here "littlest things," but not yet clearly labeled "trivial" or "insignificant" (I-4). These are fine discriminations, but below I-3 we have not seen the notion of trivial or unimportant problems, while above I-4 we have not seen the response "little things" or its obvious variations.

**1. Specific members of her family (Δ, 4; I-4, 10)
    her Husband
    her sister's children
    her son who was away
    me and my family

2. —friends; other people (Δ, 2)
   her boyfriend
   everyone

3. —herself (Δ/3, 1; I-4, 15)
   herself too much

*4. Appearance (concrete reference) (Δ/3, 3; I-3/4, 1)
   the way she walked
   what she was going to wear
   her figure
   her weight
   being ugly

*5. —her health; my health (I-3/4, 2; I-4, 10)
   my mother that is; about my getting sick and leaving
   her ulcers
   whether I got enough sleep
   my eating so little

6. —what's happening to the children (to me) (Δ/3, 1; I-4, 10;
I-4/5, 2)
how the kids and I are doing
how I am doing
how her family was getting along, if they had enough to eat,
ect.
how baby was doing

*7. —her job; her grades; school; tests (I-3/4, 10; I-4, 3, 4, 5)
Being taken out of School
what her grade would be
the finals at school
getting poor grades

*8. —money; bills; household expenses (I-4, 11)
how she would get the money to buy food
where the next meal is coming from
how the bills were going to be paid
finances

*9. —everything; a lot of things (I-2, 1; I-4, 1; I-4/5, 1)
anything that comes to mind
all kinds of goodies
a variety of things

10. —the littlest things (I-2, 1; I-4, 1; I-4/5, 1; I-5, 1)
minute things
small household things

11. Immediate concerns; concrete, free associations
the way the house looked
travling
planning meals
the rain and sleet
not being able to go out and play

12. —nothing
nothing at all

13. Evasion
who is she?
huh!
no thoughts
I do not know who she is

Unclassified
that a disaster is forthcoming

I-3/4

At the I-3/4 level social, not physical, concerns are the most prominent: "pleasing," "being popular," or "doing the right thing." Presumably
this emphasis explains why "her appearance" is I-3/4 while a specific response such as "being ugly" is I-3; the latter is more physical and the
former more social. It is not surprising, then, that concern with failure
also falls at I-3/4. A glimmer of the self-evaluation typical of the I-4 is
apparent in brief statements about worrisome personality traits or inner
states, such as "my depression," "being lonely." Responses in the category
"my late hours; me not behaving" come from Delta to I-4 protocols. The
category is placed here because such responses more frequently occur
above I-3. Like "my getting into trouble; me when I go out" (Delta/3),
however, this category may be more a function of age than ego level.

*1. —her appearance; her looks (I-3, 4; I-4, 13)

  2. —others' health, welfare (I-3, 5; I-4, 10, 17)
      his health
      her husband's health
      her mother's health
      her children's health
      the welfare of her children

  3. —pleasing, getting along with people; (not) being liked (I-4,
      13, 14; I-4/5, 4)
      how to get along with men
      whether she'd be accepted by the crowd, her date, etc.
      whether people liked her for what she is
      her relationship with her husband
      my not getting along
      not being loved
      finding love

  4. —(not) being popular; getting dates; getting married (Δ,
      3; I-4, 9; I-4/5, 4)
      her love life
      seeing Frank again
      her problems with dating
      not having any boy-friends

  5. —what others thought, would say (I-4, 13, 14)
      other people's opinions
      what the neighbors would think
      his familys' opinions
      what her friends would say

6. —my late hours; me not behaving (Δ, 1; Δ/3, 2)
   me coming home alone
   my being a tom boy
   me being out late

7. —saying the proper thing (I-4, 12)
   what she had said
   talking about others

8. —doing, not doing the right thing (I-4, 5, 6, 8; I-4/5, 5)
   not being able to do things right
   doing what should be done
   doing the right thing for Jimmy
   pleasing the wrong people

9. —getting things done (I-4, 4, 7; I-4/5, 5)
   me, if I would ever get finish with my work
   about household tasks that were undone
   finishing what she had begun

10. —failure; finishing school; getting a job (I-3, 7; I-4, 3, 4, 5, 7)
    not passing anatomy
    flunking tests in school
    Finishing college
    getting a job

11. Personality traits or inner states (I-4/5, 5)
    being smart enough
    being nervous
    the things she thought about
    fears without any reason
    her inadequacy
    her attitude toward other people
    my tendency to overwork

Unclassified
   sex
   her problems
   my lack of interest in education

I-4

Specific to this level are responses evaluating worries as trivial or unnecessary, and conceiving them as problems, decisions, or choices, rather than simply "things," "money," "her daughter." There is a genuine sense of self-evaluation, "her inability to tolerate physical illnesses" (I-4) versus "herself" (I-3) or "her inadequacy" (I-3/4). Time is a theme that runs through a number of categories at this level. Responses such as "life" or "the future" come from a wide range of ego levels and are placed here as a compromise. Besides expressing concern about time limitations and the future, the I-4 subject who says that she worries about trivial matters is implicitly criticizing herself for wasting time and energy. The theme of being liked, prominent at I-3/4, is here expressed either as concern with rejection or acceptance, or as concern with how others think of her.

*1. —unimportant, trivial things; unnecessary things (I-2, 1; I-3, 9, 10; I-4/5, 1; I-5, 1)
some of the silliest things
trifles that didn't deserve so much attention
foolish fancies
things that she souldn't
things that never happened
small unmeaningful things
me although she needn't have

*2. —the future, life (I-4/5, 6; I-5, 2)
getting old
growing up
what was going to happen next
me and my final outcome

3. —her career; getting into college (I-3, 7; I-3/4, 10)
her vocation
her vocation in life that was to come later
getting into the college of her choice
her not being accepted into college

4. Achievement; ambition; success (I-3, 7; I-3/4, 9, 10; I-4/5, 6; I-5, 2)
finding her ambition in life
whether or not I would make it a career or not
how she would accomplish all she wanted to
her ability to suceed & do anything in the world
getting boys and success

5. —(not) doing a good job (I-3, 7; I-3/4, 8, 10)
doing well on the divisions
not being competent in her chosen role
not being able to play the cello well

6. —not living up to own (others') standards (not specified)
   (I-3/4, 8)
   not doing what she felt was right
   doing what displeased her parents
   my not doing the things she thought I should be doing

7. Time limitations (I-3/4, 9, 10)
   being pushed for time
   not having enough time to do what she wanted
   having too much to do
   the pace one must keep in life
   the slow progress she was making

8. Decision, choice (I-3/4, 8)
   whether I have made the right decisions
   how her parents would feel about the decisions that she made

9. Adequacy, adjustment as wife and mother (Δ, 1; I-3/4, 4;
   I-4/5, 4)
   not having children
   how her marriage would turn out
   whether she should marry even if she "just married anyone"
   *was she going to be a good Christian, a good wife, and a good
      mother*
   the rearing of my children in a confussed world

10. —her family's problems (Δ, 4; I-3, 1, 5, 6; I-3/4, 2)
    my sister on dates
    us her children, eating, health, and welfare
    how her 2 year old daughter would feel toward her new baby
    her husband's career

11. —financial problems (I-3, 8)
    financial matters
    not making enough money
    making ends meet

12. Problems with expression, communication (I-3/4, 7)
    her opportunities to express herself
    not being able to express herself
    her inability to communicate with others

13. —what people thought of her (I-3/4, 1, 3, 5)
    the impression she had made on others
    other people's opinion of her
    how she looked to others

his feelings for her
people laughing at her

14. —being rejected; not being accepted (I-3/4, 3, 5; I-5, 3)
    whether or not people would accept her
    why she was unpopular with other people
    being left alone
    herself and why she felt left out

15. —her identity (I-3, 3; I-4/5, 6)
    herself and the kind of person she really is
    who she was

16. —social problems; the cruelty of others (I-4/5, 5)
    war
    car accidents
    the starving people, but, as many people, she took no action
    the lack of consideration people have for others

17. Death of family members or friends (I-3/4, 2)
    what would happen to her if her husband got sick or died
    something happening to her husband while he was on a business trip
    whether she would ever see her parents again

Unclassified
    whether her boyfriend would make passes. She was disappointed if he didn't, and mad if he did
    a friend who needed love and care and was not getting it
    what she could do to solve her problems

I-4/5

At this level belittling of worry takes the form of worry about "things that could not be prevented." Instead of worrying about being liked or what other people think, the I-4/5 subject is concerned about mutuality in intimate relationships with family or close friends. She is concerned about values, long-range goals, and her social responsibilities.

Some responses at this level involve an explicit or implied comparison of two views toward some worry. Clearest are the past worries that time has not shown to be justified. Others involve two agents, the inner life of two people, be it two worriers, one worrier and one nonworrier, or two people with problems. Vague as this category may sound, it captures an important aspect of ego development. The ability to see the inner life of other people in the same light as and at the same time as one's own is rare below the I-4 level, and not usual until I-4/5.

1. Unrealistic, useless worries (I-3, 9, 10; I-4, 1; I-5, 1)
   things that could not be prevented
   things that would work themselves out
   the inevitable
   things that were almost impossible
   imaginary illnesses

2. Then versus now (I-3, 6)
   whether I would stop biting my nails. And by the way, I did
   us. But we grew up without broken bones despite our skiing
      activities
   me going out with boys but soon stopped when she found out
      I was adult enough
   me, now she worries about daddy
   other people liking her. She still does.

3. Implied or explicit comparison of two points of view
   why I had worried so much about school
   me when I deemed it so unnecessary
   not being able to make friends and I tried to help her
   many of her own problems and not those of others
   me because I was more interested in Sports. than a social life
   not being accepted by the group she wanted to belong to
   her husband's worrying about her being sick
   things we did that would upset our father

4. Mutuality in intimate relations (I-3/4, 3, 4; I-4, 9; I-5, 3)
   how I'm getting along. is my husband and I real tight
   the lack of harmony at home
   her personal relationships with her closest friend
   what separation during the war would do to my husband and
      me
   why her emotions seemed to get the best of her and why she
      should be cursed with loving one person who didn't love
      her back

5. Feelings of conscience, responsibility (elaborated) (I-3/4, 8, 9, 11; I-4, 16)
   her conscience and if she was doing all she should do, or if
      she would get her period. (My best friend.)
   feeling too responsible for society's shortcomings
   her feeling of helplessness because she was not able to do every
      thing she wanted to do for others

6. —*her goals in life* (I-4, 2, 4, 15; I-5, 2)

what kind of life she would have in the future and whether
*   she would get to persue her desires*
her future and her place in life
herself, her values, and her future
her long-range future plans

Unclassified
the wart on the end of her nose
her ability to put forth her best efforts at all times
God, man, and herself

I-5

Few new themes appear at I-5, but the familiar ones are expressed
with more perspective. Many responses classed I-5 encompass contrasting
facets of a problem; for instance, worrying about small things and avoiding important ones, or concern about doing the right thing but doing as
one planned anyway. Another characteristic of I-5 responses is concern
with abstract and intangible aspects of experience, such as creativity and
meeting standards expected of one.

1. Little things rather than big ones (I-2, 1; I-3, 10; I-4, 1;
   I-4/5, 1)
   small things overlooking major ones
   the small insignificant things, and avoided thinking about im-
   *   portant things*
   little things that seemed momentous because they were so
   *   close to her*

2. Enjoyment of life; loss of zest for life (I-4, 2, 4; I-4/5, 6)
   the future so much she forgot to enjoy the present
   life becoming monotonous
   life, but usually she just enjoyed as much of it as she could
   *   grasp*
   losing her dreams and ideals and falling prey to daily "ruts"
   *   and monotony*

3. —whether she could meet the standards expected of her (I-4,
   14; I-4/5, 4)
   living up to the image of her older brothers and sisters
   her personal failings as judged by the standards of her main
   *   associates*

Unclassified
her creativity—was there any such thing as Creativity?

*whether she was doing the right thing or not but she continued
on with her plans*

I-6

One category, a diverse listing of worries, is put at I-6 on the basis
of two examples, both of which came from I-6 protocols. We have come
across only one other such response, which came from an I-5 protocol.
Listing of any kind on this item is unusual, but to be rated I-6 there must
be both concrete and abstract, both personal and social, both large and
small concerns included.

Also classified here is a poetic response placing a far-reaching social
concern within the context of one's own hopes for life.

1. Mélange (more than three diverse concerns)
    *school, grades, friends, boys, life, bombs, Russia, Goldwater,
    sisters, brothers*
    *money, health, the state of the world, and whether her son
    needed new shoes right now*

Unclassified
    *a war which destroyed the world before she fulfilled her
    dreams*

I Am—

Most answers to this item can be broadly classed as referring to one's circumstances, traits, or feeling states. The largest single category is at I-3, describing circumstances in matter-of-fact terms or the kind of information that can be recorded on an IBM card. Responses in this category rarely occur over I-4 and account for a large proportion of cases below I-3. Responses beginning "lucky" or "fortunate" are also found from I-2 through at least I-4/5, as well as responses such as "who I am" and "what I am." Where there are additional elements in such responses, the scoring should be governed by the added phrases. This item reveals the poverty of usual approaches to the self-concept, which depend only on degree of self-approval. Here we find at low levels (I-2 and Delta) both a shallow self-approval and bitter self-rejection, at middle levels (I-3 and I-3/4) predominantly self-satisfied remarks, while at high levels there are characteristic tempered self-criticisms.

I-2

Since most I-2 responses cannot be distinguished from the concrete descriptive responses at I-3, there is only one category here, stating that subject is good or nice. Theoretically the response "nothing" might be classed here or at Delta, but it is placed at I-3 because we have seen it only on I-3 and I-3/4 protocols.

1. —a good girl; nice (I-3/4, 11)
   always good and respectful
   a young lady a respect lady & nice
   a very pretty child when I want to be I am [age deleted] and
      I have been told to be good so I try
   a Very good woman

Unclassified
I don't know

DELTA

Self-critical responses classed here are global in terms and imply total self-rejection, contrasting with more differentiated and self-accepted self-criticism found at I-4. "Unlucky" is placed at this level while "lucky" is classed I-3. One may be considered lucky or fortunate for a number of reasons, and use of such terms implies a sense of gratitude, which is spelled out at the I-4 level. Unlucky, however, seems to have just one meaning: Fate frowns on me.

1. Complaints against environment
   unlucky
   a girl who no-one really understands
   sick of this place and want to go home
   completely frustrated with selfish people

2. —crazy; stupid
   really at times quite stupid
   crazy and in love

3. —boy crazy
   a sex maniac
   very wild
   a flirt

4. —careful whom I talk to
   very careful with whom I play with

5. Self-rejection (I-3, 6; I-4, 17)
conceited and mean at times when I am in a bad mood
easily hurt, ugly, nosy and not very tactful
dirty-minded, overweight (little) [age deleted]
very ugly

I-3

The largest category answers the question, "Who are you?" in terms of concrete identifying information. Another frequent group of categories answers the question, "What do you feel like right now?" Answers at this level refer to transitory states, whereas at higher levels more enduring qualities are stressed. Self-descriptions refer to socially approved traits and in some cases to socially approved negative traits such as lazy and not smart. Feelings tend to be banal.

**1. Vital statistics: name, age, sex, occupation, marital status, and so on (I-3/4, 2, 3)
a painter
a student
a young lady
a girl I am sleepy too
a married women with two children
an Anglican

*2. Role or function in family (I-3/4, 2; I-4, 14)
a wife and mother
a very proud mother
a very good cook

*3. Immediate feelings: happy, miserable, nervous, etc. (I-3/4, 1; I-4, 1)
happy, and in a good mood so please forgive my foolishness
miserable during this orientation period
bored with this
satisfied
disgusted
sorry I have to answer these questions, because I am tired of writing
very lonesome for a boy

4. Immediate physical states
tired and hungry
in need of sleep

cold
pretty comfortable, right now

5. Immediate actions (I-4, 10)
    taking a test
    going to finish if I can
    not going to go home now
    going on a vacation

6. Appearance (Δ, 5)
    too fat
    very cute
    not so worried about my complextion

7. —average, normal (I-4, 7)
    a average student

8. —friendly, easy to get along with; not very easy going
    out going & extrovertive

9. —kind, considerate, understanding (I-4, 3)
    very kindly toward people
    an understanding person

10. —modest, shy; an introvert
    a person with an inferiority complex
    a very quite person

11. Banal feelings about concrete things, animals, situations (I-3/4, 5, 12)
    glad I have a car
    deathly afraid of squirrels
    worried about getting pregnant
    tired of hearing children all day
    worried about the test next hour

12. —lucky to have the family (friends) I have; happy with my family
    lucky to have such a wonderful husband
    lucky that I have many friends
    very happy about Deborah
    very proud of my father & mother

13. —worried about my family
    anxious about my family
    concerned about my son
    concerned about Kathy
    very concern over the raising of my children

14. —lucky; a lucky person (I-4, 1)
    very fortunate to be here

15. —glad to be a woman, girl
    glad I'm a female

16. —smart, not smart
    a serious intelligent woman
    very slow in life

17. —lazy
    too lazy for my own good

18. —stubborn; determined (I-3/4, 7; I-4, 16)
    over 21 & have a mind of my own
    not the type of person to give up easily

19. —me; myself; who I am
    what I am
    me, first, last & always

Unclassified
    nothing
    getting old!
    a very nervous person
    in fair health

I-3/4

Some I-3 themes are only minimally changed at this level, such as reference to future rather than present occupation or family status, reference to long-term rather than immediate feelings. There also appear striving to do one's best, intimations of concern for long-term life plans, and replacement of social virtues, such as easy to get along with, by inward virtues, such as sincerity. Characteristic is a group of responses referring to self-consciousness and being confused by complexity, in particular, the complexity of a projective test. The I-3/4 subject who sees herself as able to take care of herself compares with the Delta subject who thinks she is old enough to take care of herself, the I-3 person who says she has a mind of her own, and the I-4 subject who talks of being independent. This progression can be seen as an increasingly inward conception of the problem of independence.

*1. —a happy person; usually happy (I-3, 3; I-4, 1)
    content most of the time
    basically happy

happy in my stage of life
about the happiest person I know

2. Status in family or group (I-3, 1, 2)
   an only child
   the youngest of my family
   a member of a wonderful club

3. Reference to future status (I-3, 1; I-4, 9)
   a potential [occupation deleted]
   studying for a career
   hoping to be a [occupation deleted]
   attempting to earn a [degree deleted]

4. —looking forward to marriage, family
   a girl of [age deleted] hoping someday to fall in love and be happily married
   going to be married in about 2 years or less to a wonderful man
   very eager to have my first child
   almost engaged

5. —in love; worried about love (I-3, 11; I-4, 11)
   In love with a wondrerful guy
   worried about my love affair

6. Thoughts, worries about life, the future (vague and general) (I-4, 9, 10)
   a graduate from [deleted] trying to figure out what I will do next
   wondering if I will "make it" the next 2 years
   pleased with my life so far
   hoping for a successful future
   beginning a completely new life
   looking for something out of life
   worried about myself & future; but mostly about myself
   worried about live because I don't know what to do or say about things my friends do
   undecided about my future career

7. —able to take care of myself (I-3, 18; I-4, 16)

8. —busy (I-4, 2)
   always in a hurry
   an active person
   up to my neck in work!
   so busy I can't find time to do the things I like
   always worried about not having enough time for what I want to do

9. —a child of God
    a woman created by God

10. —sincere; conscientious; religious (I-4, 16)
    a person with high principals & hope never to lose them
    not phoney
    frank

11. —trying to be a good person (wife, parent) (I-2, 1; I-4, 12)
    always trying to do my best
    trying to raise my children the best I can

12. Feelings about own actions (I-3, 11)
    very happy in my work
    most happy when I'm successful
    glad I'll be going home soon
    very ashamed of my past
    nervous speaking in front of a crowd

13. —self-conscious; sensitive
    very self-conscious of the people around me
    I suppose sensitive I worrie a lot

14. —unsure, confused (unelaborated) (I-4, 9)
    full of anxieties at the present time
    a worrier
    thoroughly confused right now
    insecure

15. —complex (unelaborated) (I-4, 15)
    a complex person
    impossible to describe by any one adjective or noun

16. —uncertain how to answer these questions (I-4, 19)
    a little stumped for an answer—too many possibilities
    not able to understand all this
    resentful of being asked to do this as I do not feel qualified to
    give intelligent answers

Unclassified
    a person who tries to use common sense
    odd

I-4

At I-4 one finds displayed a greater zest for life, appreciation of its blessings, a beginning sense of individuality, and explicit long-term plans for the future. Some I-4 categories differ from similar responses at I-3/4 by greater emphasis on process, a trend that continues at higher levels. For example, while the I-3/4 subject strives to be good, the I-4 strives to improve. To describe oneself in terms of a combination such as wife, mother, housekeeper is a banality and occurs frequently at the I-3 level. To combine such descriptions with ones from other universes, such as student, citizen, or even woman, is distinctive of the I-4 level. To describe oneself somewhat critically, in terms neither all good nor all bad, is very characteristic for this level. Turning this stem, which invites self-preoccupation, into a remark about society or about people in general, tends also to be indicative of a level I-4 or higher, though one notes complaints against the environment at the Delta level. Remarks about the test evolve from statement at I-3 that one is taking a test, to anxiety over the ambiguity of the task at I-3/4, to speculation at I-4 about what it might reveal.

1. —glad to be alive (I-3, 3, 14; I-3/4, 1)
   lucky, because I love life
   excited about life
   glad I am me
   and I'm glad!
   a lucky person to be whom I am and where I am

2. Interests (I-3/4, 8)
   very interested in art
   very interested in cosmetology and want to learn all I can about it
   interested in many things
   excited about being in [school deleted]

3. —interested in working with, helping people (I-3, 9)
   a relatively considerate person who cares much for people
   a woman who is interested in youth and their future
   trying to always be happy & give happiness
   a woman who cares

4. Appreciation of opportunities, privileges, blessings
   fortunate to have the opportunity to finish my education
   thankful for my many opportunities and experiences—although all of them have not been pleasant
   happy to have had the privilege of being the mother of Jeannette and Diane
   very glad to be myself. And thank God for my blessings

5. Appreciation of good health
   lucky to be able to function normally and to be healthy
   very lucky girl to have 11 brothers and sisters that are all

physically and mentally well and I am also very proud of my parents

6. —a person; an individual; a human being
   a living being
   what I am . . . mainly a human being

7. —an ordinary person (I-3, 7)
   no better than anyone else
   just like any other human female

8. Body and soul
   a thinking reasoning individual possessing a body & soul
   a human being with a supernatural soul & free will

9. Concern with direction, purpose in life (I-3/4, 3, 6, 14)
   not sure what I want to do as an occupation, or to be as a person
   struggling to find my place in life
   beginning to know what I really want out of life
   a girl who strives to reach her ultimate goal
   caught up in the quest of knowledge
   very concerned about making the right choices later on in life

10. Plans, intentions, ambitions (I-3, 5; I-3/4, 6)
    going to work to my capacity
    alive and anxious to become great
    a girl with wonderful ideas, but not the courage to do them
    a [deleted] who has been thru many misfortunes & intends to see that my children don't go through the same

11. Feelings in interpersonal relations (I-3/4, 5; I-4/5, 1)
    sorry for causing mother to worry about me
    still trying to overcome my reaction about sex because my face turns red and I get real scared
    still in love with my husband, but don't want to take him back

12. —trying to improve; more mature (I-3/4, 11)
    a girl striving to be a woman
    a very immature person. I pray that God will help me in everyway possible
    not the person I would like to be
    changing to a better person
    what I am; although I try to improve my faults

13. Social consciousness (I-4/5, 2)
    anxious to contribute something of value to mankind

very disgusted with the world situation especially in the United States

lucky to be alive and living in a free country where so many liberties are offered to me

14. Contrasting roles (I-3, 2)

a woman, wife and mother of 3

[occupation deleted], a girl, and a citizen of the United States

student, human,?—

a wife, a mother, a housekeeper, a student

15. A complex person (elaborated); contradictory attributes (I-3/4, 15; I-5, 1)

eager to be friendly, but shy with new friends

a thousand other people

many, many, people made into one individual

a successful person, but feel insecure at times. I console myself in saying everyone does

a pessimistic optimist

a happy person but discouraged at times

16. Differentiated character traits (often somewhat self-critical) (I-3, 18; I-3/4, 7, 10)

as independent as I like

a very ill-tempered, hard headed, and fun loving woman

too sympathetic when it comes to caring for children

disorganized

an aggressive person

materialistic

a coward

a very self-centered person because I don't like to be around people

inclined to be introspective

often a pessimist

17. Self-accepted self-criticism (I-2, 5)

something, yet nothing, but most of all a very lucky girl

not particularly good looking, but it bothers me not

not a leader, but feel I am a good worker

not extremely smart and try to make up for this with various other activities

useful, but not completely useful

[age deleted], crazy, lovable, and ugly and fat

18. "Secret" revelations

>*a secret spy for the Russians*
>*a witch*
>*ninty-four years old*

19. Speculation about the test (I-3/4, 16)
    curious as to the outcome of this test
    *wondering what you can possibly learn about human behavior
    or thoughts from this test*
    telling a great deal about myself with these responses
Unclassified
    lucky—more than I sometimes remember

I-4/5

The responses at I-4/5 and higher are best thought of as significant elaborations of themes found at the I-4 level. With the exception of expressions of gratification in relation to love and marriage, these responses are so unique that trying to form categories is possibly misleading.

1. Gratification in interpersonal relations (I-4, 11)
   very happy being married to and living with my husband
   *in love in an adult or "real" way and have never be happier
   or had such a sense of belonging & fulfillment*
   *the happiest when I can be in a [occupation deleted] or when
   my husband and I can sit and talk*
   *[physical description deleted] I feel that love is wonderful sex
   is pure*

2. Broad view of human race (I-4, 13)
   *striving to experience as many things as I can & get a broad
   view of how the human race lives*
   a rather complex person—as we all are, I think
   hopeful that the state of man will become universally better

Unclassified
   a woman, a wife, a student, an individual person
   a combination of many dichotomies
   *nut who writes poems scrubs floors or oil paints at 2:00 in the
   morning*
   *an individual who needs to be doing something interesting
   and challenging*
   *happy being who I am and being a woman. I wouldn't want
   to change for I enjoy being a girl*
   *lucky to have to chance to make something out of my life and
   also to be able to have my senses and facilities*

I-5

The one identifiable category here is clear expression of inner conflict.

1. Inner conflict (I-4, 15)
   in love, or so I think, and very happy when we're together, depressed about high school, and worried about college. (Naturally!)
   an introvert, shy, with a desire to be friendly & outgoing
   a very confused person in a world of even more confused people. I seek satisfaction from life in love and a career yet fear I cannot find both

Unclassified
   woman living and creating life
   at times a question mark, at times just a period, but many times an exciting exclamation mark
   too much in love with everything, and I imagine too unrealistic!
   a living, thinking, female, able and ready to compete or comfort

I-6

Unclassified
   aware of human frailty and weaknesses, yet I believe that man can, thru his own efforts, improve his own lot

Item 24

A Woman Feels Good When—

Major themes found in response to this stem are, in approximate order of increasingly interpersonal emphasis: sensual gratification, tension reduction (in a nontechnical sense), demands met, being complimented or appreciated, being loved, being wanted or needed, doing something for others. On the whole, the more interpersonal, the higher the level, but within each theme there are categories representing different levels. Typical of high levels are responses indicating fulfilling one's own inner standards, which is somewhat apart from the sequence of increasing interpersonal emphasis, and complex responses uniting several of the preceding themes.

At low levels feeling good is taken to be an immediate bodily

287

state; at higher levels it tends to refer to a frame of mind and to a longer term. Direct reference to sexual gratification is more likely at the lowest and highest levels than at intermediate ones. One Delta subject responded, "having sex. intercourse with the person she loves." This is different from the I-2 responses because of the reference to "person she loves." One I-3/4 subject responded, "she & her husband have a good sexual relationship." Here there is reference to a long-term relation, in addition to referring to a specific person. The response is, however, banal compared to one classed at I-6, "her sex life goes well, and when, in all respects she and her husband are 'sympatico.' " The latter suggests mutuality and the interrelatedness of sex and other aspects of life.

I-2

Distinctive for this level are a few responses interpreting feeling good as sensual gratification, most commonly but not always sexual. Sexual gratification here is physiological, not interpersonal or mutual. "She is happy" is a tautology; this response does of course occur occasionally at higher levels.

1. Direct reference to sexual gratification (Δ, 1)
   she gets screwed
   she has it
   she has a penis
   being kissed on her neck
   She kisses her man

2. Reference to sensual gratification (Δ, 1)
   sitting down
   eat
   she feels a good soft kitten
   she is sleeping
   she has been drinking

3. —she is happy
   shes in a good move. .

Unclassified
   she crys

DELTA

Responses distinctive for this level mostly have overtones of demands met immediately: you give her what she wants or do what she asks. Going out with a guy can be thought of as a demand met.

1. —she gets what she wants (I-2, 1, 2; I-3, 6)
   man or husband doings the right thing for her
   she gets to go out for a while
   something she wants is done
   she receives love from a man or her husband

2. —she is given something she likes (I-3, 1, 6, 16)
   she is being offered and million dollars
   you buy something for her
   her husband brings home his pay check
   she can go on a shopping spree
   she gets something new

3. —everything goes her way (Δ/3, 1, 2; I-3, 9)
   something nice happen

4. —she is with a man (no implication of continuing relation)
   (I-3, 7; I-3/4, 2)
   a guy takes her out
   she is out
   she has a man around
   she is with her husband
   she's in her husbands arms

Unclassified
   her children does the right thing
   —I take the fifth admement

DELTA/3

One or another way of expressing that everything is all right occurs from I-2 at least through I-3/4, but it is most common below I-3. We have made some admittedly fine discriminations with respect to this type of response. At the Delta level there is the connotation of getting her way. At Delta/3 the connotations are escape from difficulties, including pregnancy and childbirth, or that things are "right." At I-3 there is explicit reference to other family members and to things running smoothly. The implication of harmony is more positive and presumably higher level than that of escape from trouble. The corresponding category at I-3/4 contains translation of things going well into the subject's feelings, "she can relax," often with explicit reference to the rest of the family.

1. —her troubles are over; her problems are solved (Δ, 3; I-3, 15; I-3/4, 8)
   pressure is off of her

she has nothing to worry about
she is carefree
she is free
shes over labor

2. —things are going right (Δ, 3; I-3, 9)
   every thing is all right
   there isn't anything wrong

3. —she does the right thing (I-3/4, 11)
   has done every thing right

4. —she's clean (I-3, 13)

5. —she is at home; she's by herself (I-3/4, 8)
   they can relaxe and be alone from the children
   her doctor says: You may go home today

I-3

Taken together, the categories referring to being complimented, looking nice, and being complimented about appearance account for a sizable proportion of responses at this level. Of the other large categories, "she is loved" occurs at all levels, hence is not differentiating and is classed here as a compromise. The category concerning her family and children being happy and well is a forerunner of the altruistic theme present at higher levels. The theme of sensual gratification is referred to here in terms of having a bath. The theme of having demands met appears in less peremptory form than at lower levels, in terms of being treated well, getting married, and having money in her pocket.

The achievement motive, prominent at I-4, is presaged here in reference to finishing tasks and to being successful, either in general or in the kind of thing no one can ever quite succeed at, such as being a good mother. At I-3/4 there is reference to accomplishment rather than tasks finished. At I-4 inner components of achievement are mentioned.

*1. Concern with appearance of self or house (Δ, 2; I-3/4, 9)
    she looks good
    she has a new hat
    she is dressed neat and clean
    she has just bought a pretty dress or furniture for the house
    has her hair done
    she is noticed

*2. —she is complimented, praised (I-3/4, 5, 10)
    she is whistled at

she is flattered
she is praised for something

3. —she is complimented about her looks (I-3/4, 10)
   she is told she looks nice

*4. —a man (someone) compliments her (I-3/4, 10)
   she is praised by a man
   you praise her
   people compliment her

*5. —she is loved (I-3/4, 1, 3; I-4, 2)
   someone loves her
   she is loved by a man

6. —she is treated well (Δ, 1, 2; I-3/4, 6)
   she is pampered
   she is comforted
   her husband remembers her birthday, anniversary, etc.

7. —she gets married; she has a man (continuing relation implied) (Δ, 4; I-3/4, 2)
   she has a good husband
   she is happily married
   she has someone to love

8. Belongs to a family; is in a group (I-3/4, 7)
   she has friends
   she have her own family
   her family is to gather

9. —everything is going well at home (Δ, 3; Δ/3, 2; I-3/4, 8)
   things run smooth in the home
   things go right for all
   when her children are well & when things run smooth
   all's well with her family

*10. —her family is happy; her children are well, well-behaved (I-3/4, 13)
   her family is well and happy
   someone tells me my children are well behaved
   she has a happy home
   she feels her family is happy

11. —she has done something well; she is successful (I-3/4, 12)
   she is a good wife and mother
   she succeeds in raising a happy family
   she does a good days work

12. —she has her work done (I-3/4, 12)
all her work is done and all the family are well
she has her house clean and in order
she has prepared the evening meal cleaned the house and is entertaining friends for dinner

13. —she has had a bath (Δ/3, 4)
she bathes

14. —she is well, healthy
when there not sick
She is not Sick are dont worry about Her children

15. —she is pregnant, has had a baby (Δ/3, 1)
she learns that her baby is going to live
she first brings her new baby home from the hospital

16. —she has money (Δ, 2)
she has money left at the end of the week

I-3/4

The most frequent theme at I-3/4 is some elaboration of the I-3 response "she is loved," such as, is told or shown that she is loved, knows or feels that she is loved, feels wanted or needed, or is with a man she loves. The theme of appearance is represented by knowing she looks good and being complimented by someone who loves her or who is sincere. Appreciation and admiration are the inward aspects of the compliments that figure prominently at I-3. The altruistic theme appears here as helping others or making them happy. The theme of accomplishment appears in unelaborated form, taking the place of tasks finished (I-3). Pregnancy and childbirth are not onerous tasks to be gotten over (Delta/3) but are themselves occasions for feeling good.

*1. —she knows she is loved (I-3, 5; I-4/5, 5)
a boy shows that he likes her
she knows someone cares about her
she knows her husband loves her. No matter what his faults are
she feels loved
her husband says I love you
her children tell her they love her

2. —she is with the man she loves; she is with the man who loves her (Δ, 4; I-3, 7; I-4, 6)

3. —she is in love (I-3, 5)

*4. —she is wanted, needed
     she feels loved and needed

*5. —she is admired, appreciated; men pay attention to her (I-3, 2; I-4, 2)
     she can please
     a man is attentive towards her
     she is appealing to others

6. —she is respected, treated like a woman (I-3, 6; I-4/5, 2)
     she is looked up to
     she is treated like a lady
     she is complimented on something to do with femininity

7. —she feels secure (I-3, 8)
     she is accepted by a group
     she possess self-confidence

8. —she can relax (Δ/3, 1, 5; I-3, 9)
     she is at ease
     she can sit down and rest after a hard days work
     there are no big worries in the family
     I feel good when nothing is worrying me

9. —she knows she looks good (I-3, 1)
     she is well dressed and knows it
     she looks, feels and smells good
     she can have some pride in her apearance & stature

10. —she is complimented by her husband, by someone who loves her; she receives a sincere compliment (I-3, 2, 3, 4; I-4, 1)
     a man compliments her! for men are usually sincere
     told she looks nice—or has complimentary statements said about her—(no flattery).

11. Meeting standards (unelaborated) (Δ/3, 3; I-4, 3)
     she is right
     she's at her best
     she has a purpose
     she has a stimulating interest
     she is satisfied
     she knows she have did the best she can

12. —she has accomplished something; she does something creative (I-3, 11, 12; I-4, 3)
     she does creative things—cooking—cleaning—furniture arranging
     she has accomplished a great deal

*13. —she has helped someone; she makes her family happy (I-3, 10)

she is not thinking about herself
she is doing something to help others
she is able to make someone else happy
she makes a happy home
she feels she has made her husband happy

Unclassified
she is getting ready to go out with her man

I-4

The dominant theme at I-4 is accomplishment, particularly doing things that she herself thinks are worthwhile or that others appreciate. A compliment is cherished when it concerns achievements. Although being appreciated by itself is classed I-3/4, in combination with other ideas such as loved or accepted it is classed here empirically. Direct, explicit statements of reciprocity in love are classed here. "She is loved for herself," classed at I-4, presages the notion of individuality found at I-4/5 and I-5. When the response is elaborated, I-4 subjects contrast being loved for herself with being loved for her services, while at higher levels the notion of individuality is clearer.

1. —she is complimented for something she has done (I-3/4, 10; I-5, 1)

loved and given credit for work
she has accomplished something that is appreciated by those around her

2. —she is loved and appreciated (I-3, 5; I-3/4, 5)

she is accepted and loved, especially by a man
she is appreciated and respected

*3. Sense of accomplishment for having fulfilled goals, duties (I-3/4, 11, 12)

she knows that her work is well done and feels satisfied in seeing it appreciated
she has the love and honor of her husband or her ambision in the life she started
can do something productive and worthwhile
she fulfills her responsibilities
she is doing something worthwhile
she has done something she thinks is important

she accomplishes a task that will be pleasing to her loved one
she has accomplished a job in keeping with whatever role she
is playing

4. Accomplishments or development of children
   her children achieve
   she's got children that wants to be educated
   the family (the children) are admiered

5. —she is loved for herself (I-4/5, 3)
   she know that her husband and kids really care for her and
   not for what she can do

6. Reciprocity in love (I-3/4, 2)
   her love is returned
   she has a happy marriage as I do and they love each other
   she is loved and when she has a family to love

Unclassified
   she can truly communicate with her husband

I-4/5

Categories here referring to individuality, roles, mutuality, and communication of feelings are similar to those of other items. Remarkable is the sizable category integrating or contrasting feeling good about personal appearance with some entirely different thought. Apparently concern for appearance is not replaced but rather supplemented by other concerns at higher I-levels.

1. Contrasting aspects, such as appearance and abilities
   men nod approvingly—both when they see her and even more
   so when they hear her talk
   she has just had a shower, is wearing the proper clothes for
   the occasion and is at peace with the members of her family
   she is complimented about her looks, intelligence & cooking
   she knows she is being feminine and intelligent at the same
   time
   she knows she has developed character, charm and physical
   attractiveness
   she looks good or when she makes someone else feel good
   she is groomed well or another aspect—healthy, happy family
   she is made to feel like a desirable and worthwhile person

2. Role conception (I-3/4, 6)
   she is loved by a man and able to accept her role as a woman

a man loves her & thinks that she makes him a more complete person

she is appreciated for being a woman a wife, a mother and a good member of society in general

3. —she is loved, accepted, treated as a person (I-4, 5; I-5, 1)
   she is accepted and loved as she is
   she is accepted as a person
   she is treated as a person with rights and dignity

4. Mutuality of interests of self and others
   she leads a life that is useful to herself & others
   she can help build a good and happy life for herself, for her husband and her family
   she can please her husband & feels secure in being loved

Unclassified
   she runs in the grass on a bright day

I-5

All the responses at I-5 and I-6 are original and most of them are conceptually quite complex. The notion of individuality or identity is clearer than at lower levels. In other respects the themes are elaborations and combinations of those at lower levels.

1. Achievement of individuality (I-4, 1; I-4/5, 3)
   she has given of her unique self
   she is using her abilities to their fullest
   she is admired by a man for the qualities which characterize her as an individual, not just her physical attributes alone
   she is doing something within her own expectation of herself as a woman
   she is respected accepted and loved for what she is, not what other's think she is
   has self identy and is loved in addition

Unclassified
   when a man remembers little things, not in an extra showey way, but in a quiet, genuine expression
   she has soothed another into peace with himself

I-6

One response here illustrates enjoyment of sex in context of a relation with another person as a deeply mutual experience. The other illustrates self-evaluated standards combined with an unusual discrimination among wanting, valuing, and being adequate to fulfill.

Unclassified
> *her sex life goes well, and when, in all respects she and her husband are "sympatico"*
>
> *she is wanted, valued and adequate to fulfill a purpose that she values high*

My Main Problem Is—

$\mathbb{C}$ompared to many other
items, there are few common themes running through categories at the
different I-levels. One such theme is relations with men, with responses
ranging from simply "men" at I-2, through "loving my husband" at
I-3/4, to "my inability to have a lasting relationship with men" at I-5.
This sequence typifies the qualitative differences in the responses given to
this stem, with subjects at I-3 and lower responding primarily in terms
of externals: other people, actions, appearance; subjects at I-3/4 and
higher, in terms of internal states or attributes: temper, indecision, choices
and dilemmas. At the highest levels there is often the added element of
self-criticism or evaluation.

I-2

The I-2 woman may mention trouble or what gets her into trouble, such as fighting or boys. Also classed here are the "I want to go

home" responses. Presumably they came from institutionalized girls who already had a problem at home. What they surely mean is "trying to get people to let me go home," a response that actually came from an I-3 protocol but is classed here on content. The problem is seen in the place, not in the person.

1. Trouble; misbehaving
   fight with my brother
   running away
   I try to act smart

2. —men; boys (Δ, 3; Δ/3, 1)

3. Desire to go home (I-3, 16)
   when am I going home
   trying to get people to let me go home

Unclassified
   is I hurt men

DELTA

Classed Delta are those responses implying a pride in one's sexuality, "sex," "that I am boy crazy." The subject seems to be saying that it is a problem only because other people say so. "Getting to see boys" implies a resentment of restrictions placed on sexual behavior. There is the appearance of self-appraisal but hardly the substance of any problem in responses like "my mouth," an externalized version of the problem of talking too much (I-3). "I am stupid" is self-depreciation, hardly self-appraisal. The responses expressing hostility toward the test classed here should be distinguished from "thinking of non-revealing statements for this test" (I-4), which is directed toward the subject herself, not the test.

1. —my mouth (I-3, 12)
   controling my tongue
   keeping my mouth from getting me in trouble

2. —getting to see boys
   to get my mother to give her consent to date boys

3. —sex; love; liking men (I-2, 2; I-3/4, 2)
   that I am boy crazy
   I like boys, and they won't leave me alone, and I like it

4. Hostility, sarcasm directed toward test
   filling out this questionaire

that this takes too long
trying not to laugh when doing this "test"

Unclassified
I am stupid
my cat
going different places

DELTA/3

The naming of other people or the specification of school or particular subjects as one's main problem is quite common from subjects below I-3, but sufficiently common from subjects I-3 and above to merit a compromise rating at this level. Both categories present external labels for problems that are more specific and more internal at higher levels, for example, "learning to do math" (I-3) or "I worry too much about my son and his trouble in school" (I-4).

*1. —other people; my home (I-2, 2; I-4, 2)
   my husband
   my boyfriend
   my mother and father
   cranky teachers
   parts of my family
   relatives
   my childern

2. —school; schoolwork; arithmetic, and so on (I-3, 8)
   spelling
   geography in school and home problems
   shcool and boys
   New Mathematics
   reading I can't read very much
   going to school

I-3

Problems given by I-3 subjects are sometimes vague and unfocused, "worrying about things" or "trying to be good." More often they are concrete and immediate, often personal and touching in a way that those of lower levels are not. They are not, however, self-criticisms, as those at I-3/4 and higher tend to be. Thus the typical ones refer to appearance, particularly weight, dates, grades, money, and immediate household problems. Most problems given at this level are stated in terms of specific actions or situations. Thus instead of the trait "being outspoken" (I-4), the problem is "talking too much" (I-3); instead of the choice "deciding on the man to be my spouse" (I-4), the problem is "trying to get married again" (I-3); instead of "feeling complete responsibility for 4 lives" (I-4), the problem is "trying to keep my children in order" (I-3). The responses classed at this level that are the most self-critical are being bossy or mean to others, which are traits or actions typically proscribed at I-3. "Wish for freedom" is placed at I-3 as a compromise. It is a small category of responses given by subjects primarily at Delta or I-4.

*1. Concern with appearance (including eating)
   my weight
   dieting
   that my face is broken out

2. —smoking

*3. —money; bills; financial problems
   *I want things that I see in stores but don't have money to
      get it*
   how to make ends meet
   making a living
   I am pore

*4. —raising, caring for, supporting family; being a good mother
   (I-4, 1, 2)
   raising my family properly
   making my family happy
   trying to keep children in order
   trying to stop the children from aruguing and fighting
   seeing that my family lives well
   *will I be able to work and give my kids some of the thing
      they needs*
   being a ideal companion and mother

5. —doing housework; household problems
   planning menus
   I don't like to cook
   washing dishes
   try to get someone to keep the baby then I work
   my housework, the children won't help

6. Concrete problems related to dating, marriage
   getting ready for the wedding
   divorce
   that my fiance is in Chicago & I am in St. Louis

7. —dating; getting married, a job, an education, through school
    (I-4, 3)
    I date too much
    wanting to get married
    trying to get married again
    finding the right man
    finding a job
    getting a good job after I graduate
    getting my education
    to finish school

8. —studying; learning (Δ/3, 2)
    learning to do math
    remembering what I learned in high school
    study shorthand
    I don't study enough
    making myself study like I ought to

9. —getting good grades; passing in school (I-4, 7)
    keeping high enough grades in school
    worrying about grades
    reading enough books to please the teachers
    that my marks in school are a bit below average, and I want
      to bring them up

10. —getting along with, pleasing, getting acquainted with others
    making and keeping friends easily
    that me and my step can't get alone
    getting to know people well

11. —being bossy, mean to others (I-3/4, 10)
    I am a bit bossy
    being mean to those I don't like

12. —talking (too much, too fast, and so on) (Δ, 1; I-3/4, 12)

13. —being good; doing the right thing
    trying to be as good as I want to be

14. —worry; worry too much, about everything (I-3/4, 14)
    worried
    I worry too much about everything
    worrying about things

15. —not getting enough sleep; getting up (I-3/4, 4)
    that I love to sleep late
    "getting going" in the morning

staying awake
I don't take enough rest

16. Wish for freedom (I-2, 3)
    getting out of here!
    I'd like to get away from home
    going where I want to go all the time!

17. —none; don't have any

Unclassified
home life
my husbond isn't home enough

I-3/4

At I-3/4 there is a change in the direction of more interpersonal problems and more self-critical statements, the latter probably being best represented by "myself." The I-3/4 subject is more likely than is the I-3 subject to mention personal attributes such as emotional states ("the loneliness without my husband"), or interpersonal traits ("self-consciousness"). At I-4 traits mentioned are more likely to be related to achievement and self-esteem. Physical states—inability to become pregnant, illness, and lack of energy—are also mentioned as problems at this level. Responses concerned with the problems of talking or worrying become more evaluative at I-3/4. The I-4 concern with achievement is presaged at I-3/4 in the concern with getting things done. Empirically classed at I-3/4 is the category, "solving my problems; adjusting to life." These responses should be distinguished from those at I-4/5 in which the subject specifies the problems or situations with which she must cope.

1. —fear of pregnancy; inability to become pregnant
   I dont want to have another Baby So I will always be afraid
      from one month to another
   achieving pregnancy
   being envious of other pregnant women

2. —being in love; being loved (Δ, 3)
   that the boy I love comes from a different background than
      mine and is younger than I
   not knowing how I really feel about love
   loving my husband
   the feeling of being loved

3. —health
I'm sick
my visual handicap
illness in the family

4. —being tired, slow; lack of energy (I-3, 15; I-4, 4)
feeling tired most of the time
being so slow in doing activities
lack of energy and overweight
keeping from getting tired and nervous

5. —being bashful, shy, self-conscious (I-4, 9, 12)

6. —tension; nervousness
that I am very restless
my nerves
my nervousness with boys

7. —being moody, depressed, lonely
being too emotional
is my moods of despondency
the lonliness without my husband

8. —temper; impatience (no implication of control) (I-4, 13)
I'm not patient enough
getting angry over little things

9. —concentration (I-4, 5)
not being able to think thorougly
letting my mind wander
daydreaming when the teacher is talking on a subject I don't
like

10. —hurting others (I-3, 11)
doing what I want and not hurting others
being afraid I'll hurt someone's feelings
that I have hurt someone deeply

11. —acting, speaking without thinking, at the wrong times (I-4,
16)
I don't know when to keep my mouth shut
saying something then regretting it
saying the wrong thing at the wrong time
that I talk too much when I am not suppose to be talking

12. —talking, expressing myself adequately (I-3, 12; I-4, 15)
I don't talk enough
untalkativeness
saying what I mean

being able to talk with a large group
expressing by feelings
expressing myself in terms I like to use

13. —completing, getting things done (I-4, 6)
getting everything I take on, done
I have to much to do
getting all the things done within a day
getting everything finished that I'd like to

14. —worrying about little things (I-3, 14)
letting little matters upset me

15. —worry about the future, what to do (I-4, 17)
what I will do when I graduate
that I do not know what I want
wondering about next year
finding what I want

16. —solving my problems; adjusting to life (I-4/5, 1)
trying to solve all problem
not being able to cope with certain problems at certain times
to accept

17. Backhanded compliment
I'm too outgoing
that I'm too sincere with other people
feeling too much love for people
I am too honest

18. —myself; egocentric traits (I-4/5, 2)
I'm too self-centered and can't settle down
my pride
I'm too stuborn
myself & my husband

I-4

At this level achievement enters directly as a need and as conflicting with other needs. Listing procrastination, lack of self-discipline, trying to do too much, expecting too much of oneself or of others, all reflect the need for accomplishment and are, in addition, self-critical. Other familiar I-4 themes appear: responsibility, communication, dependence. Responses in the latter two categories imply the problem is one of interpersonal relations, one of give and take, rather than residing only in oneself, such as "saying what I mean" (I-3/4).

1. Concern with responsibility, outcome of child rearing (I-3, 4)
   *that I know that someday I'll have the great responsibility of
   caring for my family*
   feeling complete responsibility for 4 lives
   to raise my children to be assets to the world
   helping my son to develop
   *assuring myself that I am teaching my children right from
   wrong and how to grow up to be proud of themselves*

2. Family problems; worry about family (Δ/3, 1; I-3, 4)
   my Son, Clarence, who is very emotional
   trying to help a mentally ill daughter
   , my child and how she is getting along in school
   my relationship with my older son
   *as a mother, knowing how to handle my children when its
   hard to pot train or don't want to mind*
   I worry about my son and his trouble in school

3. —choosing a husband, career, school (I-3, 7; I-5, 1)
   deciding upon the man to be my spouse
   *deciding what school give me the best opportunity of prepa-
   ration in my chosen field of work*
   what college and career to choose
   choosing the right college

4. —lack of self-discipline; being lazy (I-3/4, 4)
   my lack of will-power when a situation demands self-denial
   my inability to say "no"
   sticking to my own rules
   my laziness

*5. —procrastination, indecision, inefficiency (I-3/4, 9)
   using what abilities I have wisely
   not using my head
   choosing which interest to explore first
   being unorganized
   *not being able to make up my mind about something fast
   enough and by myself*

*6. —lack of time, time to get things done; trying to do too much
   (I-3/4, 13)
   finding time to do everything I'd like to do
   getting in enough time for reading up on current events
   time marching on!
   too much to do in such a short time
   that I am apt to try to squeeze too much into a day

that I enjoy doing too many things
*limiting my activities within the bounds of my time and
energy*

7. Concern with achievement, knowledge (I-3, 9)
wondering if I'll do well
getting out of her and making something of myself
a fear of trying to succeed in a hard job
not enough ambition

8. Conflicting needs, desires
*getting my lessons at school because there are so many other
things I prefer*
finishing my education after marriage
balancing time devoted to school and to home
*financial. I prefer to be home all the time with my family
instead of employment outside the home*
*trying to care for 5 children and still have free time with my
husband*
*how to reconcile the boy back home with college, and how
to "grow him up"*
I like men, but I'm apparently afraid of marriage

*9. —lack of confidence, assurance; feeling insecure, inferior
(I-3/4, 5)
inconsistency and maintaining confidence
overcoming lack of self-esteem
that I depreciate myself

10. —being dependent, overprotected
I let my parents treat me as if I were a child
keeping a life of my own
overprotective parents

11. —being sensitive, serious

12. —my tendency to withdraw (I-3/4, 5)
*my introvertness—my tendency to listen rather than partici-
pate in large groups*

13. —temper; patience (emphasis on control) (I-3/4, 8)
my uncontrollable temper
keeping my patience
keeping calm under situations of strain

14. —routine; boredom
not caring
trying to get away from boring housework

15. Problems with communication (I-3/4, 12)
    communication with my husband
    poor communication
    not being able to communicate effectively to others
    sometimes I find it hard to convey my feelings and I feel sometimes I'm over sympathetic

16. —lack of tact; being outspoken (I-3/4, 11)
    non-conformity

17. —understanding, knowing myself, others (I-3/4, 15; I-5, 1)
    that of finding myself and what I want
    that I am still unsure of myself (desires, career, etc.)
    understanding my son lately
    understanding why other people do the things they do
    trying to understand certain people

18. —expecting too much of myself, others (I-4/5, 3)
    learning not to make snap judgments of people
    being overly aggressive and expecting others to move as quickly as I do

19. —involvement in other people's problems
    not being able to help some people
    trying to promote peace and harmoney
    my ability to know everyones business
    I become to emotionally involved with people and their problems

Unclassified
thinking of non-revealing statements for this test

I-4/5

The I-4/5 categories, all of which have some of the I-4 type of striving, involve more distance from self, more ability to see self in a context of other people and events, than those at I-4. The I-4/5 subject stands back from her difficulties, such as feelings of insecurity or disappointment, and sees the problem as one of coping with or adjusting to the difficulty. Other categories contain an evaluation of oneself as being unrealistic or too perfectionistic. In the latter case the I-4 need for achievement is itself being criticized.

1. Adjustment, coping with problems (specified) (I-3/4, 16)
    I am unable to cope with all my responsibilities
    becoming adjusted to the possibility of a career for myself

adjusting to the unfavorable occurences in my life
accepting complete defeat
trying to solve feelings of insecurity
dealing with disappointments
that I need to resolve some "strings" which hang over from
*   childhood*

2. Perfectionism, rigidity (I-3/4, 18)
   not being able to "let things ride"
   trying to be orderly
   to exacting a nature
   being stubborn and unchangeable in certain areas
   impatience and a judgmental attitude
   sticking to small detail
   my preoccupation with principles

3. Being unrealistic (I-4, 18)
   worrying needlessly
   my imagination
   I have a quick temper and tendency to daydream too much
   that I tend to be hypercondriac
   I often don't realize I have any
   thinking too much and thus creating problems for myself

Unclassified
   that I am too often happy being alone
   fear of separation from the few people whom I love

I-5

One theme at I-5, variously expressed, is to be more accepting of self and others as they are, to be more tolerant, less seeking of approval. Again, this implies an ability to stand aside from oneself and evaluate oneself as a person among other people that is rare below the I-4/5 level. The I-5 concern with self-realization is reflected in the category, "Search for goals, purpose in life."

1. Search for goals, purpose in life (I-4, 3, 17)
   seeking and settling goals and ideals for a family
   finding an interesting field and challenging career for myself
   trying to decide just what I want to do with the rest of my
   *   life so that I can satisfy myself and in some way help or*
   *   please others*
   deciding what my purpose in life is and what I can do to
   *   achieve this purpose*

shyness and a slight insecurity. I know what I want but doubt
whether I can do it. I would hate to waste a life that has
potential for something
what I am going to do or be and will I be of some use to
someone

2. Evaluation of self in interpersonal relations—with distance
    my inability to have a lasting relationship with men
    learning not to worry too much and tolerating weakness in
    those around me
    I want people to think I'm better than I am. I try to put on
    this impression but it shows up in my facial expressions
    being to concerned with seeking others approval
    I worry to much & don't have the self-confidence which I
    seem to

Unclassified
    doing what I want or what I should, living up to my mother's
    opnion of me. Keeping my boy friend for ever
    that I am not always content with my life

I-6

Classed here is a response illustrating a search for identity. A simple response such as "what will I become" would be given a somewhat
lower rating (actually we have never seen such a response), because it
does not contain enough information to merit an I-6 rating. To be rated
I-6 a response must contain additional elements characteristic of I-4 and
higher protocols, and merit at least an I-5 rating on the basis of being a
unique combination of high elements. The unclassified response shows
an unusual combination of commitment and self-criticism.

1. Identity
    I am afraid, I lack the courage to be what I want to be be-
    cause it is different from what my parents feel I should be

Unclassified
    that I will need two lifetime, (not permitted) to reach my
    goals since they aid evalutionary rather than revolutionary
    processes

Whenever She Was with Her Mother, She—

T he main themes for this stem are to feel good, to be good, to have discord with mother, to talk about things with her, to be different, especially to regress. All these themes or their variants, including negatives, appear at almost all levels, at least in terms of single responses. There is progressive decentration from being solely concerned with self, or whoever "she" is taken to be, to concern for others, especially the mother. The rare responses mentioning love illustrate this: "loved me" (Delta); "felt loved" (I-3/4); "was very affectionate" (I-4/5). Most altruistic responses are I-4 or higher, but many responses at those levels are not altruistic, for instance, "always did as she wanted to" (I-4) is selfish in content, but it describes a relation in some sense that "ask for things" (I-2) does not.

If we seek a single underlying theme in the varied manifest responses, it must be dependence. Presumably some if not all the "happy" responses reflect enjoyment or acceptance of dependence. Dependent responses distinctively I-2 are complaints or demands. At I-3 additional responses indicating acceptance of dependence refer to feeling safe or secure. Indication that dependence or the regressive pull induces discomfort can be read into such responses as "felt different," "acted like a baby," and "felt like a child" (I-3/4). At I-4 these themes are represented by the categories "was a different person" and assertion of equality and independence. At I-4/5 there are explicit discussions of feelings of regression and struggle to maintain independence. Thus, while there is no one-to-one correspondence between I-level and how one handles the problem of dependence on the mother, some of the best categories do reflect a correlation between the two variables.

I-2

Most responses classed I-2 are global, all-purpose feelings (good, nice, all right), or dependent complaints or demands. Although ambiguous grammatically, one category seems to describe the mother as being good to the subject. At I-2, the subject's behavior is described as "nice," again a global term, not necessarily carrying the connotation of obedience as does "was good" (Delta).

1. —felt good (Δ, 1; I-3, 1)
   good

2. —was, felt nice, all right, OK (Δ, 1; I-3, 1)
   was alright
   is alway nice
   acted nice
   was a very nice person

3. —was good to me
   always is kind to us kids
   would not be mean to me

4. Dependent complaining
   always tells what goes wrong
   ask for things
   cried
   didn't get it

Unclassified
always ran away
faint
thought she was bad
would tell everything

DELTA

Most responses classed Delta can be interpreted as reflecting the struggle over rules: "was good," "would never mind her," "acted like an angel." "Was ashamed," although located here empirically, accords with the theoretical expectation that the Delta subject is capable of shame but not of guilt.

1. —was good (I-2, 1, 2; I-3, 1, 10)
   was a good child

2. —acted badly; misbehaved (Δ/3, 2; I-3, 14)
   was disagreeable
   acted terrible
   tried to be bad
   would never mind her
   always acts nasty

3. —acted like an angel (I-3/4, 9; I-4, 5)

4. —was ashamed
   I was ashamed
   hid because she was ashamed of her
   turned red
   walked like she didn't know her

Unclassified
always stayed home

DELTA/3

Fighting responses are found below I-3 and at I-3/4 but not at I-3, hence this compromise rating. Fighting may have different meanings, but even when it means arguing, expressing it in this way has an impulsive ring. At all levels, except perhaps the lowest, there are responses indicating some effort to make a particular impression on the mother. At the Delta level this is expressed as "acted like an angel," leaving it ambiguous whether this represents genuine good behavior or dissimulation. At Delta/3 there are definite indications of self-consciousness about the behavior, whether good or bad: "puts on." The distinction between be-

havior and feelings is not any clearer at I-3, where the typical version
is a few responses like "acted very lady like." At I-3/4, however, the description becomes unambiguous: "put on a phony act."

1. —fought (I-3/4, 14)
   fought with everyone
   was constantly fighting and yelling

2. —showed off; acted cute, like a fool, a snob (Δ, 2; I-3, 14;
   I-3/4, 8, 9, 18)
   puts on
   bragged
   thinks she's cute
   makes a fool of herself
   is snotty, rudd, and smart
   looks down on people

I-3

Many subjects at this level merely give global feelings, usually positive ones: felt happy, fine, enjoyed self, had fun, felt safe or secure.
Conventional expressions of good behavior also occur: "was real sweet,"
"didn't smoke," "acted very lady like." Being rude and not talking are
presumably the I-3 subject's way of combating her own dependence or
her mother's request for subservience. Only a few responses mentioning
negative feelings are classed at this level, mostly vague feelings of nervousness or upset or dysphoric feelings not directly related to dependence.
More specific feelings of discomfort are given at I-3/4, and feelings that
are a direct reaction to the problem of dependence—felt dominated, repressed—are classed I-4.

**1. —felt, was happy, fine, content, etc. (I-2, 1, 2; Δ, 1; I-3/4,
   1; I-4, 2)
   was glad
   felt pleasant

*2. —had fun, a good time; enjoyed herself (I-4, 1; I-4/5, 6)
   had a ball
   had a swell time
   had an enjoyable time
   liked it

3. —got along
   got along fairly well with her

4. —laughed; smiled; joked

5. —felt safe, secure, protected
was safe

6. —was nervous, upset, afraid, unhappy, miserable (I-3/4, 10, 11, 12; I-4, 3)
was nervous as a cat
seemed frightened
felt depressed

7. —acted, felt strange (I-3/4, 6)
didn't act as normal
acted in a very unusual manner
felt unnatural

*8. —talked; discussed problems (unspecified) (I-3/4, 16; I-4, 1, 9)
was talkative
talked about problems and helped solve them
gossips all the time

9. —did not talk (I-3/4, 15; I-4, 10)
didn't voice an opinion
would not talk as much
let her do the talking
was silent
clammed up tight

10. —was obedient; watched what she said and did (Δ, 1; I-4, 4, 6)
didn't act up
behaved
did as she was told
was careful of what she did

11. Avoidance of specific actions
didn't smoke
wouldn't smoke, drink or cuss
never looked at boys

12. —was kind, pleasant, friendly, sweet, polite, courteous (I-3/4, 5; I-4, 5)
was as sweet as can be
was mannerable
seemed very friendly
was not snobbish

13. —acted like a lady (I-3/4, 7)
    acted like a respectable lady
    acted very lady like

14. —was rude, sarcastic, disrespectful; ignored her (Δ, 2; Δ/3, 2;
    I-3/4, 13, 18)
    acted fresh & insolent
    seemed to ignore her

15. —helped her (I-3/4, 5)
    would help her as much as she could
    done all she could for her
    was helping her

16. —stayed around her (I-4/5, 2)
    stayed close beside her
    doesn't want to leave

17. Specific concrete actions
    bought lots of clothes
    usually took her shopping or to visit friends
    was usually sewing
    drank coffee

18. Evasion; don't have a mother
    who?
    ?
    no comment
    my mother has passed on 40 yrs. ago

I-3/4

The I-3/4 subject focuses on more specific reactions in the mother-daughter relationship. With the mother she feels loved, uncomfortable, or like a child. She "seemed happy" rather than "was happy" (I-3), reflecting a beginning awareness that actions and feelings do not necessarily coincide, an awareness necessary for optimal ego growth and perhaps for optimal relation of an adult woman to her mother. There is more concern for the mother as a person at this level than is expressed at lower levels. Here the subject describes herself as being thoughtful, considerate of her mother, wanting to help and please her. Hostile feelings are also classed at this level as well as "quarreled, argued." There are several categories at this level concerned with being or seeming different, the same, more grown-up, like a child, reflecting an appreciation that one's behavior may be in part determined by role relations. The I-3 subject seems unaware of this relativity, "didn't act as normal," and the I-4 subject will specify alternative situations, "acted completely different than with her friends."

1. —seemed happy, contented, and so on (I-3, 1)
   seemed gay
   seemed to be the happiest person on earth

2. —felt loved; knew she was loved
   feels the love and efection
   knew someone loved her

3. —felt, seemed proud, pleased, fortunate
   was proud that her mother looked so young for her age
   is delighted
   felt was lucky to have such a nice mother

4. —tried to please her, make her happy (I-4, 5; I-4/5, 5)
   tried to cheer her up
   would do anything to please her

5. —was thoughtful, helpful, considerate; wished she could help (I-3, 12, 15)
   was always considerate and helpful
   wanted to help her

6. —acted, seemed different, the same (I-3, 7; I-4, 7, 8)
   was different
   acted so differently
   seamed to change
   changed entirely
   acted in her normal, unpretentious way

7. —acted, seemed, felt mature, more grown-up (I-3, 13)
   appeared more mature
   acts big for her age

8. —acted, seemed, felt immature, like a baby, a spoiled child (Δ/3, 2; I-4/5, 3)
   felt as if she was a baby
   acted childish
   acted like a little girl and was waited on hand & foot
   acted naive
   was a spoiled brat

9. —acted innocent; put on a huge front (Δ, 3; Δ/3, 2; I-4, 5)
   was sickening sweet and innocent
   acted so innocent and angelic
   put on a phony act

10. —was quiet, shy, reserved (I-3, 6; I-4, 3)
    stayed in the background
    appeared terribly self-conscious
    seemed timid
    became very quiet
    seemed to be more shy

11. —was tense, uncomfortable, uneasy (I-3, 6; I-4, 3)
    was restless
    felt strained
    was ill at ease

12. —felt awkward, embarrassed (I-3, 6)
    got embarrassed
    felt like a fool

13. —was irritated, hostile, antagonistic (I-3, 14)
    was angry
    was irritable
    became annoyed and wanted to get away
    was sullen

14. —quarreled, argued (Δ/3, 1)
    had a tendency to contradict her
    argues because she is hurt by neglect
    antagonized her quite a bit
    disagreed with her

15. —listened; learned (I-3, 9; I-4, 10)

16. —confided in her (I-3, 8)
    felt like she could confide in her
    sewed and talked and confided in her

17. —was like her
    resembled her
    acted like her
    identified with her
    was always mistaken for her twin sister

18. —ignored her friends (Δ/3, 2; I-3, 14)
    acted as tho she didnt know me
    wouldn't speak to anyone
    did not seek the company of others

Unclassified
    felt left out
    was very happy and yet very unhappy

I-4

Classed I-4 are those responses that state that the subject enjoyed talking with her mother or enjoyed her company, responses suggesting an enjoyment of the relation not apparent in simply "had fun" or "enjoyed herself" (I-3). The I-4 subject may assert that she is comfortable or relaxed; why is this I-4 while "uncomfortable" is I-3/4? Ideally, the problem of dependence on the mother probably should be faced and resolved between I-3 and I-4, and the subjects in this category may be among those for whom the transition has been a smooth one. To feel respect for mother is probably also a happy outcome, but asserting one's equality or independence sounds more problematic. Other responses are explicit references to conflict with the mother and the effort to avoid strife. That the dependence-independence conflict may be at the core of the relation with the mother is not explicitly stated until the I-4/5 level.

1. —enjoyed talking, the visit, mother's company (I-3, 2, 8; I-4/5, 6)
   enjoyed their talks
   liked to talk & joke with her
   enjoyed exchanging news
   enjoyed hearing her talk
   enjoyed time spent together

*2. —was, felt relaxed, comfortable, at ease (I-3, 1)
   seemed so calm
   felt confident
   felt very relieved
   didnt have any thing to wurry about

3. —was, felt dominated, inhibited, repressed, withdrawn (I-3, 6; I-3/4, 10, 11; I-4/5, 4; I-5, 1)
   was treated as a child
   appeared to be dominated by the older woman
   felt tied down
   acted as though she were afraid to breath
   was paralyzed
   pulled into her shell

4. —was on her best behavior; behaved properly, well (I-3, 10)
   always want to act her best
   behaved pretty well
   acted properly
   acted as she should
   was a ideal person

5. Effort to be pleasant, avoid strife, control temper (Δ, 3; I-3, 12; I-3/4, 4, 9)

   was trying to be pleasant

   was as her mother thought she was

   acted innocent even if she wasn't, to make her mother think good of her

   pretended domestic tranquility

   must be careful not to complain!

   tried to keep from losing her temper

6. —respected her; was respectful (I-3, 10)

   respected her wishes

   was most respectful to her

7. —was a different (the same) person; was (not) herself (I-3/4, 6)

   acted like a completely different person

   was not her true self

   was still the same person

   was herself

8. —acted, seemed different, the same (situation or behavior specified) (I-3/4, 6)

   acted differently than with friends

   was much different than when alone

   acted like the little good girl she really wasn't

   acted like an angel—but when her mother left—she sure did change

   always acted the same as she did when she was out. That's what I respected in her. (Lida, my girlfriend.)

   felt the same as if with a girlfriend

9. —talked (subject specified); talked freely (I-3, 8)

   discussed relatives

   talked about her activities and compared them

   talked about cooking

   could say whatever she pleased

10. —didn't know what to say; couldn't express herself (I-3, 9; I-3/4, 15)

    got tongue-tied and so was silent

    could not talk about many things that were important to her

    kept her innermost feelings to herself

11. Appreciation of mother's judgment, advice

    depended on her mothers good judgment

was happy because her mother is fun to be with and loved
    give her good advice
usually asked for advice

12. —is just another friend
    felt like she was with a "pal"
    felt she had a friend

13. —did what she wanted; got what she wanted
    thought she could do and say what she had a mind to
    "wrapped her around her finger"
    dominated her
    was pampered
    asserted her independence

14. Thoughts of the past, future
    recalled her childhood
    remembered wonderful family times
    wondered about her future

I-4/5

The typical category here involves explicit recognition of regressive feelings and the struggle over dependence, rather than indirect reflections in terms of vague tension or arguing. Classed at this level empirically are responses that state that the subject "seemed to enjoy it." Responses indicating a genuine concern for the mother as a person, more differentiated than simply helping her or wanting to please her, are classed here as well as responses indicating mutuality, that mother also shared the enjoyment or affection. Actually responses stating simply that the subject was affectionate or loving are also classed at I-4/5. The rarity of such responses is in itself amazing. Perhaps the ability to express one's own affection toward mother is an extension of the ability to be relaxed and comfortable (I-4) with mother; it also shows the subject as giving to, rather than receiving from, the mother.

1. Mutual enjoyment, affection
    enjoyed comparing notes on "family and household" subjects
    and her mother would talk in whatever dialects or accents
        suited their mood at the moment, resulting in much fun
    enjoyed to do things they were both interested in
    felt happy because they loved and respected each other

2. —clung to her; was affectionate (I-3, 16)
    always clung to her
    was very affectionate

wished she could hug and kiss her mother—but every one is an individual
was respectful, as well as loving

3. —regressed; became a child again (I-3/4, 8)
   regressed to childhood behavior
   became a little girl again

4. —lost her individuality, independence (I-4, 3)
   always felt less independent
   became very dependent
   could not think for herself

5. Concern for the mother's feelings (specified) (I-3/4, 4; I-5, 3)
   wanted her to be proud of her
   allowed her to feel she was needed
   tried to make her feel loved and important
   made her mother feel small and unwanted
   tried to make her feel younger than she really was

6. —seems to enjoy it (I-3, 2; I-4, 1)
   seems to be in a pleasant mood
   seemed to enjoy her company
   seemed to be having a great time you could tell they were "pals"

Unclassified

Was happy and confident that her mother would help her with whatever problem may confront her
had the feeling of being judged and found wanting
didn't show as much respect for her as she seemed to feel when she talked about her
would run around her skirts and create an unpleasant scene, she being my girlhood friend who was a bit mischevious

I-5

At I-5, the subject is able to view her relation with her mother with more distance than at lower levels. The conflict between mother and subject is knowingly replaced by an inner conflict, reflected in the tension of self-control. The complexity of interpersonal relations is recognized in that subject can respond and react to the mother's relations with others, not just to mother herself. Awareness of her mother's feelings is expressed at this level as at I-4/5, but at I-5 such responses are more complex and unique.

1. Inner conflict (I-4, 3)

   felt conflicted

   felt torn between opposing emotions

   was hostile, ill-at-ease, and defensive

   kept very quiet and our conversations were never as free

   was struggling for control

2. Appreciation of mother's relations with others

   could feel that love that made their family so close

   could be grateful her mother and husband are friends

   was irritated. In my grandmother's last years she and my mother were often at odds. I knew they loved each other deeply and it hurt me to see them treat each other that way

3. Concern for and awareness of mother's feelings (elaborated) (I-4/5, 5)

   found many things she didn't want to talk about because she knew her Mother would be upset and it would do neither of them any good to have her worry

   was comfortable and felt loved even though she knew she wasn't wanted because of a situation that existed

   tried to understand her mother's point of view so that if she objected to something she would not hurt her mothers feeling

Unclassified

   was shy and ignored her or didn't consider her mother an equal

   felt repressed, I don't with her mother or with mine

I-6

The ability to stand aside from one's relation with the mother seen at I-5 is markedly apparent in the one example placed at I-6 which reflects a unique perception of the mother as a symbol of what is worthwhile in an entire generation. The sense of time and the social awareness as well contribute to an I-6 rating.

Unclassified

   absorbed some of the patience and wisdom of a generation, which has seen two World Wars and a Great Depression

The Worst Thing About Being a Woman—

Most subjects interpret the stem correctly and give a germane reply—that is, they give an answer that applies to all women and no men (menstruation), or that they believe applies more characteristically to women than to men (less freedom, more dependence). In a few cases throughout the I-level range there is a slight shift in meaning to something like "The worst thing that can happen to a woman—" (for example, tragedies occasionally associated with childbirth), or "For a woman the worst thing to do—"

'(for example, to gossip). Even in such cases the response refers to something either essentially or typically pertaining to women or believed to do so. Only at the I-2 level is the semantic slippage so great that the stem is taken to mean something more characteristic of men than women (fighting, drinking) or not specially associated with either sex (diseases, being mean).

Discrimination on this item, particularly between I-3, I-3/4, and I-4, is not good. The most frequent responses to this stem, and ones that occur at virtually all I-levels, concern female biological functions, keeping up one's appearance, and denial that there is "a worst thing." A substantial number of responses ranging in I-level from I-3 to I-4/5 deal with a woman's lack of freedom or the social restrictions and limitations imposed on her.

Some subjects object to the role requirements of being a woman. At lower levels the objections imply self-rejection, for instance "having to act like one" (Delta). At I-3 the complaint is simply "being a woman" and at I-3/4 "being what's expected of you." Responses in terms of role conflict, especially that of career versus marriage, first appear in significant numbers at I-4. Implicit in such responses is conflict between being what is expected and being what one wants to be. At higher levels being a woman encompasses many role definitions, not mutually exclusive. One may have one role as mother and another as career girl or working woman. The conflict then becomes more abstract and can be viewed in terms of internalization. Instead of career versus marriage, the conflict at the I-4/5 level is one of dependence versus independence and at I-5 the struggle to maintain one's individuality and conflict over duty to conflicting aspects of one's role. One resolution of this conflict is seen in the paradoxical response from an I-6 protocol, "is accepting your position as a woman and an individual, but once found ceases to be the worst and becomes the best." Housework is another pervasive complaint, expressed at I-2 simply as all the hard work, at I-3 as housekeeping or specific tasks, at I-3/4 as "your work is never done," at I-4 as the routine or drudgery of housework, at I-4/5 as "the responsibility of tedious housework," and at I-5 as the fear of becoming stagnant because of the monotony of household chores.

I-2

Although we do not automatically score a response I-2 on the basis of semantic confusion without regard to content, many of the I-2 responses can be interpreted in those terms. Diseases, being mean, fighting, and drinking are by no means characteristically woman's prerogative; they are, however, typical of the I-2 notion of "worst things." "Having a baby" is a semantically correct response and given occasionally as high as I-3/4, but most often at I-2. Why it is characteristic must be guessed. It may be seen as an inevitable fate. Further, from the complex physical and psychological phenomena of pregnancy and childbirth, the I-2 subject may select the sense of depletion, of having to give for no evident return. Responses such as "is having to take care of kids all the time" may have the same implication; most women find housework more onerous than taking care of children. Men are viewed only in negative terms at I-2.

*1. —is having a baby, being pregnant (I-3, 4; I-3/4, 14)
    having babies. If you could stop it be alright
    is having to bear children
    is getting pregnant every nine months

2.—is taking care of kids; always staying home (I-3, 5; I-3/4, 4)
    is to stay at home with the baby
    you have to watch children
    is when you are marred and have kids who spank them

3. Because of men: Concrete and impulsive (Δ, 3)
    is that she have men in her bed
    is fighting c̄ men
    is a men is a dog

4. "Worst thing" not specific to women (Δ, 2)
    is drinking
    is trying not to get into fights
    is deseases
    is she is mean

DELTA

The category "hardships and troubles" sums up the Delta subject's view of the worst thing about being a woman. Two categories refer to relations with men and are apparently contradictory: "putting up with men" and "trying to find a man." In the former case there is depreciation of man, in the latter, a predatory attitude. However, "being taken advantage of" or misused is rated I-3 on this item. An unexpected category at this level is "having to act like a woman." Here there is acknowledgment that one's station requires certain kinds of behavior, that is, a role concept. Its primitiveness is shown in that the role is determined only by sex; there is in fact no office corresponding to being a woman, as there is an office of wife or mother. Also, "having to act like a woman" is obligatory, there is no implication of choice.

1. —is hard work, working all the time (I-3, 6; I-3/4, 5)

2. —is hardships and troubles (I-2, 3)
   is you get the rough end
   is grooming trouble
   is getting in trouble

3. —putting up with men; being bossed around (I-2, 3; I-3, 11; I-3/4, 13, 14)
   is having a rotten lover or husband
   is you can't say no
   is being treated like dirt by men
   is the crap they take from men
   is boys
   is guys won't leave you alone

4. —is trying to find a man (I-3, 12; I-3/4, 15)
   is the chasing of men
   the shortage of males
   is that you have to go out of your way to please a man

5. —is having to act like a woman (unqualified) (I-3, 14; I-3/4, 1, 10)
   is you have to be femine
   is living up to it
   is trying to play a part

Unclassified
   is being a dog
   is I have all the worryes
   is that she looks like a slob when she's pregnant

I-3

Some women from I-2 to I-5 will not admit that anything about being a woman is wrong or worst. Nearly half of these responses, however, occur at I-3. Similar responses on higher protocols include a positive declarative, such as "I love it" (I-4). The same wide range in ego level is found in responses about keeping up one's appearance ("fixing your hair," "wearing heels") and about menstruation or menopause. Again they occurred most frequently at I-3. As these popular responses suggest, the complaints of the I-3 subject tend toward being stereotyped, commonplace, and outward-oriented (getting married, housework, being a lady).

*1. —is nothing; I don't know (I-4, 14)
   can't relate it

means nothing to me

there is'nt any worst thing

I disagree, *because I feel to be a woman you have all good
thing*

*some women think it is the underclothes, but I don't find any-
thing wrong with being a woman*

*2. —is staying attractive (I-4, 13)
   is trying to keep up with styles
   is shaving her legs and plucking eyebrows
   is wearing a girdle
   is getting grey hairs
   is it takes to long to dress

*3. —is menstruation, change of life (I-3/4, 7)
   is once a month
   is the cramps
   is getting the curse

4. —is pain, childbirth (I-2, 1; I-3/4, 7, 16; I-5, 4)
   she bears such pains
   is the pain of the particular body processes
   *is Having a Baby to me Because I Have a Very Hard time at
   Child Birth*

*5. —is the housework (I-2, 2; I-3/4, 3; I-4, 7; I-4/5, 5)
   is having to wash, iron, and cook
   is keeping the children and the house in shape
   is not likang house work

6. —is working, responsibility, too much to do (Δ, 1; I-3/4, 3,
   5; I-4, 6)
   they are depended upon a lot
   when problems are mostly hers
   *is a lot of responsibility and not having a husband to take care
   of the children*

7. Job and money problems (concrete) (I-4, 2)
   is getting a job
   is going to work at night
   not making good wages
   lack of money for luxurys
   working two jobs

8. Concern about doing things, going places: General or all-
   inclusive (I-3/4, 4, 5, 9; I-4, 1, 2)
   She Has So much to do

is that you always have something to do
not to be able to go out and find all kinds of jobs
is never going places you want to go
is Not always being able to do all one would Like to do
is doing things you don't enjoy

9. —is worrying, being emotional (I-4, 9)
is the way she worries more than a man
is being unhappy
is having the fear of something terrible happening
is worring

10. Concern for reputation (I-3/4, 1, 2, 10)
is being a good woman
is you have to be careful what you say and do
is having to watch out for her "name"
is having to be a lady most of the time

11. —is being taken advantage of (Δ, 3; I-3/4, 13, 14)
is the advantages men take on kindness or generosity

12. —is worrying about finding the right man (Δ, 4; I-3/4, 15; I-4/5, 5)
not finding a man
is not being able to find the right man to love

13. Stereotyped faults of women (I-3/4, 18, 19)
is gossiping
is being vain
is that they often times are catty
is the jealousy between women. Ugh!!
is she is sometimes too bossy

14. —is being a woman, the weaker sex (Δ, 5; I-3/4, 10, 12)
is that you're not a man
is being secondary

15. —is being alone (I-3/4, 17)

Unclassified
is the double standard
growing up

I-3/4

Responses at this level reflect sensitivity to or insecurity about measuring up to social standards. There are complaints both about things one should do and that one should not or cannot do. Complaints about

expectations and criticisms are the precursors of complaints about stereotypes at I-4. A variety of responses at I-3/4 are objections to women's
subordinate status: dependence on, inferiority to, exploitation by men.
Concern for being dependent must be distinguished from concern about
emotional dependence, feelings of dependence, or more elaborate responses indicating greater capacity for role conception, most of which are
rated I-4/5.

At the I-3/4 level complaints about disabilities are less physically
oriented than at I-3, expressing concern for inability to have, or losing, a
child rather than about the pain of childbirth, for "physical ill health"
rather than "pains." Some subjects respond by referring to disability in
such specific situations that one must assume they mean the response as
humor, referring to mechanical ineptness; not to the pains of childbirth
but to sitting down on an episiotomy; not menstruation but being unable
to swim during it. These responses occur on I-3 and I-3/4 protocols and
are classed here somewhat arbitrarily on the assumption that the pre-
sumed humor implies some distance from immediate concerns.

1. —is being what's expected of you; is the things expected of
   you (Δ, 5; I-3, 10; I-4, 1, 5; I-5, 3)
   is bending to public opinion
   is you're expected to be a baby
   is living up to expectations of critics

2. —is being judged, misjudged; is accepting criticisms (I-3, 10;
   I-4, 5)
   is that you must be at your best all the times
   *is when you aren't judged on personality or brains but just
   looks*
   is being contridicted fault being found by others
   *watching your step—so nobody gets the wrong idea. Always
   trying be nice I please people*

3. —is fulfilling your responsibilities; is the responsibility of rearing a family (I-3, 6; I-4, 6; I-4/5, 4)
   responsibility to your family, but I like it
   is the role of household "supervisor"
   is trying to be mother & father both
   *is when she has to support herself & her family and can't
   be a wife & mother*

4. —is being tied down (I-2, 2; I-3, 8; I-4, 6, 7)
   is being stuck at home
   is being tied down after she is married

having a baby and not having enough time for oneself
is she is tied to the house when her childrens are little

5. —your work is never done, finished (Δ, 1; I-3, 6, 8; I-4, 7)
Trying to keep up with all my work

6. —is getting old

7. Physical limitations; physical ill health (I-3, 3, 4)
lack of strength
is so many things go wrong with you
is not being able to work as hard as a man
is that she experiences more physical problems than men

8. —you can't do things men do
you can hardly ever be wild and enjoy the pleasures that boys do
is you can't play football

9. —not being able to go out alone at night, to go out without a date (I-3, 8; I-4, 1)
is she can't go to certain places without an escort & still be a lady
is that she always has to escorted

10. —is trying to act like one (Δ, 5; I-3, 10, 14)
is staying feminine
not bening one
is when she don't act as a woman should

11. —is being dependent (I-4, 12; I-4/5, 2, 3)
is being a dependent on her husband
is not being able to stand on our own two-feet
is not being able to be independent and free
is having to follow instead of lead

12. Feeling inferior to men; being considered inferior (I-3, 14; I-4, 2, 3)
is the low social prestige
being considered stupid by lots of men
is you are suppose to be the weaker sex
she has to take a back seat so often
is that there's a tendency to discriminate against them by men

13. Being misused or mistreated (Δ, 3; I-3, 11)
is being teased
is being dominated
is men don't always treat you as such

is being the object of lust
is that she does the dirty work

14. Sexual exploitation (I-2, 1; Δ, 3; I-3, 11)
    is the thought of getting pregnant
    is the constant threat of getting pregnant
    is that sometimes men give you a line and make a fool of you
    *Is sometimes boys take advantage of you and it wrecks your
    whole life*
    *is that she is the one who has the most problems if she has
    an illegitimate child*

15. —is waiting to be picked (Δ, 4; I-3, 12; I-4, 12)
    is not being married yet
    having to sit back and wait
    is that you can't make the first move
    is depending on men to ask for dates
    is you can't ask the boys you want to go out with

16. —is not to be able to have children; is losing a child (I-3, 4;
    I-5, 4)

17. Being unwanted, unloved, without friends (I-3, 15; I-4/5, 5)
    not being loved or thinking this way!
    is likeing someone you know doesn't like you
    is the possibility of being an old maid
    she can be left a widow

18. Interpersonal traits (I-3, 13)
    is you must be understanding
    is being too sympathetic or trusting
    is the contrary nature
    is not being able to be quite as dominant a person as a man

19. —is competition with other women (I-3, 13)
    is living with other women
    *is that there is so much competition in wearing clothes at
    school or anywhere*

Unclassified
    is the worry about figure, face, etc.

I-4

Instead of complaining about living up to expectations, the I-4
subject is more apt to complain about being judged by stereotypes or hin-

dered in being what she wants to be. General statements to this effect are
not uncommon below I-4 ("is her restricted freedom," I-3), but occur
more frequently at I-4 and I-4/5. Instead of seeing herself as "being" subordinate to men, the I-4 subject attributes her subordination to external
circumstances, such as discrimination or prejudice in the business world,
or sees herself as assuming a dependent role.

Traits or emotional states mentioned are more evaluative than at
lower levels ("is you must be understanding," I-3/4, versus "is knowing
how to understand a man," I-4). Role conflict is a complaint at I-4, but
is usually expressed in stereotyped or "women's magazine" terms, such as
career versus marriage or the many roles women have to fill. These responses contrast with more differentiated references to role conflict at the
I-4/5 level and corresponding references to inner conflict at I-5. Similarly, the I-4 complaint about never-ending chores and the routine or
drudgery of housework is a less explicit version of the higher level concern
that the duties required of a woman do not encourage fullest development
of inner life.

*1. —is restriction, lack of freedom (I-3, 8; I-3/4, 1, 9; I-4/5, 1,
        2; I-5, 1)
        are the limitations set by society
        is the cultural and social restraints put upon her
        is the position females have held in the world for so long
        is that you are suppressed incessantly
        is the handicap of etiquette
        is being restricted in going places & needing protection
        is not being able to be as free to do things

2. Limitations in opportunities, jobs, careers (I-3, 8; I-3/4, 12)
        is that most every business is run by a man
        is that her services are not valued as highly as a man's
        the difficulty in proving your ability in many areas
        *is that she usually does not get the career she has always
        wanted*
        *is that men have some advantages that women don't and that
        some women would like to have*

3. Limitations in her standing as a thinking person (I-3/4, 12;
        I-4/5, 2)
        not being able to stand up for what is right
        is being unable to express yourself
        is frequently being intellectually demoralized
        her opinions often aren't respected as highly as a mans

is not being expected to achieve as much as men in the same field

4. —is being taken for granted

5. Being judged by, overcoming stereotypes (general) (I-3/4, 1, 2; I-5, 3)
    is overcoming the male image of a woman
    is that people expect all of them to act alike
    is having to overcome stereotypes of the past
    is that some people think you must be femine most of the time

6. Burden of responsibilities (specified) (I-3, 6; I-3/4, 3, 4; I-4/5, 5; I-5, 1)
    is the problems you must face
    having to do things she doesn't want to do
    are the moral obligations that restrict her
    is being tied down with the responsibility of many small children
    is that you are depended upon at all times

7. —is the routine, drudgery of housekeeping; is the endless chores of the home (I-3/4, 4, 5; I-4/5, 4; I-5, 2)
    is having a million and one things to do
    is being saddled with small trivial jobs
    is getting into a rut around the house
    is that you always feel there is more to do than there is time

8. Role conflict (I-4/5, 1, 3; I-5, 1)
    is that she must engage in so many various roles
    is that she is often required to play several "roles" all at once
    is being torn between domesticity and a career
    is compromising career and desire for marriage and a family
    is that it is difficult to manage a home, raise a family and work at the same time

9. —is emotional pressures; a tendency to be too emotional (I-3, 9)
    is feeling so helpless at times
    is feeling insecure
    is the monthly emotional cycle
    is that she is always supposed to be calm and smiling

10. Not understanding, wondering about men (I-4/5, 5)

11. Sexual, dating, marriage problems (emphasis on external aspects) (I-4/5, 5; I-5, 2, 4)

is you have to except your sexual problems for what they are
is being single & still having to put up with mentrael periods
is having your parents remind you of all the trouble that you
can get into because you are a woman
is that people—society try to marry her off before she's ready
to know what she wants

12. —is playing the passive role (I-3/4, 11, 15; I-4/5, 3)
learning when not to be so independent
is that she should always play the passive role rather than an
aggressive & independent one
is the inability to sometimes be the aggressor in relations with
men who have the upper hand

13. Time necessary to maintain good appearance (I-3, 2)
is having to take two hours to get dressed to go out
is the times that has to be spent on such things as putting
rollers in her hair

14. —I love it; I like being a woman (I-3, 1)
I feel fortunate to be a woman
I am glad and cannot think otherwise
I still enjoy it thoroughly, except monthly periods
I can't think of anything wrong with being a woman. I en-
joy it

Unclassified
is you can't haul off & hit somebody

I-4/5

Most I-4/5 complaints are similar to those found at I-4, but are viewed with greater perspective. Restrictions and expectations are seen in terms of roles versus impositions of society. One response about the complexity of filling several roles simultaneously is put in this same category partly because of the unusual combination, wife, mother, daughter instead of wife, mother, maid, and partly because of the juxtaposition of complexity and simultaneity, a combination we have not seen at I-4. There is essentially the same I-4 complaint about housework, but also acceptance, "responsibility of tedious housework." Role conflict expressed at I-4 is experienced at I-4/5 in terms of conflict between being dependent and independent, a more internalized version of essentially the same problem. Problems of love and marriage also emphasize more internal issues, "deciding what love is," or concern adjustment to or happiness in marriage.

1. Restriction or confusion in woman's role (I-4, 1, 8; I-5, 1, 3)
   is being confined by roles
   is the ambiguous definition society has of her role
   is the confusion in society's expectations of women today
   is the complex roles she tries to fulfill as wife, mother, daughter all at once

2. Limitations in making decisions (I-4, 1, 3)
   is having to wait for men to make decisions
   is having to wait until men (boys in my case) decide they're going to notice you
   is the not always being free to make decisions and follow through on them

3. Dependence as a problem (I-3/4, 11; I-4, 8, 12)
   the conflict of being independent and self sufficient and being expected to be dependent such as on dates, etc.
   is that its often difficult to reconcile feminity and desire to have a successful career
   a feeling of insecurity. You give up your wage earning potential when you marry, and yet you may need to earn a living some day

4. —responsibility of tedious housework (I-3/4, 3; I-4, 7)
   is that she must perform certain menial tasks that have only indirect values

5. Emotional difficulties concerning love and marriage (I-3, 12; I-3/4, 17; I-4, 10, 11; I-5, 2, 4)
   is deciding what love is
   is finding the right man to marry and knowing for sure that he is the right man for you
   is her poor ability in knowing how to understand and cope with the opposite sex
   is that she might not find the right husband and so wind up a bitterly unhappily married woman or a frustrated old maid
   is the difficulty women often have coming to adjust to the fact that marriage is not all romance, & love, & "a bed of roses"

Unclassified
   is being healthly aggressive and yet not controlling in what society

I-5

Where the I-4 subject sees the many obligations placed on women, the I-4/5 woman emphasizes the context from which they result; for the I-5 subject the urgent aspect is the inner conflict that results, for example, a conflict of duties. At this level household chores and other pressures are seen as threats to maintaining one's individuality. Similarly, specific stereotypes are singled out as obstacles to being the person one wants to be. Elaborated concerns about tragedies of childbearing seem to come from I-5 protocols, whereas simple statements about "losing a child" come from lower ones.

1. Inner conflict (I-4, 6, 8; I-4/5, 1)
    is being torn between her duty as a creature of the modern world, and her duty to be an old-fashioned wife
    is being in conflict over the changing female role

2. Difficulty in maintaining individuality in the face of pressures, household duties (I-4, 7)
    is that one can get into a domestic rut without constant vigilance
    is that after she is married with kids her mind may go to waste (my mother's isn't)
    is that there is a greater chance of her becoming stagnant intellectually if she gets overwhelmed with household chores
    is that she is often made to conform, and is frowned upon if she attempts to be individualistic
    is the internal and external pressure to submerge one's personality

3. Criticism of stereotypes (explicitly stated) (I-3/4, 1; I-4, 5; I-4/5, 1)
    is being considered too weak in character to carry burdens
    is that some people treat you like a dear little girl and some like a cruel scheming shrew
    is trying to buck the traditional ideas surrounding the feminine mystique
    is being lumped into a general category labeled "Women"
    is that most men expect them to be perfect

4. Personal tragedies related to childbearing (uniquely expressed) (I-3, 4; I-3/4, 16)
    is birthing a child and losing it or seeing it a helpless cripple
    is not being able to be proud of a child born out of wedlock

I-6

Both responses classed I-6 state, in separate ways, that what is best or worst depends on what each woman makes of her circumstances.

Unclassified
> *cannot be generalized, as one woman makes an asset of the same situation decried by another*
> *is accepting your position as a woman and an individual, but once found ceases to be the worst and becomes the best*

A Good Mother—

This stem has the virtue that it draws many identifiable high responses, but it has the defect that many completions are given over a wide range, for example, "is loving" (I-2 to I-5), "is like mine" (I-2 to I-5), "is my goal" (Delta to I-4/5). The most frequent themes at all levels are versions of: is good to have, is unselfish, takes care of her family, is loving and understanding, and guides and disciplines. Directly or implicitly hostile statements about the mother are less common than for other stems concerning mother. These statements tend to be ones saying what a good mother should not do or be, and are more easily seen as criticisms of the subject's own mother than anything else: "shouldn't run out on her children" (Delta), "should put love before pride" (I-4). Below I-3 such negative remarks have a complaining or demanding tone; many at Delta also are sarcastic or sardonic. The few rated I-3 are paradoxical, saying essentially that a good mother may not be good. At I-4 the corresponding negative remarks are

339

criticisms concerning more or less abstract qualities, capacity to show love, building up daughter's self-confidence, being fair. In making such specific criticisms the subject seems to indicate that mother is not totally rejected even though there is resentment against irritating traits. The touchstone for assigning an I-4 rather than a Delta rating is the abstractness of the conception. Negative statements can occur even in a context rich enough to merit I-4/5 rating: "loves her children, never compares them to someone else and doesn't make it impossible to talk to them. They should also have outside interest."

Since there is not much disagreement about the qualities of a good mother, and there is as much variation within as between I-levels on what qualities are mentioned, an important clue is the number of really different themes or qualities mentioned, whether in a series or in combination. At higher levels one knows that no single quality makes a mother good; the requirements, in fact, are somewhat contradictory.

Some of our subjects are mothers, some are adolescent girls. However, there is no necessary relation to whether this item is answered in the role of mother or daughter. Below I-3 responses in many cases sound like demands for unlimited attention. At I-4 and above many responses sound like aspirations or admonitions to oneself.

I-2

A subject at this level tends to describe a good mother in terms like fun, nice, kind, and sweet, which are not only restatements of the "good" in the stem but also somewhat false emotionally here. Probably a reflection of the unlimited demands of the I-2 subject are "is always good to her children," "buyies mostly ever thing you want." One category, similar to some found at higher levels, puts emphasis on the mother as a source of supply: "always takes care," as opposed to the more evaluational "takes good care of her children" (I-3), or the more inward "cares for her family" (I-3/4).

*1. —takes care of, looks after her children; stays home and takes care (I-3, 3, 7; I-3/4, 5)
   sees after the children
   feeds her children, and stay home at night
   stay home and look after her children
   is a woman who stay at home and cook, wash, iron, make bed and take care of him

2. —is good, nice, sweet (I-3, 2, 8)
   is always good

3. —is good, nice, sweet, kind to her children; gets them things
(Δ, 6; I-3, 2)
is always kind to her children
is very sweet to her child
is a mother who see to that her child gets things before she do and etc.
buyies mostly ever thing you want

Unclassified
would feel good

DELTA

Most responses classed at this level have in common a demanding or complaining tone. There are complaints about intrusiveness, lack of attention, and the mother's misbehavior. "Thinks of children, not herself" is contrasted with the cliché classed at I-3, "thinks of her children first." The category, "is always with her children; shouldn't leave," is a demand for constant physical presence as opposed to the more general, "always has time for her children" (I-3/4). The category dealing with complete loyalty and trust and "loves her child no matter what" may reflect a resentment of the mother's demands and control.

1. —is loyal; trusts her child; loves her child no matter what (I-3, 1; I-3/4, 2)
is loyality with her children and does good things for the family
should trust her child

2. —doesn't pry into her child's private life
leaves her daugher alone on a date

3. —is always with her children; shouldn't leave (I-3, 6, 7; I-3/4, 4)
shouldn't leave her kids alone
is always keeping an eye on her children
shouldn't run out on her children

4. —shouldn't run around
is one that never goes out every night to the hotel or something like that
is a mother who doesn't make eyes at other happily married men

5. —thinks of children, not herself (complaining tone) (I-3, 5)
isn't always thinking of social statis

6. —lets her children do what they want (I-2, 3; I-4, 11)
should always please her children
should respect her children's wishes

7. —is hard to find

Unclassified
went that way
should not hesitate to speak up when she thinks her daughter
   might be in the wrong company
is a married mother
keeps her house clean. I hate a sloppy mother!

DELTA/3

Responses placed at this level deal with mother as being a house-keeper or with her functions as a housekeeper: cleaning house, feeding children, and the like. Thus a good mother is defined by concrete, visible actions.

1. —should be a good housewife; makes a good home; does housework (I-3, 10; I-3/4, 8)
is a very good housekeeper
wants to see that her Kids have a happy home and food on
   the table
will keep her house and children clean
should make good food and care for others

I-3

The I-3 subject tends to describe a good mother with broad compliments, wonderful, important, and so on, or by clichés, "thinks of her children first," "loves her children equally." Statements that she loves and understands her children come from protocols covering the entire I-level range, but predominantly from I-3 protocols. Many categories classed at this level focus on behavior, describing what one should do to be a good mother. She is strict, she punishes, she stays home, she talks, helps, guides and teaches. She does what is good or right, implying an absolute external standard as opposed to the relative standard, "does what's best" (I-3/4), or to internalized standards evident in "does her best" (I-4). Responses stating that a good mother has good, happy children are concerned with the children's present state as opposed to responses concerned with future outcomes, ". . . tries to help them become good young men and women" (I-4). Traits described at this level are behavioral ones, such as "hard working," unlike the more internal ones classed at I-3/4: warm, thoughtful, and so on. At I-3, the subject may mention other roles, wife, friend, companion, but without the implication that these are alternatives, "is a friend as well as a parent" (I-4).

**1. —loves, understands her children (Δ, 1; I-3/4, 1, 14; I-4, 11)
       should love her kids
       has to understand her kids
       trys to understand her children

*2. —is, should be loving, kind, understanding (I-2, 2, 3; I-3/4, 1)
       is very understaning
       is a loving person

3. —takes good care of her children; loves and takes care (I-2, 1; I-3/4, 5)
       takes loving and tender care of her children
       loves her children and takes good care of them
       should take of care of her children well
       takes good care of hersef and kids if she has any

*4. —is fair, impartial; loves all her family equally
       should treat her children equally
       loves her husband as much as her children
       is fair in dealing with her children
       has equal concern for all her children

*5. —thinks of, puts her family first (Δ, 5; I-3/4, 11; I-4, 10)
       always puts her family before herself

6. —cares about, worries about her children (Δ, 3; I-3/4, 6)
       is the care of her family
       always worries and watches her children

7. —stays home; never neglects her children, her responsibilities (I-2, 1; Δ, 3)
       never neglects her responsibility as a parent

*8. —is wonderful, lovely, an asset, good to have (I-2, 2; I-3/4, 3)
       is the best yet

9. —is important, essential, necessary
       mean a lot to a famialy
       is most desirable

10. —is a good wife; has good, happy children (Δ/3, 1; I-4, 3, 9)
       is a good woman
       usually has well-brought up children

makes for a good wife and will have good children
makes her children happy

11. —does what is good, right, proper (I-3/4, 9; I-4, 14)
    should try to rear her children right
    raises her children properly
    brings up her children in the right way

12. —is strict; punishes (I-3/4, 10)
    always corrects her child
    does spank her children

13. —helps, guides, teaches children; teaches right from wrong
    will teach her children about God
    sets limits, controls and directs
    is one who teaches and loves her children
    is also a teacher
    is always willing to help
    is one who teaches her children good manners, keeps them
    clean & sees that they gets a good education

14. —helps, is there when needed
    is one who will always help when it is needed
    tries to help when you ask her
    is always around when trouble comes

15. —is a friend, companion; is close (I-4, 3)
    tries to be friends with her child
    is a girl's best friend
    is a close mother with her children

16. —talks with her children (I-3/4, 13)
    is a wonderful person to talk things over with
    talks to her children

17. Behavioral traits
    is a church going mother
    is a hard working one

18. —is me, my mother (I-4, 18)
    is something I hope I am
    I sure try to be
    is what I have
    is one like mine

Unclassified
    is happy
    is a wise mother

should see that they have well balances meals
is sometimes too good

I-3/4

Responses classed at I-3/4 begin to take into account more interpersonal aspects of the mother-daughter relation. The verb "cares" in the
response "cares for her family" has both the behavioral connotation of
"takes care" (I-2) or "takes good care" (I-3) and the interpersonal connotation of "is concerned" (I-3/4). Where the I-3 subject speaks of loving her child, the I-3/4 subject may speak of giving or showing love. A
good mother is one who listens (I-3/4) rather than one who talks (I-3).
Interpersonal traits are classed at this level though these responses are
given by subjects at all I-levels, including a fairly large number of I-3
subjects. Women who say, "is a blessing," "is a treasure," suggest that all
mothers are not necessarily good mothers, an idea made explicit at I-4:
"is a rare one!" The responses dealing with a good mother as a goal
come from a wide range of protocols but can be differentiated from those
describing the subject, "I hope is me" (I-3).

*1. —is, should be patient, thoughtful, considerate (I-3, 1, 2;
   I-4, 13)
   should be considerate and love children
   is a thoughtful, kind and gracious woman

2. —is, should be consistent, dependable, honest (Δ, 1)
   is consistent, patient, and above all, loving
   is usually consistent in child-rearing practice
   should be consistent and loving

3. —is a blessing, a treasure, a precious possession (I-3, 8)
   cannot be replaced
   an unforgettable and priceless one is a blessed thing to be
   is a Joy forever

4. —devotes time to her family (Δ, 3)
   is with her family often
   is available to her children and husband at all times
   always has time for her children
   gives her child time as well as things

5. —cares for, provides for her family (I-2, 1; I-3, 3; I-4, 4)
   is one who cares for her family as well as others
   cares well for her husband and children

is one who care & looks out for her child in all respects
will provide for her family

6. —is interested, concerned, devoted to her family (I-3, 6;
   I-4, 10)
   has her family at heart
   's whole life is her family
   is constantly concerned for her family
   is interested in all that her children do

7. —wants, keeps her family happy
   wants her children to be happy
   always sees that her family is contended

8. —makes a happy home (Δ/3, 1)
   provides a home for her children filled with love, acceptance,
       etc.
   tries to make the home a haven
   provides a wholesome environment for her children
   strives to make a happy & devoted home & family

9. —does what's best; wants the best for her children (I-3, 11;
   I-4, 10, 14)
   tries always to know what's best for her children
   does the best thing for her children
   trys always to provide the best for her children

10. —doesn't spoil her children (I-3, 12)
    should never pamper her child
    should not give a child everything he wants

11. —is unselfish, self-sacrificing (I-3, 5; I-4/5, 5)
    gives as much and even more than she receives
    has considerable selflessness
    loves her family and except responsibilities with out a grumble

12. —enjoys children, her family; is proud of her children
    is one who enjoys fully being a mother

13. —listens to her children; is attentive; is one you can confide
    in (I-3, 16)
    is a good lisener
    can listen to a childs tales of woe
    always listens to what her children has to say
    pays attention to her children
    a loving and understanding person. and one you could tell
        everything you feel

14. —gives love, security; shows her love to her family (I-3, 1)
    gives a lot of love and security and wants to be a mother
    will give her child everything; especially love & understand-
      ing
    should show love to her husband and children always
    not only loves her children, but shows it

15. —is an adviser, counselor
    is a good psychologist

16. —gains satisfaction, rewards
    realizes much satisfaction
    reaps rewards in many ways

17. —is my goal, what I want to be
    is what I'm going to do my best to be
    is a desired goal

18. —is hard to define; is many things
    follows no particular mode. (standard)
    varies
    there are all kinds, but they have in common a love for their
      children and a desire to aid them in every way possible

Unclassified
    is a mother that feels a child's hurt
    is one who is understanding whenever possible

I-4

Many I-4 responses combine ideas which stated alone or without qualification are classed at lower levels. When compound responses are found at lower levels, the responses are usually elaborations of a single theme: "is understanding, kind and loving" (I-3), "loves, worries and cares for her husband and children all her life" (I-3/4). The I-4 subject typically balances contradictory ideas, such as love and discipline, friend and parent, helps but does not interfere. These responses reflect what seems to be a typical process of ego development: becoming aware of contradictory ideas at one's current level and then combining them to form more complex ideas, thus achieving a higher level. The traits of a good mother mentioned at this level are traits one might expect of a person who can balance and weigh contradictions: tolerance, acceptance, being broadminded. At I-4 there is a sensitivity to the child's inner life not apparent at lower levels. A good mother "is alert to the needs of her children" (I-4), rather than "understands her child" (I-3); "makes her children feel secure" (I-4), rather than "gives her children love and security" (I-3/4). Ideas which first occur at I-4 are those concerned with the development and future outcome of childrearing, with recognizing the individuality and independence of the child. Definite responses about teaching and encouraging individuality are classed at higher levels. The categories dealing with the development of children and the outcomes of childrearing not only contain an orientation to the future, but along with a second category, "is respected, loved, admired by her family," contain the implied contingency, "if one is a good mother, then . . ." one will be loved, or one will raise healthy children.

*1. —uses both love (understanding, patience) and discipline (I-5, 5)

affectionate, understanding but firm
is one who loves her children but does not spoil them
will be understanding but strict with her children
loves her children, and knows when to and when not to punish them, and is open to give advice when the child wants it
is someone who loves her children and wants them to be happy but also believes in obedience

2. —loves, helps, guides without domineering, interfering (I-4/5, 5; I-5, 5)

will not domineer her children but will keep control in an understanding and tactful manner
is one who helps without interfering

3. Fills other roles: wife, friend, father, and so on (I-3, 10, 15; I-5, 5)

is also a good wife
is a friend as well as a parent
should be a friend and companion as well as a mother
is both mother and father in trying times
is something pretty hard to find nowdays. good house keeper or home maker, yes! but good mother, no!

4. —also loves, cares for her husband (I-3/4, 5)

is devoted to her children, but never forgets her husband
tries to give each child the same amount of attention & discipline & still look after her husband
loves her children as much as she does her husband and she cares enough for him to make a few sacrifices for them
is one that takes care of her children, but does not fail to notice her husband

5. —considers herself also (I-5, 4)
   loves her home children and husband and still has outside interest
   forgets not herself

6. —allows children to grow up, think for themselves, make their own decisions (I-4/5, 2, 3; I-5, 1)
   loves and lets go
   is one who lets her children grow up
   lets her children live
   does not force her opinions on her grown children
   knows that her children must learn to make their own decisions
   never makes her kids feel babyish and she should give them the right to speak for themselves and make their own decisions

7. —loves her children in spite of faults; sees them as individuals (I-4/5, 2; I-5, 1)
   loves her children but tries to understand their actions good or bad
   understands her children's problems and treats them as different individuals
   sees her children as separate beings rather than as extensions of her own personality
   cares about her child as an individual

8. Concern with development of her children (I-4/5, 1)
   shows interest in all phases of her child's life
   tryes to raise her child instead of just letting it grow
   derives great pleasure from her family and enjoys watching them grow and develop
   watches both the spiritual and educational growth of her children
   is interested in her childrens fulfilling their potentials

9. Concern with eventual outcome of childrearing—healthy, happy, well-behaved (I-3, 10; I-4/5, 1)
   knows she is a good mother when her children are happy and feel loved when they become adults
   raises physically and mentally healthy children
   is one who has succeeded in giving her child the things he needs most to become a welladjusted individual
   is one who loves and understands her children, and who tries to help them to be good young men & women

10. —is concerned with, aware of her children's needs, problems, welfare, happiness (I-3, 5; I-3/4, 6, 9; I-4/5, 4)

knows when her child is unhappy

is alert to the needs of her children

takes an active interest in the welfare of her children

has a deep concern for her children's happiness as well as their health and safety

is one who always considers the interest & good of her family

is concerned with what's good for the child

thinks of her family first—which includes health—etc.

is someone who thinks of the welfare of the child and his needs rather than her own

puts the needs & good of her family before everything—at times even herself

11. —respects her children; gives them the feeling of love, security, being wanted (Δ, 6; I-3, 1)

will treat her children with respect, but the reverse must be present also

is one who tries to give her children stability and the feeling security and love

makes her children feel secure

always takes the best care of her children as she possibly can & makes them feel wanted

12. —is respected, loved, admired by her family

arouses the respect and love of her children

commands respect from her family, is a devoted wife and a sincere friend to her children

13. —is, should be tolerant, accepting, broadminded (I-3/4, 1)

is an acceptant mother

has understanding, patience, love and tolerance

sees all sides of the problem

kind understanding and not to jump to and conclusion

is open and consistent in dealing with her family

14. —does her best, all that she can (I-3, 11; I-3/4, 9)

is a person who does her best

tries to rear her children as good as she can

is one that loves her Children and does her best to make them happy

should give as much time, attention and devotion to her children as she possibly can

15. —is relaxed, self-confident; does not try too hard to be one
(I-5, 3)
relaxes & enjoys her children
is one who believes in herself
doesn't worry about doing the right thing for her children
conceals the fact

16. Does not have certain specific character flaws (implied criticism)
is not possessive
is someone who does not criticize
should put love before pride
does not try to have a career and be a mother too

17. Difficulties and imperfections of motherhood
has good and bad moment in her life
has many responsibilities
train and raise her children propperly sometimes with help
from other who may know a little more
is something one must work at

18. —is (not) the description of my mother (I-3, 18)
is personified in my mother
, is a category were my mother fails in

Unclassified
is a rare one!
sets a good example
is one who shares herself with her family
does what she can and accepts the inevitable

I-4/5

Several categories placed at this level deal with the growing independence of the child. One is concerned with the eventual emotional
independence from mother. Another is concerned with teaching individuality and self-sufficiency. The similar category at I-5, "allows, encourages individuality, independence," does not contain the implication
that independence is imposed on the growing child, as do the responses
placed here, but rather that independence develops naturally unless
squelched. Perhaps "does not dominate, overprotect" is the I-4/5 version
of this idea. Also classed I-4/5 are those responses concerned with the
ability to put herself in her child's position, responses more inclusive than
"is a mother that feels a child's hurt" (I-3/4). There is concern for the

child's development at this level, as there is at I-4, but at I-4/5 it is stated in terms of moral and social development.

1. Concern with outcome of childrearing, with social or moral development (I-4, 8, 9)
    is what usually makes good, devoted parents of her own children in the future
    cares for her children with the thought of making them respectable citizens
    both disciplines and spoils her children and raises them up with a good sense of values and morals
    teaches her child values from a very early age
    helps her children grow emotionally & socially by providing numerous experiences

2. —teaches independence, self-sufficiency (I-4, 6, 7; I-5, 1)
    helps her children grow to be self-confident and independent
    will raise her children so they are ambitious, independent and know right from wrong
    works to make her family happy and teaches discipline and individualism

3. Separation as a developmental phase (I-4, 6; I-5, 1)
    cares enough for her children, to let them go when they are ready
    trys to allow her children to grow up without excessive discipline and without making them feel that they are hurting her when they leave home
    prepares both herself and her children for their eventually leave taking
    knows how to untie gradually the apron strings and shift responsibility to young shoulders
    gives her children emotional freedom

4. Tries to see the child's view (I-4, 10)
    tries to remember back to her own girlhood before passing judgment or punishing
    tries to understand her children's viewpoint even if she can't always agree
    is patient, & able to put herself in her child's position

5. —does not dominate, overprotect (I-3/4, 11; I-4, 2)
    is one who is neither neglectful or over-protective
    does not overprotect her child and smother it in love
    is warm without smothering her children

Unclassified

> *loves her children tangibly as well as intangibly; she knows how to and does set limits*
>
> *is one who communicates deeply with her family, has trust when in doubt & loves*
>
> *is sacrificing, seeing in her children the attainment of her unachieved goals*
>
> *is a child's dream and a woman's goal*
>
> *loves her children, never compares them to someone else and doesn't make it impossible to talk to them. They should have outside interest*

I-5

Most responses classed I-5 elaborate and combine ideas found at I-4 and I-4/5. The category, "helps make decisions, solve problems," contains a recognition that growing children need help and advice given in an atmosphere of mutuality, thus combining the ideas found at lower levels of guiding and respecting the child's growing independence. Where an I-4 subject may say that a good mother also fills other roles, the I-5 subject recognizes the resultant conflicting demands that may be imposed on the mother and that must be accepted to be a good mother; the same responses can be seen as elaborations of the I-4 idea of giving both love and discipline. The new ideas classed here are the growth of independence and individuality as being inherent in the child and the necessity to strike a balance between one's own needs and the needs of the family. Both ideas are expressed clearly and explicitly at I-6.

1. —allows, encourages individuality, independence (I-4, 6, 7; I-4/5, 2, 3; I-6, 1)

   > *loves her children but gives them freedom to be independent —which isn't always easy*
   >
   > *should not only care about her children and show interest in them but should encourage them to develop on their own*
   >
   > *helps her children to grow in mind and spirit, but allows and encourages them to develop ideas of their own*
   >
   > *provides consistent discipline for her children and allows them to grow up without over protecting them*
   >
   > *is one who shows trust in her children and gives them responsibility and knows and trusts them to do it without actually saying so*
   >
   > *tries to understand her children as individuals, is honest, and behaves naturally around them*

*is one that balances protective love with larger and larger
amounts of freedom as the child matures*

2. —helps make decisions, solve problems (mutuality)

*looks after her family and cares for it by being aware of their
needs and letting them go at their own speed and helping
them to solve problems and have fun together*

*understands problems of her children and can talk to them
about possible solutions*

3. Is relaxed, confident (elaborated); accepts her limitations
(I-4, 15)

relaxes, and lets her children know it

*has a warm feeling toward her children and a confidence in
herself*

*is not always perfect and it is better if she does not pretend
to be*

*can be a woman who believes in her task and, who is open
enough to except what life gave her*

4. —balances her needs and her family's (children's) (I-4, 5)

*thinks first of her children but can not neglect her own con-
tinued development*

is first a good wife; and happy

5. Both love and discipline (original and elaborated) (I-4, 1,
2, 3)

*should be loving, patient, should have fun with her children,
but always remember she is the mother and not another
child, the voice of authority*

*has an unselfish interest in her children. She stimulates them
and is their companion as well as an ever present disciplinarian*

*must teach her children early in life that there are things they
cannot do and yet still be a loving and forgiving person*

*is a kind and understanding person who can sympathize and
still obtain respect as well as love*

*establishes ideals, is a firm disciplinarian, and is available to
listen constructively and with love*

Unclassified

*is one who has an interest in her children's welfare physically,
spiritually, emotionally and socially*

*loves and cares for her children in spite difficulties which she
personally can have physically or emotionally*

I-6

Here we have a few responses that indicate both the complexity of being a good mother, that different requirements must be met, and that ultimately the child must find his own identity. These responses convey in unique language a glimpse of the difficulty in reconciling the parents' responsibility and the child's need to find himself and achieve eventual autonomy, hence, in a sense, the impossibility of being a good mother.

1. Several aspects, including respect for child's unique identity
   (I-5, 1)

   lets go, loves without demanding conformity to her own ideals and standards—and helps to guide if possible

   is kind, consistent, tender, sensitive and always *aware a child is master of its own soul*

   is one whose bounty of love extends to and influences her children that they, too, may become integral and loving persons

Unclassified

   is able to arrive at some kind of balance between her ambitions and hopes for her family and what she thinks each and all of them can work toward and helps in any way she can

Sometimes She Wished That—

This stem contains an invitation to regression; so one must not be surprised when subjects at any level respond in terms of typical weaknesses rather than strengths. Most responses are clauses beginning with "she" or "I." Where the response begins "she," in most though not all cases the subject seems to be referring to herself. Where the response begins "I," in many cases the "she" of the stem seems to mean the mother; thus, the subject is giving the mother's wish for the subject. In other cases, however, one has the feeling that it is simply a matter of semantic slippage; the "she" of the stem is the same person as the "I" of the response. The latter instances are similar to the kind of thinking one finds on the lowest protocols and hence are rated I-2. There is of course no guarantee that we shall always make such inferences correctly.

Many of our subjects, like the fisherman's wife in the fairytale, waste their wish on hostile thoughts ("there weren't any boys") or anti-wishes ("she was dead," "she had never been born"). One cannot always discriminate hostile from anti-wishes ("I was dead"), but both are clearly anhedonic. Almost half the responses on I-2 and Delta protocols are either hostile or self-destructive in content. Such wishes are rare at the I-4 level and probably nonexistent at higher levels. Should they occur above the I-4 level, one would therefore suspect depression or other pathology; there may be such unfavorable connotations even at I-4, but we have no data on the matter.

The unpleasant tone of the I-2 and, less uniformly, Delta responses is striking. Escapist wishes, neutral in tone, are of next greatest frequency, while wishes expressing some kind of happiness or fulfillment, appearing first at Delta, increase at I-3 and higher levels. Wishes that dwell on unpleasant aspects of life occur at all levels but they change from self-destructive ones to wishes for specific and limited changes at high levels, thus expressing both self-criticism (which self-destruction does not) and a greater sense of choosing or having chosen one's own destiny.

I-2

All the categories at this level are anhedonic. We have two hypotheses about the category "I was dead." One is that it is derived from the more common "she was dead" (Delta/3) by semantic slippage, substituting "I" for "she." It could be rated I-2 for that reason. A more intricate but perhaps more apposite hypothesis is also compatible with the I-2 rating. If one's hostile feelings toward mother appear as undisguised death wishes, one would perceive the same in mother, whether justly or not. Only one subject put such a thought clearly: "I was dead and I wished she was." Some responses apparently indicating the mother's displeasure with the subject's behavior are classed at this level ("I wouldn't do the things I do"), contrasting with rudimentary self-criticism at I-3 ("she hadn't done it"). A hypothetical connecting theme in the I-2 categories is perception of the mother as rejecting the subject.

1. —I was dead; I was not her child (Δ/3, 1; I-3, 9; I-3/4, 11)
   dead
   I was dead and I wished she was
   I wasn't born

2. —she didn't have any children (I-3/4, 3)
   she had never had children

3. —I would do what she wanted (I-3, 10)
   I wouldn't do the things I do
   you do all the thing she ask you to

Unclassified
   my brother and I don't fight

DELTA

The dependent complaining of the Delta subject is usually directed against the mother or her husband. The subject not only wants to be taken care of, she wants to be understood, which often seems to mean given permission. The wish to be happy or to get what one wants is a bit redundant of the stem; at the Delta level such responses are simple, un-elaborated, and passive in tone compared to similar thoughts at higher levels. Hostile wishes are not frequent, but when they do occur they are characteristic for this level.

1. —I'll be happy; I'll get the things I want (passive tone) (I-3, 1; I-3/4, 7; I-4, 3)
   good things would happen

2. Dependent complaining
   she had a different mother
   her mother wasn't so square
   her mother would understand
   her husband would leave her alone
   my husbin would stay home sometime
   someone els would cook supper

3. Hostile wishes
   there weren't any boys
   there was no school
   she could make her x best friend jelous
   her grandchildren would be 10 times as mean as her children
   she slamed the door in her face

DELTA/3

The categories classed at this level are negative in tone. They are put here as compromise because they are relatively more frequent on low protocols but not infrequent at I-3 or even I-4. An exception to the fore-going remarks is the wish for a car or bicycle. One thinks of the old ex-pression, "If wishes were horses, then beggars would ride." Apparently modern wishes have wheels.

*1. —she were dead; she had never been born (I-2, 1; I-3/4, 11)
   she never was alive
   she could die
   all her troubles were over. (6 ft. under)

2. —she were a boy, man
   I had been a boy
   I could have been a boy

3. —she could leave, run away, never come back (I-3, 5, 7, 9)
   she left home
   she wouldn't never have to go home
   she could get out of here, too
   she could leave and get married and never come back
   I would leave
   I would leave and don't come back again
   we were gone

4. —she were out of school; school was over (I-3, 8; I-3/4, 8)
   she could quit school
   she didn't have to go to school

5. —she were not married (I-3/4, 3)
   she never married
   she was single

6. —she had a bicycle, car (I-3, 1)
   she do not have to ride the bus

I-3

Pleasurable wishes predominate at I-3, often concrete and conven-tional ones, riches, good looks, popularity, health. Projected antagonism, from the mother or other women, takes the moderate form, "I was not around." Escape wishes refer to being alone or getting away. One cate-gory is interpretable as regret over a sexual episode; the most common example is "she hadn't done it." The combination of a vague sense of regret and yet apparent reference to something concrete would be rated here even if the presumption of sexual reference were incorrect.

*1. Desire for money, material possessions (unelaborated) (Δ, 1; $\Delta/3$, 6; I-3/4, 7)
    she was a millionaire
    she had a rich man
    she was born rich

2. Reference to appearance, popularity
    she were taller and better looking

3. —she were older, younger (I-4, 8, 11; I-4/5, 4)
    she was a child again
    she was grown up

*4. —she could be alone
    I could go somewhere by myself
    she could be left alone
    she was alone
    she could just run away from people

5. —she were someplace else; she could get away ($\Delta/3$, 3; I-3/4, 5)
    she lived in another city
    she could go where she wanted to
    she were a thousand miles away
    she could get away from it all

6. —she could get out of problems, troubles (I-4, 1)
    she could forget her problems
    she could get out of all her troubles

7. —she could go home, be with her mother ($\Delta/3$, 3)
    she was back home
    they were all home again
    I had stayed home
    mother was here

8. —she could quit work; she was finished ($\Delta/3$, 4; I-3/4, 8)
    her children were grown
    she could retired
    she didn't have to do all these things
    it was finished
    she had help

9. —I was not around (I-2, 1; $\Delta/3$, 3)
    I would no longer be her friend
    some times she wished that I was a long way from here

10. Wish for concrete actions (I-2, 3; I-3/4, 2)
    she could go out
    I would study more
    I would call her
    my brothers were more neat

11. —she was better behaved; she could forget (probably veiled reference to a sexual experience) (I-4, 6)
    she hadn't done it
    she hadn't been too forward with the boys
    she had never gone on the date
    she had never heard of the male sex
    she'd never met him
    people would forget some things
    she could ignore certain things
    sometimes I wished that—some people didn't even know me
    she would never see him again

12. Health
    her mother would never die
    she had been born strong

13. Evasion (I-5, 4)
    no thoughts
    ?
    I don't know what you mean she

Unclassified
    she was of another race
    she was a princess
    her parents weren't as strict
    she were free
    she was lucky

I-3/4

Although as a general rule we class at the same level two responses that differ only by insertion of a negative, there are exceptions here. Wishing to be rid of a family one already has ("she didn't have any children," I-2; "she were not married," Delta/3) is vastly different from wishing to have a family. Although there are no large and clear differences between I-3 and I-3/4 responses on this item, the I-3/4 answer tends to be more positive and more purposeful, as illustrated by the difference between getting away from things (I-3) and taking a vacation (I-3/4). Altruistic wishes, both in the form of wishing benefits for other people and of wishing for the solution of concrete social problems, such as war or starving children, are a new element at this level. Concern for more abstract social problems is rated higher.

*1. —she were married
   I was married
   she had accepted his ring
   she were through school and happily married
   she could get married and have a baby

2. —she had a boy friend (I-3, 10; I-4/5, 3)
   she would meet the guy
   her lover was home from the Navy
   her boyfriend would write
   he would kiss her

3. —she had a large family; she had married earlier, later (I-2, 2; Δ/3, 5)
   she had had more children
   she hadn't had so many children
   her children had come earlier
   she had brothers and sisters

4. —things were different, better, easier
   everything is smooth sailing
   times were a little easier
   life had turned out differently
   things were better for her children

5. —she could travel, take a vacation (I-3, 5)
   she could take a trip
   she could go to Europe

6. —she had more spare time (I-4, 1, 2)
   she had time to herself
   she had more time to spend with her children for recreation
   she had more time to travel

7. —she could afford more things (Δ, 1; I-3, 1)
   we had more money for a home of our own
   she could buy more for her children & herself

8. Dissatisfaction with education or career (Δ/3, 4; I-3, 8; I-4/5, 4)
   she had gone to college
   she could go to school
   she had never gone to school
   she had stayed at home instead of going to work

she had gone some where else for her education
she could be a pediatrician
she were a pioneer
she was on her own

9. —she were different, more capable (I-4, 6, 7)
   she could do more
   she were more talented
   she could paint
   she had common sense
   she could be more expressive
   she was twins

10. —she were someone else (Δ/3, 2)
    she was another person

11. Wish for death in response to particular problems
    she was dead because no one loved her
    she was dead during hours of labor

12. Desire for fame or glamor
    she were beautiful and could become an actress
    she was a model
    she were a great personality

13. Altruistic wishes: social or moral issues or benefits to individuals (I-5, 3)
    war was an unknown word
    people expressed religious values honestly
    she had more money or was a better Christian
    all people could be as happy as she
    she was able to give them more
    she could be a missionery

I-4

In some ways the I-4 categories sound more like the I-3 than like the I-3/4 categories, for there is again a rather magical desire to escape responsibilities. What is different at I-4 is that the subject specifically states that she would like to shed responsibility, or worry, or decision, rather than just wanting to get away from it all, as does the I-3. Other I-4 subjects make it plain that they are playing with fantasies in their responses. Thus, the distinguishing feature of these responses is not the nature of the wish but the evident sense of choice or of participation. The aspiration to be a better, more mature person, with more of some differentiated trait, is a new theme at I-4. A frequent I-4 fantasy is that

there should be more hours in the day; at I-4/5 subject makes explicit
that she wants more time in order to be able to do more interesting
things.

1. Wish for relief from responsibilities or from expectations of
   self and others (I-3, 6; I-3/4, 6; I-5, 1)
   she did not have to take care of her children all the time
   she could be something completely frivolous
   someone would make her decisions for her
   life were not so real and earnest
   her tasks werent so over-whelming
   she was a child again, with no decisions to make
   she could move out of her house and not have to worry

*2. Change or escape—fanciful fantasy (I-3/4, 6; I-4/5, 2)
   there were more hours in the day
   time would stand still
   winter would never come
   she could fly away to never-never land
   she would always be young
   she had lived in another time
   all her problems could be solved in one day

3. Capturing or recapturing joy (Δ, 1)
   she could stand on a mountain top and shout for joy
   life was a bed of roses
   *she were back in the comfortable, happy surroundings that
      she had known*
   she could have more fun
   she could always be so happy

4. —she could live her life over again (I-4/5, 1)
   she could start from the beginning
   we had more than one life

5. —she had done some things differently, made different choices
   (I-4/5, 1)
   she had tried her hand at interior decorating
   *she could do some of the things she missed doing when she
      was younger*
   she had acted differently
   she had said or thought of what another had
   she had not been so hasty with some of her decisions

6. —she were a better person (I-3, 11; I-3/4, 9)
   *she could be a different sort of person, just the opposite of
      what she is*

she could have the qualities she felt dear
she could be prefect and do everything right. also make de-cisions that were right and pleased people
she had no faults
she was capable of more love and understanding for her family

7. Wish for more (less) of specified traits (I-3/4, 9)
   she had been more sensitive
   she were more aggressive
   I wouldn't be so shy and try to have more self-confidence
   she was more adventuresome and spirited
   she was more charitable
   her husband would be aggressive

8. Wish to be more independent, mature, self-motivated (I-3, 3; I-4/5, 4)
   she did not have to be dependent on her parents
   she had followed her own inclanations more
   she didn't have to depend on other people and inconvenience them
   the world could not control her actions

9. —she knew more; she could see into the future (I-4/5, 1)
   she knew more about people
   she could know everything
   she could live in a foreign country to get to really know the people
   she could be sure of what she was doing, at least once

10. Concern with accomplishment (I-4/5, 2)
    she could really make her mark in the world
    she'd applied herself more
    she could do more useful things
    she had more things to do

11. Reason for wanting to be older, younger, a boy, married, etc.
    she was a never a woman because of all the problems we have
    she was older, so she could hurry and date
    I would have been a boy because boys aren't that fussy about clothes
    she were as free as a college girl
    she was married—just in order not to study any more
    she were married to get away from everything

12. —people were kinder, more considerate (I-4/5, 3; I-5, 3)
    the world was charitable

I-4/5

Although the themes at I-4/5 are chiefly elaborations of ideas found at I-4, the view of life as a whole is much clearer than at I-4. The interest in life experiences and in relations with other people is more vivid and more vital.

1. View of life as a whole (I-4, 4, 5, 9)

   she could gain a greater depth in her response to life

   she could live several lives in different ages and different countries

   she had insisted on working instead of being just a housewife to change her whole way of life

   she could have become aware of the importance of an education earlier in life

   she had not persued education, but had chosen a more domestic, simple life

   she had married and had a family

   she knew where she was going

   she knew what she is

   life were not such a consistent series of decisions

   she would be grown up and never go through the phases of growing up to an adult

2. —she could do more interesting things (I-4, 2, 10)

   days were longer so she could do all of the things she wanted to do

   life was more interesting

   she was doing something interesting and challenging

   she could do some of the things she wanted to do and not be restricted by inadequate funds (e.g. go to the opera)

   there were more hours in the day in order to do more things

   she had more opportunities to express her own personality

3. Wish for closer interpersonal relations, renewal of past relations (I-3/4, 2; I-4, 12)

   she had a sister closer to her own age to talk things over with

   his mother would accept her and love her as her own did

   she could visit old friends

   she could sit down with all the people she liked and just talk a long time

   she could tell people how much she really liked them

4. Independence contingent on change in circumstances (I-3, 3; I-3/4, 8; I-4, 8)

> *she were already working and more on her own*
> *we were married and on our own*
> *she was no longer a child but a woman and on her own*

Unclassified

> *she could just get out and walk or just even climb a tree if*
> *she wishes*

I-5

Most characteristic of the I-5 level is a rather direct coping with inner conflict. Many of these responses are elaborations of the idea at I-4 that one would like to escape responsibility, but there is a clearer indication of there being two sides, and the responses are more original. A similar category expresses a wish and then retracts it or expresses some reservation about it. Not included in this category are responses just saying that it is impossible ("Sometimes I wish that—I had Chuck but it's impossible," from a Delta protocol). The thoughts expressed at the I-5 level assert rather that even getting one's wish would not suffice. We have seen no distinguishable I-6 responses.

1. Coping with inner conflict (I-4, 1)
   > *she did not see life at a depth she does because it would mean*
   > *less responsibility*
   > *she could give up her desires for a career and just be a woman*
   > *she was smarter or else too stupid to know the difference*
   > *she'd feel less guilty about things undone or unsaid regarding*
   > *the mother-daughter relationship—the she being me*
   > *she could feel void of any emotional ties with the opposite sex*
   > *and that she wasn't expected to ever marry*
   > *she could stop worrying for just a little while and just have*
   > *some hedonistic pleasure*
   > *she were neither so intelligent nor so discerning*
   > *she could escape from the apparently unbearable problems*
   > *she faced*

2. Renunciation or retraction of wish
   > *she could see but she got along well and was very happy*
   > *she had things she would not be happy with if she had them*
   > *she could be completely alone, although she knew this was not*
   > *normal or ideal*
   > *she could run away and hide from everything and everybody*
   > *but she knew that running was not the answer*

I would be just like my sisters; now she's glad I'm not
she could go back, but she realized this would not bring hap-
piness the second time

3. Social problems, abstract (I-3/4, 13; I-4, 12)
   people were less prejudiced & that she had greater faith in
   God
   there were not so many tight, closed-in minds in the world

4. The question is too indefinite, too hypothetical (I-3, 13)
   (I can no longer tell you about "she" it is too hypothetical)
   Sometimes I wish I had more native ability

ITEM 30

When I Am with a Man—

Responses concerning the subject's feelings occur at all levels for this stem. But the kinds of feelings described change, and one acts a part before feeling it: "I act myself" (I-3), "I remain myself" (I-3/4); "I act like a woman" (I-3), "I feel like a woman" (I-3/4). In general, the feelings described at one level are made contingent at the next higher level; for example, "I am happy" (I-3), "that I like I feel happy" (I-3/4); "I am at ease" (I-3/4), "who enjoys my company, I am at ease" (I-4); "I am stimulated" (I-4), "depending on the man, of course, I generally feel intellectually stimulated" (I-4/5).

At lower levels, particularly I-3, answers refer primarily to mo-

369

mentary actions and feelings. Going up the scale, an increasing proportion of responses also refer to aspects of the situation or people that extend beyond the limit of the date or occasion, such as enduring attachments, comparison of feelings or actions with those on other occasions, standards of conduct, enduring traits, sharing of interests, sense of continuing identity.

The relation implied in being with a man appears to be interpreted primarily as sexual below I-3 and as social at I-3 and above. Appreciation for several facets of the relation, social, sexual, professional, is clearly expressed at I-5. As one goes up the scale there is a deepening sense of reciprocity: "I have fun" (I-3), "I like, I have a good time" (I-3/4), "I enjoy his company," especially if he is an interesting person, and I hope he enjoys my company (I-4). At I-4 there is also concern for the man's interests. At the I-5 level the selectivity of the I-4 subject, enjoying him if he is intelligent or interesting, is combined with a clearer indication that how the subject feels depends on how he feels about her, a deeper form of reciprocity than simply mutual enjoyment of a date. Concern with whether the man likes her is remarkably rare below I-5, considering that not all of our subjects can be among the most popular girls. Feelings of being shy (I-3) or uncomfortable (I-3/4) may reflect this concern.

I-2

Almost all the responses classed I-2 can be interpreted as responses to "When I have intercourse with a man—." The subject may flatly deny this has occurred, she may describe dysphoric reactions, or she may openly describe sexual arousal or hostility. The Delta subject may be just as open about sex but emphasizes enjoyment (". . . never a dull moment good sex appeals and laughters") or describes what she does ("I like to make out"). Responses stating "I think about sex" are classed I-3/4 along with thoughts about love or marriage.

1. Sexual arousal or hostility (Δ, 1, 2; I-3/4, 19)
    I get hot
    I get excited
    I get hot and bothered and want to be loved
    I get goose-bumps
    something goes all over me
    I am mad
    I want to shoot him

2. —I am never with a man (I-3, 16)
   I don't be with mens
   I never was

3. —I feel bad, sick, unhappy, afraid (I-3, 4)
   I don't like it
   I get scared
   I'am shaking to death

Unclassified
   I can leave the house
   obey him

DELTA

The Delta subject tends to view being with a man in terms of potential (rather than inevitable?) sexual relations. She may express enjoyment of sex, or express a fear of and a need to control her own impulses ("I keep a straight head"). "I act like a girl should" may also be related to impulse control and can be distinguished from responses describing polite, ladylike behavior (I-3).

1. Sexual pleasure (impulsive tone) (I-2, 1)
   boy!
   When I am with my husband never a dull moment good sex appeals and laughters
   I go wild
   I usually have a riot

2. —I kiss, neck, make out with him (I-2, 1)
   if he is my husband I wood kiss he
   I usually just sit around and listen to records and neck
   I like to make out

3. —I am careful, take precautions, behave myself (I-3, 9)
   I be careful but enjoy myself
   I keep a straight head
   I hole myself togather
   I always say "Cool it!"
   I'm scared and don't know how to handle myself sometimes

4. —I (don't) act nice, right, like I should (I-3, 9)
   I think I should act right and don't act silly
   I act like a girl should
   i guess I'm not very nice

5. —nothing; it doesn't bother me (I-3, 1, 18)
   nothing!
   it doesn't even bother me one way or the other
   I feel no pain

6. —it's none of your business (I-3, 18)
   I think that is my own business
   This is also none of your business

Unclassified
   theres trouble
   I start laughing
   lose my appetite completely

DELTA/3

Responses placed at this level indicate that the subject views being with a man in terms of sexual relations, typical of the I-2 and Delta levels, yet she expresses concern for the approval of others, typical of the I-3 level. These responses may illustrate the development of a protoconscience; one feels guilty and thus controls one's impulses because one *expects* sanctions from others.

1. Concern with what others think
   I think every one will say oh look at them two
   I get a guilty conscience of what my mother would think if she saw me now
   I don't like other people staring at us

I-3

At this level the usual response is undifferentiated pleasant mood: "happy," "feel good," "have fun." Closely related to these responses is "I enjoy it," which is classed empirically at I-3/4. Not all I-3 subjects who describe their feelings describe positive ones. Those who respond with negative feelings are likely to say that they are bashful, shy, nervous, or upset. A conventional view of relations between the sexes is expressed in responses reflecting conventional expectations of men, or in responses asserting that the man is her husband, brother, and so on. The subject may also describe her behavior in conventional terms: she is polite, friendly, ladylike. When these actions are stated as feelings or desires they are rated higher, for instance, "I want to be pleasant," "I feel like a lady" (I-3/4). I-3 responses containing comparisons or contingencies are rare. Although the I-3 subject may say that she feels or acts the same or differently, the I-3/4 subject is more likely to specify the difference, "I feel prettier," or to compare her feelings and actions to those in other situations, "act no different than when I am with a woman." "I act accordingly" is classed I-3 and seems more like "I act like a woman" (I-3) than like "I act according to how I feel about him" (I-3/4).

*1. —I feel happy, fine, good, wonderful (Δ, 5; I-3/4, 4, 12; I-4, 7)
I am contented
feel great
I feel alright

2. —I have fun, a good time (I-3/4, 1, 12; I-4, 7)

*3. —I feel safe, secure, protected (I-3/4, 12; I-4, 7)
I feel well taken care of

4. —I am bashful, shy, nervous, upset (I-2, 3; I-3/4, 3, 13, 14; I-4, 6)
I am usually very shy
I often get upset
I blush

5. —I feel proud, important (I-3/4, 4, 18)

6. —I act (feel) the same, different, natural, normal (I-3/4, 9, 10)
I feel nothing special
I try to act non-shalant
stay the same
I guess I am as any normel women!
I don't feel any different
sometimes act different

*7. —I talk, converse, listen to him (I-3/4, 15; I-4, 3, 4)
I am usually talkative
I try to hold a good conservation
I let him talk

8. —I try to look my best, attractive (I-3/4, 7; I-4, 11)
I like to look my best
I put my best face forward
feel like dressing up

9. —I am polite, on my best behavior (Δ, 3, 4; I-3/4, 16; I-4, 5)
mind my manners
I keep my place
I am my best

10. —I am friendly, sociable, a companion (I-3/4, 16)

11. —I act ladylike, feminine, like a woman (I-3/4, 7; I-4, 10)
    I remember that I am a lady and act accordingly
    I try to act like a lady
    I try to act feminine
    I conduct my self in a femine way
    I act like a woman

12. —I act accordingly (I-3/4, 11)

13. —we get along (I-4, 1)
    we work well together
    I usually get along fine

14. Expectation of conventional male behavior: be a gentleman, take me places (I-4, 13)
    I like for him to suggest where to go
    I like him to take the initiative
    I like for him to be very pleasant

15. Specification of situation, companions
    there is alwas another person or two along
    I love being with married couples
    there's mixed company
    I am at work
    I like to go to expensive places

16. Assertion that man is husband, father, or the like (I-2, 2)
    I'm usually never, unless it is my husband, or doctor, or min-
        ister. No comment!
    I hope it's my husband
    (Ive never been with a boy either except my reletives)
    I am never with a man (in the sense of a older male) except
        my father or friend of family
    it's usually my steady

17. —I think of my husband; I remember I'm married (I-4, 14)
    think only of the man I love

18. Evasion (Δ, 5, 6)
    I don't know
    ?

Unclassified
    I'm never alone with men, my husband would be angry
    I figure he is thinking of sex

I-3/4

The I-3/4 subject has begun to perceive being with a man as interaction, though reciprocity and concern for the man's enjoyment are not as apparent as at I-4. Feelings classed I-3/4 are typically feelings of comfort or discomfort. The moods found at I-3, happiness, nervousness, and so on, appear at this level but are contingent on the man involved. The I-3/4 subject may also give comparative responses, "I am happier," "I can talk easier," or specify other situations, "it's no different than being with a woman." When specific feelings or actions are related to other situations the rating is higher: "I can talk more easily than with a woman" (I-4), "I feel comfortable and at ease as I do with women" (I-4/5). Many responses classed at this level appear to be reactions to the man's interest and attention, "I sparkle," "I feel wanted," "I feel womanly," "I am flattered." The potential sexual nature of the relation is recognized but is stated in terms of motives or thoughts, "I want to know his intentions," "I think of sex," rather than of actions (Delta) or of impulses (I-2).

*1. —I enjoy it, myself (I-3, 2; I-4, 1, 3, 8, 9)

*2. —I feel relaxed, comfortable, at ease (I-4, 8)
   then I am calm

*3. —I feel tense, uncomfortable, self-conscious, out of place (I-3, 4; I-4, 6)
   I am on edge at all times
   I feel jittery
   I am unsure
   I feel a bit uncomfortable
   I am sometimes ill at ease

4. Sense of exhilaration, self-enhancement, idealization (I-3, 1, 5; I-4, 2, 8; I-4/5, 1; I-5, 4)
   When I am with my husband I feel I am the luckiest person in the world
   I feel good like the center of attraction
   I sparkle
   I am animated
   I am very scintilating
   my world is complete

5. —I am flattered, complimented (I-4, 8)

6. —I feel wanted, needed, loved (I-4, 8)
   I feel wonderful and wanted

7. —I am aware of being feminine; I feel feminine, attractive, like a woman (I-3, 8, 11; I-4, 11)
   I usually enjoy being a woman
   I feel like being very feminine

I feel extra feminine
I feel more of a woman
I feel womanly

8. —I feel, act different (specified) (I-4, 4; I-4/5, 3)
   I act more mature
   I feel prettier
   I am happier
   I act more feminine

9. —I act, feel the same as (different from) with a woman
   (I-3, 6; I-4, 4; I-4/5, 3)
   act no different than when I am with a woman
   I fell the Same way if I am not with a man
   it's no different than being with a woman

10. —I remain, act myself (I-3, 6; I-4/5, 4)
    I try to be myself
    I'm the same person as always
    I try to act myself

11. —it depends on the man I am with (I-3, 12)
    what man?—that all depends
    I act according to how I feel about him
    I adapt my feelings to the situation

*12. —I'm happy (feel good, have fun) if I like him, if he's the
    right one (I-3, 1, 2, 3; I-4, 8, 9)
    if it's the right one, I'm very happy
    my husband I am happy a content
    I feel great. (if I like him)
    I feel wonderful, especially with a certain one
    that I love, I feel secure

13. —I am nervous (shy, self-conscious), depending on who I
    am with (I-3, 4)
    I get nervous sometimes espseally if I like him
    I am ill at ease, unless it is my husband
    I'm not usually as much at ease, unless he is a good friend
    other than my husband, I'm not too comfortable

14. —I don't know what to say; I become quiet (I-3, 4)
    I sometimes don't know what to talk about or say
    I don't know, I don't talk much
    I get quiet
    I am reserved
    I get tonguetied

he has to do most of the talking
I feel rather nervous, not knowing what to talk about

15. —I talk too much, more freely (I-3, 7; I-4, 4)
    I can talk easier
    I feel myself free to talk

16. —I want to be (try to be) pleasant, charming, interesting (I-3, 9, 10; I-4, 5)

17. —I try to figure him out; I wonder what he thinks (I-4, 14; I-4/5, 2)
    I study him
    I wonder what opinion he has of me
    I want to know his intentions
    I wonder if he is like all the rest

18. Concern for man's regard (I-3, 5; I-4, 13)
    I like for him be proud of me
    I like to feel important to him

19. —I think of sex, love, marriage (I-2, 1; I-4, 14)

I-4

At this level there is increasing concern for the man's feelings, comfort, and enjoyment, reflecting an awareness of the situation as an interaction. Thus the subject may say she enjoys his company or the conversation, or she may emphasize mutual enjoyment. At I-4 feelings of pleasure and enjoyment classed I-3/4 are made contingent on the man involved. The subject's enjoyment is also dependent on the traits he possesses or on her regard for him. For the most part, the content of the responses classed I-4 is not very different from that at lower levels. In general, I-4 responses are more elaborated, thus more specific, perhaps combining alternative reactions. New ideas classed I-4 are assertion that the subject is the man's equal, desire for respect, comparison of the man to other men, and consideration of him as a prospective mate.

*1. —I enjoy his company, his attention; we both enjoy ourselves (I-3, 13; I-3/4, 1; I-4/5, 7; I-5, 3)
    try to make the date as enjoyable for him as well as having a good time myself
    I expect him enjoy my company
    I have a good time. We have the same interests besides sex
    I enjoy any compliments or extra attentions

2. —I am stimulated (I-3/4, 4; I-4/5, 1)
   I am usually stimulated
   I am sometimes stimulated sometimes not

3. —I enjoy the conversation, talking to him (I-3, 7; I-3/4, 1; I-4/5, 2)
   it can mean an enjoyable time talking
   I love listening to him talk and I am a very good listener also
       I add a few of my own comments

4. —I can talk more easily than with a woman (I-3, 7; I-3/4, 8, 9, 15; I-4/5, 3)
   I can speak with honesty more than I do when with women
   I speak and not about the same as when I am with a woman
       (but I study him)

*5. Focus on man's feelings, comfort, enjoyment (interaction implied) (I-3, 9; I-3/4, 16; I-4/5, 6)
   I show him respect
   I try to be interested in what he talks about
   I like to be able to converse with him intelligently
   we talk about things we have in common, etc.
   I try to be an interesting conversationalist

6. Feelings of discomfort, elaborated (comparison, time perspective, alternatives) (I-3, 4; I-3/4, 3)
   I get very nervous until I know him
   I feel ill-at-ease if we have nothing in common
   I tend to become either too talkative or too quiet
   I feel very unsure of him
   I am not always as calm as I should be

7. —I am happy, feel good, have fun, if I respect, admire, am proud of him (I-3, 1, 2, 3)
   that I respect and like I have a very good time
   I admire, I feel secure
   that I can be proud of I am very happy & satisfied

8. Differentiated feelings of pleasure contingent on man involved (I-3/4, 1, 2, 4, 5, 6, 12)
   who enjoys my company, I am at ease
   I feel normal, according to who the man is and what he means to me
   I love, I'm in a complete new world
   whom I love, I feel very proud and happy to be at his side
   I feel ill at ease, or relaxed, depending on the person I am with

9. Enjoyment contingent on man being interesting, intelligent (I-3/4, 1, 12)
   who thinks I enjoy conversing with him
   I enjoy his company unless he is a "bore"
   that is intellegent and kind I like talking with him
   I enjoy myself if he has a sense of humour and is somewhat attractive

10. Acting up to ladylike standard, elaborated or qualified (I-3, 11)
    I try my best to give a good impression, but still be relaxed
    I try to act lady like, unless I am playing a sport
    along, I try to enjoy myself and yet still act like a lady

11. —I am conscious of my appearance (I-3, 8; I-3/4, 7)
    I am concerned of my appearance
    I feel very good but self cautious of how I look

12. —I feel I am his equal

13. —I want to be respected (I-3, 14; I-3/4, 18; I-4/5, 7)

14. —I think of him in terms of a prospective husband; I compare him to the men I love (I-3, 17; I-3/4, 17, 19)
    I think of what it would be like to be married to him
    I look to the future, either with or without him
    I often compare him with my father and brothers
    I compare him to my husband

15. —I am aware of it
    I know he is a man
    I know it

Unclassified
feel good sexually and emotionally

I-4/5

At this level are classed responses indicating a more integrated concept of oneself and of the man, ideas made more explicit at I-5. At I-4/5 are statements that the subject feels whole, alive, and complete, that she dislikes assuming a role, and that she is concerned with the man's beliefs and point of view. Also classed I-4/5 are responses implying an appreciation of the complexity of the interaction: an explicit statement that one's own behavior may affect the man's feelings and reactions or that the attitudes of others may affect one's own feelings toward the man.

Finally there are composite responses concerned with respect, attention, and consideration, though any single one is I-4.

1. —I feel alive, complete (I-3/4, 4; I-4, 2; I-5, 4)
   I come alive
   I feel revitalized
   I feel whole & complete & I thoroughly enjoy myself, generally

2. —I enjoy learning about his beliefs, point of view (I-3/4, 17; I-4, 3)
   I enjoy getting to know his feelings and beliefs
   I enjoy talking and seeing his point of view
   I enjoy his conversation and different viewpoint
   I am anxious to hear his views on ideas, etc.

3. —I feel differently than (the same as) with a woman (specified) (I-3/4, 8, 9; I-4, 4)
   I am relaxed and have the self confidence that I have with a woman
   I feel comfortable and at ease as I do with women
   I'm happier than with a woman
   I feel more stimulated than with a woman
   I feel as lonely and with anyone else

4. —I remain myself (elaborated) (I-3/4, 10)
   I'm still Mrs. [deleted] and I want to be respected as that
   I usually have a good time just being myself
   try to be myself and not put on a show for him
   I dislike assuming a role
   , I act nice, but like myself, because I feel that if he doen't like me for myself then he is not worth my love
   I feel as though I'm the same as all way, because I try to be at my best all the time

5. Subject's reaction contingent on feelings of others
   whom my parents approve of, I myself feel more secure
   I find that I react to him in terms of my husband's feeling about the man

6. Concern with effect of own behavior on man's feelings (I-4, 5)
   I don't hide my brain or opinions but I don't trot them out either, especially if he is sensitive
   I am shy but pray that he doesn't notice it or if he does he doesn't dislike it and regret being with me

I like I am happy but if I don't like him I try to be pleasant and endure it without hurting his feelings

7. Concern with respect, attention, considerateness (composite responses) (I-4, 1, 13)
    I expect to be treated with dignity, respect—and attention
    I want to be desired and respected
    enjoy their attention and considerateness
    I first try to be respected then (in some cases) I try to gain his love

Unclassified
    depending on which man, of course, I generally feel intellectually stimulated

I-5

At I-5 and I-6 one finds original self-perceptions, usually expressing enjoyment of being with men. The interaction is viewed as a complex process with no simple formulas to be applied for enjoyment. The capacity for role-conception is prominent. This is shown by the clear distinction of business and social or personal roles. A related distinction is that between the sexual and the social aspect of personal relations with men.

1. Business versus social roles: relativity to the situation
    I'm properly flirtous, confident of myself, or usually having a good time—this applies to social situations, otherwise a man simply represents a business, ex. "milkman"
    in what way do you mean husband or any man? What situation. Can't answer
    I react in relation to whether I'm fulfilling a professional role, or am "being a woman"
    I am almost always able to treat him on a business like basis as I have worked with men all my life

2. Contrast of sexual with personal relation
    I enjoy their company in stimulating conversation, and on a strictly platonic level, but men in general are not staisfied with just that
    I am not always conscious of his maleness
    I try to view him as I would another person rather than constantly being aware of the sex difference

I like I feel secure and yet a little fearful that his only inter-est is physical

if he makes me feel like it is important to be a woman—I love it but if he treats me as just a sex symbol I'm repulsed

3. Concern with interaction, reciprocity going beyond enjoyment of date (I-4, 1)

   I enjoy his company if he is intelligent and likes me

   I want him to dominate the conversation, but allow me to express an opinion. I want to feel that he is watchful for me and knows I'm along

4. Original expression of enjoyment (I-3/4, 4; I-4/5, 1)

   I am delighted and (often) delightful

   I feel excitingly feminine

   If I love him, I glow I'm happy and I cherish our time to-gether

   I shine—not really—I wish I did

Unclassified

   who is humorous, intellighent and an idealist, I feel alive and vital

   I enjoy men very much, more so as I get older

   I've never cared enough for a man to put something here. I like being beside a man but that's all I can say

I-6

Unclassified

   I often enjoy the chance to better understand how male and female can complement each other

   I enjoy it if he is interesting, but am uncomfortable if he tries to compliment me for I feel I am no longer very attractive

When She Thought of Her Mother, She—

Most subjects respond to this stem in the third person. Those who do not usually are I-3 or above. Objection to the ambiguity of the stem is rare, but when it occurs, it is on higher protocols. A few popular responses, "cried," "smiled," "was happy," account for about 20 per cent of the total number of responses; they are rare above I-4.

Discrimination on this item is only fair. Responses at I-2 and Delta are mostly popular ones. The content of I-3 responses is popular or bland or vague, "felt good," "had nice thoughts," "called her." The majority of I-3/4 responses are positive—frequently idealized—thoughts and memories about mother ("thought of a great lady," "remembered how much she loved her"). Differentiated traits of both mother and subject appear at I-4, "felt remorse," "saw a domineering, selfish, exact person." A significant number of I-4 responses concern the subject's relationship with her mother, "thought of pleasant hours shared," "wished they had been closer." Perspective and recognition of both subject and mother as distinct individuals are notable in responses rated higher than I-4.

Two types of responses found at almost every level are negative reactions and expressions of homesickness. At the Delta level the negativism is action-oriented or derisive, "threw up," "thought of Blatz Beer." Comparable reactions at Delta/3 and I-3 are mild in tone and ambiguous in meaning, "was upset" (Delta/3), "frowned" (I-3). As at the Delta level, responses above I-3 sometimes reflect intense feelings; with increasing ego level, however, distance from one's feelings is more evident ("felt a series of frustrations," I-4; "felt repulsed, but ashamed," I-5). Below I-3 homesickness is most commonly represented by action, "cried," "went home." At I-3 one misses the mother, wants to go home, or almost cries. Above I-3 more explicit descriptions of longing for mother or home appear: "felt homesick," "wanted to be with her," I-3/4; "felt nostalgic," "thought of homey things," I-4.

I-2

No doubt for many I-2 subjects the mother is seen primarily as a source of supply for their needs. As one I-2 subject stated it: "think of the good thing she done for her." However, we cannot discriminate such responses from similar ones at I-3/4, which anticipate explicit appreciation and gratitude at I-4. The distinguishing mark of the I-2 categories seems to be a slight conceptual inappropriateness.

1. Reaction as if mother is there (Δ, 1)
   is good
   looked at her
   walked away

2. —loved, liked her (I-3/4, 4; I-4, 5)
   I love my mother

3. —wondered; wonders about things (I-3, 4)
   thought of a good thing

Unclassified
   is when she get sick

DELTA

Distinctive Delta responses appear to be reactions against dependence on the mother. Although the most discriminating Delta responses are the blatantly derogatory ones, nearly half of the Delta subjects give the popular response, "cried." The unclassified responses can be construed as dependent complaining.

1. Expression of hostility, disgust (action-oriented or derisive) (I-2, 1; Δ/3, 2; I-3, 10)
   burned inside
   thought of Blatz Beer
   threw up
   had a trantrum
   called her an old witch
   wept bitter, bitter tears on her mink coat

2. —laughed (I-3, 1)
   started to swear and laugh

3. Keeping a distance from mother (I-3/4, 17)
   thought of a stranger
   When she think of mother,—it doesn't bother me I never knew her
   thought of her as a good Christian lady. She's nice as long as she don't bother me

Unclassified
   was in need for mama
   complained that she was not loved

DELTA/3

Categories at this level imply a close identification with the mother similar to the I-2 dependence on mother, but the apparent security of the I-2 is missing. Although "cried" is the most frequent response to this stem, it appears proportionately more frequently on protocols below I-3, and thus is placed here as a compromise.

**1. —cried; began to cry (I-3, 8; I-3/4, 15)
   always cried
   cried because she's dead
   often cried

2. —was, got upset; felt, became nervous (Δ, 1)
   felt disturbed
   worried

3. —went home (I-3, 7)
   went to visit her
   started to drive home to where she lives

I-3

Stereotyped feelings and reactions that substitute for feelings are the most frequent I-3 responses to this stem, "cried" (but rated Delta/3), "smiled," "was happy." A small number of these responses are negative: "shuddered" or "felt badly." More differentiated feelings, such as homesickness, contentment, or pleasure do not appear until I-3/4. Subject's thoughts about the mother are banal or nonevaluative, "thought of many good things" or "thought about how she treated her." Other categories concern the subject's behavior consequent to thinking about mother, "called her" or "said wonderful things about her." Such responses as "hated her" and "got very angry" are more frequent at Delta and at I-3/4 than at I-3; the category is not discriminating and is placed here as a compromise.

*1. —smiled (Δ, 2)
   had a smile on her face
   smiled fondly
   smiled contentedly

*2. —was glad, happy; felt good (I-3/4, 2)
   get happy or the thought just make her happy
   feels wonderful
   was a very happy person
   seemed to be very happy

3. —had nice, good, wonderful thoughts (I-3/4, 1, 5)
   thought of many good things
   thought of something nice

4. Simple nonevaluative thoughts (I-2, 3; I-3/4, 7, 12; I-4, 12)
   thought of what she looked like
   thought about how she brought her up
   thought about how she treated her
   thought of the person who brought her into the world
   remembered a lot
   thought about her a lot

5. —loved to talk about her; seldom talked about her
   said wonderful things about her
   said "My Mother does"

6. —called her; didn't call her; wrote her a letter (I-4, 13)
   would buy a gift and sent it to her
   remembered her birthday

7. —missed her, home; wanted to go home (Δ/3, 3; I-3/4, 13, 14; I-4, 10, 12)
   would think of home
   she thought she should go home
   felt like going to see her
   wish she was there again
   felt how she missed her

8. —almost cried; wanted to cry (Δ/3, 1; I-3/4, 15)
   felt teary-eyed
   would fight back her tears

9. —cringed; winced
   shuddered
   frowned

10. —got angry, mad; hated her (Δ, 1)
    got cross
    expressed her dislike for her

11. Evasion (I-3/4, 17)
    who?
    ?
    I don't know
    thought of her mother

Unclassified
   felt badly
   always told her mother what she thought of her

I-3/4

There is a decline in all-purpose words like "happy," "nice," "good," and "things" at I-3/4. "Feeling" and "felt" are borderline words, typical for the I-3/4 who is very conscious of feelings but in banal combinations not unusual at I-3 ("felt very happy"). Rather than just feeling happy, at I-3/4 one specifies feelings such as warmth, contentment, homesickness. Rather than just thinking of nice things (I-3), one has pleasant thoughts or memories. Crying (Delta/3), an action, is replaced by feeling sad or lonely.

A beginning awareness of the mother as an individual is evident at I-3/4 in the subject's desire to be like her mother and in her concern for her mother. Although one I-3/4 category concerns thoughts of good times together, appreciation of the relation between mother and subject does not appear until I-4.

1. —had pleasant, happy, fond thoughts, memories (I-3, 3; I-4, 5, 7)
   thought of happiness
   thought kind thoughts of her

2. —felt warm, content, pleased (I-3, 2)
   felt comfortable
   felt colm & at ease
   got a warm inner glow

3. —was proud; admired her (I-4, 5)
   felt a sense of pride

4. —thought of love; thought in a loving way (I-2, 2; I-4, 5)
   thought of love and understanding and this helped her through hard times
   remembered how much she loved her

5. —thought of a wonderful woman, of near perfection (I-3, 3)
   thought of a great lady
   thought of an angel in heaven
   thought of the most wonderful person God can give
   would rave how wonderful her mother was

6. —thought of a good, kind, sweet, understanding woman (I-4, 1)
   thought of understanding and affection
   thought of someone who is warmhearted & kind
   thought of of thoughful & loving person

7. —thought of all the work her mother did; thought of how much mother did for her (I-3, 4; I-4, 3)
   thought of the nice things she has done
   thought of the responsibilities she had
   thought of someone who had experience in most everything
   thought of all the children she had & how she lived through it
   would say my mother was good to me

8. Self-evaluation (general) (I-4, 15)
   thought of things she should have done

tried to do better
knew that she had to do right
remembered what she was supposed to finish
felt ashamed

9. —wanted to be like her (unelaborated) (I-4, 17)
   hoped she could be the same
   wondered if she could ever be such a person

10. —thought of the good times, wonderful times, fun they had
    had (I-4, 7)
    smiled & thought of many things they had done together

11. —remembered (thought of) her childhood (I-4, 11, 12)
    recalls happy childhood and past
    remembered childhood misery
    saw herself as a small girl
    began to think of old memiors

12. —thought of the whole family (I-3, 4)
    also thought of her father
    *thought also of her sister and brothers and how much fun
    they have together*

13. —felt, got homesick (I-3, 7; I-4, 10, 12)
    felt so homesick she broke down and cried

14. —wished she could see her; wanted to be with her (I-3, 7;
    I-4, 13)
    wanted to talk to her
    felt sad that she lived so far away
    wished she had lived longer
    looked forward to seeing her again

15. —was sad, lonely, unhappy (Δ/3, 1; I-3, 8)
    became blue
    became sorrowful
    Became depressed
    shrugged in despair
    appeared sad, for her mother passed two years ago

16. —felt sorry for her; wondered how she was (I-4, 2; I-4/5, 1)
    wondered if anything was wrong
    felt concerned
    felt pity

17. —stopped thinking about her (Δ, 3; I-3, 11)
    quickly changed her mind

pushed the thought from her mind
cringed and changed her thoughts

I-4

At I-4 the mother appears as an individual, sometimes with problems of her own, and as a friend as well as a mother. Subject expresses appreciation for her advice and help and for her good qualities and traits, such as gentleness, patience, and efficiency, more differentiated than the qualities perceived at lower levels. Similarly, the subject's feelings for her mother, like tenderness, respect, guilt, and gratitude, are more complex. Although acknowledgment of conflicting feelings ("had mixed emotions") is most characteristically I-4 for this item, somewhat to our surprise it may occur even at the Delta level. To specify what the conflicting emotions are is rated I-4/5.

At I-4 memories of home and childhood are expressed more vividly than at I-3/4: one yearns for her childhood (I-4) instead of remembering it (I-3/4); one grows nostalgic or sentimental instead of homesick; and one thinks of "home, laughter and good food" instead of "old memories." Since some of these I-4 responses are more concrete than parallel ones at lower levels, and vice versa, the inadequacy of abstractness alone as a measure of ego development is illustrated.

1. Thought of specific traits (I-3/4, 6; I-5, 1, 2)
   thought of a small, neat organized woman
   thought of an honest loving person, trying her best to do
     the right thing
   thought of an attractive, wholesome, intelligent, loving, and
     understanding lady with gray hair
   saw a domineering, selfish, exact person

2. —thought of some of her mother's problems (I-3/4, 16; I-4/5, 1)
   worried about her health
   wished that she could have walk and got well

3. —was grateful; appreciated all that she had done for her (I-3/4, 7)
   wishes she could repay her for all the things she has done
     for her
   realized she had been a very lucky daughter

4. Appreciation of mother's good advice, help, love, and so on (I-5, 1)

remembered all the acts of kindness that had been done for her

thought of one who loved her and was proud of the things she had done

knew that her mother did her best in raising her

thought of someone on whom she could depend

5. Feelings of respect, affection, tenderness for mother (I-2, 2; I-3/4, 1, 3, 4)

   was filled with tender memories

   felt a deep love and affection

   was touched by her spunk

   smiled because her mother was cool and loved her very much

6. —thought of a friend

   thought of her more like a sister

7. Thought of shared experiences (I-3/4, 1, 10)

   thought of pleasant hours shared

   remembered many enjoyable times they'd had together

   remembered long walks in the woods and along the shore

8. Thoughts about subject's relationship with mother

   wished they had been closer

   wished she knew her better

   began to wonder what happened between them

   wished she could be more friendly with her

   always remembered her childhood relationship with her mother

   realized she still influenced her life

9. Regret mother died while subject was young

   always felt sad because she died why she was so young

   cried because she was only twenty-three when she died from childbirth

   I feel that I missed something in life because she died, when I was 11

10. —felt, grew nostalgic (I-3, 7; I-3/4, 13)

    became sentimental

    fell into a pit of nostalgia, and longed to visit her home

11. Wish to recapture the past (I-3/4, 11)

    yearned for her childhood

    grew sad and lonesome for the more carefree days of her childhood

    wished she could have re-lived some of her years again

12. —thought of home, homey things (I-3, 4, 7; I-3/4, 11, 13)
had wonderful thoughts of love and home
thought of a happy home and childhood
thought of her home town
thought of the warm smell of cookies and food from a kitchen
usually thought of her home and the feelings there

13. —wanted to telephone her; was sorry she had not written
(I-3, 6; I-3/4, 14)
realized she would call soon
thought, "I should write her some time."
remembered she owed her a letter

14. —had mixed emotions, feelings (I-4/5, 3)
was confused
thought of both good and bad times
had good thoughts as an adult, but not so as a child

15. —felt guilty, regretful (I-3/4, 8)
felt remorse
wished she had been more kind
realized she had been wrong (the girl)
was sorry she had been so hard to get along with

16. Negative feelings, memories (I-4/5, 3)
had unpleasant thoughts
felt a series of frustrations
felt hurt at the memory of old pains
was filled with thoughts of anger and pity

17. Desire not to be like her mother; desire to be like her mother
in some respects (I-3/4, 9; I-4/5, 2)
was glad not to be her
loves & respects her but doesn't want to be exactly like her
thought of how she would like to be when she became a
mother
reflected on her goodness and tried to conduct herself in the
same manner

Unclassified
sometimes tried to analyzed her actions
felt sad she had had to work so hard
was quiet

I-4/5

Although on other stems concern for the mother's feelings, especially more common ones such as happiness, is not uncommon at lower

levels, on this item it usually does not occur until I-4/5. In general, responses here elaborate or combine I-3/4 and I-4 ideas. To take one unclassified example, not only does the subject love her mother (I-3/4) and vice versa (I-4), the love is mutual. Particularly characteristic are those responses that combine positive and negative feelings or recognition of faults and virtues.

1. Concern for the mother's feelings, well-being (I-3/4, 16; I-4, 2, UC)
   wondered if she were happy
   tried to understand her feelings
   wished she had more interests
   regretted those four last years illness for her
   wished she could take back things done and said before which hurt her

2. —hoped she would be like her in some ways and different in others; remembered her good features and her faults (I-4, 17; I-5, 2, UC; I-6, UC)
   tried to think of only her good features and not her faults
   remembered what a wonderful person she was but was not oblivious to her faults

3. Mixed, conflicting feelings (specified) (I-4, 14, 16)
   felt repulsed, but ashamed
   felt tenderness, admiration, at times exasperation—"she" is me
   felt both pride and depression

4. Emotion contingent on a specific memory or quality in the mother
   only got very angry—for remembering the time that she bawled her out
   did it kindly and remembered her goodness and driving spirit
   grew sad to think of how she had mistreated her

Unclassified
   remembered the wonderful childhood she had, of the strong, loveable leadership her mother had
   was proud that her mother was hers, and realized how much they love each other
   remembered all the good advice she received from her that helped her to adjust to life

I-5

Responses at the I-5 level present thoughtful appraisal of the mother's motivations, values, and ideals. There may be explicit or implicit concern for the mother's attitudes toward life as a whole, as there may also be at I-4/5 but rarely lower. Responses may go beyond the statement that mother has faults and virtues to give a picture of differentiated positive and negative traits.

1. Appreciation of mother's values, ideals, abstract qualities (I-4, 1, 4)

   remembered the high standards and values of her mother

   appreciated many of the intangible things her mother had given her

   remembered her justice and calm

   was overawed at her mother's insight and capabilities—things she never realized as a child

   (again, may I avoid "she" for about "her" there is no end of fabrication) When I think of my mother, I think of devotion and duty

2. Perception of mother as a complex person (I-4, 1; I-4/5, 2)

   thought of her as an intelligent sensitive, but nervous person

   saw wiseness mixed with humor

Unclassified

   always felt a similar approach as her mothers to life

   felt an almost sad feeling at the thought of her mother's goodness & the emptiness of losing her

I-6

The one I-6 response completes the line of thought beginning at I-3/4 with wanting to be like the mother. The response is quite similar to the I-4/5 idea of wanting to be like mother, yet different, too. What merits the I-6 rating is the explanation of the thought in terms of personal identity.

Unclassified

   hoped to be like her in some ways, but different in others, because she was herself, not her mother

If I Can't Get What
I Want—

This stem does relatively well at drawing low-level responses and poorly at drawing high-level responses. Responses above I-4 are mostly combinations of those at I-4 rather than new thoughts. The stem presents a childish thought in childish words. How does one handle frustration of a wish? Our subjects are under no obligation to tell us how they act, but some of them probably do. Below I-3 the stem is often interpreted as if it read, "If my parents won't give me what I want—." Thus they answer that they ask a boyfriend (I-2) or take it (Delta). As we go up the scale, an increasing proportion of subjects take the stem as reference to an abstract situation, a part of the human condition, rather than as reference to intrafamily conflict.

At I-2 there is no program for dealing with the feeling of frustration except denial: "I don't want noting." The Delta subject may be angry or upset; to stage an outburst (deliberately?) is rated Delta/3. So far as dealing with feelings goes, the I-3 formula is "forget it" rather than the I-2 denial. At I-4 the feelings are seen as there to be dealt with even if one accepts the situation. In general, responses at the I-4 level contain an element of detachment, of distance from the situation, at times in the form of self-criticism ("I usually pout, til I see my silliness"). Some subjects misread the stem, usually by omitting the negative. As some of the unclassified examples illustrate, we have rated such responses according to their content. There is only one such category, at I-3, with responses like "I will be pleased."

I-2

At this level there is no mechanism for dealing with an ungratified wish. You rebel against parent or authority, you cry, or you deny the wish.

1. Rebellion against parents
   I run away
   I ask my boyfriend or some other boys
   get bad

2. —I cry (Δ/3, 3)
   I usually cry
   I cry to myself

3. —I don't want anything; I won't get anything (Δ/3, 2)
   I dont want it

Unclassified
   I don't to anything, not even cry

DELTA

At the Delta level the wish is still immediate and paramount. There is a somewhat paradoxical advance in the direction of control implied in the greater focus on the desired object. Anger is more focused than crying, and taking it is more focused than running away. In distinguishing Delta responses from search for another means at I-3/4, one looks for the emphasis on getting it at Delta, as if it is inconceivable that a wish be denied. At worst, the Delta subject is prepared to buy it, as if the stem read, "When they won't give me what I want—." To work for it or earn it is I-3.

*1. —I get mad, angry, upset (Δ/3, 5; I-3/4, 1)
   I get angry sometimes
   I get mad and then I usually get it

2. —I take it; I fight for it
   I go get it
   I take something

3. —I get it one way or another (I-3, 6, 7; I-3/4, 4)
   I ask my father for it!
   don't give up I get it!
   I'll find another way of getting it (honestly)
   I'll find a way to get it
   Ill have to buy it
   I work harder and do a better snow job and I eventually do get it

DELTA/3

The transition from Delta to I-3 is also more or less the transition from denying the situation to coping with it. Most categories are placed at this level as a compromise, because they are relatively more frequent below I-3 but absolutely about as frequent at I-3 or I-3/4. Responses like "I have a tantrum" are particularly nondiscriminating, coming from protocols ranging from I-2 to I-4/5. To keep on begging for it may be a type of response distinctive for this level.

*1. —it doesn't bother me; I don't worry (cry, care) about it
   I won't get mad
   sometime I do not care

2. —I don't get it (I-2, 3; I-3, 1)
   I just don't

3. —I pout, sulk (I-2, 2; I-3, 9)
   I mope around

4. —I keep begging for it
   I start to talk about the kids that have everything
   I keep asking or hinting
   I usually keep on pressing, till I get it
   talk until I get it

5. Stage an outburst (Δ, 1)
   I have a tantrum
   I usually throw a fit until I get it
   I usually get angry and start cursing

I blow my top
I yell and stomp

I-3

At I-3 the predominant type of response is passive acceptance of the situation. Next most frequent is trying again or trying harder. The notion that one works for it is not passive but is again a denial of the stem, as are many responses below I-3.

**1. —I do without ($\Delta/3$, 2; I-3/4, 3, 6)
    I settle for what I have
    I manage
    I learn to do without
    I live without it

*2. —I forget it (I-3/4, 6)
    I try very hard not to think about it

3. —I give up
    I stop asking
    I let it go

*4. —I try harder; I try again (I-3/4, 2)
    I work that much harder for it
    I try harder the next time

5. —I wait until I can (I-3/4, 2)
    I wait
    I'll just have to wait until I can

6. —I work for it (Δ, 3)
    I earn it
    I try hard to save so I can

7. —I usually do (Δ, 3)
    I get it eventually

8. —it bothers me; I worry (I-3/4, 1)

9. —I sometimes (usually) pout (sulk) ($\Delta/3$, 3; I-3/4, 1, 7)
    I often sulk

10. —I pray for it
    I pray about it

11. —I'd be pleased, satisfied, happy

Unclassified
    I would get a 3 bath room house
    I get a Job

I-3/4

The predominant tone at this level is acceptance of the situation. Expression of dysphoric feelings is classed here but the category is non-discriminating. Perseverance (we distinguish "keep trying," I-3/4, from "try again," I-3) is classed here; more common is settling for something else. To try another way is classed I-3/4, but if the response indicates either another method of approach to the same goal or changing to a new goal, it is classed I-4.

*1. —I am unhappy, hurt, disappointed, depressed (Δ, 1; I-3, 8, 9; I-4, 9, 10)
  I sometimes become discouraged
  I feel bad, cause I cant afford the things I want & need
  I usually get unhappy for a while

*2. —I keep trying; I try until I do (I-3, 4, 5)
  I'll work until I get it
  I will keep trying untill I see if I can get it

**3. —I'll settle (try) for something else, the next best thing (I-3, 1; I-4, 6)
  I'll try for something just as good
  I will take what I can get
  I just take a substitute
  I try for a good alternative
  I find a substitute

4. —I try another way (Δ, 3; I-4, 8)
  I try a different approach
  I try to do the next best thing
  I go about it in another way
  I attempt something else
  I try an alternative solution
  I try to figure how I can
  I try another angle

5. —I compromise, compensate (I-4, 6)
  , then I have to compromise
  I substitute

*6. —I accept the fact; I make the best of the situation (I-3, 1, 2; I-4, 4, 7)
  I can usually adjust myself to the fact
  I reconcile myself to the fact
  theres nothing I can do about it

I try to forget about it and concentrate on what I already have

7. —I sulk (am unhappy, angry) but soon get over it (I-3, 9)
   I am unhappy at first, but adjust rapidly
   I am sad but must learn to accept it
   I usually pout until I get bored and forget about it
   I sulk awhile and then forget it

8. —that's that
   Well I am not expected to have every thing
   it's too bad
   you cant allways get what you want

9. —it is for the best, God's will (I-4, 2)
   I'm glad because I don't like being spoiled
   I know it is because God doesn't want me to have it, even if
       I get mad at the time
   I tell myself I dont deserve it

10. Feelings with interpersonal reference (I-4, 10, 13)
   I sometimes am jealous
   I feel mistreated
   I sometimes feel rejected

Unclassified
   I try to get over it quickly
   I would help the poor

I-4

At this level the subject is concerned with reasons, contingencies, and choices between alternatives. While at I-3 many responses indicate an acceptance of the stem (often lacking at lower levels), at I-3/4 the subject states that she accepts the situation. This line of development is carried further at I-4 to accepting or being content with or adjusting to what one can get or already has. A number of responses combine alternatives rated separately at lower levels. The response "I'll wait ore do without" is rated I-3; the two parts of the response are not really alternative. The response ", I sometimes save for it, or sub." (presumably meaning substitute) is rated I-4, since these are genuine alternatives.

*1. —I (want to) know the reason; I try to find out why
   '(I-4/5, 2)
   I sulk until I understand why

*I try to get something else or reason out why I didn't get
what I first wanted*
I think logically and consider a compromise
*I first become angry; then reason out why or why not I should
really have it*

2. —I rationalize (I-3/4, 9)
   I try to reason why it is best
   I am disturbed at first, and then I begin to rationalize
   I'll try to look ahead to find out I really don't need it
   I keep trying or rationalize
   I try to find the advantages in not having it

3. Reaction contingent on circumstances or on value of goal
   at the time, if it's reasonable I wait until I can
   I try again if it is worthwhile
   I earn it myself if it seems important
   I might be angry (according to the situation) but I accept it
   I pattern my behavior according to the situation
   I keep trying until I no longer want it

4. —I accept the situation only after I have tried again, every
   way (I-3/4, 6)
   I shall find a way to get it before settling for second best
   I try until I have it or if it is looks impossible I let it alone
   then I try harder, unless it is a hopeless cause
   I sometimes quit, but usually not without trying once more

5. Contrasting alternative reactions (I-4/5, 3)
   I either nag or accept it
   I sometimes forget it or else try again until I do get it
   *at all times, but I can be easily satisfied with what I have or
   a substitute for what I want*
   *I either agree that I shouldn't really have it or throw a good
   fighting arguement*

6. —I change goals (I-3/4, 3, 5; I-4/5, 1)
   I just forget about it and concentrate on something else
   I try to set a goal for something more attainable
   *I'll make a compromise which may be better than my first
   desire*
   I try to find a satisfactory substitute
   I channel my energies to some other task
   I become interested in other things
   sublimate

7. —I try to be content with, accept what I have, can get
   (I-3/4, 6)
   then I have to accept that which I can have
   I'll try to adjust for something else
   I'm usually mature enough to accept the fact
   I content myself with something else
   I think of what I have

8. Different approaches to the same goal (I-3/4, 4)
   in one way, I think of others
   I'm upset and try "devious" methods to obtain it
   I forget about it for the most part but try whenever a new
   occasion (or way) arises

9. —I am unhappy (disappointed) but then try again, for some-
   thing else (I-3/4, 1)
   I become discouraged, but try again
   I'm very perturbed, and try again

10. —I feel frustrated (I-3/4, 1, 10)
    I usually become frustrated and angry

11. —I boil inside
    I usually become quiet, but I'm boiling inside

12. —I feel sorry for myself; I'm spoiled
    sometimes I feel self pity
    I'm usually grumpy. I guess I'm spoiled
    I feel sorry for myself for awhile but get over it in a short
    time. On occasion I have blamed my husband

13. Differentiated feelings (I-3/4, 10)
    I become very impatient
    I feel resentful
    I may be disappointed, but seldom disillusioned

14. Combination responses with unique elements (I-4/5, 3)
    I become quiet, ignore my family and lock myself in my room
    I pout—then I try to be sweet and pleasing
    it is sometimes for the best, but not always easy to realize at
    the time
    I don't quit trying, I drop the subject then bring it up at a
    later date
    I usually pout, but good sense always comes to me, and I can
    see I'm wrong

> *I feel despondent, but a good cry and a talk with my husband make it ok*
> *I usually pout, til I see my silliness*

Unclassified

> *to make something of myself*
> *then it may be I'm not working hard enough for it*
> *it hurts because i never want for me. Most of the time it for the children*

I-4/5

Conceptual complexity is the chief clue to high level for this item. Most responses above I-4 are combinations of I-4 responses, showing a sense of choice or contingency, acknowledgment of unpleasant affect, and some distance from the situation, often in terms of acknowledgment that this is a situation to which one must adjust, not just a personal conflict. "I try to change my goals" (I-4) may sound much like "I try to change my wants" (I-4/5), but there is a difference. The latter is one step further in the internalization of the problem, in changing self rather than the world outside or one's relation to the world.

1. —I change my wants, desires (I-4, 6)
   I change direction and aim for something else
   I try to substitute or else rationalize the desire away
   I'll change my desires to something else, because I'm not too hard to please
   I wait till I can get it or re-evaluate my desire for wanting it
   I will have to learn to be satisfied with what I can get

2. Evaluation of situation (I-4, 1; I-5, 1)
   then perhaps I should reevaluate the situation
   I need to do some evaluation of my goals and the obstacles in their way
   I try to figure out why and then take the next best course
   I try to understand why not and make mental adjustments
   I try to understand why and then change it if possible
   I ask myself, what will be the benefit of it in terms "10 years from the present time when I am so eager to get it."
   I try to evaluate another way to do it or hunt for a substitute
   I wonder why—and then (1) try again (2) settle for something else (3) forget it
   I try to be realistic about the situation

3. Combination of I-4 ideas (I-4, 5, 14; I-5, 1)

   I feel depressed, frustrated or disciplined—depending upon what I couldn't have & why

   I either try to forget about it, rationalize by saying I can do without it, or find some way to get it without hurting anyone

   I try another way or another subject

   I am disappointed, but don't press my point. I may try again to get it later when I think the time is right

Unclassified

   It doesn't bother me too much. I'd rather forget it than create tension

   I often feel like stomping my feet & screaming, but I generally try harder or seek a substitute

   I try to find a fatalistic rationalization for it, but I don't always succeed

I-5

For this item we have not seen any responses on I-6 protocols that we could clearly distinguish from those of I-5 and I-4/5 subjects. The single I-5 category carries further the conceptual complexity that characterizes most I-4/5 responses. Additional aspects that are shown in these responses are seeing multiple facets of situations and distinction between desire and need.

1. Evaluation of the situation: two or more I-4 or I-4/5 ideas (I-4/5, 2, 3)

   I re-examine my desire for it, my need for it, and the methods I used to achieve

   it depends. If it's a school grade I try again. If I don't deserve it I say "thats life." If I really want it I try again

   I analyze the desire and the interference: if the former seems sound I use other means to achieve the end or a satisfying modefication of it

Usually She Felt That Sex—

T his item elicits both pos-
itive and negative attitudes towards sex at every I-level. Ignoring neutral
remarks, we may note, nonetheless, that negative responses are about as
common as positive ones for subjects below I-3, while there are very few
negative responses from subjects above I-4. More germane to ego level,
the pleasure of sex is seen as physiological excitement below I-3, as part of
an interpersonal relation above I-4. At I-3 and I-3/4 conventional values
predominate, and positive feelings are usually expressed in a muted way.
At I-4 values are more personal than conventional, positive feelings are
usually expressed more convincingly, and sex, whether viewed positively
or negatively, is seen in a larger context. There is no one-to-one relation

between experience and ego level. Many responses rated above I-4 are most likely to occur to experienced women ("can be a positive beautiful thing as years of marriage add up," I-4/5), but some obviously are given by the inexperienced ("was a glorious mystery, about which she wanted to know," I-4/5).

I-2

Interpersonal emphasis is noticeably absent at I-2. Sex may be seen as a physical act or equated with people, but recognition of interaction between persons is absent. The unique responses, "was between her and no one else" and "was two men together," illustrate vividly the lack of interpersonal reference.

1. —was bad, evil, not good (Δ/3, 3, 4, 5; I-3, 9, 10)
   a very bad thing
   was impure

2. Sex is girls, men, or the like.
   only meant girls
   is a male a female
   was two men together
   is a girl

3. —is her own business (I-3/4, 6)
   was between her and no one else

Unclassified
   don't matter
   she do not like
   is good to me because I get hot
   was the Best thing she ever done

DELTA

For the Delta subject sex is a commodity or a means to some end. It may get her in trouble or be what she needs.

1. —is all she had; is what she needs (Δ/3, 1; I-3/4, 11)
   is al she like
   was what she wanted
   is 90 per cent of my life Sixual relation causes child

2. —got her in trouble
   does her wrong

3. —was a game
   was a part time game

4. Exciting because forbidden (Δ/3, 3; I-3, 5; I-3/4, 12)
   was desirable but forbidden
   esciting before marriage but different after marriage

Unclassified
   was a thing expected of her
   helpes me on up the road farther
   that what marrage and babys ar about

DELTA/3

Responses like "was good" can occur at almost any level but occur proportionately more often below I-3. The category "is nothing, boring, stupid," is characteristic of Delta/3 subjects. The remaining responses, all negative, are infrequent ones found on protocols ranging from I-2 to I-4, classed here because of their relative frequency on I-2 and I-2/Delta protocols.

*1. —was good, a good thing (Δ, 1; I-3, 4)
   was good for her

2. —is nothing, boring, stupid (I-3, 3; I-3/4, 14)
   was for the birds
   is wasted time
   Just don't bother a woman
   was for Kinsey to write about

3. —was sinful, wrong, not right (I-2, 1; Δ, 4; I-3, 9)
   was a wrong word

4. —was nasty, not nice (I-2, 1; I-3, 9, 10; I-3/4, 14)
   was not a nice subject
5. —was horrible, terrible, awful (I-2, 1; I-3, 2; I-3/4, 14)
   was a terrible thing
   was a nightmare

I-3

Subjects at this level choose conventional, bland statements, such as "is natural," "is necessary," "is unimportant." The predominant tone of the positive statements is an approving cliché. There is considerable range in the degree of enthusiasm implied in the positive remarks, from "is OK," to "makes the world go round." Negative attitudes such as "was shameful," "is dirty," are less frequent but not uncommon. The negative statements at I-3/4 are usually more interpersonal ("was not to be discussed") or indicate greater distance from one's feelings ("was not appealing").

*1. —is natural, normal, wholesome (I-3/4, 7; I-4, 1, 8)
Is normal in life
is normal (using discretion)
is not unhealthy
was a healthy function of normal people

*2. —is for married people; should be left to adults (I-3/4, 6, 7)
was only pertaining to marriage
is for married people to enjoy
was horrible outside of marriage
should not be encouraged before marriage

*3. —is necessary, important; is unnecessary, unimportant (Δ/3, 2; I-3/4, 8, 14; I-4, 11)
was secondary
plays an important role
was unimportant to herself
was less important than love
is not important at a Certain Age

*4. —was fine, wonderful, interesting (Δ/3, 1; I-4, 4)
is something wonderful and worth waiting for
is great

5. —was fun (Δ, 4; I-3/4, 12)
"makes the world go round"
was to be liked

6. —is nice, something nice (I-4, 11)
is very pretty

7. —is OK, all right (I-3/4, 13)

8. —was not to be ashamed of (I-3/4, 3; I-4, 9)

9. —was shameful, naughty, vulgar (I-2, 1; Δ/3, 3, 4; I-3/4, 1, 2, 14)
was ugly
was something to be ashame of
was a very naughty subject

10. —is dirty, unclean (I-2, 1; Δ/3, 4; I-3/4, 14)
was a dirty word
was a dirty subject

is unsanitary. (the way the act)
was something dirty and looked down on

11. —was a necessary evil (I-4, 6)

12. —is, could be a problem
    sometimes is nerve wrecking
    is a gread problum for teen ager
    was a problem for her

13. —was for others; was not what she wanted (I-2, UC; I-3/4, 14)
    was just for men
    was just for other people, not her
    didn't concern her

14. Evasion
    I don't know
    Who?
    cant relate

Unclassified
    was right
    could be good or bad
    was to be respected
    was a bother
    was confusing
    Was a secret

I-3/4

Many responses at this level make implicit or explicit references to normative attitudes and behavior; sex should or should not be discussed, is overemphasized, is personal, is OK at the right time or place. Most of the remaining responses are more differentiated versions of conventional I-3 feelings: instead of being natural (I-3), sex is a part of life; rather than being fun (I-3), sex is exciting or pleasant.

*1. —was not to be discussed, mentioned; is to be avoided (I-3, 9)
    was something to hide
    was to be suppressed
    was not a good topic of conversation
    was a subject to just know about
    shouldn't be talked about in public
    was taboo for small children to learn about

2. —was embarrassing, an embarrassing subject (I-3, 9)

3. —was a good topic to talk about (I-3, 8)
   was not an unpleasant or dirty topic
   was for open discussion
   was a topic to talk over with the girls
   should be discussed with children at home by parents

4. Concern with understanding, knowing about sex (I-4, 10)
   is something one must learn about
   was something she didn't understand
   was something that everyone needs to know about
   was something that had to be understood in the right way

5. —was overemphasized, overpublicized (I-4, 8)
   was exposed too much
   was written about to much
   was being over-emphasized in today's society
   should not be referred to so much in Advertisements, movies, etc.

6. —was personal, a private thing; is between husband and wife (I-2, 3; I-3, 2)
   was to be with one person
   was something secretive between her and her husband

7. —was a part of life, marriage (unqualified) (I-3, 1, 2; I-4, 1, 7)
   was merely a function of life
   was just a part of life
   was apart of her
   is a part of nature

8. —was an important, necessary part of marriage, life (I-4, 1, 7)
   plays an important part in her life
   was a big part of marriage
   is one of the necessary things in life
   was a necessary part of every human's life
   was necessary for a happy home

9. —was sacred, a God-given gift (unelaborated) (I-4, 5)
   was meant to be
   was a sacred and holy thing
   was pure and good

10. —was beautiful, a beautiful thing (I-4, 3)
    was treasured and beautiful
    was the beauty of life
    was the most beautiful act on earth

11. —was special, the greatest; is love, life (Δ, 1; I-4, 2, 4)
    held a special significance
    was romantic
    was the best thing on earth
    is one of the greatest things ever

12. —was exciting, pleasant, enjoyable (Δ, 4; I-3, 5; I-4, 3)
    was desirable
    was just for pleasure
    was something to enjoy

13. All right, OK, contingent on time, place, or use (I-3, 7; I-4, 12)
    OK at times
    is good at the right time (marriage)!
    was important in its place
    was enjoyable at the correct time and place
    was a pretty good thing, if used properly

14. —was overrated; was not appealing (Δ/3, 2, 4, 5; I-3, 3, 9, 10, 13; I-4, 6)
    was disgusting
    was of the animal order

Unclassified
    is wonderful with the right man
    was not the most important thing in the world

I-4

Evaluation of the role of sex in life is prominent at I-4, but stated in simple terms: sex is essential for life, an expression of love, part of a relationship. Contingencies are explicit rather than general as at I-3/4, but not conventional as at I-3. Conventional attitudes or practices may be denied, such as "was not an evil or sinful feeling" or "was not to be degraded as it has been." Negative feelings about sex are infrequent and typically expressed in terms of resignation or toleration. Sex is seen as cause and as consequence for other aspects of life.

*1. Normal, natural part of life, marriage; necessary to life (I-3, 1; I-3/4, 7, 8)
    was a normal part of life
    was a natural part of marriage
    was a normal thing occurring in the human being
    was as basic as eating and sleeping
    is essential to the procreation of life

2. —was an expression of love (I-3/4, 11; I-4/5, 1)
   is an expression of affection
   should be an expression of love

3. Enjoyable, pleasant, wonderful, beautiful (elaborated) (I-3/4, 10, 12)
   is a beautiful thing if respected
   was a beautiful part of life
   just part of my married life which I enjoy
   is interesting and enjoyable
   was a desirable experience
   is something that is healthy and is to be enjoyed

4. —was rewarding, satisfying, fulfilling (I-3, 4; I-3/4, 11)
   makes life richer
   was meant for happiness and fulfillment
   is wonderful and makes her feel that is is glad that is a woman
   was one of life's great joys

5. Sacred (elaborated) (I-3/4, 9)
   was a sacred thing to be saved for marriage
   was enjoyable and in accordance with the fullfillment of God's plan
   is something that is a sacred trust
   was sacred and beautiful

6. —was a duty; must be accepted (I-3, 11; I-3/4, 14; I-4/5, 2)
   was a thing to be tolerated
   was just another chore
   was just like a job
   was not to be avoided

7. Seen as part of a relation (I-3/4, 7, 8; I-4/5, 1)
   was a part of love
   was enjoyed by both partners
   was something only to be shared with her husband
   a vital and necessary part of a successful marriage relationship is the right perspective
   brought her and her husband closer together
   was a beautiful thing if love is involved

8. Should be taken seriously and not misused (I-3/4, 5)
   was a natural thing, but that control is needed
   was a natural, normal thing, and not a subject for dirty jokes
   was not to be degraded as it has been

was a sacred thing, not something for public display
*was used for the wrong thing when it is used for trash and
not the beautiful thing that it is*

9. Denial of negative feelings (I-3, 8)
should not involve guilt
was normal and not to be feared
was not an evil or sinful feeling
was normal and something not to be embarrassed about
was part of life which shouldn't be thought of as evil

10. Concern with communication, teaching (I-3/4, 4; I-4/5, UC)
talks were interesting
could have been better prepared for
should be taught at home and in the school
was not handled well in most magazines
*should be talked about openly so that teen-agers could learn
about it in a healthy way rather than an unhealthy way*

11. Contrasting attitudes
was wonderful and sometimes dirty
was very irratating but at other times she enjoyed it
was a priviledge in marriage sometimes not
was hard to discuss, though understood
was nice but mysterious
was more exciting than it was
was not ecstasy but pleasant
is important to some and unimportant to others

12. Approval with reservations (I-3/4, 13)
was worthwhile in the appropriate moral context
was great but subject to too many social pressures
was all right if excessive demands were not made upon her
*was okay, but you have to have a lot of love for the person
you sleep with or its a chore*
*was something wonderful if she was old enough & mature
enough to except sex*

Unclassified
was good and a part of being herself

I-4/5

Responses classed here add a little conceptual complexity to the
I-4 categories. Evaluation of attitudes towards sex or of the part sex
plays in marriage, love, or life, are more explicit than at I-4. Recognition

of change in one's own attitude over time is characteristic, as well as coping with disparate aspects (necessity and pleasure).

1. An expression of love (elaborated) (I-4, 2, 7)
   was an expression of love and respect
   was an expression of love and very pleasurable
   was a beautiful expression of deep love
   is one of the best ways of demonstrating love for a man
   properly used was God's greatest gift—as it demonstrates perfect love

2. Feelings change with time and experience (I-4, 6)
   was not as important as I know it is now
   can be a positive, beautiful thing as years of marriage add up
   was something to put up with. She changed her mind when she met her second husband

3. Evaluation of others' opinions
   was something very funny in movies—I disagree
   was a dirty word (sister in law)
   was underrated by many of her married friends whenever it was discussed
   was a vital part of life for others but not for her until after marriage

Unclassified
   was emphasized too much in proportion to other phases of marriage
   was quite necessary—in fact without it life would be rather dull and dreary
   is an interesting subject but has no set answer. It just goes on and on with no end. Its a vicious circle
   was a glorious mystery, about which she wanted to know
   has something to look forward to

I-5

Characteristic responses here involve coping with contradictory aspects, seeing sex in uncommon contexts, and in terms of mutuality. Mutuality is of course implied by saying that sex is an expression of love. To be scored at this level, however, it must be expressed more clearly and unambiguously.

1. Concern with sex as a basic part of a relationship (elaborated)

> *was glorious and beautiful, and a bond (after love) between a man and his wife*
>
> *was an important part of a genuine love between man and woman*
>
> *is something that can contributes toward marital satisfaction or discord*
>
> *was something that a husband and wife should have a thorough understanding of and agree with each other*
>
> *is also an essential thing in marriage and should be enjoyed by both or you might as well not expect a very happy marriage*

2. Sex viewed as an abstract cause

> *was a facet of living that had endless possibilities, both for creativity & destruction*
>
> *was a fearful, awful thing because she had a common wrong value*
>
> *was good and could act as a healing and soothing balm to life*
>
> *was delightful in itself, but made a difficult problem by the culture*

Unclassified

> *was delightful, intriguing, and very, very boring*
>
> *was a fine institution*

I-6

These responses are rated here because of their unique breadth of perspective. There are conflicting and contrasting thoughts as well as original and unconventional ones.

Unclassified

> *was an integral part of life and only over—or under-emphasized in neurotic individuals and situations*
>
> *was something she knew technically but had not experienced either physically or mentally, and she shouldn't she wasn't old enough in any sense of the word*
>
> *(May I again speak for myself?) Sex is a basic interest and motivation at every age*

For a Woman
a Career Is—

Use of the term "career" rather than "job" in this stem may produce a middle-class bias; secretaries are career girls, but a housemaid is not. Even though trends on this item are consistent with those on others, they are capable of socio-economic explanation here. Thus, the response category "working; hard work" (I-2) is somewhat redundant, but also realistic for lower social classes. The emphasis on earning money (Delta and I-3) is also realistic in many cases, though one should not overlook that the same concerns can be expressed at a higher level ("a fortress for life against poverty,"

416

I-4; "a useful necessary thing. There is no substitute for the feeling that one can earn one's own bread and butter," I-5). Only at I-3/4 and higher is there emphasis on a sense of choice; one can choose to have a career or not in accord with one's needs and abilities. This feeling, distinctive for higher levels, can also be a realistic function of class status.

Little or no relation exists between I-level and approval or disapproval of a career. There is a relation, however, between I-level and insight into the problems or benefits a career brings to a woman. Blanket statements are predominant up through I-3, but decrease thereafter. Unequivocally disapproving statements are infrequent at any level. Instead of disapproval at I-3, a career is more likely to be seen as "unimportant" or "secondary." The largest group of responses comprises stereotyped expressions of approval, "wonderful," "important," "necessary" (I-3). Awareness that a career poses difficulties for women, particularly in relation to marriage, is implied at I-3/4 and I-4 in contingent or uncertain statements such as, "good if her children are all grown" (I-3/4), "good as long as you don't neglect your family" (I-4), "somewhat debatable" (I-3/4). Above I-4 the responses are more likely to concern problems or advantages of combining career and marriage ("very desirable to avoid being lost when her family grows up and has a life of their own," I-4/5).

Four views about a woman's career are frequently expressed. A career is a job to be given up at marriage: this view holds from the lowest levels through I-4 but is strongest at I-3/4. Being a wife, mother, and homemaker is a woman's career: this view, expressed simply, is more characteristic of subjects below I-3; it is rare above I-4/5. A career is a kind of self-indulgence, hence must remain secondary to a woman's duty to her family: this view is anticipated as low as the Delta level, but is expressed with increasing force and clarity at each subsequent level ("secondary," I-3; should not interfere with her home, I-3/4; "secondary to her family," I-4; "something she would like to have but will give it up to make a happy and solid home," I-5; "very satifying if she has the time, energy and ability to fit it comfortably into the rest of her life, assuming she is married," I-6). Finally, a career is viewed as a means of self-expression, whether it is job or home: this idea is prominent above I-3/4, but anticipated at lower levels ("her life," I-3; "something she likes to do," I-3/4; "something she wants to achieve," I-3/4).

To see a career in a wider social context than simply self and family is unusual. At the I-3/4 level one category involves a self-centered concern, social approval and prestige. One I-4 subject sees a career as a contribution to society. At I-5 one response considers the conflict between duty to family and to society. For some of the responses rated I-6 recognition of the social context is one factor.

I-2

Most I-2 responses are classified at Delta/3 or I-3. Some responses at I-2 are somewhat redundant. There is also a question, unanswerable on our data, whether some of the responses classed I-2 and Delta indicate semantic confusion or failure to understand the stem.

1. —a good job (Δ, 1; I-3, 8)
   very good work
   a good Job to have
   a job

2. —working; hard work (I-3, 8)
   heavy
   hard for them
   is hard to pull
   hard because she has to work hard

3. —being good, clean (Δ/3, 1)

Unclassified
   easy
   doing as she please
   stay single

DELTA

To see a career purely in terms of money is typical for a Delta orientation. The category "exciting" is an empirical one, difficult to rationalize; for the Delta subject excitement may be a reward like money. "Everything" and "her future" have been classed here somewhat arbitrarily. Some of these responses may be a condemnation of marriage, and some may indicate misunderstanding of the stem.

1. A way to get money (I-2, 1; Δ/3, 4; I-3, 7)
   money
   a job worth lots of money
   money in her hand and a good job
   a teacher because you earn quite a lot of money

2. —everything; her future (I-3/4, 12)

3. —exciting (I-3, 1; I-3/4, 10)
   adventure
   the life

Unclassified
   prostitution if she feels neglected
   something you work very hard for and then blow it all by
   getting married

DELTA/3

The Delta/3 categories, like those at I-2 and Delta, are either very global or extremely concrete. They occur over a wide range of I-levels, but are proportionately more frequent below I-3. Qualification of "good" is enough to raise the rating to I-3, for example, "sometimes good."

*1. —good; nice; a good thing (unqualified) (I-2, 3; I-3, 1, 2, 3)
   a very good thing

2. —nothing; silly (I-3, 10; I-3/4, 18)
   for the birds
   stupid
   not good
   She should not work

*3. —being a wife, mother, homemaker (I-3, 9)
   her family
   having children
   taking care her family
   making a good home
   being a good wife and mother
   being with a man

4. Naming of specific occupations (Δ, 1)
   modeling
   a good nurse or typist
   teacher archelogy
   to be a teacher

I-3

Responses in the starred categories, all global adjectives, have occurred on protocols ranging in I-level from I-2 to I-4/5, but peak at I-3. Even the more descriptive I-3 responses are simple and unequivocal, such as "necessary to make ends meet" or "raising a family." For the I-3 a career is a thing you have; many I-3/4 subjects see it as a process or goal. Alternatives, contingencies, inner aspects and interpersonal factors are mentioned above I-3.

*1. —fine; wonderful; OK (Δ, 3; Δ/3, 1; I-3/4, 10)
   just great
   delighteful
   an enchanting thing
   the best thing in life
   alright to a certain extent

*2. —good (nice) to have; helpful (Δ/3, 1; I-3/4, 6)
   something you should have
   sometimes a good thing to have
   a good idea
   her best bet
   a good experiance
   helpful to daily living

3. —sometimes good (Δ/3, 1)
   good for a while
   often a good thing
   sometime best for the woman
   sometimes enjoyable

*4. —important, necessary (with no contingencies) (I-3/4, 14)
   sometimes necessary
   usually important
   important to some
   important to an extent

*5. —secondary, unimportant, unnecessary (with no contingencies) (I-3/4, 4; I-4, 1; I-4/5, 1)
   secondary in her life
   not always necessary
   second best
   incidental

6. Value compared with that of marriage (I-3/4, 16; I-4, 1)
   good but marriage is better
   just as important as being a housewife
   not as important as a man
   better than being married

7. —an economic aid; a means of support (Δ, 1; I-3/4, 3)
   something to do to earn money of her own
   necessary to make ends meet
   necessary if she needs money
   her living
   something to live off

8. —a big job for her (I-2, 1, 2; I-3/4, 9)
   a full time job
   a heavy load

9. —raising a family (Δ/3, 3; I-4, 7)
   My career was Rasing Kids
   being married and raising a family
   that of raising a family and establishing a home

10. —not satisfactory; not enough (Δ/3, 2; I-4, 4)
    unrewarding
    not entirely fulfilling

Unclassified
   her life
   I don't know

I-3/4

A broader and less dogmatic view of a career is evident in many of the responses classed at this level. The I-3/4 subject recognizes certain contingencies, such as marital status and whether or not a career interferes with her functions at home. She sees that a career is "a matter of choice" and that it may be good or bad. Specification, however, that the choice is an individual decision is I-4, and that it is contingent upon the individual's unique characteristics and circumstances, I-5. Rather than simply stating a career is important or unimportant, the I-3/4 subject expresses her feeling in some context, for example, "a must in today's world," "not as important as for a man." A career is most often seen in a positive light, but is so described in more differentiated terms than at I-3, for example, "desirable," "her goal," or "something she wants to achieve." Appreciation of a career is more diverse at I-3/4 ("interesting," "satisfying," or "prestige") but not so differentiated as at I-4 ("fulfilling," "an escape from the tediousness of being a housewife"). Descriptions of a career as an insurance against emergencies peak at I-3/4, but are not uncommon at I-3 and I-4. To be rated higher than I-3/4 something more than security must be included, such as "something that she must be prepared for in case of need but does not always use" (I-4).

*1. Importance, value contingent on marital status (I-4, 1, 4, 5; I-4/5, 3)
   wonderful if you don't fall in love
   fun until she gets married & wants a family
   stupid if your married
   a handicap if she is rearing a family

>nice if she is single, but should be dropped after she is a wife
> and mother

2. Should not interfere with marriage; difficult to mix with raising a family (I-4, 2)
>fine if it does not take her away from her family and children
>nice but shouldn't be mixed with raising a family
>taking something away from her home

*3. —an insurance policy; something to fall back on, rely on
(I-3, 7)
>something to fell back on if something happens to her mar-
>ried life
>very helpful if her husband should die, and some self-support
>is needed
>something to live by later

4. —temporary; a side-line (I-3, 5)
>a hobby
>just a means of passing time
>not her lifes work
>sometimes a frill
>between her schooling and marriage
>a time filler until marriage

5. —an outlet; important if keeping a home isn't (I-4, 4, 6,
10, 11)
>an outlet from everyday housework
>something to give her an outlet from mother hood
>important if she can't have children or can't stand housework

6. —an asset; worthwhile (I-3, 2)
>sometimes advantageous
>desirable

7. Positive and negative aspects (simply stated) (I-4, 14; I-5, 3)
>perhaps desirable, perhaps not
>good but not always useful
>important but not essential
>not always necessary but sometime helpful
>sometimes good sometimes disrupting to the family

8. —somewhat debatable; a conflict (I-4, 13)
>unsure
>a difficult decision to make
>not always the best thing

9. —demanding; time-consuming (I-3, 8; I-4, 5)

    sometimes difficult to attain
    hard to hold onto after marriage and she is trying to raise
      a family

10. —interesting, challenging, satisfying (Δ, 3; I-3, 1; I-4, 6, 8, 12)
    a stimulating adventure
    interesting, and necessary
    something of unattainable interest
    a satisfying experience

11. An opportunity to achieve, get ahead (I-4, 9)
    her way of rising up in the world
    the step toward higher prestige

12. —(good, important if it is) something she wants to do, likes to do (Δ, 2; I-4, 8; I-4/5, 6)
    O.K. for whoever wants one
    important only if she desires one
    something she wants to achieve
    anything that she really wants to make a career of
    whatever she feels comfortable doing
    a field where she finds herself very dedicated

13. —her goal; something to look forward to (I-4, 10)
    something she has always longed for
    of something to think and dream
    her wish come true
    something to work for

14. —an important part of life; important, necessary today (I-3, 4)
    a must in today's world
    of utmost importance
    the most important step in her life

15. —only a part of her life; not her whole life
    part of her life
    not the most important aspect of her life

16. Comparison with a man's career (unqualified) (I-3, 6)
    not as important as for a man
    just as important as a man's career
    important, but not as important as a man career
    often as important as for a man

17. —is what she makes it; a matter of choice (I-4, 14; I-5, 3)
    an option
    up to her
    her own perogative

as important as she makes it
what every she feel is best for her

18. —something I care nothing about (Δ/3, 2)
    good, but it's not for me
    unattractive to me

19. Society's views (stated simply)
    generally looked on unpleasantly
    not universally sanctioned
    becoming more acceptable and actually desirable
    becoming more important

20. —any number of things
    many and varied things
    a number of fields

Unclassified
    nursing, I think this, because that is what I want to be

I-4

The responses classed at this level show that the importance given a career is not a function of ego level. One large group of responses clearly gives marriage priority over a career and another group emphasizes that a career is a vital expression of a part of oneself, otherwise stunted by marriage and home. A third view transcends the marriage versus career stand; a career is whatever allows self-expression or is a prominent interest. However, to state explicitly that a career is whatever she really wants to do, whether in the home or an outside job, is rated I-4/5.

Responses at I-4 are more personal in emphasis than those at lower levels. A career is stimulating, enriching, challenging, and a sign of success and recognition. Its desirability may be contingent on the individual's plans, intentions, desires, or abilities, a less conventional and more personal set of contingencies than marital status (I-3/4). Seeing a career in relation to inner needs rather than external situations is typical ("lovely if you are happy in your field of work" or "what is most self-fulfilling").

*1. —secondary to marriage, her family, her home (I-3, 5, 6; I-3/4, 1; I-4/5, 1, 3; I-5, 1)
    not as important as being a good mother
    only 2nd to marriage & family
    and should be secondary to the rearing of her family
    important and exciting, but secondary to her homelife

2. —good if she considers her husband and family first (I-3/4, 2; I-4/5, 3; I-5, 1)

fine if she does not have a family whom she is neglecting

sometimes necessary but should not be placed above her husband and family if she has a husband & family

fine, providing adequate care is taken care of any children there may be

3. —fine as long as she can be housewife and mother (I-4/5, 2, 4; I-6, 1)

good, but I feel that it should be combined with marriage; children

4. (Not) An alternative to or substitute for marriage and family (I-3, 10; I-3/4, 1, 5; I-4/5, 3, 5)

a substitute

sometimes a compensation

very important if she is not the domestic type

something she must have, if she has no family

very important & rewarding but no substitute for a husband & family

good and provides excitement and may be better for some women than marriage

5. Value contingent on her plans, intentions, wishes (I-3/4, 1, 9)

"out" of she plans to raise children

alright if she's intending on staying single

not advisable unless she intends not to marry

sometimes difficult to follow through with when she also wants to raise a family

6. —an interesting outside experience (I-3/4, 5, 10)

a great outlet and added attraction

stimulating to the routine of her life

an interesting addition to her family life

the thing that gives her the spark

only to occupy spare time and provide pleasure

7. —either marriage or a profession (I-3, 9; I-4/5, 6)

a home, husband and children or a life all her own

not necessarily a job—a home and family can be a rewarding one

needed. Either a family to keep you busy, or outside work

8. —(good, important if it is) something she can do well, suited to her abilities (I-3/4, 10, 12; I-4/5, 6)

good if she can handle it
desireable if she has the capabilities and drive it takes
whatever she is best suited for
doing what she likes to do well

9. A sign of success, achievement, accomplishment (I-3/4, 11)
   success of one part of life
   showing success in doing a good job
   wonderful recognition for her mind

10. A way of satisfying inner needs (I-3/4, 5, 13)
    an escape from housework or lonliness
    vital if she is intelligent and hates to keep house
    an escape from the tediousness of being a housewife
    to fulfill her desires—either raising a family or going into the business world
    something she can turn to when she becomes bored

11. —the expression of herself (I-4/5, 5; I-5, 1)
    one way of expressing her abilities
    nice to have for she too needs to be able to express her individuality
    an expression of a side of her personality which cannot be expressed in the home
    perhaps an important aspect of her total self expression
    as important as it is necessary to her way of life or need to express herself

12. —rewarding, fulfilling (I-3/4, 10; I-4/5, 4, 5; I-5, 1)
    a means of fulfilling her capacities
    what is most self-fulfilling

13. Personal or inner reservations (I-3/4, 8; I-4/5, 3, 4)
    wonderful if she wants it and can have a satifying one
    not always entirely satisfying—if she sacrifices her personal life for it
    sometimes joyous and honerable. Other time utterly redicules
    lovely if you are happy in your field of work
    good, if she is capable of balance between personal and business life

14. —an individual decision; good for some & not for others I-3/4, 7, 17)
    a decision which every woman has to make up her own mind about
    essential to some—not to others—marriage, in it self, is a career

Unclassified
> *something she should choose wisely*
> *not always necessary, a good education is still necessary though*
> *a valuable experience and can help her become a more well-rounded individual*
> *an opportunity to make a contribution to society*
> *a fortress for life against poverty*

I-4/5

Most responses at this level are combinations or elaborations of typical I-4 ideas: instead of being secondary to family, a career is secondary to a family's happiness; a career may be something to rely on, but also can be hell; emphasis is on growth or fulfillment as a person, rather than on self-expression or simply "fulfillment." There is more awareness that a career and marriage involve separate but not necessarily incompatible roles. Thus marriage and a career may be combined, eliminating the necessity implied at I-4 to choose between two alternatives. This is not to say that conflict is absent at this level, but it is a more indirect form of the expression of conflict between various role expectations found at I-5. Unfortunately we have no clear formula for excluding clichélike references to "woman's role," which ought to be classed lower.

1. Secondary to family's happiness, welfare (I-4, 1; I-5, 1, 2)
   > *second to making the home a happy place for her husband*
   > *her family and their problems and their needs*
   > *secondary to a happy home life, if she is wise*
   > *secondary to running a happy & rich household & being a wife and mother*

2. —compatible with marriage (I-4, 3)
   > *possible in conjunction with marriage and family rearing and can be kept along with marriage*

3. Evaluation in relation to marriage, family life (I-3/4, 1; I-4, 1, 2, 4, 13; I-5, 1, 2; I-6, 1)
   > *most important if she doesn't have a husband to rely on for security, but it can be hell*
   > *very desirable to avoid being lost when her family grows up and has a life of their own*
   > *secondary to a husband and family but necessary should she ever need to support the family*
   > *important only if it is not at the expense of her family. In*

some situations it contributes to the emotional stability of a family
often deciding it is more important to her than marriage
a substitute or a supplement secondary to being a wife and mother

4. Evaluation in context of identity or role as a woman (I-4, 3, 12, 13; I-5, 1; I-6, 1)
    important but secondardly to her role as a woman
    doing that which makes her happy and fulfills her as a woman
    sometimes so important that she loses her identity as a woman
    as important as for a man, but I feel no woman should deny her femininity or herself the opportunities of motherhood

5. A means of self-fulfillment, self-development, self-identity (I-4, 11, 12; I-5, 1; I-6, 1)
    a part of growth as a person & a valuable experience
    one way to fulfillment as a person
    necessary to give her a sense of fulfillment that a family alone does not supply
    very necessary. If she doesn't have one at some time she will only have half-lived
    important for growth qualitatively in order to deal with her personal life and make decisions in the outside world

6. Whatever she really wants to do: whether being a housewife or having an outside job (I-3/4, 12; I-4, 7, 8; I-6, 2)
    her greatest interest, whether it be her home or a profession
    important, whether it be in the business world or in a maternal way
    doing the most with her talents and it can range from being a wife to having an important position
    something she wants to do more than anything else in the world no matter if it is only raising a family

Unclassified
    excellent if she is tempermentaly suited for one
    one means of finding an outlet for any frustration that she might have

I-5

Two categories at I-5 reflect an awareness that obstacles to a career result from the conflict generated within oneself and within the family. A career is an individual matter contingent on individual needs

and circumstances, about which there are no general rules such as "good
if she is not married" (I-3/4), and " 'out' if she plans to raise children"
(I-4).

1. Awareness of own needs, goals, as well as family's (I-4, 1, 2,
   11; I-4/5, 1, 3, 4; I-6, 1)
   *something she would like to have but will give up to make
   a happy and solid home*
   *tolerated, until she finds an inner security for herself and
   her children*
   *a duty to the world which she cannot often fulfill because of
   her previous duty to her family . . .*
   *important to continue to develop, stimulate & express her
   interests, to keep her mind alert, but not at the expense of
   her family*
   *difficult because of the conflicts of the role of woman—as
   a wife and a self-sufficient person*

2. Evaluation in the context of her relationship with her husband
   (I-4/5, 1, 3; I-6, 1)
   *a good ambition if it does not conflict with a couple's life
   after marriage*
   *hazardous if married I feel it would probably conflict with
   the husbands sense of importance*
   *dependent on the cooperation of her husband if it is pursued
   after marriage*

3. —it depends on the woman (I-3/4, 7, 17; I-6, 2)
   dependent upon her need for it
   a debatable subject and depends on individual circumstances
   sometimes good, sometimes not—depending on the woman
   the right thing but this also depends on the woman
   necessary or a time "bider" depending on that woman
   *a matter of choice to be followed or avoided according to
   individual needs*

Unclassified
   *a useful, necessary thing. There is no substitute for the feeling
   that one can earn one's own bread and butter*

I-6

The responses classed at I-6 are unique elaborations of ideas found
at I-4/5 and I-5. Prominent elements are that it is a matter of personal
choice, depending on the particular woman, and that it can be integrated

with rather than being necessarily in conflict with her functions as wife and mother.

1. Integration of career with identity or role as woman (uniquely elaborated) (I-4, 3; I-4/5, 4, 5; I-5, 1, 2)

   a blessing at the proper time and an extension of her basically female role for living in today's world

   a means of fulfillment, helping make her an intellectual, interesting person, so that she may be a better wife-companion

   very satifying if she has the time, energy and ability to fit it comfortably into the rest of her life, assuming she is married

2. Value, choice contingent on individual (uniquely elaborated) '(I-4/5, 6; I-5, 3)

   an individual matter—I admire women who truly have a career the love

   a matter of choice with respect to her assessment of her self in terms of the world in which she lives

My Conscience Bothers Me If—

Although this stem has probably the hardest word in our test form, most subjects give clear, pertinent replies. Failure to comprehend can be a sign of low I-level; denial that conscience ever bothers (Delta) probably indicates some comprehension. We have not asked the subject what bad things she usually does, nor would it be realistic to expect an honest answer to such a question. Therefore we do not ask ourselves what kind of transgression a subject at the given level might commit but rather what she would consider a transgression. We attempt to reconstruct the value system that would lead to the response. Since the stem is an embarrassing one, particularly to those with a severe conscience or with severe misdemeanors, some disguise may be expected and a corresponding amount of inference needed. "I am unpure" (I-2) is assumed to refer to a sexual act. "I don't have know money and have seen something I want" (Delta) is assumed to refer to stealing. In general, progress is from actions classed as bad per se, to disobeying external rules, to bad consequences for others, to breaking the social compact or to violating inner standards.

I-2

Theoretically the I-2 subject has no conscience in the sense that more mature people do. Distinctive I-2 responses seem like naming taboo acts, usually sexual. Any implication of violation of general rules or standards, loss of control, or concern for interpersonal consequences, raises the rating above this level.

> 1. Sexual acts (I-3/4, 8)
> *I am out with a boy*
> *stay out all night*
> *when I like a nother boy or get into trolbe*
> *I am unpure*
> *I do something with a man and not tell my mother about it*
> *or a preist*

Unclassified
> *the house is not clean*
> *I drank*

DELTA

Characteristic Delta reactions displayed on this item are callousness ("I let it") and willful demanding ("always do what I want to do"). "I have to lie to someone who trusts me" displays also denial of responsibility for one's actions. "I can't have my own way" is illogical as an answer but clear as an expression of willfulness. Answers based on not succeeding or on being talked about indicate a lack of conscience almost as clearly as saying one does not have one. The one category here that names transgression of a rule refers to stealing; one may surmise that it is the concrete character of this transgression that impresses it on people earlier in development than lying or cheating.

> 1. —I steal
> *If I take his money*
> *I take something that is not mine*
>
> 2. —I don't have a conscience; my conscience never bothers me
> *none*

> *it doesn't*
> *I don't have any bothers*
> *always do what I want to*

3. —I let it
   I realise it

4. —I am being talked about, suspected
   my mother is suspisious of what I have been doing
   I feel that someone is watching me

5. —I happen, have to lie, cheat, etc. (I-3, 1)
   I have to lie to someone who trusts me
   I happen to lie about something
   I am forced into a white lie

6. —I don't succeed in what I want to do (I-3, 13; I-3/4, 14)
   I can't have my own way
   I'm unconsiderate & don't succeed in making a fool out of Jan
   do something stupid

Unclassified
   I waste precious time taking tests like this

DELTA/3

While many low-level subjects give responses of the "I do wrong" type, so do others, especially at I-3; hence the compromise rating here.

*1. —I do something wrong, bad (I-3, 2, 3, 8)
   I do wrong
   I don't do the right thing
   I have done something
   I've done something wrong
   I am bad

2. —I get mad (I-3, 5; I-3/4, 10)
   I get mad at my family
   get angry

I-3

For most I-3 subjects rules are more specific than doing right and not doing wrong, but the rules still tend to be absolute, external standards. At I-3/4 awareness of the relativity and origin of standards is often implied, but it is not stated until higher levels. Responses at I-3 usually

refer to infractions of specific rules such as those against lying and cheating, and for studying and doing chores. The rules may be quantitative
("I talk too much"; "spank my baby too hard"), which is an advance
over the taboo acts at I-2. A concern for appropriateness or consideration
of causes and effects, particularly interpersonal ones, indicates a higher
level.

**1. —I lie, cheat (Δ, 5; I-4, 13)
   lie to my husband
   tell a story
   I am untruthful about something
   I cheat on tests
   I am not honest

2. —I do something I shouldn't (Δ/3, 1; I-3/4, 3)
   I do something I'm not suppose to

*3. —I mistreat someone; I do people wrong; I am mean (vague
   or unspecified) (Δ/3, 1; I-3/4, 1, 2; I-4, 2)
   I say something mean to someone, preferably my husband
   I am cruel to others
   I do something to someone else
   I treat someone badly
   I harm someone
   I have done wrong to any one
   I am mean and conceited

4. —I talk too much; I say something I shouldn't (I-3/4, 5)
   do or say the wrong thing

5. —I fight, argue, nag (Δ/3, 2; I-3/4, 10)
   I have a fight with my friend
   I nag my husband too much
   I argue with my mother
   I fuss too much

6. —I am too hard on the kids (I-3/4, 12)
   spank my baby too hard
   I spank my son
   I scream at the kids to much

7. —I don't do my chores (I-3/4, 11, 15)
   I miss classes
   I Forget to brush my teeth
   I dont cook

8. —I violate a rule (Δ/3, 1; I-3/4, 9; I-4, 8)
   I disobey

I commit a mortal sin
I speed too much
I drink too much
I break God's will's and commands

9. —I spend too much money (I-3/4, 16)
    I don't pay my bills
    I owe money
    I buy anything for myself

10. —I do certain things (vague)
    I let something go on
    I forget to do something

11. —I think of bad things (I-3/4, 6)
    I am trouble about something
    I worry about something
    worry about something I really want to do
    I think what I won't say

12. —I think of my past
    I think about my past which is a sad one

13. —I make a foolish mistake (Δ, 6)
    Ive made a wrong decision
    I act foolish

14. —my children misbehave
    my son acts up in public or school
    my Kids are out late
    my son won't try to do some home work

15. —I don't help people (I-3/4, 13)

Unclassified
    sometimes
    something went worng between me & someone
    my husband is upset with me

I-3/4

The most conspicuous new element at I-3/4 is awareness of one's own and others' inner life. What is wrong is to hurt someone else's feelings. It is not just doing wrong but knowing that one has that bothers one's conscience; at I-4 this becomes a concern for the intention of the act. Rather than the absolute rules of the I-3 subject, the rules the I-3/4 subject sees will often be related to their source: parents, school, church, society. The existence of standards is implied: not only must chores be done (I-3), but tasks should be done well (I-3/4). Explicit statement of living up to standards is rated I-4.

*1. —I hurt someone's feelings (I-3, 3; I-4, 3, 4)
   I hurt someone
   I've done something wrong—especially if its hurt another person
   I hurt my mother & dad
   I do something wrong or hurt someone else

2. —I am rude to people; I speak harshly to others, to those I love (I-3, 3; I-4, 2, 6)
   I ridicule others
   I'm nasty to the ones I love
   I am cold to someone
   I am crabby and mean to people—especially those I love
   lash out at people
   I have insulted someone

*3. —I do what I know is wrong; I do things I know I shouldn't; I don't do what I think I should (I-3, 2; I-4/5, 2)
   I felt I did the wrong thing
   I do something I think is wrong
   I do something wrong and I know it is wrong
   I don't do something I know I should
   I do something I know I shouldn't of done, but I couldn't say one
   I realize I've done something wrong
   I do something for which I am later sorry

4. —I do something (wrong) without admitting it (I-4, 5)
   I do something & don't tell
   I do something behind my mother's back
   I don't tell my husband certain things which happen
   I lie, especially to my boyfriend or my best girlfriend until I tell him the truth
   I am not honest with my parents

5. —I talk about someone (I-3, 4; I-4, 2)
   I speak badly about another individual

6. Taboo thoughts (I-3, 11; I-4, 8)
   I think about sex
   I doubt my religious training
   I think about something that seems contrary to my religion

I swear against God
I know I've said something or heard something which is obscene

7. —I don't go to church (I-4/5, 3)
I should go to confession but rationalize and don't go

8. Sexual transgressions (implied standards) (I-2, 1)
I go out of my line as a woman
I lose my temper or step out of line
I would go out with a man besides my husband
I go & "make out" more than I should

9. —I disobey my parents (I-3, 8; I-4, 8)
I do something mother doesn't approve of
I talk back to my mother
my parents tell me not to do something and I do it anyway
I do something which is expressly against my parents' wishes
I do something I've been taught against

10. Lack of self-discipline, self-restraint (Δ/3, 2; I-3, 5)
I lose my temper
I go off my diet
I nag just because I'm tired
I get angry w/ people when I am worried about something else

11. —I neglect my family (I-3, 7)
I leave my children too often
I can not do For my children What is Needed
I leave my son alone

12. Inappropriate discipline (I-3, 6)
spank my children and then find they were not to blame
I'm irritable & impatient with my children & if I've hit them for small things
I raise my voice when correcting the children
I scold my daughter unnecessarily

13. —I don't help people when they need it, when asked, if I could (I-3, 15; I-4, 7)
fail to do a favor of some one that need a favor

14. —I don't do a task well (unelaborated) (Δ, 6; I-4, 11)
I flub up in classes
I do not keep house well
I stick my foot in my mouth or do badly on a test

*15. —I neglect my work; I don't finish a task; I waste time (general) (I-3, 7)

    I procrastinate

    I know I've cheated someone or etc. or if I've neglected my work or if I've lied

    I donot do enough

    I don't get everything done I think I should

16. —I buy something I don't need, can't afford (I-3, 9)

    when I go shopping and forget to tell my husband first if I by something

17. Differentiated emotions (I-4/5, 4)

    I am not sure of myself

    feel self-pity

    I am coy & jealous

    I become impatient

Unclassified

    I think anyone disapproves of me

    I displease my God

    I do things that I don't approve of others doing

I-4

The I-4 subject is concerned with intentions and purposes. Usually this takes the form of feeling guilty about having done something wrong deliberately, but occasionally a subject will say her conscience bothers her when she has unintentionally done something wrong. To say one's conscience hurts *even though* the act was unintentional is rated I-4/5. At I-4 many responses refer to fulfilling obligations and responsibilities. There is a corresponding decrease in responses referring to prohibitions. It is not enough to refrain from lying (I-3); one must also be sincere (I-4). Reference to integrity is found at higher levels. Reference to standards or principles, whether religious, moral, or even standards of achievement, merits an I-4 rating. Where the standards are clearly self-evaluated rather than imposed by having been taught or by membership in an institution, usually a religion, the rating is I-5.

*1. Statement about intentionality of actions (I-4/5, 1)

    I hurt someone on purpose

    I do or say something to hurt someone

    I do something I know will hurt someone later

    I did something intentionally

through erro I have misused anyone
Offend some one, unintentionally

*2. —I have been unkind, inconsiderate, selfish (I-3, 3; I-3/4, 2, 5; I-4/5, 4; I-5, 2)
I feel I have been selfish
not alway considerate of others
I have spoken thoughtlessly
I'm uncharitable to my family
I say unkind things about another person
I think bad things about other people

3. —I have hurt someone unnecessarily (I-3/4, 1)

4. —I feel that I have hurt someone (I-3/4, 1)
I know I have caused some one unhappiness
I know I have hurt someone's feelings

5. Do wrong without atoning, making amends (I-3/4, 4)
I do something wrong & don't make up for it
I do something I shouldn't and I haven't been punished
I go to bed before I make up with anyone I've argued with
I offended someone and had no opportunity to appologize

6. —I have been unfair, unjust (I-3/4, 2)
I don't do what I believe is fair or right
I say something unfair about someone else
Ive told a lie, or have done an injustice to someone
I feel I have hurt someone who didn't deserve this treatment

7. —I have failed to help (elaborated) (I-3/4, 13; I-5, 2)
I feel I was needed to help someone and was unable to do so
I fail to give the right amount of help to Someone who comes to me for help, advice or comfort
I know I haven't really tried in helping others
I miss church or feel I haven't done as much as I should for my loved ones or anyone

8. —I act contrary to my principles, to the principles I was taught (I-3, 8; I-3/4, 6, 9; I-4/5, 3; I-5, 1)
I do something contrary to the value system I was taught
I do not follow my "standards"
I know I've done something against my moral standards
I preach one thing and do the opposite

9. —I don't fulfill my responsibilities
shirk responsibility
I do not tell the truth or face up to my responsibilities

10. —I break a promise, let someone down
    I disappoint those whom I respect
    I feel I have failed to do what is expected of me
    cannot keep my word
    I forget an obligation

11. —I have not done my best (I-3/4, 14)
    I do not work up to my capabilities
    *I write a test that does not show the teacher what I really
    know*
    I feel I have not tried as hard as I might

12. —I am not true to myself, honest with myself, sincere
    I try to fool myself
    I am not sincere in what I say
    I fail to express myself frankly

13. —I deceive, betray others (I-3, 1)
    I feel I've deceived someone
    I betray my family or friends
    I betray someone's confidence
    I deliberately deceive or cheat
    I break the trust of someone who trusts me

Unclassified
    *I do something which I know isn't right; it's usually nothing
    major; but little minor things*

I-4/5

Responses rated here are mostly elaborations of I-4 responses.
Note that to "do something I feel is wrong" is not the same as feeling
that I have done something wrong, though our I-3/4 subjects use these
responses interchangeably. The emphasis at I-4/5 is on internalization of
standards; only responses elaborated to make that aspect clear are scored
I-4/5. Another similar category refers to doing what I believe in. Where
it is plainly stated that the standards are my own or internal, the rating
is I-5. The I-4/5 "even if" category is an interesting one. Going up the
scale to I-4, one notes the growth of concern for intentions that Piaget
has pointed out. At I-4/5 there is a responsibility for consequences, regardless of intentions, but that by no means returns one to the starting
point of absolute rules. The I-4/5 subject also feels guilty about insignificant things and things she only thought of; hence she is describing how
she attains some distance from categorical imperatives. This too is an
evaluation of standards. In effect, the subject is saying that her conscience may bother her when it should not.

1. Even if action is unintentional, insignificant, unavoidable (I-4, 1)

   I feel I've hurt anyone's feelings no matter how unimportant it may seem at the time

   I even tell a tiny little lie that is insignificant

   I even think about doing something I know is wrong

   I have to "back down" on a promise—even if it is unavoidable

   I willfully or unwillfully hurt anyone

2. —I do something I feel is wrong (elaborated) (I-3/4, 3)

   I do something I consider is seriously wrong—integrity is important

   I do something I feel is wrong & not if someone else feels it's wrong

   I do or say something which I feel was wrong or inappropriate

3. —I neglect to do those things in which I believe (I-3/4, 7; I-4, 8; I-5, 1)

   I fail to follow my religious principles

   I do not do what I believe in or if I neglect my own son

4. Hurt others' feelings, elaborated, differentiated (I-3/4, 17; I-4, 2)

   I feel I slight someone

   I'm petty or I disregard the feelings of others

   I do not really listen to a person

   I display an unnecessary lack of tact

   I am a little belligerent or unnecessarily curt toward someone

Unclassified

   I do things that interfere with my long term goals

   allow myself to enhance a story by extra details

   I exploit someone

   prejudge other people before I really know them

   I do that which is contrary to what I was taught as a child

I-5

Elements which conduce to an I-5 rating are a sense of the complexity of conscience, self-analysis of motives, positive injunctions rather than prohibitions, and sometimes a vivid sense of regret. The clearest criterion is the combination of internalization and generalization: one has set one's own principles, ideals, or values.

1. —I violate internal standards (I-4, 8; I-4/5, 3)

   I do not put my best efforts into activities I deem *important*

   I have not lived up to the standards I have set for myself

   I am not honest with myself and do not follow my own moral code

   I do something that is against my basic *religious belief. I am not a deeply religious person in the sense of running to church everytime the bell rings, but I do have a deep and abiding respect for God*

   in some small way, I do not live up to my ideals, or if I have given the wrong impression

2. I did not help others for selfish reasons (I-4, 2, 7)

   I do not do the extra thoughtful or ethical acts I have no excuse for not doing

   I realize how I might have been unselfish and helped another person when it was necessary

   I had chance to help some where and for selfish reason I did not take the oportunity to do so

   I nag my husband or have selfish motives for what I do

3. At least three contrasting possibilities, at least one at I-4/5

   I waste too much time or if I act too willing on a date or if I ignore people

   I compromise my intellectual integrity or am mean or don't try and understand or don't really try new things

Unclassified

   I lie—but I don't know if it bothers me because I'm sorry or because I'm afraid I'll be caught

   I scold my children over minor faults, then later realize how trivial it was

ITEM 36

A Woman Should Always—

This stem invites the subject to respond in terms of her ideas about woman's role or place and also to respond in terms of rules. The "should" in the stem can be taken to mean cautionary rules, usual at Delta; rules of social norms, usual at I-3; duties, at I-4; or a kind of self-actualization, a combination of rights, duties and destiny, at I-5. Subjects who object to the imperative, "should always," are likely to be at high I-levels: "realize that there is nothing she 'should always'" (I-4/5).

Responses concerned with woman's role, particularly clichés like "be feminine," "act like a woman," come from subjects at all I-levels but are most frequent at I-3/4 or higher. Be, talk like, remain, act like a

443

lady or woman, while in principle not identical, are used interchangeably and are classed I-3/4. To feel like a lady or to remember that one is a lady or woman (I-4) is different from being or acting like one. At I-5 the admonition is to look, feel, *and* act like a lady or woman. This distinction between looking, acting, and feeling is not customarily made by subjects at lower levels, particularly at I-3 and below, even though it is well within the intellectual capacity of our subjects.

Direct references to sexual relations are rare, but two high-level ones can be contrasted: "be well groomed, a willing sexual partner to her mate, and constantly boardening her mind" (I-5) and "be a lady in the parlor and a whore in the bedroom" (I-4). The former indicates acceptance of sex in a context of mutuality and as one part of life; the latter, while recognizing role differentiation, does so in context of a severe moral dichotomy often found at I-4 but not expected at I-5 or I-6.

I-2

The I-2 subject tends to think in terms of absolute, primitive moral dichotomies, here particularly clean versus dirty. Some subjects actually tie clean body to pure soul: "Keep herself clean and pure in body and soul."

> *1. —be clean
> *Keep herself clean and pure in body and soul*
> *try to be clean about herself*
> *bathe*
>
> 2. —be nice (Δ, 1; Δ/3, 1; I-3, 2)
> *Nice*
>
> Unclassified
> *smile*
> *feed her children and keep them clean*
> *feel good when she has a family*

DELTA

Responses classed Delta have a wary, watchful flavor, as if others are always about to harm one or to take advantage. "Take care of herself," classed here empirically, could have several meanings but probably means not count on anyone else to take care of her. There is a fine line between being careful because you might be caught and being concerned for the consequences of one's actions. The former is classed Delta, the latter I-3/4. Responses stating that a woman should act her age or not act phony may be given by girls dissatisfied with behavior of their mothers or other women. Empirically classed Delta are concrete actions related to appearance, a category which includes some obviously sarcastic responses such as "wear clothes."

1. —be good; keep a good reputation (I-2, 2; I-3, 4)
   be careful not to get a bad reputation
   value her reputation
   be a good woman
   be diecent

2. —be careful with men; be in control with men (I-3/4, 6)
   watch a man
   be ware of men
   keep one step ahead of the man
   have control over her body and not the man

3. —be smart, thinking; be careful; know what she is doing (I-3/4, 6, 9)
   be alert
   look farther than her nose
   be sensivetive and know what she is doing
   look before she leaps
   watch what she does
   watch her step

4. —take care of herself (I-3, 8)
   look out for herself
   protect herself from some things

5. —act her age, like an adult; don't act phony, funny (I-3/4, 7)
   be mature
   act femine & not phoney
   be natural and not talk real funny and walk funny
   be herself & don't be fake

6. Concrete actions related to appearance (I-3, 1)
   comb her hair
   put makeup on if she's ugly
   wear clothes
   keep seams straight on stockings
   dress like a woman

Unclassified
   give in to her desires

be sweet and nice Ha Ha
be psychoanalyzed
have a rest

DELTA/3

Responses concerned with looking and dressing nice come from the range I-2 to I-3/4, but mostly from Delta/3 and below; so placing this category here is less arbitrary than in some other cases. The poverty of these responses is betrayed by the all-purpose word "nice." Unlike some other stems where, for example, many subjects respond to "wife" as if it were "mother," relatively few subjects respond to this stem in terms of such specific roles. There are, however, responses dealing with concrete functions of a mother or housewife; they are classed here because they tend to be given by subjects below I-3.

1. —look, dress nice (I-2, 2; I-3, 1)
   look and act nice
   have a nice appearance and should get along with other people
   look nice and neat in appearance
   appear nice

2. —stay home; take care of home, family (I-3, 5; I-3/4, 12)
   be at home when she is needed
   keeps a nice home
   care for the house and cook
   clean house
   be good to her family
   do her best with her family

I-3

For the I-3 subject a woman should always get married, love and obey her husband, and be a good mother. "Be attractive, well-groomed" is a category that does not differentiate among the I-levels. Variations on this theme which can be distinguished are feelings about appearance (I-4) and responses saying she should look her best or be as attractive as possible (I-3/4), responses which are less categorical and absolute than those at I-3. The traits mentioned at this level, "be loving," "be agreeable and friendly," "be a good sport," all serve to make one nice to get along with, while traits with inward connotations, understanding, consideration, and the like (I-3/4), are less often mentioned at I-3 or lower. The I-3 subject tends to specify banal moral virtues, "be virtuous," "be honest," "be faithful," rather than inner ethical standards from which they might be derived, "try to live according to her conscience" (I-4).

**1. —be attractive, well-groomed (Δ, 6; Δ/3, 1; I-3/4, 2; I-4, 1)
be neat and clean in her appearance
keep herself neat and attractive for her husband
be presentable
keep her figure
keep herself looking good
look like a woman

2. —be friendly, pleasant, polite (I-2, 2; I-3/4, 4, 5)
be companionable
be loving
be sweet
be a good sport
be well mannered
be fun and gay
watch her manners

3. —be happy, content, secure (I-3/4, 15)
be made happy
be happy in what she is doing
be contented at home
feel secure

4. —be respectable, virtuous (Δ, 1; I-3/4, 5; I-4, 7)
retain he modesty
be pure and modest. Unless she is married
keep her morals high

5. —get married; be a good wife and mother (Δ/3, 2; I-3/4, 12)
try to find a husband
become a mother
strive to be a good mother
be a clean Kind and good. a housewife A good mother

6. —love (please, respect, obey) her husband (I-3/4, 13)
make a man happy
listen to her husband
please the man she loves
love her man
obey

7. —be faithful, honest, loyal, true (I-3/4, 7)
be sincere

be true to her husband in love and sex
be truthful

8. —keep herself in good health (Δ, 4)
   take care of herself, physically & mentaly
   be in good health

9. —pray; be religious
   look toward God
   depend on the Lord

I-3/4

The leading category here refers to being feminine, a woman, or a lady. Behavioral qualities advocated are slightly more differentiated than the nice, friendly sort at I-3, and refer to traits such as reserve, modesty, and gentleness that are included in one meaning of femininity. There is also a category of more inward, less behavioral traits, concerning sensitivity to and consideration for others; although this category peaks at I-3/4, it is not rare at higher levels. Concern for others is also reflected in the categories referring to keeping her family happy and with thinking of them first, presaging the more realistic I-4 category concerning assuming responsibilities to her family. The category concerning having outside interests and helping others presages the search for self-fulfillment mentioned at I-4/5 and unique expressions of social concern at I-4/5 and higher. "Be herself," or "be true to herself," and "have a mind of her own," all classed I-3/4, imply that one should be an individual; in a sense, this injunction is the opposite of "be a lady." At higher levels occur responses that are more clearly related to individuality, as well as responses related to self-awareness, "know herself" (I-4), or to self-acceptance, "accept herself" (I-5). The category most difficult to rationalize is the one concerning respecting herself and demanding respect from men; this occurs on a few cases ranging from Delta to I-4/5. Self-respect in general is an I-4 notion, but there is a colloquial meaning to having respect for a girl, something like "no heavy petting."

**1. —be feminine, a lady, a woman; act feminine, like a lady, like a woman (I-4, 2, 3, 4, 5; I-5, 1)
       try to maintain her feminine role
       try to be a woman
       act like one
       act in a lady-like manner
       try to be a lady

be feminine and not masculine
look and act like a woman

*2. —look her best, as attractive as possible (I-3, 1; I-4, 1)
  be as neat as possible
  try to look her best
  make the best of her face and figure
  look her loveliest

3. —be a good example; be a credit to her sex
  try to be an asset to her sex
  set a good example

*4. —be sensitive, kind, understanding, thoughtful, patient (I-3, 2; I-4, 12)
  be kind, considerate and friendly to everyone whom she comes in contact with
  be compassionate
  be attentive, warm and attractive towards others
  be gentle, cheerful and helpful
  love and understand

*5. —be quiet, reserved, modest (I-3, 2, 4; I-4, 12)
  listen and never talk unless she has something important to say
  act in her place
  watch her language
  speak quietly and forcefully, and gently

6. —think before she speaks (acts); be careful of what she says (does) (Δ, 2, 3)
  think twice before she speaks
  listen before speaking and be sure she understands what she hears
  think before she does anything
  careful of her conduct
  consider the outcome
  watch what she does around her children

*7. —be herself; be true to, honest with herself (Δ, 5; I-3, 7; I-4, 5, 6; I-5, 2)
  act like herself
  be herself and only herself
  be good & honest with herself
  be truthful to herself and others
  be herself, not try to be somebody else

8. —respect herself; be respected (I-4, 6; I-4/5, 5)
   have respect, for herself and her neighbors, be a good Christian
   demand respect from a male

9. —use good judgment; act with good sense (Δ, 3)
   do the wisest thing
   use her talents wisely
   act seniblely

10. —stick up for her rights; have a mind of her own (I-4/5, 3)
    stick up for her rights, because now a days women are taking over many jobs which man have held
    be a bit stubborn and be someone who doesn't give in to things easily
    lead her own life. Be free and loving in the right manners

11. —do the right thing; do what she thinks is right, best (I-4, 7, 8)
    do as she feels is right and proper
    learn to teach others the right things instead of always the wrong

12. —make a good home life; keep her family happy (Δ/3, 2; I-3, 5; I-4, 14)
    make as good a home life as possible for her family
    try her best to keep her family healthly and happy
    attempt to keep her home peaceful
    try to keep a reasonably clean house, good meals, a contented husband & children

13. —think of her family first; submit, cater to her husband (I-3, 6)
    think of her family before herself, something that is not often done
    put her husband above everything else
    make her husband feel like he is adored
    try to let the man feel superior
    be willing to allow her husband to play the dominant role

14. —have outside interests; help others (I-4/5, 2)
    be ready to do her work in her community
    Be willing to give a helping hand whenever needed. When time permits it
    try to think of others first
    feels she is able to contribute to society

15. —be optimistic; enjoy life; get the best out of life (I-3, 3; I-4, 9; I-4/5, 1; I-5, 3)
look on the happy side of the picture
keep smiling even when things go wrong
think in a positive manner
live life to the fullest
fell that life is what you make it

I-4

The I-4 turn toward inner life is shown here in the categories that concern a woman's feelings about her appearance, her feelings about being a woman, and remembering that she is a woman. Striving and coping are shown in the themes of responsibility and helpfulness toward family, of self-improvement and growth, of obeying her conscience, and of being and doing her best. Subjects who say "be herself at all times" seem to imply that one should never play a part, which can be thought of as contrary to "act like a lady under all circumstances"; both are classed here. Conceptual complexity is shown in categories referring to psychological causation, to balancing of opposites ("be a woman but still be her *own* self"), and to combinations of three or more traits. In the latter category there should be at least three clearly different traits, and at least one that would be rated I-3/4, whether it fits some I-3/4 category or is one like a sense of humor that seems to be mentioned only in combination with other traits for this item. Note that mere use of the word "because" does not suffice to qualify a response as exhibiting psychological causation: "stick up for her rights, because now a days women are taking over many jobs which man have held" is rated I-3/4.

1. Feelings about appearance (I-3, 1; I-3/4, 2)
take pride in her appearance
try to be as attractive as possible and never forget that her physical appearance is important
be aware of her appearance

2. —remember to be feminine, a lady, a woman (I-3/4, 1)
remember to act like a lady
remember she's a woman & act accordingly
remember her feminine qualities
try to keep in mind she is one
be aware she is a woman

3. —be as feminine as possible, under all circumstances (I-3/4, 1)
remain as feminine as possible

be as feminine as the situation will allow
be as womanly as possible
try to be femine in every way
be a lady at any cost
look and act in a feminine way, even when she is washing the car
try an be a woman and a lady at all time no matter what
be feminine, though she is in careers where there are a majority of men

4. —enjoy being a woman; be proud, thankful to be a woman (I-3/4, 1; I-5, 1)
   be proud she is a homemaker
   be happy she is a woman
   realize that she is lucky to be a woman
   be proud of her body and of her sex

5. —be a woman but still be herself (I-3/4, 1, 7; I-5, 1)
   remain feminine but stand up for her rights as a woman
   be herself and never try to act like a man. She should be feminine

6. —know, trust, understand herself; be herself at all times (I-3/4, 7, 8; I-5, 2)
   believe in herself
   strive to understand herself and others
   know herself before she contemplates marriage
   trust her capabilities
   have patience with herself
   be herself in the presence of anyone or even when she is alone

7. —set high goals; follow her conscience (I-3, 4; I-3/4, 11)
   stick to her convictions
   stand behind her beliefs

*8. —do, be her best (I-3/4, 11)
   be at her very best
   do her best at whatever she does
   work to her ability
   take care of herself, by keeping herself clean, and composed, be at her best all the time

9. —fulfill her potential; develop her abilities (I-3/4, 15; I-4/5, 1, 2)
   strive to satisfy her own interests and develop her own potentials

strive to improve herself in every way

strive to do what best suits her nature whether it be raising a family and/or following a career

be clean, strive for better intelligence and happiness

try to make the most of her abilities especially giving and receiving

10. Concern with ambition, accomplishment

be ambitious

have a feeling of accomplishment

take pride in her accomplishments

11. —be realistic, adaptable (unelaborated) (I-5, 3)

face reality

be resourceful

be pleasant, refined and able to adjust to everyone

12. Three different traits, at least one at I-3/4 (I-3/4, 4, 5; I-5, 4)

be honest, understanding & gracious

be alert, attractive, intelligent and gracious

be honest, neat and clean, friendly, and possess a sense of humor

carry herself in a woman way—neat respectful—pride—and many other I could name

try to keep herself neat, "on the ball," and thoughtful of others

be neat, alert, polite, a good conversationalist, have good common sense

13. Her actions, feelings, appearance, determine her own, others' response (psychological causation)

try to remain calm in the face of family crisis for her family depends on her

stand by the man she loves, for trust men and they will be true

act like a woman and she'll always be treated as one

Carry herself in a way that she is always respected

love herself in order to love her husband

devote some time away from her home and children as it will make her a better wife and mother

Try to be an example for her children for their home life is their pattern for their adult life

be dressed neatly, act properly and be in a good mood because smiles attract many people

want respect. Respect is necessary for love

14. Fulfill her responsibilities to her family; have a good relation
    with husband (I-3/4, 12)
    *be very helpful to her husband, encourage but never push
    too hard*
    *think of her home responsibilities before taking on other ac-
    tivities*
    try to fulfill her role
    be open about things to her husband
    keep her husband in love with her
    *get married, and marry only a man she loves and feels she
    could live with as a compassionate love-mate*
    *try to make a happy marriage for both herself and her hus-
    band*

15. —be loved
    be made to feel she is loved and needed

16. Balancing of opposites (one or both from I-3/4)
    be a lady in the parlor and a whore in the bedroom
    try to be happy without being selfish
    be considerate of others and yet be an individual
    try to look her best without trying to overdue it
    give of herself yet keep part of herself all to herself
    be friendly, but a little reserved before others

Unclassified
    *try to understand what she expects of herself and what others
    expect of her*
    be a woman first, a wife second, and a mother third

I-4/5

Major themes at this level are self-fulfillment and rejection or
transcending of stereotyped role expectations. Some interesting and
thoughtful answers contradict the stem: "nothing is that absolute and
universal."

1. Self-fulfillment (I-3/4, 15; I-4, 9)
    be confident and have a purposeful, eventful life
    strive for growth and increasing depth in her marriage
    try to fulfill her desires
    be as mature and well developed person as she is able to be

2. —be aware of the outside world (I-3/4, 14; I-4, 9)
    be aware of the things surrounding her life

> *try to use all her abilities in dealing with her husband &*
> *children and also live outside the world of her home*
> *find some interests to share with her husband other than her*
> *own immediate little world of her household*
> *try to keep her mouth shut when everyone else around her*
> *gossips. She should always keep up to date in world events*
> *so that she doesn't have to talk about the washing she did*

3. Concern with overcoming stereotypes (I-3/4, 10)
   > *set her sights high and ignore what people say about what a*
   > *woman can't do*
   > *keep her temper and never allow the fact that she is a woman*
   > *stop her from doing something in which she is very talented*
   > *be womanly but not "typically feminine," i.e., scatterbrained,*
   > *silly, mediocre, etc.*

4. Share human qualities with men
   > *be allowed to be human the same as anyone else*
   > *be a person first*
   > *be considerate, thoughtful and kind which applies to men also*

5. —respect herself as well as respecting men (I-3/4, 8)
   > *have pride in herself as an individual, as well as pride in her*
   > *husband and family*
   > *remember to respect a man's ego but also expect him to re-*
   > *spect hers*

6. —nothing is that absolute and universal
   > *realize that there is nothing she "should always"*

Unclassified
> *maintain her own code of morals—a sense of individuality*
> *Try to make the world a little bit of a better place because*
> *she is in it*

I-5

Most responses classed here refer to acceptance of self and others and of one's situation, particularly the situation of being a woman. As compared to similar responses at lower levels, such as "be herself" or "be feminine," there is less exhortation and more reconciliation, in addition to less banal expression. Conceptual complexity appears in responses contrasting three distinct ideas, at least one of which must be separately classifiable at the I-4 or I-4/5 level. In contrast to the similar category at the I-4 level, which lists three or four traits, usually with the highest at I-3/4, the component parts of the composite are activities rather than just traits.

In doubtful cases, originality of response can tip the scales toward the higher rating.

1. —accept her role (I-3/4, 1; I-4, 4, 5)
   learn to accept her role
   understand, accept, and appreciate her unique role as a woman
   value and treasure those qualities which make her a woman
   be a woman, let the men do their jobs stay in their places, put the men in theirs and live

2. Accept herself or others as they are (I-3/4, 7; I-4, 6)
   accept herself
   try to live so she can tolerate herself above all else
   be herself whether she's intelligent or a "dumb broad"
   try to understand her husband's many moods as best she can
   look for the best in her children—and that way she can help them more

3. —be able to adjust to life (elaborated); strive for inner happiness and harmony (I-3/4, 15; I-4, 11)
   make the best of any situation in the most intelligent way that she can
   try to be ready to face, handle and accept what life has to give. She shouldn't just accept everything she should be able to use her judgment
   remember that everyday is important; happiness is important and problems don't last
   strike a balance between her own wants and satisfactions and those of her family

4. Conceptual complexity: three contrasting ideas, at least one at I-4 (I-4, 12)
   act like a lady, as well as think like one and look like one
   remember that she is first a woman and look like it, act like it, and feel like it!
   be well groomed, a willing sexual partner to her mate, and constantly boardening her mind
   be ready to give according to her nature, but she should never let herself be taken advantage of. She should remain charming both in body and spirit
   care about her husband first; love intensely be an aid to the community and be made to be happy by her husband
   be true to what she believes is right, keep her intellect alive, & be loving with her family

Unclassified
> *take time to reason and try to be objective*
> *try to do something about cruelty, dire poverty and the un-*
> *happiness of others*

I-6

Since this stem calls for responses about a woman's role or be-havior or rights, responses expressing an abstract social concern are rare and come only from high protocols. Some such responses are listed in the unclassified group at I-4/5 and I-5. The single response listed at the I-6 level is remarkable in that it links this social concern with the sentence stem by the clause "as should a man." Perhaps even more telling is that it transcends the polarity of working for social betterment and accepting others as they are.

Unclassified
> *as should a man, treat other individuals with respect and*
> *work toward the betterment of the whole of people, not*
> *just of herself*